Jamey Romesburg

Teaching
and Learning
in the Middle Grades

Teaching
and Learning
in the Middle Grades

K. DENISE MUTH
The University of Georgia

DONNA E. ALVERMANN
The University of Georgia

ALLYN AND BACON
Boston London Toronto Sydney Tokyo Singapore

Series Editor: Sean W. Wakely
Series Editorial Assistant: Carol L. Chernaik
Production Administrator: Annette Joseph
Production Coordinator: Susan Freese
Editorial-Production Service: WordCrafters Editorial Services, Inc.
Manufacturing Buyer: Megan Cochran
Cover Administrator: Linda K. Dickinson
Cover Designer: Suzanne Harbison

Library of Congress Cataloging-in-Publication Data

Muth, K. Denise.
    Teaching and learning in the middle grades / K. Denise Muth, Donna E.
Alvermann.
        p.   cm.
    Includes bibliographical references and index.
    ISBN 0-205-13302-9
    1. Middle schools—United States—Curricula. 2. Teenagers—
Education—United States. 3. Teaching. 4. Learning.
5. Adolescence. I. Alvermann, Donna E. II. Title.
LB1623.5.M88   1992
373.2′36—dc20
                                      91-37991
                                        CIP

Printed in the United States of America

10 9 8 7 6 5 4 3 2   97 96 95 94 93 92

To our husbands,
Shawn Glynn and Jack Alvermann

BRIEF CONTENTS

CONTENTS

Part Three Instruction and Learning

PREFACE

Teaching and Learning in the Middle Grades is designed primarily for students enrolled in undergraduate and graduate teacher education programs at the middle-grades level. Its purpose is to prepare teachers of young adolescents.

An important feature of this book is its relevance. For example, most of the examples and sample exercises throughout were designed by pre- and in-service middle-grades teachers like yourself. Additionally, descriptions of middle-grades classrooms and examples of dialogue between teachers and young adolescents are actual samples collected during visits to middle-grades schools. As such, this book reflects what can and is being done by teachers in today's middle-grades classrooms.

A second important feature of this book is its research base. Each chapter is grounded in the most current theory and research on the teaching and learning of young adolescents. If teaching is to evolve into a profession, it must do so in part on the foundation of a professional knowledge base. The decisions you make in your classroom should be based on professional knowledge rather than on the notion that "this is what I've always done." We hope that the chapters in this book prepare you to use that knowledge base to make important decisions about the teaching and learning of young adolescents.

We believe that effective middle-grades teachers are able to link their knowledge of young adolescents with their awareness of middle-grades content and sound instructional practices. Accordingly, we have divided this book into three parts. In Part One, you will learn about young adolescents and the schools they attend. The historical development of middle-grades schools in the context of current thought is presented in Chapter 1. Chapter 2 provides an in-depth look at the many developmental changes that young adolescents undergo. Chapter 3 identifies a variety of ways in which you can provide for the individual differences among your students.

Part Two is designed to heighten your awareness of the important role that the middle-grades content plays in the teaching and learning of young adolescents. The issue of the middle-grades curriculum is examined in Chapter 4, which compares a traditional curriculum with an alternative curriculum built around the personal concerns of young adolescents. Chapter 5 highlights the content that should be taught in the academic core subjects to prepare young adolescents for the twenty-first century.

Part Three will aid you in applying your insights about young adolescents and your knowledge of the middle-grades curriculum to designing and implementing effective instruction. Chapter 6 serves as the foundation for this part of the book by depicting the teacher as a decision maker. Chapters 7 through 15 highlight the many decisions teachers make, such as how to plan effectively, how to assess students, what teaching strategies to use, how to interact with young adolescents, and how to manage classrooms.

Acknowledgments

This book would not be possible without the help of many people. We wish to thank the following individuals for their thorough and critical reviews of the manuscript:

Mark W. Conley, Michigan State University; Esteban Diaz, California State University, San Bernardino; Thomas Erb, University of Kansas; Art Garner, Memphis State University; Judith L. Irvin, Florida State University; Dale H. Schunk, University of North Carolina; Greg P. Stefanich, University of Northern Iowa; and Karen D. Wood, University of North Carolina, at Charlotte.

In addition, many of our colleagues at the University of Georgia provided excellent suggestions from their readings of the various chapters. In particular, we thank Laurie Hart, Cy Hawn, Elizabeth Pate, Beverly Payne, David Payne, and David Reinking. Thanks are also due to Stephanie Bales, Faith Downey, and Tracy Pharr for their help in typing the manuscript.

We are also indebted to Patricia Clifton, principal, and to the teachers and students at Hilsman Middle School in Athens, Georgia, for so graciously allowing us to photograph them for this book. Sixth-grade teacher Taylor McKenna and photographers Richard Pomante and Rick O'Quinn deserve special thanks for their time, effort, and endless patience in organizing, scheduling, and shooting the photographs.

Finally, we are deeply grateful to Carol Wada, who guided us initially, and to Sean Wakely at Allyn and Bacon, who helped us finish this project.

Teaching
and Learning
in the Middle Grades

1

Introduction: Young Adolescents and Schools

The education of young adolescents has emerged as an area of critical need for the 1990s and into the twenty-first century. The middle grades, which serve young adolescents from ages 10 to 14, play a crucial role in these students' preparation for later life. But the reform recommendations of the 1980s have virtually ignored this group of students and the schools they attend. In its report, *Turning Points: Preparing American Youth for the 21st Century* (Carnegie Council, 1989), the Task Force of the Carnegie Council on Adolescent Development warned that we cannot continue to ignore the schooling of young adolescents. As Jackson and Hornbeck (1989) point out, "For many youth, early adolescence is one of the last real opportunities to affect their educational and personal trajectory. The middle grades school, one of the key socializing institutions for early adolescents, represents a critical 'turning point' in the lives of American youth'' (p. 831).

This introductory chapter serves as a framework for the other chapters in this book. Our goal in this chapter is to familiarize you with middle-grades schools as they exist today, compared to the junior high schools of the 1960s and to the way educators envision them in the future. In the first section of this chapter, we provide you with a brief history of the development of middle-grades schools. Next, we describe middle-grades schools as they exist today. In the third section, we discuss the most recent recommendations for restructuring middle-grades schools for the twenty-first century. After reading this chapter, you will have a sense of how far middle-grades schools have come in the past few decades and how far they still have to go to become the types of schools from which all young adolescents can benefit.

Historical Development of Middle-Grades Schools

Melton (1984), Alexander and McEwin (1989), Lounsbury (1990), and Moore and Stefanich (1990) all provide excellent summaries of the historical development of middle-grades schools. Much of what we present in this section draws from their summaries.

Around the turn of the twentieth century, the first seeds of the middle-grades school were planted by the Committee on Economy of Time in Education. The committee recommended that the current 8-4 organization of America's schools be reorganized into a 6-6 plan. The committee also suggested that the second 6 years might be divided into two 3-year periods. The result was that, instead of attending one school for 8 years and another school for 4 years, many of the nation's students would now attend one school for 6 years and another school for 6 years. Even more important, some students would now attend one school for 6 years, another school for 3 years, and another school for 3 more years. Over the next few decades, the first of these 3-year schools evolved into the junior high school.

By 1920, there were 883 junior high schools in the United States, and that number eventually climbed to approximately 7,000 (Melton, 1984). Some of these schools contained grades 7 through 9, and other contained grades 7 and 8. The number of junior high schools increased dramatically in the second half of the century. "By 1960 approximately four out of five high school graduates had gone through an elementary-junior-senior high school organization (usually 6-3-3)'' (Alexander & McEwin, 1989, p. 1).

Dissatisfaction with junior high schools became evident in the early 1960s. More and more educators came to realize that these schools were not serving the needs of young adolescents as they were originally designed to do. Regardless of the grades they encompassed, the schools tended to look pretty much the same; that is, they were exactly what their name implied—*junior* high schools, or high schools for young adolescents. Many of the features of high schools had inappropriately been incorporated into the junior high schools. The result was that many of these junior high schools had "full departmentalization, interscholastic athletics at the expense of intramurals, inappropriate social activities, premature emphasis on academic requirements at the expense of discovery and exploration, [and] the confusion of sophistication for maturity'' (Melton, 1984, p. 7). In essence, these schools were failing dismally in their task of educating young adolescents.

Melton (1984) identifies three additional reasons why junior high schools were failing in their mission: lack of recognition, reasons for reorganization, and lack of knowledge of young adolescents.

Lack of Recognition

Despite the fact that junior high schools were located in just about every state, the junior high school movement was unable to get recognition from many state departments of education. Without such recognition, there was no mechanism by which teachers could become certified to work specifically with young adolescents. As a result, those colleges and universities that prepared teachers had little incentive to offer programs or even courses specifically designed for those who would work with young adolescents. Despite the widespread 6-3-3 reorganization that had occurred throughout the first half of the century, instruction was being carried out in much the same ways as in the old 8-4 organization. In other words, the needs of the young adolescents in these schools were not always being met.

Reasons for Reorganization

Despite all good intentions of those involved in the junior high school movement, many states created junior high schools for reasons other than the needs of young adolescents.

> A major problem was that much if not most of the reorganization was done for administrative not educational purposes. Fluctuating enrollment figures, building utilization, staffing and budgetary problems, and other like factors, usually took precedence over the need for a unique intermediate program. (Melton, 1984, pp. 8–9)

Lack of Knowledge of Young Adolescents

Many people, particularly those in the general public, did not understand young adolescents and their needs. To many of these individuals, young adolescents represented an age group marked by problems, and junior high schools represented schools where problems happened. As Melton (1984) speculates, there may actually have been an unconscious hope among some people that if junior high schools went away, so would the problems of the young adolescents who attended them.

Amidst these problems, however, there were some good things that came out of junior high schools. In particular, in some junior high schools around the country, the dropout rate among seventh- and eighth-graders was reduced, the concept of exploration was introduced, guidance services were provided, cocurricular activities were scheduled, and many innovative programs were implemented (Melton, 1984).

Middle-Grades Schools Today

In the early 1960s, educators who were dissatisfied with the lack of accomplishments of the junior high schools longed more and more for schools that would actually serve the needs of young adolescents. These educators wanted schools that would take into account the physical, cognitive, social, emotional, and moral development of the young adolescents who attended them. They wanted schools that would prepare young adolescents to make the transition from elementary school to high school. William Alexander and Donald Eichhorn were two of the educators among this group. William Alexander is frequently called the father of the middle school, and Donald Eichhorn was "perhaps the first major implementor of the middle school concept" (Lounsbury, 1984, p. 3).

Results of a survey administered by Alexander and McEwin (1989) indicate that, perhaps because of the strength of the middle-school movement, the number of junior high schools in the country is decreasing significantly. Their survey shows that between 1970 and 1987, schools for young adolescents containing grades 6 through 8 have increased from 1,662 to 4,329, whereas schools containing grades 7 through 9 (i.e., junior high schools) have decreased from 4,711 to 2,191 during the same time period.

At this point, we feel it is necessary to clarify our use of the term *middle-grades schools*. As you have just learned, in the early 1960s, due to dissatisfaction with junior high schools, the middle-school concept was born. Many schools adopted this concept but may not have changed their names. Therefore, today we have many schools throughout the country that do an excellent job of serving the needs of young adolescents but do not have the term *middle school* in their name. For example, some of these schools are still called *junior high schools* and others are called *intermediate schools*. Similarly, there are many schools that changed their name to *middle school* but actually still operate under the old junior high school concept.

Accordingly, throughout this book, we use the term *middle-grades schools* to represent all schools—whether they are called middle schools, junior high schools, or intermediate schools—that serve the needs of young adolescents. In short, it is not the name of the school but rather the unique features it offers that determines whether or not it actually serves the needs of young adolescents.

What are some of the unique features that help a middle-grades school serve the needs of young adolescents? The following have been identified as key components of effective middle-grades schools: interdisciplinary teams, advisory programs, and exploratory programs (George & Lawrence, 1982). In addition to the following descriptions of each of these components, each component is also discussed throughout the other chapters in this book when appropriate.

Interdisciplinary Teams

Mac Iver (1990) describes interdisciplinary teams as "a keystone for effective education in the middle grades" (p. 460). *Interdisciplinary teams* are small groups of teachers, generally representing each of the content areas, who teach the same group of students. Interdisciplinary teams usually consist of a mathematics teacher, a science teacher, a social studies teacher, and a language arts teacher. In some middle-grades schools, special education teachers, reading teachers, art teachers, music teachers, and physical education teachers may also be part of a team.

The teachers on a team all teach the same group of students. The effect is that a number of small "schools," or communities, are created within a school. All teachers on a team should have the same planning time so that they can plan together. It is also advantageous if all teachers on a team are housed in one area of the school, particularly if the school is large, so that students do not have to spend a great deal of time going from one part of the school building to another.

Flexible block scheduling is an important characteristic of interdisciplinary teams. With this type of scheduling, teachers on a team are not locked into a fixed number of periods per day or a fixed amount of time per period. For example, an interdisciplinary team of teachers might have a four- or five-period block of time devoted to the academic subject areas. Teachers on the team plan together to determine how they might best use that block of time. Figure 1.1 illustrates a schedule for a school with three sixth-grade, three seventh-grade, and three eighth-

FIGURE 1.1   Sample Schedule Illustrating Team Planning and Block Scheduling

TEAM	1	2	3	4	5	6	7
6A (4)						Plan	SGG
6B (4)		ACADEMIC BLOCK				Plan	SGG
6C (2)						Plan	SGG
7A (4)	BLOCK	SGG	Plan				
7B (4)	BLOCK	Plan	SGG	ACADEMIC BLOCK			
7C (2)	BLOCK	SGG	Plan				
8A (4)				Plan	SGG		
8B (4)	ACADEMIC BLOCK			SGG	Plan	ACADEMIC BLOCK	
8C (2)				SGG	Plan		
Physical Education (5)	Plan	7	7	8	8	6	6
Exploratory (7)	Plan	7	7	8	8	6	6
Reading (3)	6-7-8	6-Plan-8	6-Plan-8	6-7-Plan	6-7-Plan	Plan-7-8	Plan-7-8
Art and Music (4)	6-7-8-6	6-8-6-Plan	6/Plan/8/6	6/7/6/7	6/7/6/7	Plan/7/Plan/8	7/Plan/7/8
Special Education (6)	Planning Varies Depending upon Exploratory and P.E.						

Source: From *Handbook for Middle School Teaching* by Paul George and Gordon Lawrence. Copyright © 1982 by Scott, Foresman and Company. Reprinted by permission of HarperCollins Publishers.

School day for students: 7:30 a.m.–1:55 p.m.

Periods: approximately 45 minutes long

Student body: 1,100

grade teams. Notice that all teachers on a team share a common planning time. In this figure, SGG (i.e., small-group guidance) represents the advisory program, which we discuss in the next section.

There are several important advantages of interdisciplinary teams. First, because all teachers on a team teach the same students, the needs of each individual student can be met more easily. For example, if Angeline has a particular home problem that is interfering with her school work, then the teachers on her team can plan together various ways to help her. Thus, Angeline is supported and helped in each of her classes and all teachers can monitor her progress.

Second, interdisciplinary teams of teachers who plan together can design lessons and units that help students see connections among the various disciplines. For instance, a team of teachers may plan a unit on justice that includes lessons and activities in mathematics, science, social studies, language arts, art, and music. (We discuss the idea of interdisciplinary units in detail in Chapters 4 and 7.)

Next, because the teachers on a team all teach the same group of students, the opportunities are increased for improving interpersonal relationships among the students and between the teachers and the students. Students on a team frequently develop a team spirit, which allows the possibility of improving students' attitudes toward school and their motivation to learn. Additionally, teachers on a team can plan lessons and activities that focus on such topics as responsibility, self-esteem, and cooperation.

Fourth, in addition to the advantages they provide students, interdisciplinary teams also offer support to the teachers on the team. This is particularly true for first-year teachers and teachers who are new to a school. Since interdisciplinary teams of teachers frequently plan together, hold parent conferences together, team teach, and discuss individual student's strengths, weaknesses, and problems, all teachers are part of a powerful support group. First-year teachers who work on teams tell us that they do not experience the isolation felt by many of their peers who are not part of a team.

The concept of interdisciplinary teams appears to be gaining in popularity among the nation's middle-grades schools, but it is still not used to the extent that middle-grades educators would like. Mac Iver (1990) reports that only "about 42% of early adolescents . . . receive instruction from interdisciplinary teams of teachers at some time between grades 5 and 9" (p. 460). Additionally, Mac Iver reports that "more 6–8 middle schools (just over 40%) use interdisciplinary teams than do other types of schools" (p. 460).

Advisory Programs

In order to promote interpersonal communication between teachers and students and among students themselves, and to focus more on the affective development of young adolescents, many effective middle-grades schools have incorporated advisory programs into their daily schedule. Frequently, these programs are called *advisor-advisee programs*. One type of advisory program involves all teachers in the school being assigned a small group (10 to 20) of students with whom they meet every day. The rationale behind advisory programs at the middle-grades level is that

Advisory groups promote communication between teachers and students.

all students know they have at least one adult who knows them personally, cares about their happiness and success, and is willing to listen to their problems and concerns.

George and Lawrence (1982) suggest that advisory time be scheduled at the beginning of the day, for a minimum of 20 uninterrupted minutes. When advisory time is scheduled at the beginning rather than at the end of the day, administrators, teachers, and students are more likely to view it as an important component of the school day. An additional benefit of scheduling advisory time at the start of the day is that it provides students, particularly those with personal or home problems, with an opportunity "to work through difficulties before beginning their academic work" (George & Lawrence, p. 177).

During advisory time, teachers spend time working with the whole group and with individual students on affective goals that the school, the teacher, and/or the students have set. The teacher's role varies from leading discussions to being a sounding board for students' problems and concerns. Advisory sessions can revolve around a variety of topics, including self-awareness, group dynamics, sharing time, and, when appropriate, just plain old-fashioned rap sessions. For example, several days could be planned around a variety of activities centering on the following components of group effectiveness:

Group Effectiveness
1. Helping the group care about the group itself.
2. Helping the group learn to work/play together.
3. Helping the group to talk/listen together.
4. Helping the group be self-directed. (George & Lawrence, 1982, p. 178)

Advisory programs are becoming more prevalent in today's schools for young adolescents. For example, 66 percent of the schools in a recent survey administered by the Center for Research on Elementary and Middle Schools (CREMS) reported that they had one such period and 9 percent reported that they had two (Mac Iver, 1990). Unfortunately, however, in some schools, these advisory periods are used more often for the mechanical tasks of keeping school (e.g., taking attendance, distributing notices, making announcements, orienting students to rules and programs) rather than social or academic support activities that use teachers' talents as advisors and that help students feel someone is looking out for their interests and needs. (p. 459)

These "mechanical tasks of keeping school" are important tasks that need to be handled, but they should not replace an effective advisory program. Results of a recent survey administered by the Association for Supervision and Curriculum Development (ASCD) indicate that only about 29 percent of the schools that serve young adolescents have a true advisory program (Cawelti, 1988).

Exploratory Programs

Earlier in this chapter, we mentioned one of the benefits that came out of the junior high school movement was a focus on exploration. Such a focus is still a critical component of today's schools for young adolescents. As you will learn in the next chapter, young adolescents are at an age when they are beginning to learn how to consider options and make informed choices. Exploratory programs are designed to help students in this endeavor, as well as learn about and pursue their interests and talents.

Exploratory programs offer regularly scheduled classes in a variety of special interest areas. Ideally, exploratory classes should be offered daily as a part of the regular school schedule. Students should be free to choose their own courses and should be encouraged to base their choices on their own interests rather than on the interests and choices of their friends. George and Lawrence (1982) identify four areas in which exploratory courses could be offered: unified arts, academic inquiry, independent learning, and discipline expansion.

Unified Arts

In an effort to expose young adolescents to areas beyond the basic academic areas, many middle-grades schools offer exploratory courses in unified arts, such as "art, choral music, instrumental music, physical education, home economics, career education, industrial arts, foreign language" (George & Lawrence, 1982, p. 152). In most cases, specially trained teachers are hired to teach such courses. Ideally, these teachers structure their courses with a focus on exploration rather than on content and competition.

Academic Inquiry

Academic-inquiry courses are tied to the regular academic areas of mathematics, science, language arts, and social studies and are taught by the respective academic area teachers. But academic-inquiry courses differ from regular academic courses in that they offer students opportunities to go beyond the basics by delving more deeply into a particular topic. An exploratory course titled "The Wild, Wild West," for instance, would allow interested students to learn more about early American pioneers (George & Lawrence, 1982). Similarly, a course titled "Great Books" provides interested students with a chance to read and discuss classic literature.

Independent Learning

Independent learning allows students to work on an independent project under the guidance of a particular teacher on a topic of interest to both the teacher and the student. Such projects help students develop responsibility, self-discipline, and planning skills. An important guideline for independent learning is that it is "open to all students regardless of previous grades" (George & Lawrence, 1982, p. 152).

Discipline Expansion

Exploratory courses in discipline expansion provide students with a chance to learn about the various areas within a discipline. Teachers in the basic academic areas of mathematics, science, language arts, and social studies offer introductory courses to their disciplines.

> In social studies, for example, students are able to explore anthropology, sociology, economics, psychology, and political science as well as traditional world history, geography, and American history. In science, students are introduced to oceanography, ecology, zoology, astronomy, and other new sciences, as well as earth science, and "general science." Other areas of the curriculum follow suit. (George & Lawrence, 1982, p. 152)

Exploratory courses (sometimes referred to as *minicourses*) are being offered in many of the nation's schools for young adolescents. But, as is the case with interdisciplinary teams and advisory programs, such courses are not being offered to the extent they could be. For example, referring to the survey conducted by CREMS, Becker (1990) states:

> Only a minority of principals (39%) report that their middle-grade schools offer minicourses. And some of these schools offer minicourses to only a portion of their students. Overall, only about 30% of students have had an exploratory or a minicourse during the seventh or eighth grade. (p. 452)

Recommendations for Middle-Grades Schools of the Twenty-First Century

From their beginning in the early 1960s until the present, middle-grades schools have made tremendous progress toward meeting the needs of the young adolescents they serve. However, there is still much progress to be made. For example, research indicates that when young adolescents make the transition from an elementary school to a middle-grades school, their "achievement-related attitudes, values, and performance" (Midgley, Feldlaufer, & Eccles, 1989, p. 247) deteriorate. Additionally, research also suggests that these students are provided with fewer opportunities for interaction and decision making (Feldlaufer, Midgley, & Eccles, 1988).

Despite such compelling evidence that changes were needed, the reform recommendations of the late 1970s and early 1980s virtually ignored the education of young adolescents. It was only at the end of the 1980s that the problems of educating young adolescents began to receive national attention. This national attention was brought about primarily by the release of a report by the Carnegie Corporation's Council of Adolescent Development (1989). This report recommended sweeping changes in the ways young adolescents are educated. These changes are described in Figure 1.2.

As you can see in Figure 1.2, the recommendations include several of the features of effective middle-grades schools that we discussed in this chapter. In particular, the report recommends "teachers grouped together as teams," "small group advisories," and "flexibility in arranging instructional time." Hopefully,

FIGURE 1.2   Recommendations of the Task Force on Education of Young Adolescents

- *Create small communities for learning*   where stable, close, mutually respectful relationships with adults and peers are considered fundamental for intellectual development and personal growth. The key elements of these communities are schools-within-schools or houses, students and teachers grouped together as teams, and small group advisories that ensure that every student is known well by at least one adult.
- *Teach a core academic program*   that results in students who are literate, including in the sciences, and who know how to think critically, lead a healthy life, behave ethically, and assume the responsibilities of citizenship in a pluralistic society. Youth service to promote values for citizenship is an essential part of the core academic program.
- *Ensure success for all students*   through elimination of tracking by achievement level and promotion of cooperative learning, flexibility in arranging instructional time, and adequate resources (time, space, equipment, and materials) for teachers.
- *Empower teachers and administrators to make decisions about the experiences of middle grade students*   through creative control by teachers over the instructional program linked to greater responsibilities for students' performance, governance committees that assist the principal in designing and coordinating school-wide programs, and autonomy and leadership within sub-schools or houses to create environments tailored to enhance the intellectual and emotional development of all youth.
- *Staff middle grade schools with teachers who are expert at teaching young adolescents* and who have been specially prepared for assignment to the middle grades.
- *Improve academic performance through fostering the health and fitness*   of young adolescents, by providing a health coordinator in every middle grade school, access to health care and counseling services, and a health-promoting school environment.
- *Reengage families in the education of young adolescents*   by giving families meaningful roles in school governance, communicating with families about the school program and student's progress, and offering families opportunities to support the learning process at home and at the school.
- *Connect schools with communities,*   which together share responsibility for each middle grade student's success, through identifying service opportunities in the community, establishing partnerships and collaborations to ensure students' access to health and social services, and using community resources to enrich the instructional program and opportunities for constructive after-school activities.

Source: From *Turning Points: Preparing American Youth for the 21st Century* by Carnegie Council on Adolescent Development, 1989, Washington, D.C.: Carnegie Council on Adolescent Development. Reprinted by permission.

these recommendations will provide the impetus for those middle-grades schools not currently using these features to begin to do so. Ideally, they will also motivate schools currently using these features to begin to think about additional ways they can meet the needs of the young adolescents they serve.

You may have noticed as you read Figure 1.2 that this report calls for help from all areas of society. The members of the committee call on those in the education sector, such as teachers and principals, leaders in higher education, health educators and health-care professionals, youth-serving and community organizations, statewide task forces, the president and other national leaders, leaders in private and philanthropic sectors, parents, and all others concerned about the future of our nation's youth to work together for the education of all young adolescents. It is only by working together, as a nation, that we will be able to ensure success for all young adolescents.

Summary

Our goal in this chapter was to provide you with a sense of how middle-grades schools began, where they are today, and where they need to go in the future in order to begin to meet the needs of all young adolescents. This chapter serves as a framework for the other chapters in the book. Hopefully, by understanding how far middle-grades schools have come and how far they still need to go, you will realize the important role that effective teaching plays in the future of today's young adolescents.

REFERENCES

Alexander, W. M., & McEwin, C. K. (1989). *Schools in the middle: Status and progress.* Columbus, OH: National Middle School Association.

Becker, H. J. (1990). Curriculum and instruction in middle-grade schools. *Phi Delta Kappan, 71,* 450–457.

Carnegie Council on Adolescent Development (1989). *Turning points: Preparing American youth for the 21st century.* Washington, DC: Carnegie Council on Adolescent Development.

Cawelti, G. (1988, November). Middle schools a better match with early adolescents' needs, ASCD survey finds. *Update,* 1–5.

Feldlaufer, H., Midgley, C., & Eccles, J. (1988). Student, teacher, and observer perceptions of the classroom environment before and after the transition to junior high school. *Journal of Early Adolescence, 8,* 133–156.

George, P., & Lawrence, G. (1982). *Handbook for middle school teaching.* Glenview, IL: Scott, Foresman.

Jackson, A. (1990). From knowledge to practice: Implementing the recommendations of *Turning Points. Middle School Journal, 21*(3), 1–3.

Jackson, A. W., & Hornbeck, D. W. (1989). Educating young adolescents: Why we must restructure middle grade schools. *American Psychologist, 44,* 831–836.

Lounsbury, J. H. (1984). *Perspectives: Middle school education, 1964–1984.* Columbus, OH: National Middle School Association.

Lounsbury, J. H. (1990). Middle level education: Perspectives, problems, and prospects. *Educational Horizons, 68,* 63–68.

Mac Iver, D. J. (1990). Meeting the needs of young adolescents: Advisory groups, inter-disciplinary teaching teams, and school transition programs. *Phi Delta Kappan, 71,* 458–464.

Melton, G. E. (1984). The junior high school: Successes and failures. In J. H. Lounsbury (Ed.), *Perspectives: Middle school education, 1964–1984* (pp. 5–13). Columbus, OH: National Middle School Association.

Midgley, C., Feldlaufer, H., & Eccles, J. S. (1989). Change in teacher efficacy and student self- and task-related beliefs in mathematics during transition to junior high school. *Journal of Educational Psychology, 81,* 247–258.

Moore, D. W., & Stefanich, G. P. (1990). Middle school reading: A historical perspective. In G. G. Duffy (Ed.), *Reading in the middle school.* Newark, DE: International Reading Association.

_2

Young Adolescent Development

Early adolescence is a time of great physical, cognitive, social, personality, and moral change. These five areas of development are interrelated and frequently overlap. As a result, a change in one area can bring about a change in another area. To illustrate the relationships among these areas, we present case studies of two young adolescent students, Clarence and Maria. The case study of Clarence is an adaptation of a case study written by Andy Forbes, a University of Georgia student. As you read through each case study, make a note of the physical, cognitive, social, personality, and moral characteristics of Clarence and Maria and how these characteristics change over time.

In the next part of the chapter, you will learn about self-concept and the role that it plays in young adolescent development. In the third part of the chapter, you will learn about young adolescent physical, cognitive, social, personality, and moral development and you can compare Clarence's and Maria's development to how the so-called average young adolescent develops.

Case Studies

Clarence

When he first enters sixth grade, Clarence is short for his age and overweight. He is exactly 5 feet tall and weighs about 135 pounds. He has virtually no body hair and his penis and testicles are not as developed as that of other boys he sees in the locker room after P.E. Also, his breasts are getting pudgy and some of the boys tease him and say he looks like a girl. Clarence is so self-conscious about his appearance that he starts to make excuses and pretends he is sick so he does not have to go to P.E. Several times he has even forged a note from his mother, asking the P.E. teacher to excuse him for one reason or another. But after a few months he stopped writing the notes because he was afraid his mother would find out. On top of all this, he has a rather squeaky, little boy's voice, which makes some of the girls laugh when he talks in class. So, he does not volunteer to answer very often.

Emotionally, Clarence is doing okay, all things considered, because he has two friends who have not yet begun to develop either. These boys have been his best friends for years, so he has gotten used to their teasing him about being fat. But most of the other boys are developing very rapidly and it bothers him when they tease him about his height and weight. Clarence does not really have any friends who are girls, except his younger sister's friends, and they do not count.

In the classroom, Clarence does very well, particularly in mathematics and science. Since he is too overweight and clumsy to participate in sports, he has a lot of time to study. This year, he even joined the science club. He finds that a lot of the other kids in the club ask him for help and want to be his partner when they work on projects. Clarence really likes doing experiments in science class because he gets to make predictions about what is going to happen and then see if he is right. During science club meetings, the other boys don't tease him about his appearance.

He also likes his mathematics and science classes because the teachers let the kids work in groups a lot. Group work is okay with Clarence because he's not as shy about speaking up in a small group as he is about talking in front of the whole class. Also, he is getting to know a few of the girls in his groups better. Maybe if they see how smart he is, they will like him better. He likes helping the kids in his group because it makes him feel needed. He is very good at planning exactly what he and his group members should do when they work together. For example, he tells them how much time they should spend on things and what order they should do them in. The kids in the group think he was born smart, but Clarence keeps telling them that he just thinks everything through very carefully before he gets started. Also, he has little games that he plays with himself when he studies for a test to help him remember all the important information.

Upon entering seventh grade, Clarence's sex organs finally begin to develop. His penis gains some size and his testicles "drop," much to his relief. But he is still unable to coax any hair to grow, especially on his face, while some of the other boys are sporting shadowy moustaches. To his horror, he is beginning to develop acne on his face instead of hair! Unfortunately, Clarence has gained more weight (he now weighs 142 pounds) but little height. The other boys wear jeans with holes in the knees, but Clarence's mother insists on putting patches on his jeans where his thighs still rub together when he walks. None of the boys laugh about his patches, though. Clarence thinks they are starting to feel sorry for him, which only makes everything worse. He does not mind getting dressed in P.E. class so much any more because he has decided the other boys are always in a rush and they do not have time to look at him anyway.

Emotionally, Clarence is having real problems because his two best friends have dropped him from their social circle. They both grew over the summer and one of them even plays on the soccer team now. They hang out with the athletic guys now and do not have time for Clarence. Clarence is beginning to feel like a freak. He constantly gets angry at his mother when she tries to baby him. He is pretty close to his little sister, though. They talk a lot and he helps her with her homework.

Clarence still does well in mathematics and science. One class that he is starting to really like is language arts. The class gets to read a lot and Clarence enjoys reading about kids like himself, especially when the kids seem to turn out just fine when they get to high school. Clarence constantly tells himself that it is okay the kids do not like him. He tells himself that he does well in school and he will be rich and famous some day and then they will all be jealous.

Another thing Clarence likes about language arts class is that the teacher lets the students keep a journal and nobody ever gets to read it, not even the teacher. Clarence usually talks to himself as he writes down everything he is feeling. Writing it down makes him feel better. Sometimes Clarence feels his journal is his best friend.

Maria

When she first enters sixth grade, Maria is very shy. She is friendly with all of the girls and they all seem to like her, but she is not best friends with any of them. She talks to the other girls in the hallways but she doesn't really interact with them much. She does not have a best friend or talk on the phone for hours like some of the other girls do.

Maria knows she is not a very good student because her grades are usually lower than the grades of most of the other kids, but she tells herself it is because she does not study and school is boring. But deep down, she knows that she does not understand a lot of what the teachers are talking about. Most of the time she has trouble even paying attention in her classes. Her mind seems to wander to other things. Of all her classes, she does the best in science because they do lots of experiments. Actually seeing things happen, like chemicals mixing and solutions dissolving, seems to help Maria make sense of a lot of new ideas. Still, she does not study, so even her science grades are not that hot. When she tries to sit down at home and do her homework, it is just too hard. She does not understand a lot of what she is supposed to read.

Maria likes social studies the least of all her classes. Some of the things the class talks about seem so remote to her life. Who cares what happened in England in the 1800s? When her teacher asked her to describe what it would be like to live on the island of Crete, she really could not answer. Her teacher was not too happy when Maria said she did not know because she had never been there. She cannot understand how some of the kids find social studies so exciting.

When she was in fifth grade, Maria started to develop before any of the other girls. Now she is tall (5 feet, 6 inches) and thin, and is beginning to develop curves. She started her period this year. She doesn't like having it but she is glad she doesn't have to worry about not getting it, like some of the other girls she hears talking about it.

Some of the boys are starting to talk to her in the halls between classes, and Maria likes that. Several of the older boys have asked her to go out, but Maria's parents say she is too young now and has to wait until she's in eighth grade to date. Once she told her parents she was going to the library to study but she really went to the movies with Alfredo. She didn't have a good time, however, because she was so afraid that her parents would find out.

By the time she begins eighth grade, Maria is pretty happy with herself. The fact that she does not do well in most classes does not bother her. She has developed into a pretty girl with a wonderful body! The other girls seem to be jealous and do not talk to her too much, but the boys all like her. She has already gone out with several of the high school boys, which is great because they have cars and can drive. Sometimes they even drink beer in the car. She likes it when they kiss her and touch her. It makes her feel special because she does not hear any of the other girls talking about doing this.

Maria does not dare tell her parents about the boys being in high school, or the cars, or the beer. And she certainly does not tell them about kissing the boys or letting them touch her. She usually tells her parents that she is going to a football or basketball game at school and then she meets her date somewhere in town. As long as she gets home on time, her parents never question her.

As these two case studies illustrate, during early adolescence a variety of changes are occurring. Quite frequently, a change in one area is associated with a change in another area. For example, Maria's physical development certainly affected her social development. Additionally, it looks as though Maria's physical and social development are starting to affect her moral development. What other relationships among the various areas of development can you identify for Maria? For Clarence? In the next section, we discuss self-concept and the role that physical, cognitive, social, personality, and moral development can play in young adolescents' self-concept.

Self-Concept

One factor that plays an important role in the relationships among the various areas of young adolescent development is self-concept. Before describing the specifics of young adolescent development, we will briefly discuss some of the ideas researchers have learned in the last decade about self-concept. This discussion will serve as the framework for the rest of the chapter, because, as you will see, self-concept plays a critical role in young adolescent physical, cognitive, social, personality, and moral development. As you read through the discussion of self-concept, think back to Clarence and Maria and see if you can identify specific ways that their development in the various areas might have affected their self-concepts.

Self-concept is defined as "a person's perceptions of his/herself" (Marsh, 1990, p. 83). In the last decade, work by Marsh (e.g., Marsh, 1984, 1986, 1989; Marsh & Shavelson, 1985) and Shavelson (Shavelson & Bolus, 1982; Shavelson & Marsh, 1986) has led to the belief that the idea of a single, global self-concept is not as useful as was previously believed. Instead, these researchers have provided evidence to support two important characteristics of self-concept: its multifaceted structure and its hierarchical structure. These two characteristics of self-concept are illustrated in Figure 2.1.

The various rectangles in Figure 2.1 represent the **multifaceted structure** of self-concept. Each rectangle signifies a facet of an individual's life and has a self-concept associated with it. Within the notion of general self-concept (sometimes referred to as *self-esteem*), Marsh and Shavelson have found evidence for three more specific self-concepts: nonacademic self-concept, math/academic self-concept, and verbal/academic self-concept. Within these three specific self-concepts, there are numerous subareas of self-concept. For example, nonacademic self-concept can be broken into a physical ability self-concept, a physical appearance self-concept, a peer relationships self-concept, and a parent relationships self-concept.

As individuals move toward adulthood, the number of facets in their self-concept increases. For example, Clarence and Maria probably would not have a foreign language self-concept until they started to learn a foreign language. Similarly, when they get jobs later in life, Clarence and Maria will probably have a vocational self-concept composed of several more specific self-concepts, such as a job performance self-concept and a colleague relationships self-concept.

The lines on Figure 2.1 represent the **hierarchical structure** of self-concept. Self-concept in the various subareas is determined by individuals' perceptions of themselves in specific situations and on specific criteria. Each individual determines the situations and criteria that are important to him or her, but, as Marsh points out, these perceptions "are influenced by evaluations by significant others, reinforcements, and attributions for one's own behavior" (1990, p. 83).

For example, Clarence's physical science self-concept would be determined by a number of factors, including the recognition he got from his peers during group work, the fact that he did well in science and got good grades, and the fact that he attributed his success to good planning and study habits rather than just being born smart. Clarence's physical appearance self-concept would also be determined by a number of factors, including his relatively short height, his excess weight, his acne, and the fact that his peers made fun of him. If the opinions of his peers were not important to Clarence, then the fact that they made fun of him would not play a major role in his physical appearance self-concept.

Thus, individuals' self-concepts in the various subareas are used to form their

FIGURE 2.1 Self-Concept

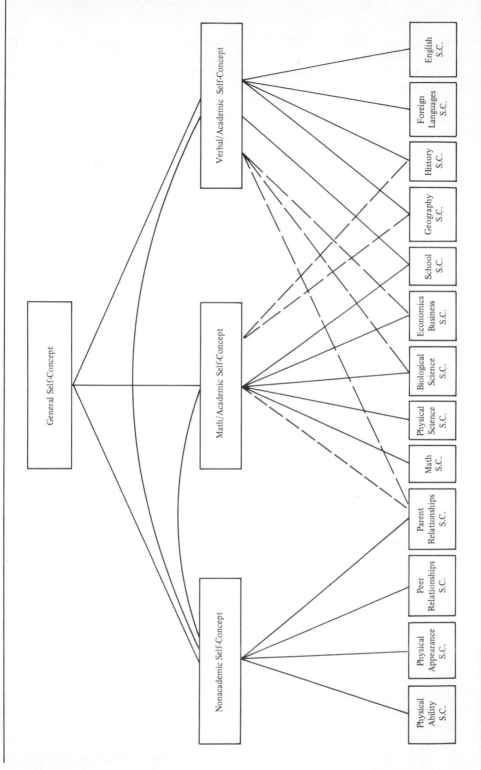

Source: Adapted from "A Multidimensional, Hierarchical Model of Self-Concept: Theoretical and Empirical Justification" by H. W. Marsh, 1990, *Educational Psychology Review, 2,* pp. 90, 93. Used with permission of Plenum Publishing Corporation and the author.

self-concepts in the three more specific areas of self-concept, which in turn are used to form a general self-concept. Taken together, Clarence's nonacademic self-concept, math/academic self-concept, and verbal/academic self-concept would help to form his general self-concept.

In the next portions of this chapter, we describe the physical, cognitive, social, personality, and moral changes that young adolescents go through. For each of these areas, we present several perspectives that explain how theorists think these changes occur. As you read about the various areas of development, think back to the case studies of Clarence and Maria to see how they reflect the ideas presented. You may also want to think back to when you were a young adolescent and recall the changes that were happening to you during your middle-grades years. Keep in mind the role that self-concept plays in young adolescent development and how Clarence's and Maria's self-concept at various times during their middle-grades years may have affected the choices they made. Additionally, try to think of things that you can do as a teacher to help your students adjust to the various changes they are going through and what role you might play in your students' developing self-concept.

Physical Development

Physically, young adolescents undergo more change than at any other time of their lives except infancy. Unlike infants, however, young adolescents are keenly aware of these changes and how they affect their daily lives. In addition, since many of these changes are more related to weight than age, there is wide variation among the changes that students of the same age may be going through. For example, while visiting middle-grades schools, we have noticed height differences as much as 18 inches among boys in the same classroom. This variation among individual students is a possible source of stress.

Research has shown that young adolescents can and do make comparisons among themselves and their peers in terms of physical development (Brooks-Gun, Samelson, Warren, & Fox, 1986). We discuss some of these comparisons later in the chapter. In sum, there is no so-called normal age at which students undergo the various physical changes associated with early adolescence. Therefore, throughout this section, the ages we give represent averages that can vary greatly.

Puberty

When we talk with teachers and parents about young adolescent physical development, the term *puberty* always comes up. Puberty has been defined in many ways, and some researchers differentiate between puberty and pubescence. For our purposes, we define **puberty** as that stage of development when an individual becomes capable of reproduction and we define **pubescence** as the 2 years prior to puberty. Pubescence can be thought of as the onset of puberty. Taking this span of time together, it is easy to see that puberty is not a single event but rather a gradual process that continues over several years.

It is during the onset of puberty that young adolescents usually grow in height and weight and develop secondary sex characteristics. It is during puberty that

puberty

primary sex characteristics develop. Primary sex characteristics (i.e., menarche and ejaculation of sperm) are necessary for reproduction, whereas secondary sex characteristics (e.g., breast development, body hair growth) are not. Maria is in puberty because she has reached menarche. Do you think Clarence is in pubescence or puberty? Why?

The onset of puberty begins, on average, at around age 10½ for girls and at around age 12½ for boys. Approximately 2 years later, age 12½ for girls and 14½ for boys, sexual development begins. It is interesting to note that the age of the onset of puberty is earlier now than it was several centuries and even a generation or two ago. In fact, there are reports of girls in the seventeenth century beginning puberty at around age 17. Improved nutrition and health care are frequently listed as factors associated with the age change in the onset of puberty over time (Tanner, 1971).

We have defined puberty and discussed the average age when it begins, but how does puberty begin and what exactly is involved? Puberty is thought to be triggered by an increase in the hormone levels associated with physical development. These hormones are secreted into the bloodstream by the various endocrine glands. As mentioned earlier, this increase in hormone level appears to be more related to weight than to age. The major physical and sexual changes that occur during puberty are growth in height, weight gain, breast development, body and pubic hair growth, penile and testicular development, and menarche. As you read about each of these five changes, think back to Clarence and Maria and see if they fit the patterns being described.

Girls and boys undergo a growth spurt during early adolescence. Typically, this spurt begins about 2 years earlier for girls (at around age 10½) than boys (at around age 12½). Girls grow about 3½ inches a year, whereas boys grow about 4 inches a year (Faust, 1977; Tanner, 1966, 1970). As a result, girls are, on average, taller than boys until about age 14. Even up to seventh grade, Maria was quite a bit taller than Clarence.

Much of the increase in weight during early adolescence is due to growth in muscles and body fat, although increases in bone size and body organs also play a role. Until around age 14, girls usually weigh more than boys. Around this age, boys' body weight is comprised more of muscle, whereas girls' body weight is comprised more of fat. Unfortunately for Clarence, he and Maria do not fit this pattern.

For girls, breast development is usually one of the first visible signs that sexual development has begun. Breast development can begin anywhere from age 8 to age 18 but it typically begins around age 11 and ends around age 15. It is not unusual for one breast to develop faster than the other. Interestingly, about 80 percent of boys also show some breast development at this time. Unfortunately, Clarence did not know this fact and as a result he thought he was pretty odd.

Growth in pubic and body hair usually begins for girls between the ages of 10 and 12 and for boys between the ages of 11 and 13. Pubic and body hair growth generally begins around the time of the height and weight spurt in both girls and boys. Pubic hair typically grows before axillary (underarm) and other body hair. For boys, axillary and facial hair growth begin at the same time.

Testicular development is usually one of the first signs of sexual development in boys. This growth generally begins about 6 months later than breast development begins in girls. The testes, which produce sperm and testosterone, usually begin to grow around age 11. Development of the penis begins about a year after the testes have begun to grow. The penis grows in length and width and the head becomes larger. The first ejaculation frequently occurs through masturbation or during sleep.

The average age for the beginning of menstruation is 13 years (Faust, 1977). Menarche usually occurs after the growth spurt and about 2 years after breast development has begun. Menarche appears to be highly correlated with weight. Research has shown that menarche occurs around 106 pounds, regardless of age (Frish, 1974). This relationship between menarche and weight may account for the fact that menstruation begins early in obese females and stops completely when weight drops below a critical point, as in the case of females who have anorexia nervosa.

Psychological and Social Effects of Physical Development

Taken together, all of the changes just described represent an enormous amount of change for young adolescents to go through in a relatively short period of time. Also, the fact that individual students may not be going through these changes at the same time as their peers can affect their psychological and social development. The case study of Clarence provides us with some excellent examples of these effects. Three areas that have received the attention of researchers are the effects of physical development on body image; the effects of being early, on time, or late in relation to peers; and the reactions to menarche and ejaculation.

Young adolescent girls are especially concerned with their hair and their facial features.

Body Image.   Young adolescents spend a great deal of time thinking about and looking at their bodies. Research has shown that young adolescents who have positive images about their bodies also tend to have positive feelings about themselves in general. For example, Brooks-Gun and Warren (1988) found that breast growth was associated with superior adjustment, positive peer relations, and positive body image for girls between ages 9 to 11. The researchers speculated that this physical change has a high social value that causes others to respond positively, which results in a positive image of oneself. This was true for Maria, who was extremely pleased with her body to the extent that her low grades did not even bother her. With Maria, however, it was the boys who responded positively to her. The girls were jealous of her, or so she speculated.

Timing of Puberty.   Research has shown that being early, on time, or late in physical development in relation to peers can greatly affect a student's psychological and social development. In addition, the effects differ for girls and boys. Where would you place Clarence and Maria in physical development in relation to their peers—early, on time, or late?

In general, girls who mature early tend to be dissatisfied with their height and weight; most want to be thinner (Duncan, Ritter, Dornbusch, Gross, & Carlsmith, 1985). Girls who mature early are also less satisfied with their body image than girls who mature on time or late (Blyth, Simmons, & Zakin, 1985). Parents perceive better relations with late-maturing daughters than with early-maturing daughters (Savin-Williams & Small, 1986). This could be due to the fact that early-maturing girls tend to date more and spend more time with friends—activities that could lead to conflicts with parents (Susman, Nottelmann, Inoff-Germain, Dorn, Cutler, Loriaux, & Chrousos, 1985). Girls who reach menarche earlier than their peers worry more about their periods than girls who reach menarche on time or late in relation to their peers (Stubbs, Rierdan, & Koff, 1989). We have placed Maria as early in relation to her peers. Which of the characteristics of early-maturing girls apply to her? For the ones that do not apply, can you think of some reasons why they do not?

On the other hand, boys who mature early tend to be more positive about physical changes than girls who mature early. For example, research shows that early-maturing boys are more satisfied with their height and weight than boys who mature on time or late (Duncan et al., 1985). However, boys who mature early are more prone to deviant behavior (Duncan et al., 1985), date more, and spend more time with their friends (Susman et al., 1985) than boys who mature on time or late. Despite this finding, parents still perceive better relations with early-maturing boys than with late-maturing boys (Savin-Williams & Small, 1986). We have placed Clarence as late in physical development in relation to his peers. Which of the characteristics of late-maturing boys apply to Clarence? Which ones do not?

Reactions to Menarche and Ejaculation.   Girls and boys appear to react differently to the development of their primary sex characteristics. Stubbs, Rierdan, and Koff (1989) report that girls have mixed feelings about menarche. On the one hand, they view it as normal and accept it; on the other hand, they worry about it and dislike it. Does Maria fit this description? Those who worry fear that they will have an embarrassing accident or that someone will find out about it. Boys, however, have strong, positive feelings about ejaculation (Gaddis & Brooks-Gun, 1985).

In terms of preparation, girls frequently discuss menarche with their mothers and eventually talk about it with their friends. However, Gaddis and Brooks-Gun (1985) found that only about half of the boys in their study felt well-informed about ejaculation. Those who did reported that they learned about ejaculation by reading books. Only rarely was ejaculation explained to them by an adult male. None of the boys in the study reported that they talked about ejaculation afterwards with their peers.

Problems in Physical Development

Despite the fact that most young adolescents develop quite normally, there are several factors that can disrupt normal physical development. These include general health and diet; eating disorders; and cigarette, alcohol, and drug use.

General Health and Diet.   Although young adolescents are typically healthy, many of them have poor eating and sleeping habits. In 1971, Biehler estimated that only about 10 percent of young adolescents have a proper diet. Unfortunately, the eating habits that are formed during early adolescence have a tendency to turn into life-long habits. Although his case study does not provide any information about Clarence's eating habits, what he eats could play a role in his weight.

Poor eating and sleeping habits can lead to poor health in general. Students who have poor general health are at a disadvantage in the classroom because they are less attentive and absent more often than their more healthy peers. Students who are chronically absent from school and not very attentive when they are at school are quite often the ones who eventually drop out.

Eating Disorders.   A recent Gallup poll (1985) revealed that 12 percent of adolescents girls and 4 percent of adolescent boys suffer from eating disorders. Eating disorders common among young adolescents include obesity and anorexia nervosa. Currently, about 15 percent of young adolescents are obese, and girls outnumber boys in obesity. Young adolescents who are obese do not necessarily eat more than their peers of normal build; rather, they tend to be less active than those peers. Clarence's case study supports the notion that he was not physically active. He cut P.E. whenever possible, and he did not participate in sports because he was clumsy.

Young adolescents who are obese frequently exhibit other physical problems, such as excessive perspiration, skin problems, and reduced mobility. Recall that Clarence had two of these problems. In addition to the present and future (e.g., cardiovascular disease, hypertension) physical problems associated with obesity, this condition can affect social relations, emotional development, and sex identity. Research shows that obese adolescents tend to remain obese as adults. Unfortunately, it appears that if Clarence does not achieve a normal weight by the end of his adolescence, the odds are extremely great that he will develop into an obese adult.

People who suffer from anorexia nervosa have the desire to be thin. Anorexia nervosa can lead to a variety of physical problems, including menstrual problems, hormonal imbalances, infertility, and even death. This disease affects primarily girls from the middle to upper classes (Gilbert & DeBlassie, 1984). Anorexia nervosa is becoming more prevalent as the American culture becomes more fascinated with the idea of slim women. Young adolescents who become anorexic usually do so because they feel they have no control over their lives. In many cases, these young adolescents also have a low physical appearance self-concept. Anorexia nervosa is an excellent example of how self-concept can affect physical development in young adolescents.

Cigarette, Alcohol, and Drug Use.   There is increasing evidence that students who smoke, drink, or use drugs begin these habits during the middle grades. For example, when high school graduates who smoke, drink, or use drugs were surveyed, 51, 56 and 29 percent, respectively, reported that they first experimented during grades 6 through 9 (Johnston, O'Malley, & Bachman, 1988). These statistics are disturbing, given the fact that students who begin to use cigarettes, alcohol, and drugs during the middle grades and continue to use them throughout high school are at risk for long-term dependency.

Even putting future problems aside, the use of cigarettes, alcohol, and drugs can have immediate adverse effects on the physical development of young adolescents, including permanent damage to the central nervous system. Maria is already drinking beer and, if her social life continues in the direction it is going, she will probably continue to do so throughout her high school years. What role do you think Maria's peer relationship self-concept is playing in her willingness to drink beer at such an early age?

Peer pressure is one of the major reasons why young adolescents begin to smoke, drink, or use drugs. Faced with the desire to be like their friends or to be accepted by the "right" group, many young adolescents succumb to peer pressure. Deciding whether or not to smoke, drink, or use drugs is just one example of an important decision that students are being forced to make at an increasingly younger age. Unfortunately, many young adolescents are not capable of making informed decisions because they are unable to see the long-term ramifications of their decisions. Informed decision making, with a particular emphasis on peer pressure, is an appropriate topic for discussion during small-group advisory sessions. Such sessions can be extremely beneficial to students like Maria.

Educational Implications

Given the timing and pace of young adolescent physical development, coupled with the potential for problems, there are a number of things that middle-grades administrators, in general, and middle-grades teachers, in particular, can do to make this process easier.

Middle-grades administrators can design a comprehensive health and physical fitness program that is relevant to the specific needs of young adolescents. Such a program was designed by educators at the Louis Armstrong Middle School in East Elmhurst, New York, in conjunction with faculty members from Queens College in

New York City. The program has two primary goals: education of the physical and education through the physical. Throughout the program, students in grades 5 through 8 are involved in three phases: exploration, exposure, and selection and concentrated work (Catelli, 1990). Figure 2.2 illustrates the phases of the program.

If Clarence had attended the Louis Armstrong Middle School, this program, with its emphasis on physical, emotional, and social development, would have been ideal for him.

Middle-grades administrators can provide appropriate sex education classes in their schools. Because of the variation in the time that students undergo physical changes, early as well as late maturers need to be prepared for these changes. In addition, early and late maturers need reassurance that they are "normal." Along similar lines, nutrition and hygiene classes should be routine in schools for young adolescents.

Young adolescents need sufficient time each day for physical activity and for interacting with their peers outside of the classroom. Unfortunately, many middle-grades schools seem to have abandoned the practice of daily recess or outdoor time after lunch. As a result, young adolescents have very little time (except in P.E., which in many cases is very structured) for physical activity of their own choice. In addition, they have very little time to socialize with their friends. The three or four minutes between classes must usually be devoted to getting books from lockers and getting to the next class on time. During lunch, students barely have time to eat, much less converse with their friends.

Within their classrooms, middle-grades teachers can do a variety of things to help students cope with the physical changes their bodies are going through. First, just by being aware of the wide variations of physical, cognitive, social, personality, and moral development among their students, teachers can recognize and be prepared for any problems students might encounter. For example, if Clarence's teachers had been aware of what he was going through as a result of his physical development, they could have made extra efforts to ensure that he received recognition and support in other areas.

Since they will have students of a variety of heights and weights, teachers can try to have chairs, tables, and desks in their classrooms that are appropriate for their students. Students who are in desks that are too large or who are squeezed into desks that are too small can hardly be expected to concentrate for very long.

Teachers can also ensure that they have appropriate expectations for all students, regardless of their physical development. For example, research (Brackbill & Nevill, 1981) has shown that taller students are expected to be more socially adept than their shorter counterparts. Teachers should remember that physical maturity does not necessarily indicate social or intellectual maturity. In addition, teachers should avoid activities that make comparisons among students and should avoid using nicknames (e.g., Stretch, Shorty) that are based on the physical characteristics of their students.

Finally, teachers can vary the pace and nature of their lessons and activities. Due to their physical development, young adolescents easily become uncomfortable and restless when asked to sit for a long period of time. Teachers can avoid this problem by planning short breaks throughout their lessons, planning activities in

FIGURE 2.2 A Working Model for the Louis Armstrong School Curriculum in Physical Education

---

CURRICULUM THEMES, PHASES AND GOALS

Exploration *Phase I*	Exposure *Phase II*	**Selection and Concentrated Work** *Phase III*

A. *Education of the Physical*

  Physical Development

▪ Awareness of Individual Fitness Levels and Ways of Measuring Health and Skill Related Fitness (Grades 5 & 6)	▪ Exposure to and Participation in a Variety of Activities that Develop Fitness Components (Grades 6 & 7)	▪ Design and Conduct a Personal Fitness Program —Knowledge and Understanding of Health and Fitness Principles (Grade 8)
▪ Awareness and Exploration of Individual Motor Abilities (Grades 5 & 6)		OR
▪ Exploration of a Variety of Movement Patterns and Fundamental Motor Skills and Games (Grades 5 & 6)	▪ Exposure to and Development of Minimum Competence in a Number of Sport, Game and Dance Activities (Grades 6 & 7)	▪ Mastery of at Least *One* Participatory Sport, Game, or Dance Activity (Grade 8)

B. *Education Through the Physical*

  Emotional Development

▪ Experience Some Degree of Joy and Success so that the Student is Motivated to Continue Physical Activity (Grades 5 & 6)	▪ Development of a Positive Self-Image Relating to Personal Movement Capabilities (Grades 6 & 7)	OR
	▪ Demonstration of an Ability to Accept the Winning and Losing Aspects of Competition (Grades 6 & 7)	▪ Plan for and Conduct Recreational Involvement for Self and Others (Grade 8)

  Social Development

▪ Exploration of Human Relations Through Group Activities (Grades 5 & 6)	▪ Development and Demonstration of Positive Social Behaviors— Cooperation, Fair Play, Sportsmanship (Grades 6 & 7)	

Source: From "School-College Partnership: Developing a Working Model for an Inner-City Physical Education Curriculum" by L. Catelli, 1990, *Middle School Journal, 21*(4), pp. 36–39. Reprinted by permission.

which students can interact with their peers, and planning active lessons that involve some physical movement.

Cognitive Development

As was the case with physical development, young adolescents are also experiencing change in their cognitive abilities, that is, changes in the mental activities they are capable of engaging in. In this section, we begin with a brief description of cognition and cognitive development. We then present three different perspectives on cognitive development along with the educational implications of each perspective. Next, we describe a relatively new area of cognition, social cognition, which is concerned with thoughts about social matters. We conclude this section with a discussion of the educational implications of social cognition.

What do we mean when we talk about the cognitive development of young adolescents? You may recall from your psychology or educational psychology courses, references to the terms *stimulus* and *response*. A young adolescent observes a stimulus and makes a response. According to cognitive psychologists, learning is more than just making a response in reaction to a stimulus. Cognitive psychologists believe that individuals are actively involved in their own learning because they are trying to understand their world better. In order to do this, they use all of the resources available to them.

To put it very simply, cognitive psychology is concerned with the activities that occur in the mind between the time of the stimulus and the time of the response. Cognitive development refers to how these activities become more sophisticated as a person gets older and gains more experience. The activities that occur between the stimulus and the response are sometimes referred to as *mechanisms, processes,* or *events.* Some of the mental activities that cognitive psychologists think are important include attention, perception, memory, decision making, and planning. Despite the fact that it is difficult to study these cognitive activities because they cannot be directly observed, a great deal can be inferred from the research that has been done in this area. As a result, there are several theoretical perspectives about how these cognitive activities shape the stimulus before a response is made.

We will now present three of these perspectives: Piaget's developmental perspective, Vygotsky's social perspective, and an information-processing perspective. We will also discuss the educational implications of each of these three perspectives. As you read through each of these three perspectives, try to identify ways in which Clarence's and Maria's academic self-concepts were affected by their cognitive development.

Piaget's Developmental Perspective

You probably are already somewhat familiar with Piaget's (1952, 1972, 1973) theory of cognitive development. Piaget believed that cognitive development takes place as an individual progresses through four stages: sensorimotor thought, preoperational thought, concrete operational thought, and formal operational thought. Biological maturation, coupled with experience, is responsible for moving an individual from one stage to the next. According to Piaget, the order of the stages is always the same, but the age at which individuals move from one stage to another varies greatly. We will review the last two stages, since most young adolescents are at one of these two stages or in transition from one to the other.

As you read through the descriptions of these two stages, think about Clarence and Maria. See if you can find any characteristics of either of them that coincide with descriptions of these two stages of cognitive development.

Concrete Operational Thought.   On average, this stage of cognitive development encompasses ages 6 to 12. Children who are capable of concrete operational thought are able to perform mental operations such as classifying, identifying relationships, and understanding spatial relations. These operations are central to many of the topics taught in the middle grades, particularly topics in mathematics and science. At this stage, children are able to *decenter,* which involves thinking about two or more characteristics of an object simultaneously. They are also able to understand that one characteristic of an object can be changed while other characteristics remain the same (*conservation*) and that these changes can be reversed.

The limitation of this stage is that children can only perform these operations and think logically about **concrete** objects and experiences, that is, objects that they can see, manipulate, or have direct experience with. As such, they are much better at visual problems than verbal problems. Maria had first-hand experience with this characteristic of the concrete operational stage. She realized that being able to see things happen helped her in science class. Students at this level have both feet firmly planted in reality and many of them are not able to deal with the abstract or hypothetical (e.g., "Suppose you are an ant") without some concrete experience first.

Working with concrete objects and manipulatives helps young adolescents who are at the concrete operational level of cognitive development.

Formal Operational Thought. On average, this stage encompa__
through adulthood. Formal operational thought is characterized by the
deal with the abstract, engage in hypothetical deduction, and perform
reasoning. What evidence can you find in Clarence's case study to indicate tha__
was capable of performing some of the operations?

At this stage, individuals are no longer confined to concrete objects. In
addition to being able to deal with abstract concepts, they are also able to think
about and analyze their own thoughts (*metacognition*) and appreciate the fact that
others may think differently than they do (*perspective taking*). Maria was not very
good at perspective taking, at least in social studies. Recall that she could not
understand how some of the kids could find social studies exciting.

Also characteristic of formal operational thought is the ability to form and test
hypotheses. Forming and testing hypotheses is exactly what Clarence liked about
science class. Additionally, an individual can be a formal thinker in one area but
not in another. For example, Clarence was clearly capable of formal thought when
it came to forming and testing scientific hypotheses, but he may not have been so
good at interpreting figurative language in poetry.

Timing of Piaget's Stages for Young Adolescents. Research suggests that young
adolescents may not be as capable of formal operational thinking as was once
believed. Brooks, Fusco, and Grennon (1983) report that only about 15 percent of
young adolescents are even early formal thinkers by age 14, the *end* of their middle-
grades years. Given this statistic, Clarence appears to be in the minority compared
to his peers. In fact, there are some reports of only 17 percent of college students
engaging in formal operational thought. These figures have important educational
implications, which we will now discuss.

Educational Implications of Piaget's Theory. One of the most important things
for teachers of young adolescents to keep in mind as they plan and implement their
lessons is that they will most likely have students capable of a wide range of
cognitive ability in their classrooms. The differences between Clarence and Maria
are a good indication of the variations in cognitive ability in middle-grades classrooms. On the whole, the majority of the students in middle-grades classrooms will
be more like Maria than Clarence. Most will be on the concrete operational level; a
few may be early formal thinkers.

Teachers can informally assess the cognitive levels of their students on activities of varying difficulty by paying careful attention to the types of questions
students ask, the manner in which they respond to questions, the strategies they use
to carry out activities, and the ease or difficulty with which they complete activities.
Maria's thoughts about social studies and the response she gave to one of the
questions her social studies teacher asked are just two examples of how teachers can
informally assess the level of thinking among their students.

Along similar lines, since most young adolescents are concrete thinkers or early
formal thinkers, middle-grades teachers can use concrete examples and hands-on
experience as much as possible. For example, pictures, films, field trips, manipula-

...hould be used to *introduce* new or difficult concepts. Maria was ...ls-on approach in her science class.

...ld also pay careful attention to the ways in which the students' ...e new ideas and concepts. Frequently, new information is pre-...lents in abstract, unfamiliar ways, and teachers may have to ...d information or involve students in relevant discussions before ...cted to tackle the textbook. This does not imply that teachers ...m challenging their students to think abstractly. They just need to ...ts have grasped the basic concepts involved before they move into the abstract. Keeping in mind that not all students will be able to deal with the abstract, teachers should adjust their expectations and lessons accordingly.

Finally, teachers should ensure that young adolescents are actively involved in learning. The students should have ample opportunity to interact with each other and with the teacher about new ideas and concepts. By talking and interacting with those around them, young adolescents will gain valuable insights into how others think and learn. Clarence's experiences working with his peers during science class and science club attest to the benefits of social interaction during learning.

Vygotsky's Social Perspective

Vygotsky (1978) extended Piaget's theories by underscoring the role that other people play in an individual's cognitive development. For young adolescents, these other people can be parents, peers, teachers, or any other persons who can serve as teachers and role models. According to Vygotsky, cognitive development occurs for young adolescents when they interact with other people who provide the necessary support for learning to take place. Language is an essential component of this interaction. Clarence's experience working with his peers in small groups is the type of interaction that Vygotsky felt was critical for cognitive development to occur. Clarence's positive feelings about working with his peers probably played a major role in his science self-concept since the opinions of his peers were important to him. Two factors that play a role in Vygotsky's theory of cognitive development are the zone of proximal development and private speech.

The *zone of proximal development* can be described as the level at which an individual can be successful at a task *if given appropriate guidance*. The zone of proximal development underscores the value of social interaction because, as Vygotsky pointed out "what children can do with the assistance of others might be in some sense even more indicative of their mental development than what they can do alone" (1978, p. 85). The zone of proximal development varies at different stages of an individual's cognitive development and it can also vary depending on the nature of the task or the subject area involved. For example, a young adolescent's zone of proximal development may be different for solving mathematics word problems than for reading expository text. The zone of proximal development can be thought of as the midpoint between an individual's independent level and frustration level. It can also be thought of as the student's instructional level, since this is the level at which the individual should receive instruction.

The notion of independent, instructional, and frustration levels has long been

*Young adolescents use
private speech to select
and implement learning
strategies.*

recognized in the area of reading, but it should be kept in mind in the content areas
as well. It is important to realize that young adolescents will most likely be
frustrated if they are left on their own when they are given tasks that are in their
zone of proximal development. Can you recall a task that Maria was expected to do
on her own that might have been in her zone of proximal development? Likewise,
students will probably be bored if instructed at a level below their zone of proximal
development. As you can see, interaction with others is crucial if young adolescents
are going to be challenged to operate within the zone of proximal development.

Also critical to Vygotsky's theory is the role that speech, particularly private
speech, plays in cognitive development. *Private speech* is defined as "all speech that
is not obviously aimed at others" (Zivin, 1979, p. 16). Thus, private speech can be
either covert (i.e., spoken to one's self) or overt (i.e., spoken out loud). In very
young children, private speech is typically overt because they verbalize their inner
thoughts. By about age 7 or 8, children have learned to internalize their thoughts
rather than verbalize them. When put in particularly difficult or stressful situations
(e.g., working alone on a task in one's zone or proximal development), however,
individuals of any age can revert back to covert private speech. For example, if you
are running late for an important appointment, you might find yourself saying out
loud, "Calm down. A few minutes won't matter. They'll understand."

In Vygotsky's theory, private speech, regardless of whether it is overt or covert, is important because it is always used as a means of regulating one's behavior. In terms of young adolescents' cognitive development, private speech is important because it helps students formulate goals, and select and implement strategies for reaching those goals. Private speech also helps students evaluate their progress and, when goals are not being reached, select alternate strategies for reaching them. Private speech is an important component of several of the learning strategies we discuss in Chapter 12.

In summary, private speech is critical for cognitive development because it allows students "to provide for auxiliary tools in the solution of difficult tasks, to overcome impulsive action, to plan a problem solution prior to its execution, and to master their own behavior" (Vygotsky, 1978, p. 28). Can you identify any instances where Clarence or Maria engaged in private speech? If so, why did they use it? Was it effective? Can you identify any instances where private speech might have been useful but wasn't used by either Clarence or Maria?

Implications of Vygotsky's Theory. Many of the implications we discussed for Piaget's theory can also apply to Vygotsky's theory. In addition, teachers of young adolescents should pay careful attention to the levels at which they instruct students, as well as the levels of the tasks they ask students to do on their own. Students should be instructed at levels that challenge them to do new things and lead them toward independent learning. When working independently, students should be given material that is appropriately challenging but not to the point that it is frustrating. Unfortunately, it appears that Maria's homework was too difficult for her to do on her own. But if she had someone to help and guide her, she might have been quite capable of doing it.

Interaction with peers can also be used to help students operate in their zone of proximal development. Having students work as much as possible in small, heterogeneous ability groups or pairs can enhance their cognitive development as well as their social development. Some of the students in Clarence's group might not have been able to do the work independently, but he provided the support they needed. Capable peers are excellent role models for young adolescents as they work toward becoming more autonomous learners.

Middle-grades teachers can help their students realize the importance and value of private speech by thinking aloud themselves in appropriate situations. For example, when working with students on problem solving, teachers can verbalize their own strategies and reasons for selecting various strategies. If a particular strategy doesn't work, a teacher might say, "Okay, that did not work. What I usually do when I run into a problem like this is. . . ." Teachers can also encourage their students to verbalize their own thoughts and strategies either to themselves or out loud, depending on the situation. For instance, it was appropriate for Clarence to verbalize his planning strategies when he worked with his peers in small groups because he served as a model for the other students. But if Clarence had been taking a test, it would have been more appropriate for him to talk through these strategies to himself.

Information-Processing Perspective

A somewhat different view of cognitive development is taken by psychologists who subscribe to an information-processing perspective. *Information processing* is a term borrowed from computer science, and this perspective makes the analogy between the mind and a computer. Over time, people develop sophisticated systems for absorbing, organizing, and using information. Clarence's case study indicates that he had developed some very effective planning strategies that helped him when he tackled new and difficult problems. Earlier in this chapter, we discussed the activities or processes that take place between the stimulus and the response. Information processing is concerned with learning more about the exact nature of these processes. Two important processes that cognitive psychologists are interested in are attention and memory. It is believed that these processes play a major role in the way a stimulus is shaped before a response is made.

Attention.   Young adolescents frequently have to make decisions about how they are going to allocate their attention. This allocation of attention can affect how information is processed (Britton, Muth, & Glynn, 1986). For example, when trying to solve a mathematics word problem that is being presented to thcm orally, young adolescents may be required to attend to several things at once, and how they allocate their attention can affect how successful they are at solving the problem.

It appears that the ability to attend to several things simultaneously increases with age, making young adolescents better at complex tasks than young children. In addition, young adolescents are better at deciding what is important to attend to and have longer attention spans than young children, but not as long as older adolescents or adults. Maria was unable, in most of her classes, to focus her attention on the material being presented. As a result, she did not understand most of it.

Memory.   Obviously, memory plays a major role in how information is processed and stored in the mind. You may recall the terms *short-term memory* and *long-term memory* from previous courses. Short-term memory is thought to be limited in capacity; young adolescents may have difficulty performing tasks that overload their short-term memory. It appears that there are developmental differences in memory. For example, the short-term memories of young children may get overloaded more quickly than those of young adolescents. Although strategies to enhance memory, as well as speed and efficiency of processing information, are believed to play a role, the exact reasons for these differences are still being researched.

Clarence's case study mentions that he developed little games to help him remember important information when he studied for a test. These games were probably memory strategies that he devised. Can you speculate on what some of these strategies might have been? In Chapter 12, we describe some effective memory strategies that young adolescents can use to help them remember important information.

Another area of memory, metamemory, is currently receiving much interest among information-processing theorists. *Metamemory* refers to the ability to be aware of your own memory processes. It appears that this ability increases with age, although even young children are capable of it in some situations. Do you think either Clarence or Maria were knowledgeable about their memory processes?

Educational Implications of Information-Processing Theory.   The information-processing perspective of cognitive development offers valuable information for the ways new information should be presented to young adolescents and for the ways we expect them to understand and apply this information. First, since knowledge seems to play a major role in processing information, teachers should ensure that young adolescents possess both the prerequisite knowledge and new knowledge necessary to be successful at the tasks they engage in. For example, Maria did not seem to have adequate knowledge to answer her teacher's question about the island of Crete. Determining whether or not a particular student possesses prerequisite knowledge can be done in a variety of ways, which we discuss in more detail in Chapter 9.

Second, teachers can identify the various components of the tasks they assign their students. Sufficient time should be spent on presenting each component, allowing students to practice before moving on to the next component, and finally putting all of the components together (Case, 1985). For instance, when learning how to write a persuasive letter, students can be taught first to make a list of all their arguments, then put the arguments in some type of order, next put the arguments in sentences, and finally attend to mechanics such as spelling, punctuation, and grammar. Trying to perform all of these components on the first draft could result in poorly designed letters.

Along similar lines, if a student is encountering difficulty with a particular task, the teacher can try to determine which component of the task is causing the difficulty and then have the student practice that component. This method is typically used in mathematics but can also be used in other content areas as well.

Third, teachers should keep in mind that the process is just as important, and sometimes more important, as the product. Remember that information processing is concerned with how information is processed and used. For example, the final answer in a word problem may not be as important as the various methods that the students used to get the answer. Focusing as much as possible on process instead of product can also have a positive effect on students' academic self-concepts. And, since young adolescents are at an age when they are just beginning to be able to consider more than one alternative, this is an excellent time for challenging them to think of alternative methods and procedures for the various tasks they work on.

Last, since young adolescents are becoming increasingly able to think about their own thought processes and mental strategies, teachers can encourage them, given the right situation, to think aloud and verbalize what they are thinking, what strategy they used to remember certain information, why they selected that strategy, if the strategy worked, and so on. Teachers are also encouraged to spend some time teaching mental strategies (e.g., rehearsal, imagery) to young adolescents. Clarence was capable of designing his own mental strategies, but many young adolescents are not. Direct teaching of mental strategies may increase the likelihood that students will begin to use them. (We talk more about strategy use in Chapter 12.)

Young Adolescents' Perceptions of Their Academic Ability

Social learning theorist Albert Bandura has looked extensively at young adolescents and adolescents. Bandura's (1986, 1988) social-cognitive theory illustrates the important role that self-perceptions play in academic learning. Bandura's work shows that people's perceptions of their own capabilities are quite often different from their actual capabilities. For example, given similar capabilities, individuals with higher perceptions of their capabilities may actually perform better than individuals with lower perceptions of their capabilities.

Bandura's theory emphasizes the role that self-appraisal plays in the development of accurate self-perceptions of one's own capabilities. Self-appraisal involves judging a number of factors (e.g., task difficulty, circumstances surrounding the task such as time limits, past performance on similar tasks) simultaneously. Self-appraisal is often difficult for young adolescents because they lack experience at it. One strategy that Bandura recommends to develop more accurate self-appraisals is to observe social models (e.g., teachers, parents, peers) who have developed this skill. In middle-grades classrooms, the use of small, cooperative groups is an excellent mechanism for providing young adolescents with peers who can serve as appropriate social models.

When students work cooperatively in small groups, they have an opportunity to observe the processes their peers use in making self-appraisals. For example, since Clarence was very organized and planned carefully before he attacked problems, he was an excellent role model for the other students in his group. Additionally, he liked working with the other students, so he was probably very patient with them and explained things clearly to them. In fact, Clarence seemed to like helping others with their school work so much that he even helped his little sister, something not many young adolescent boys would probably do. Do you think Maria could have benefitted from working in small groups with other students?

Given the fact that many young adolescents are not proficient at self-appraisal, how do these students go about making judgments about their academic ability? Unfortunately, evidence suggests that young adolescents rate their academic ability and the academic ability of their peers in terms of the grades they receive. For example, Nicholls (1979) found that when young adolescents were asked to rate their academic ability, their answers correlated with their grades. Blumenfeld, Pintrich, Meece, and Wessels (1986) reported that students mentioned grades twice as often in the fifth grade than in the second grade when asked how they knew if someone was smart.

In addition, it appears that young adolescents tend to compare their academic performance with that of their peers. In particular, Feldlaufer, Midgley, and Eccles (1988) found that comparison of report cards increases when young adolescents enter junior high. How did Clarence and Maria go about appraising their academic ability? Which of the two do you think was more accurate in his or her appraisal? Why?

Given the prominent role that grades appear to play in young adolescents' perceptions of their academic ability, coupled with the idea that self-perceptions can affect performance, what do you think about (1) the type of goals you might set for your students, (2) the methods you might use for communicating progress toward goals to your students and their parents, (3) the role that grades might play in your evaluations of student progress, and (4) the criteria you might use for assigning grades?

On a more positive note, Steinberg, Elmen, and Mounts (1989) found that adolescents who feel their parents are warm, democratic, and fair tend to develop more positive attitudes and beliefs toward their achievement than their peers. This finding, however, came from a sample of primarily white, middle-class families. Can you think of a reason to explain these results? Do you think the results would be the same if the students were from minority groups or from low socioeconomic families? Do either Clarence or Maria fit this profile? What implications do you think the results of this study have for middle-grades teachers?

Social Cognition

A relatively new area of interest among psychologists is how young adolescents learn about social matters. This area, called *social cognition,* is concerned with how individuals learn about others and their viewpoints, and how they see themselves in comparison to others (Shantz, 1975). Kohlberg's (1963, 1969) theory of moral development (which we discuss later in this chapter) can be thought of as one component of social cognition. In addition to the research that has been done in the area of social development, two of the perspectives on cognitive development that we discussed previously (i.e., Piaget's developmental perspective and the information-processing perspective) have also influenced the area of social cognition.

Developmental Perspective.   Influenced by Piaget and Kohlberg, Selman (1976, 1980) proposed that social cognition develops in stages. These stages revolve around role-taking skills that involve the ability to distinguish between one's own and others' perspectives. Selman has identified five stages of role taking, with young adolescents falling into the fourth stage. Young adolescents at this stage are capable of seeing beyond their own and others' perspectives in order to look at social situations from a neutral perspective.

Another important component of this perspective, especially for young adolescents, is egocentrism (Elkind, 1967; Looft, 1971). *Egocentrism,* which can be thought of as the opposite of role taking, is the inability to separate oneself from others and the rest of the world. Egocentric young adolescents consider only their own point of view and they consider it as the only point of view. In addition, young adolescents who are egocentric tend to focus on an imaginary audience (Elkind & Bowen, 1979). The *imaginary audience* is defined as the feeling that everyone is as concerned about your behavior as you are. Perhaps the belief in an imaginary audience can explain our previous discussion about young adolescent girls who worry about menarche because they fear everyone will know.

According to Elkind (1967), egocentrism declines developmentally as individuals progress through Piaget's cognitive stages. For example, in the sixth grade,

Young adolescents who are egocentric have the feeling that everyone is looking at them.

Clarence thought everyone was looking at him in the locker room, to the point that he lied to get out of P.E. But by seventh grade, Clarence had figured out the other boys were actually in too much of a hurry to get to their next class to take time to look at him. Do you think Maria exhibited any egocentrism?

Information-Processing Perspective. The information-processing perspective of social cognition, referred to as *social information processing*, is concerned with how individuals process information about their social world. Researchers who hold this perspective of social cognition are interested in such questions as how attention, memory, planning, and other mental activities affect an individual's ability to process information about social matters. As such, social information processing looks at social development in much the same way as cognitive information processing looks at cognitive development. Clarence was very good at using attention, memory, and planning when it came to academic matters. Do you think he was skillful at using these mental activities in social situations? What about Maria?

Educational Implications of Social Cognition. Selman (1976) encourages teachers to become aware of the stage of social cognition that each of their students are in because it will give them a better understanding of the social relationships in their classrooms. Also, by determining the social cognition stages of their students, teachers can set more realistic expectations for the students and, as a result, will be more likely not to overestimate their social abilities.

Teachers can also put their students, as much as possible, into situations that require them to take various roles and think about the perspectives of others. In addition, teachers of young adolescents may want to consider giving students duties in the classroom and in the school that would help them gain a sense of responsibility and provide them with opportunities to interact with other people.

Finally, discussions and activities concerning egocentrism, others' perspectives and feelings, developing a sense of self-identity, and other related issues may help young adolescents become less egocentric. These discussions and activities would be extremely appropriate for advisory sessions in the middle grades and would probably have been very beneficial to Clarence. In addition to classroom activities and discussions, teachers can expose students to the wide variety of books written about young adolescents like themselves. Besides helping students develop their reading skills and gain an appreciation of reading for pleasure, these books can help students become less egocentric. Many of the novels written for young adolescents help students identify with others who are encountering problems similar to theirs. Clarence and Maria might both have benefitted from reading some of these books.

Social, Personality, and Moral Development

School for young adolescents involves much more than academic matters. During their young adolescent years, students are going through changes with respect to their social, personality, and moral development. Contrary to popular notions, early adolescence is not necessarily a time of enormous emotional stress for all young adolescents (Bandura, 1964). More recently, in a study involving lower-, middle-, and upper-class 9- through 15-year-olds, Larson and Lampman-Petraitis (1989) found "little support for the hypothesis that the onset of adolescence is associated with increased emotionality" (p. 1250).

Before we discuss each of these three areas of development, we will define them and discuss their interrelated nature. *Social development* refers to changes that occur in the ways that individuals interact with others. *Personality development* refers to changes that occur within individuals in the way they view themselves. *Moral development* refers to changes that occur in the rules and principles that individuals use to guide their interactions with others. As you read these definitions, you probably noticed that these three areas of development overlap. For instance, it is hard to imagine a young adolescent changing socially without undergoing some personality change at the same time. Similarly, it seems likely that moral development would also be accompanied by some social changes and vice versa.

Social Development

A great deal of young adolescents' thoughts and actions are devoted to social matters. It is at this time that young adolescents are beginning to change in the ways that they relate to and interact with other people. This process is generally referred to as **socialization**. A fairly new line of research in the area of social development is called **social learning theory**. Social learning theorists are concerned with "the whole spectrum of the socialization process by which children learn, often through indirect teaching, to conform to the cultural expectations of acceptable behavior" (Muuss, 1982, p. 271).

Social learning theorists believe that the situation and the environment are more important in social development than other factors such as maturation. In a sense, Clarence learned indirectly that it wasn't cool to wear jeans with patches on the thighs, especially if he had any hope of ever being accepted by the other boys.

Unfortunately, there wasn't much Clarence could do about it since his mother didn't seem to be very flexible when it came to wearing jeans.

Social learning theorists such as Bandura (1977) believe that individuals watch and then imitate the behavior of models, who may or may not know they are being imitated. Behavior that is rewarded is more likely to be modeled than behavior that is punished. Three very influential models for young adolescents are parents, peers and peer groups, and teachers.

Despite the fact that young adolescents are at a stage when they are seeking more autonomy, parents still play a major role in the socialization process of their children. Young adolescents report that their parents have more influence on their attitudes, behavior, and performance in school than their best friends (Berndt, Miller & Park, 1989). Most young adolescents' ideological beliefs parallel those of their parents (Newman & Newman, 1988).

In addition, despite widely held beliefs to the contrary, young adolescents' relationships with their parents are quite strong and harmonious. This is not to say that young adolescents and their parents always agree on things, but their disagreements tend to arise over everyday matters such as chores, dress, and regulating social activities (Smetana, 1989). This was certainly true for Clarence, who disagreed with his mother over clothes. Smetana also reported that parents and their children tend to agree on the causes of these disagreements and that disagreements over homework and academic achievement peak during early adolescence. Smetana speculated that this last finding may be the result of the transition to a new school when grades typically decline.

Peers and peer groups can have a significant influence on young adolescents' social development. Being part of a group can mean support, friendship, and access to social activities, but it can also lead to conformity (Brown, Eicher, & Petrie, 1986). Young adolescents report that when peers do influence them, they tend to be a positive rather than negative influence (Berndt, Miller, & Park, 1989). Interestingly, students who perceive themselves as being part of a group value group membership more than students not part of a group (Brown, Eicher, & Petrie, 1986).

Gavin and Furman (1989) report that the desire to be in the popular group increases during early adolescence and that the pressure to conform is higher, groups are less permeable, and groups have a clearer hierarchical structure in early and middle adolescence than in late adolescence. Peer groups appear to be more important to girls than boys, especially in terms of conformity in appearance (O'Brien & Bierman, 1988). We found the exact opposite was true for Clarence and Maria. Can you think of any reasons why acceptance by a peer group was more important to Clarence than to Maria?

Teachers have the potential to serve as important role models for young adolescents. At a time when many young adolescents are beginning to seek independence from their parents, other adults such as teachers can serve as the stepping stone between parent and peer models. Unfortunately, the little research that has been done in this area indicates that young adolescents do not perceive their teachers in this way. For example, in a recent review of the research on teachers as significant others, Galbo (1989) notes that teachers account for only "ten percent or less of all the significant adults mentioned in research studies'' (p. 550). Galbo also notes that when teachers are listed as significant others, it is usually for academic rather than social reasons.

Since most of the research in this area is based on self-reports from students, it is not clear whether teachers really are not significant in young adolescents' lives or whether teachers do play a role but students see that role as less significant than the role of their parents. Some optimistic researchers think that young adolescents underestimate the role their teachers play in their social development.

Except for a few references to academic matters, neither Clarence's nor Maria's case studies even mention teachers. If you were Clarence's or Maria's teacher, how do you think you could serve as an effective role model? Do you think it would be a good idea to talk to Clarence's or Maria's parents about how their children are developing socially? Would you give their parents any recommendations about things they could do as parents to help their children develop socially? If so, what recommendations would you make?

Personality Development

Young adolescents are faced with numerous choices, all of which have the potential to shape their personality. One of the most comprehensive theories of personality development is that of Erik Erikson (1963). Erikson identified eight stages of personality development, each of which is identified by conflict between the individual and the outside world. Presumably, as individuals pass from one stage to the next, they are able to cope more successfully with life. The stage that is probably of most importance to middle-grades teachers is stage five, identity versus role confusion. The majority of young adolescents will enter and remain in this stage during their middle-grades years. In the next section, we describe stage five and two of its important components: identity and self-concept, and sex-role identity.

At stage five of Erikson's (1963) theory, identity versus role confusion, individuals search for a personal identity, or an answer to the question: Who am I? Although they never directly asked themselves that question, both Clarence and Maria were searching for the answer. This search for identity involves the notion of self-concept, which we described in detail in the beginning of this chapter. Self-concept is greatly influenced by experience, especially experiences with parents, peers, and schools.

As individuals pass through stage five, they develop a better sense of who they are and this sense of who they are becomes more consistent with how others view them. The development of a general self-concept is an extremely slow process. Although large changes may be observed in the more specific facets of self-concept, general self-concept is rather stable in young adolescents (O'Malley & Bachman, 1983). How do you think Clarence and Maria are progressing in terms of developing a sense of who they are? Do you think their sense of who they are is consistent with how others view them? Why or why not?

Sex-role identity is another important component of personality development. *Sex-role identity* refers to individuals' ideas about what it means to be male or female. As was the case with self-concept, sex-role identity is also greatly influenced by parents, peers, and school. During the elementary school years, except for a few traditional differences, such as boys being more aggressive than girls, surprisingly few differences between boys and girls are observed. However, during adolescence, several differences begin to emerge. For example, females perform better on verbal creativity tests, whereas males perform better on some tests of mathematical reasoning and spatial-visual tests. Also, males take credit for their successes more than females, but females are more helpful than males. How do Clarence and Maria fit this pattern?

During the past decade or two, psychologists have begun to look at sex-role identification in a different light. Traditionally, males were expected to demonstrate male characteristics and females were expected to demonstrate female characteristics. In more recent times, however, some psychologists, such as Bem (1975), advocate a model of sex-role identification in which individuals demonstrate the positive characteristics of both males and females. For example, males can be athletic and also emotional, and females can be gentle and also ambitious.

Educational Implications of Social and Personality Development

There are a number of things that middle-grades teachers can do to help young adolescents develop a better sense of who they are and how they relate to other people. Probably one of the easiest and most effective things teachers can do is to keep in mind that all students develop differently and at different rates. Hence, the students in your classes are likely to exhibit a wide range of development. Therefore, the goals and expectations you set for students should be developmentally appropriate.

Students should also be encouraged and taught how to set realistic goals for themselves. Goal setting is a topic that could easily be discussed with young adolescents in a small-group advisory session. For example, Maria seemed to be moving through early adolescence with no goals in mind, particularly in the area of academics. A program on setting realistic goals might well prevent Maria from becoming a dropout at some time during her high school years. Her academic progress so far, coupled with the apparent indifference of her parents, puts her at risk of dropping out.

As much as possible, teachers should provide opportunities in their classrooms for social interaction. Young adolescents need time to talk with their peers about social matters as well as academic matters. Students need to be exposed to the ideas and opinions of others in order to develop socially as well as personally. Perhaps if Maria had spent more time with other students her age, instead of older boys, she would have engaged in more age-appropriate social activities. Interacting with other students her age in nonthreatening classroom settings might have encouraged her to spend more time with them outside of school.

Teachers can also provide opportunities for students to be recognized for their achievements and accomplishments, especially in front of their peers. For example, during group work, Clarence got recognition from his peers for his academic ability and his organizational and planning skills. This seemed to satisfy Clarence, but it also might have been helpful for his teacher to tap those skills in such a way that he would have received recognition from all of the students. All students have strengths and weaknesses, and teachers need to make it a point to identify and recognize each individual student's strengths. Teachers can also encourage creativity and individuality instead of conformity as much as possible in the classroom.

In order to avoid constant conflicts with young adolescents who are looking for autonomy, teachers should have clear, reasonable classroom rules. These rules should be enforced consistently and in the same manner for all students. Some teachers may also want to involve their students in determining class rules and penalties at the beginning of the school year. (This topic will be discussed in detail in Chapter 15.)

In order to avoid sex-role stereotyping, teachers are encouraged to treat boys and girls the same in the goals and expectations they set, in the activities they assign, and in the responsibilities they give. Boys and girls should be given the same options and choices in the classroom, especially in academic matters.

Moral Development

Moral development refers to changes in how individuals reason about right and wrong in their interactions with others. Due to changes in our society, young adolescents are being forced to make critical choices at an age when many of them do not have the ability to make informed decisions. For example, young adolescents are faced with choices about smoking, drinking, taking drugs, engaging in sex, and joining gangs that encourage violence and crime. The development of morals in young adolescents is complicated by the many physical, cognitive, social, and personality changes with which they are struggling.

Being thrust into difficult social situations with a developing body and a low self-concept can play havoc with a young adolescent's sense of right and wrong. This is exactly what appears to have happened to Maria. We will discuss two perspectives of moral development: a cognitive-developmental perspective and a social-learning perspective.

Cognitive-Developmental Perspective.   One of the most well-known theories of moral development is that of Lawrence Kohlberg (1963, 1976, 1980), who extended previous work by Piaget. This theory posits that moral development is determined by an individual's level of cognitive development. Moral development is seen as a progression through a series of six stages. Most young adolescents are in stages two, three, or four. Individuals in stage two are usually still egocentric and they view everything in terms of their own needs. At this stage, individuals' actions are determined by their own, and occasionally other's, desires. They also interpret good and bad in terms of the consequences associated with their actions.

For example, in the sixth grade, Clarence forged his mother's signature on notes excusing him from P.E. because of his desire to avoid getting dressed in front of the other boys. Similarly, in the sixth grade, Maria lied to her parents because of her desire to go out with Alfredo. Both Clarence and Maria stopped this behavior because of their fear of the consequences of getting caught, not because of any feelings that it was wrong to lie to their parents.

At stage three, good and bad are determined according to what pleases other people. For example, in eighth grade, Clarence might try very hard during P.E., exercise after school, and participate in a weight-control program because his parents asked him to and he wants to please them. What type of behavior do you think Maria might engage in at stage three?

At stage four, young adolescents determine good and bad as a sense of duty, which overshadows their own personal desires. For example, Clarence might continue his exercise and diet throughout his high school years because he knows how important physical fitness is and how it will affect his health throughout his entire life. Describe what Maria might do at stage four. At the end of the case studies, what stage do you think Clarence is at? Maria? Why?

Social-Learning Perspective. Social-learning theory is not developmental in nature. Social-learning theorists, such as Albert Bandura, maintain that moral behavior, just like any other behavior, is learned. Parents, peers, teachers, and significant others serve as models and their behavior is observed and imitated. Behavior that is rewarded is more likely to continue than behavior that is punished. For example, Maria was getting social recognition by going out with the older boys, especially since she was riding in cars and drinking beer. In a sense, this social recognition was a reward for her, so she continued to date the older boys. What do you think Maria might have done if her parents had punished her for engaging in these activities?

Social-learning theorists distinguish between knowing what should be done (moral reasoning) and what is actually done (moral behavior). This distinction is not made in Kohlberg's developmental perspective. Do you think Maria actually distinguished between what she should be doing and what she was doing?

Educational Implications. The issue of moral education in the classroom is an extremely controversial one. Nevertheless, there are several things that teachers can do to encourage appropriate moral development in their students. First and foremost, teachers can serve as good role models for their students. Teachers should follow the same rules that they expect their students to follow and obey. If students are not allowed to eat in the classroom, then the teacher should not eat there as well. Teachers should also ensure that students understand the rationale behind all class rules. If students see a good reason for a rule, they are more likely to obey it for social reasons rather than for fear of punishment.

Middle-grades teachers can also use small-group advisory sessions to discuss the process of making informed choices. Along similar lines, sessions on goal setting can be planned to help young adolescents to think about the people and things they value and to begin to think about how to prioritize future goals. Roleplaying can be used as a means of helping students understand the viewpoints of others as well as a means of teaching them how to resolve conflicts.

Young adolescents also need to be provided with opportunities for choice in the classroom. They should be encouraged to weigh alternatives when they make academic and social choices and to consider the outcomes of their choices.

Teachers can also help their students develop a sense of social responsibility. This can be done by giving each student some responsibility within the classroom that makes him or her answerable to others. Social responsibility can also be encouraged through the curriculum and through after-school and community activities. Special programs have been designed in many cities to help young adolescents become more involved in their communities. Figure 2.3 describes the Early Adolescent Helper Program designed by The City University of New York. This program assigns young adolescents as helpers in community places such as Head Start and senior citizen centers. The helpers work under the supervision of a trained adult and attend weekly seminars to help them reflect on their experiences.

Finally, teachers should be aware of the stages of moral development. By knowing that students can be at different levels of development, teachers may be better able to understand their students' behavior in the classroom.

FIGURE 2.3   Student Helpers Form Community Ties

Connections between the community and the school are one important result of the Early Adolescent Helper Program (EAHP) initiated by The City University of New York. School personnel get to know the people and resources in their community as they seek placements for the Helpers. Community agency staff gain understanding of the schools in their area through what may be their first formal agency contact with the school system. Thus, while the young adolescent Helpers are gaining a sense of belonging to the community, adults in the program are doing the same.

The EAHP trains middle grade students as Helpers and places them in the community for after-school assignments in safe and supervised places. Helpers are sent to child care or Head Start centers, where they read to the children, supervise the playground, assist with the snack, conduct arts and crafts or music activities, and help with math games. Other Helpers are placed in senior citzen centers, where they join in projects with the elderly, such as interviewing one another on audio or videotape about life experiences of different generations.

An adult, usually a teacher or guidance counselor, trains Helpers in weekly small-group seminar with hands-on activities designed to build Helpers' skills and prepare them for their role in the community. The seminars emphasize reflection and encourage Helpers to talk about themselves, think about their futures, and take responsibility for their daily lives. Helpers share experiences, ideas, and approaches and discuss their feelings about being a Helper as well as appropriate dress and behavior on their assignments.

Developing trust within the seminar enables Helpers to discuss concerns that are not usually addressed in school. As young adolescents, for example, they have had little experience in exercising authority or power, and they are able in the seminar to exchange views on this subject.

In one newsletter on the program, Helpers said they learned to listen to others, to trust and be trusted by others, to be patient and reliable, to accept responsibility, and to meet new people who became important to them. They enjoyed getting to know adults at their school outside the usual teacher-student relationships, and especially liked being treated as co-staff, feeling valued for their efforts and opinions, and feeling important to others.

Adults reported in the newsletter that the Helpers acted without exception in a professional manner, attended regularly, and assumed their work roles with complete seriousness. The adults also noted positive attitude and behavior changes.

Source: From *Turning Points: Preparing American Youth for the 21st Century* by Carnegie Council on Adolescent Development, 1989, Washington, D.C.: Carnegie Council on Adolescent Development. Reprinted by permission.

Summary

As illustrated through the case studies of Clarence and Maria, young adolescents go through enormous physical, cognitive, social, personality, and moral development during their middle-grades years. All of these areas of development interact, so that a change in one area can affect any or all of the other areas. The multifaceted and hierarchical structure of self-concept plays an important role in the interrelationship among the various areas. The numerous facets of self-concept can affect young adolescents' development and vice versa.

Because development in these areas proceeds at different rates for different individuals, young adolescents make comparisons between themselves and their peers. These comparisons can cause anxiety for young adolescents who feel they are not normal. These comparisons can also affect the self-concepts of young adolescents. Middle-grades teachers can help their students by becoming aware of the specific variations that can occur in young adolescent development, making their students aware of these variations, and then reassuring them that peer comparisons are not always an accurate measure of their own development.

In summary, middle-grades teachers are encouraged to become aware of the various stages of physical, cognitive, social, personality, and moral development and keep in mind that the students in their classroom will not all be on the same level. Teachers should treat all students as individuals and provide tasks and opportunities that are developmentally appropriate for them.

REFERENCES

Bandura, A. (1964). The stormy decade: fact or fiction? *Psychology in the schools, 1*, 224–231.

Bandura, A. (1977). *Social learning theory.* Englewood Cliffs, NJ: Prentice Hall.

Bandura, A. (1986). *Social foundations of thought and actions: A social cognitive theory.* Englewood Cliffs, NJ: Prentice Hall.

Bandura, A. (1988). Self-efficacy conceptions of anxiety. *Anxiety Research, 1*, 77–98.

Bem, S. L., (1975). Sex role adaptability: One consequence of psychological androgyny. *Journal of Personality and Social Psychology, 31*, 634–643.

Berndt, T. J., Miller, K. E., & Park, K. (1989). Adolescents' perceptions of friends' and parents' influence on aspects of their school adjustment. *Journal of Early Adolescence, 4*, 419–435.

Biehler, R. F. (1971). *Psychology applied to teaching.* Boston: Houghton Mifflin.

Blumenfeld, P., Pintrich, P., Meece, J., & Wessels, K. (1986). Children's concepts of ability, effort, and conduct. *American Educational Research Journal, 23*, 95–104.

Blyth, D. A., Simmons, R. G., & Zakin, D. F. (1985). Satisfaction with body image for early adolescent females: The impact of pubertal timing within different school environments. *Journal of Youth and Adolescence, 14*, 207–225.

Brackbill, Y., & Nevill, D., (1981). Parental expectations of achievement as effected by children's height. *Merrill-Palmer Quarterly, 27*, 429–441.

Britton, B. K., Muth, K. D., & Glynn, S. M. (1986). Effects of text organization on memory: Test of a cognitive effort hypothesis. *Discourse Processes, 10*, 475–487.

Brooks, M., Fusco, E., & Grennon, J. (1983). Cognitive levels matching. *Educational Leadership, 40*, 4–8.

Brooks-Gun, J., Samelson, M., Warren, M. P., & Fox, R. (1986). Physical similarity of and disclosure of menarcheal status to friends: Effects of age and pubertal status. *Journal of Early Adolescence, 6*, 285–300.

Brooks-Gun, J., & Warren, M. P. (1988). The psychological significance of secondary sexual characteristics in nine-to-eleven-year old girls. *Child Development, 59,* 1061–1069.

Brown, B. B., Eicher, S. A., & Petrie, S. (1986). The importance of peer group ("crowd") affiliation in adolescence. *Journal of Adolescence, 9,* 73–96.

Case, R. (1985). A developmentally-based approach to the problem of instructional design. In R. Glaser, S. Chipman, & J. Segal (Eds.), *Teaching thinking skills* (Vol. 2, pp. 545–562). Hillsdale, NJ: Erlbaum.

Catelli, L. (1990). School-college partnership: Developing a working model for an inner-city physical education curriculum. *Middle School Journal, 21*(4), 36–39.

Duncan, P. D., Ritter, P. L., Dornbusch, S. M., Gross, R. T., & Carlsmith, J. M. (1985). The effects of pubertal timing on body image, school behavior, and deviance. *Journal of Youth and Adolescence, 14,* 227–235.

Elkind, D. (1967). Egocentrism in adolescence. *Child Development, 38,* 1025–1034.

Elkind, D., & Bowen, R. (1979). Imaginary audience behavior in children and adolescents. *Developmental Psychology, 15,* 38–44.

Erikson, E. (1963). *Childhood and society* (2nd ed.). New York: Norton.

Faust, M. S. (1977). Somatic development of adolescent girls. *Monographs of the Society for Research in Child Development, 42* (1, Serial No. 169).

Feldlaufer, H., Midgley, C., & Eccles, J. (1988). Student, teacher, and observer perceptions of the classroom environment before and after the transition to junior high school. *Journal of Early Adolescence, 8,* 133–156.

Frish, R. E. (1974). Critical weight in menarche, initiation of the adolescent growth spurt, and control of puberty. In M. M. Grumbach, G. D. Grave, & F. E. Mayer (Eds.), *Control of the onset of puberty.* New York: Wiley.

Gaddis, A., & Brooks-Gun, J. (1985). The male experience of pubertal change. *Journal of Youth and Adolescence, 14,* 61–69.

Galbo, J. J. (1989). The teacher as significant adult: A review of the literature. *Adolescence, 24,* 549–556.

Gallup, G. (1985, November 8). Poll of adolescent eating disorders. *USA Today.*

Gavin, L. A., & Furman, W. (1989). Age differences in adolescents' perceptions of their peer groups. *Developmental Psychology, 25,* 827–834.

Gilbert, E. H., & DeBlassie, R. R. (1984). Anorexia nervosa: Adolescent starvation by choice. *Adolescence, 19,* 839–853.

Johnston, L. D., O'Malley, P. M., & Bachman, J. G. (1988). *Illicit drug use, smoking and drinking by America's high school students, college students, and young adults.* (DHHS Publication No. (ADM) 89-1602). Washington, DC: U.S. Government Printing Office.

Kohlberg, L. (1963). The development of children's orientations toward moral order: Sequence in the development of moral thought. *Vita Humans, 6,* 11–33.

Kohlberg, L. (1969). Stage and sequence: The cognitive-developmental approach to socialization. In D. A. Goslin (Ed.), *Handbook of socialization theory and research* (pp. 347–380). Chicago: Rand McNally.

Kohlberg, L. (1976). Moral stages and moralization. In T. Lickona (Ed.), *Moral development and behavior: Theory, research, and social issues.* New York: Holt.

Kohlberg, L. (1980). *Recent research in moral development.* New York: Holt.

Larson, R., & Lampman-Petraitis, C. (1989). Daily emotional states as reported by children and adolescents. *Child Development, 60,* 1250–1260.

Looft, W. R., (1971). Egocentrism and social interaction in adolescence. *Adolescence, 6,* 485–494.

Marsh, H. W. (1984). Relations among dimensions of self-attribution, dimensions of self-concept, and academic achievements. *Journal of Educational Psychology, 76,* 1291–1308.

Marsh, H. W. (1986). Global self-esteem: Its relation to specific facets of self-concept and their importance. *Journal of Personality and Social Psychology, 51,* 1224–1236.

Marsh, H. W. (1989). Age and sex effect in multiple dimensions of self-concept: Preadolescence to early-adulthood. *Journal of Educational Psychology, 81,* 417–430.

Marsh, H. W. (1990). A multidimensional, hierarchical model of self-concept: Theoretical and empirical justification. *Educational Psychology Review, 2,* 77–172.

Marsh, H. W., Byrne, B. M., & Shavelson, R. (1988). A multifaceted academic self-concept: Its hierarchical structure and its relation to academic achievement. *Journal of Educational Psychology, 80*, 366–380.

Marsh, H. W., & Shavelson, R. J. (1985). Self-concept: Its multifaceted, hierarchical structure. *Educational Psychologist, 20*, 107–125.

Muuss, R. E. (1982). *Theories of adolescence* (4th ed.). New York: Random House.

Newman, P. R., & Newman, B. M. (1988). Differences between childhood and adulthood: The identity watershed. *Adolescence, 23*, 551–557.

Nicholls, J. (1979). Development of perception of own attainment and causal attributions for success and failure in reading. *Journal of Educational Psychology, 71*, 94–99.

O'Brien, S. F., & Bierman, K. L. (1988). Conceptions and perceived influence of peer groups: Interviews with preadolescents and adolescents. *Child Development, 59*, 1360–1365.

O'Malley, P., & Bachman, J. (1983). Self-esteem: Change and stability between ages 13 and 23. *Developmental Psychology, 19*, 257–268.

Piaget, J. (1952). *The origins of intelligence in children*. New York: Basic Books.

Piaget, J. (1972). Intellectual evolution from adolescence to adulthood. *Human Development, 15*, 1–12.

Piaget, J. (1973). *The psychology of intelligence*. Totowa, NJ: Littlefield, Adams.

Savin-Williams, R. C., & Small, S. A., (1986). The timing of puberty and its relations to adolescent and parent perceptions of family interactions. *Developmental Psychology, 22*, 342–347.

Selman, R. (1976). Social-cognitive understanding: A guide to educational and clinical practice. In T. Lickona (Ed.), *Moral development and behavior: Theory, research, and social issues*. New York: Holt.

Selman, R. (1980). *The growth of interpersonal understanding*. New York: Academic Press.

Shantz, C. (1975). The development of social cognition. In M. F. Hetherington (Ed.), *Review of child development research* (Vol. 5). Chicago: University of Chicago Press.

Shavelson, R. J., & Bolus, R. (1982). Self-concept: The interplay of theory and methods. *Journal of Educational Psychology, 74*, 3–17.

Shavelson, R. J., & Marsh, H. W. (1986). On the structure of self-concept. In R. Schwarzer (Ed.), *Anxiety and cognitions*. Hillsdale, NJ: Erlbaum.

Smetana, J. G. (1989). Adolescents' and parents reasoning about actual family conflict. *Child Development, 60*, 1052–1067.

Steinberg, L., Elmen, J. D., & Mounts, N. S. (1989). Authoritative parenting, psychosocial maturity, and academic success among adolescents. *Child Development, 60*, 1424–1436.

Stubbs, M. L., Rierdan, J., & Koff, E. (1989). Developmental differences in menstrual attitudes. *Journal of Early Adolescence, 4*, 480–498.

Susman, E. J., Nottelmann, E. D., Inoff-Germain, G. E., Dorn, L. D., Cutler, G. B., Loriaux, D. L., & Chrousos, G. P. (1985). The relation of relative hormonal levels and physical development and social-emotional behavior in young adolescents. *Journal of Youth and Adolescence, 14*, 245–264.

Tanner, J. M. (1966). Galtonian eugenics and the study of growth: The relation of body size, intelligence test score, and the social circumstances in children and adults. *Eugen Rev, 58*, 122–135.

Tanner, J. M. (1970). Physical growth. In P. H. Mussen (Ed.), *Carmichael's manual of child psychology*, Vol. 2 (3rd ed.). New York: Wiley.

Tanner, J. M. (1971). Sequence, tempo, and individual variation in the growth and development of boys and girls aged twelve to sixteen. *Daedalus, 100*, 907–930.

Vygotsky, L. S. (1978). *Mind in society: The development of higher mental processes*. Cambridge, MA: Harvard University Press.

Zivin, G. (1979). Removing common confusions about egocentric speech, private speech, and self-regulation. In G. Zivin (Ed.), *The development of self-regulation through private speech* (pp. 13–49). New York: John Wiley and Sons.

3

Providing for Individual Differences

Students in the middle grades represent a broad range of abilities, backgrounds, and motivations to learn. In this chapter, you will learn about exceptional, or special needs, students and the use of adaptive instruction to meet those needs. You will also become aware of multicultural influences on the development of young adolescents' thinking and learning. Finally, you will learn about the importance of linking motivational goals to student outcomes.

A common thread running throughout this chapter is the need for middle-level educators to be responsive to the individual differences of a broad range of students. In the course of their physical, cognitive, and social development, young adolescents face obstacles to learning that tend to be magnified by the differences discussed in this chapter—differences in ability, background, and motivation.

Exceptional Students

Exceptional, or special needs, students include those for whom regular classroom instruction is insufficient or inappropriate. In the past, these students would most likely have been segregated into special classes. Currently, however, the emphasis is on integrating students as much as possible, sometimes with resource room teachers and special education teachers offering supplemental instruction to special needs students and/or support to the regular classroom teacher. Practices vary from one school district to another and from one area of exceptionality to another.

In this chapter section, you will discover how middle-grades educators address the varying needs of at-risk students, the handicapped, the gifted and talented, and those who have limited English proficiency. You will also learn about the feasibility of implementing and maintaining adaptive instruction to meet these diverse learners' needs.

At-Risk Students

Why some students succeed in school and others do not is one of the major questions under investigation by researchers working on a large-scale longitudinal study conducted by the National Center for Education Statistics (NCES). Known as the National Education Longitudinal Study of 1988 (NELS:88), it began with a survey of 25,000 eighth-graders in 1,000 public and private schools across the United States. In 1990, researchers from NCES revisited the students, who were then tenth-graders. Follow-up surveys will be conducted at 2-year intervals from this point forward.

The results of the NELS:88 survey indicated six at-risk factors that may determine whether a student stays in school or drops out. These factors are listed here with the percentage of eighth-graders possessing each of them. It should be noted that 53 percent of the eighth-graders surveyed had none of these risk factors, 47 percent had one, and 20 percent had two or more (Rothman, 1990).

- Single parent family—22%
- Family income less than $15,000—21%
- Home alone more than 3 hours a day—14%
- Parents have no high school diploma—11%
- Sibling dropped out—10%
- Limited English proficiency—2%

(U.S. Department of Education, 1990, p. 1)

Socioeconomic status, although an important factor in identifying at-risk students, is not the sole determinant of who will succeed in school and who will drop out. We all know of young adolescents who are not from low-income homes, yet are at risk of dropping out of school because of drugs, truancy, and the like. Similarly, it is not only the underachieving minority student who drops out of high school. According to Ralph (1989), "5% of white dropouts had literacy skills that exceeded those of the average college graduate" (p. 399).

Another factor, the graded-school concept, may do more to ensure that at-risk students drop out of school than socioeconomic status, drugs, truancy, and under-achievement combined. Cuban (1989) argues:

> The graded school, with its imperative to sort out differences in order to preserve uniformity, hardens low-status labels (derived from poverty and racism) in the minds of well-meaning teachers and administrators and makes it more difficult for the students to succeed. For those labeled "at risk," graded schools are poised to produce failure. (p. 782)

Although Cuban acknowledges that "many students [succeed] by dint of personal resilience and the luck of having one or more teachers who could see strengths when the school saw only failure" (p. 782), he holds the traditional structuring of U.S. schools as responsible for the high dropout rate, largely because it tolerates such enduring practices as ability grouping, differentiated curricula, and periodic promotions. Moreover, Cuban believes that present attempts to redesign schools in this country are bound to fail if they leave unexamined the assumption that graded schools adequately serve at-risk students.

These are some facts and opinions related to at-risk populations. What are some of the solutions? More specifically, what are some findings from research, as well as programs for at-risk youths in the middle grades, that attempt to intervene on their behalf?

Findings from Research on At-Risk Students

Not surprisingly, report card time produces depression and anxiety among low-achieving students. However, recent research by Mac Iver (cited by the Center for Research on Effective Schooling for Disadvantaged Students, 1990) suggests that handwritten comments and progress grades, in addition to the usual performance grades, have a positive effect on low-achieving students.

Specifically, Mac Iver estimates that in a middle-grades school with 650 students, 10 additional students will be promoted each year if the school uses both handwritten comments and progress grades. Similarly, his research shows that lower dropout rates are associated with middle-grades schools that use comments and progress grades as supplemental information to the usual performance grades.

> Progress grades, notes Mac Iver, allow low achievers who are displaying consistent improvement to get A's or B's in progress even if their performance is low relative to other students. Handwritten comments may let low-achieving students know that "teachers are paying attention to them and recognizing their contributions to the class." Thus both of these grading practices are effective in motivating students. (Center for Research on Effective Schooling for Disadvantaged Students, 1990, p. 10)

Mac Iver found no positive effects on at-risk students for report card entries that dealt with performance, effort, conduct, and computer-generated comments. In fact, he noted that conduct grades have particular drawbacks when used with young adolescents. Middle-grades students tend to view conduct grades as controlling and punitive; they see them as tools adults use to force conformity.

Mac Iver and Epstein (Mac Iver's colleague at the Center for Research on Effective Schooling for Disadvantaged Students) conducted another study that looked at differences in the instructional opportunities provided to at-risk students.

Mac Iver and Epstein found that disadvantaged middle grades schools that were predominantly minority—African-American or Hispanic—were less likely to use hands-on or higher-order learning instructional methods and were less likely to offer as much opportunity to explore fine arts, practical and life skills, and other enriching curriculum areas. (Center for Research on Effective Schooling for Disadvantaged Students, 1990, p. 5)

Programs for Middle-Grades At-Risk Students

Interestingly, and perhaps wisely, the sentiments of middle-grades reformers are no longer centered on finding "model" middle-grades programs that can be replicated (but rarely are) elsewhere. Instead, there seems to be a movement *away* from prescriptive program models *toward* the specification of objectives that require school districts to work out their own programs for ensuring that at-risk students are no longer discriminated against by low expectations, unchallenging curricula, and nonsupportive organizational structures.

One of the largest contributors to making this new philosophy of educational change work is the Edna McConnell Clark Foundation. Originally focused on supporting programs to alleviate youth unemployment, the Foundation now commits millions of dollars to support interventions at the middle-grades level that will keep students in school, promote positive self-esteem, and provide challenging curricula (Fleming, 1990).

What spurred this new focus on at-risk middle-grades students? There are several reasons, all of which are related to what you learned about young adolescents' development in Chapter 2.

1. Middle-grades students seek peer approval and independence from home and school influences. When studying and academic achievement are not valued by their peers, at-risk students' grades may decline. They may also find themselves being graded on the curve, a practice that further intensifies their feelings of low self-esteem.
2. Although middle-grades students seek independence, they also miss the guidance and support provided in their elementary school years. This is especially true of at-risk students who find themselves scurrying from class to class, attempting to meet the expectations of several teachers rather than one or two as in elementary school.
3. Young adolescents are self-conscious of themselves, and this self-consciousness is compounded in at-risk students. When their performance does not measure up to the school's expectations, at-risk students in middle grades retreat into their own world and virtually shun the activities that their teachers have planned (Fleming, 1990).

Handicapped Students

Landmark legislation, passed in 1975 in the name of Public Law 94–142, the Education of All Handicapped Children Act, was not the start of special education, but it was the beginning of a new era (Ferguson, Ferguson, & Bogdan, 1987). Some 15 years later, the title of a 1990 commentary in *Education Week* read, " 'Backlash' Threatens Special Education'' (Zirkel, 1990, p. 64). What has happened in the education of handicapped youth that threatens to reverse the gains made possible by Public Law 94–142? To answer that question, we need to look briefly at the years preceding 1975 and then at the intervening years since Congress passed the legislation favoring special education.

Brief History

According to Ferguson, Ferguson, and Bogdan (1987), "The history of disabled people is, to a large degree, the history of poverty" (p. 395). Until the early part of the nineteenth century, individuals with handicapping conditions depended on their immediate family for care, and if that care was not forthcoming, then the local almshouse was the likely alternative. However, in the 1820s and 1830s, the state began to assume financial responsibility for the education of handicapped children, largely through segregated schooling at state-run institutions (e.g., residential schools for the deaf and blind).

At the turn of the twentieth century, three developments occurred that focused more attention on disabled individuals.

1. Compulsory school attendance laws resulted in the introduction of special education classes during the Progressive Era.
2. The importation of the Binet intelligence test from Europe made it easier to "sort" students into regular and special education classes.
3. Social Darwinism laid the foundation for segregated special education classes.

Quite often this segregation led to the tracking of students from special education classes to asylums, where they remained until they passed away. A supervisor of special classes in Boston in 1916 described the process this way:

> Most will agree that the ideal condition would be for . . . the mentally defective to go from the school directly to the institution, and thus safeguard the public from inefficiency, unemployment . . . and all the other social consequences of feeble-mindedness. (Ferguson, Ferguson, and Bogdan, 1987, p. 398)

The same researchers wryly noted, "That was said by a friend of disabled children; the enemies were not as hopeful" (1987, p. 398).

It was not until the 1970s, with the advent of the civil rights movement and the passage of Public Law 94–142, that the concept of *least restrictive environment* came into being. Under the least restrictive environment clause, handicapped students are placed in educational settings that enable them to be integrated as much as possible into regular education, while they still receive the necessary academic support from special education teachers.

Integration

Integration (a term now preferred over *mainstreaming*) has physical, functional, social, community, and organizational connotations associated with it. For example, it is not enough that handicapped and nonhandicapped students are physically housed in the same building. Rather, full integration means that handicapped and nonhandicapped individuals should have functional access to all the facilities of a school (e.g., swimming pool, cafeteria, gym), although for safety reasons, the two groups of students may be restricted to using these facilities at different times.

Social integration, such as extracurricular clubs for nonhandicapped tutors and their handicapped peers, is one example of how middle-grades educators can integrate severely handicapped students with their nonhandicapped peers (Hanline & Murray, 1984). Finally, community integration and organizational integration are needed if handicapped individuals are to function in a way that allows them to use their self-care skills and vocational training in a society where *separate* is no longer thought of as *equal*.

There are several approaches to teaching handicapped students the content of a middle-grades curriculum. Developmental, functional, basic skills, and clinical treatment, are the most common. Ferguson, Ferguson, and Bogdan (1987) prefer the functional-skills approach for the following reasons:

1. It encourages teaching skills in clusters rather than in isolation.
2. Only skills that handicapped students will need to master to function in their home, school, and community environments are taught.
3. The functional approach does not presume a stage of "readiness," thus aiding in the teaching of young adolescents whose chronological age and practical needs may not coincide with a specified set of competencies.

With seemingly so much progress being made in the field of special education, what prompts Zirkel (1990) to warn of a backlash? Citing pressures building from economic, legal, and demographic factors as some of the potential threats to Public Law 94–142, Zirkel notes that the cost of educating a handicapped youth is two and a half times that of educating a nonhandicapped youth. This economic burden falls almost exclusively on the states. Litigation costs are also rising, sometimes astronomically. Finally, the number of special education teachers is shrinking while the demand for their services is increasing.

Gifted and Talented Students

Just what the terms *gifted* and *talented* mean cannot be agreed upon by experts in the field. Some define the terms interchangeably and ascribe such characteristics as "demonstrated or potential ability in intellectual, creative, or specific academic areas, leadership, or the performing and visual arts" (Maker, 1987, p. 421). According to Maker's review of the literature on the gifted and talented, "these are students who, because of their ability, require services or activities beyond those normally provided by the school" (p. 421). Others differentiate between the two terms, ascribing high intellectual and academic ability to giftedness, and abilities in other areas (such as leadership, athletics, and the arts) to talentedness. For the purposes of this chapter, we do not distinguish between the two terms.

Identification and Grouping

There is no consensus on the best way to identify gifted and talented students, nor is there agreement on the best programmatic placement for students once they are identified. Despite the lack of consensus, it appears from the research on identifying the gifted and talented that multiple instruments are better than single ones.

The effectiveness of different programmatic placements has been the object of continued investigation, but with little that is generalizable from one study to the next. For example, studies have compared the relative effectiveness of ability grouping within the regular classroom, resource or *pull-out* teacher programs, special classes and seminars, and separate schools for the gifted. No one placement was found to be consistently superior to another. However, what can be learned from this research is that changing the grouping of students without altering the curriculum or methods used to teach them cannot be expected to make a significant difference in the students' educational experience (Maker, 1987, p. 432).

Likewise, the search for the better program type—enrichment or acceleration —has been largely unproductive in terms of generalizing to the gifted and talented population at large. Generally, the answer to which is better seems to depend on the characteristics of the students and teachers, the desired outcomes, and the instructional methods used (Maker, 1987). When the question is asked about the most effective program type for middle-level students, *given specific conditions and desired outcomes,* there is somewhat better agreement from the research.

For example, the results of a study conducted by Passow, Goldberg, and Link (1961) indicated that an accelerated program in which middle-grades gifted students were exposed to mathematics content at an accelerated pace was superior to an enrichment program. In a follow-up study conducted by the same researchers, similar results were obtained. In a recent study of seventh-grade mathematically talented students, Dark and Benbow (1990) found that these students excelled not because of their high verbal ability but rather because of their "ability to transform linguistically presented information into a mathematically useful format" (p. 427). Knowledge of findings such as this can aid in making decisions about appropriate placements of gifted and talented middle-grades students.

Guidelines

Perhaps the most helpful guidance to middle-grades teachers in search of ways to develop gifted students' talents can be found in Torrance's (1966) guidelines for fostering creative thinking in the classroom. These guidelines have been summarized by Ingersoll (1989) and applied to adolescent development (see Figure 3.1).

FIGURE 3.1   Guidelines for Fostering Creative Thinking

1. *Value creative thinking.*   The adolescent should see that the parent or teacher values and appreciates creative thinking.
2. *Make children more sensitive to environmental stimuli.*   To be fluent and flexible, the adolescent must have a wide range of responses available and must have skills to observe a wide variety of characteristics. By teaching adolescents to be sensitive to variations and changes in their surroundings, you also increase their ability to consider alternative aspects of a situation.
3. *Encourage manipulation of objects and ideas.*   Adolescence is a time when young people normally engage in mental games and play with thoughts. Instructors need to encourage this tendency.
4. *Teach the adolescent how to evaluate each idea systematically.*   As an individual begins to develop divergent thinking abilities, the patterns of intellectual thinking may be unorganized and unsystematic. Sometimes concept flexibility can be encouraged through the use of heuristic techniques. A *heuristic* is a systematic procedure that serves as an aid to problem solving and originality, such as brainstorming, synectics, and so on.
5. *Develop a tolerance of new ideas.*   Adolescents and children tend to be intolerant of uncertainty. Tolerance of ambiguity and uncertainty is fundamental to originality. Often such tolerance involves holding off judgment about the value of ideas. Sometimes what initially strikes you as a widely silly idea may develop into an original and creative solution to a problem. (It may also remain a silly idea.)
6. *Beware of forging a set pattern.*   Creative and original thinking is hindered when people think there is one right way to go about solving a problem. Once again, to be flexible means to be able to "break set," to be able to think about a problem in alternative modes.
7. *Develop a creative classroom atmosphere.*   Part of the learning process involves seeing how creative people act. Teachers should practice considering alternatives, withholding judgment on unusual ideas, and maintaining a tolerant attitude about uncertain areas, if adolescents are expected to behave similarly. (Practice what you preach!)

Source: From G. M. Ingersoll, *Adolescents* (2nd ed.), © 1989, p. 152. Reprinted by permission of Prentice Hall, Inc., Englewood Cliffs, New Jersey.

Limited English Proficiency Students

The special needs of students for whom English is not the native language are met in typically one of two ways. In the first, the bilingual education approach, limited English proficiency (LEP) students are taught the content of the curriculum (e.g., mathematics, social studies, science) in the language they already know; at the same time, they are taught English. This approach differs from the so-called English as a second language (ESL) approach, in which students attend special pull-out classes where they are instructed in English, the language of all their classes (Fillmore & Valadez, 1986).

Proponents and Critics

Proponents of bilingual education argue that ESL programs are ineffective because they teach students the language of the school but not the subject matter of the core curriculum. When students are unable to comprehend their core courses, they are at risk of failing those courses and eventually dropping out of school. Critics of bilingual education, on the other hand, argue that the use of one's native language in school can inhibit the learning of English. Other critics claim that allowing students to speak their native language in school encourages them to maintain cultural differences that work against their entering the mainstream of U.S. life. Still other critics argue that expecting students to learn in two languages may cause needless cognitive confusion.

Although Fillmore and Valadez (1986) acknowledge that the research is mixed on whether or not bilingual education is effective, they stress the need for students to hold on to their native language for cultural reasons.

> The immigrant groups whose children are the LEP students in our schools today have enormous cultural resources and talent to contribute to their adopted society. These contributions can help to invigorate and enrich the society as they have in the past. The learning of English will give LEP students access to the opportunities offered by the society, but if the unique resources that their cultures have given them are lost in the process they will have less to give back to the society as adults. (p. 680)

Strategies for Teaching LEP Students

Many LEP students in the middle grades who have learned to read and write in their native language experience minimal difficulty in learning English. Those who are not literate in another language, however, will need special help in acquiring the requisite skills for learning from their content area textbooks. Thonis (1989) offers the following strategies for teachers working with these LEP students:

1. Seat the student close to the front of the room where directions and instruction may be given with fewer distractions.
2. Speak naturally, but slowly, to allow for comprehension to develop.
3. Use a lower *register,* that is, shorter sentences, simpler concepts, and fewer multi-syllabic words.
4. Repeat the explanations, directions, or instructions as needed.
5. Support content area instruction with visual material such as pictures, diagrams, stickmen and drawings.
6. Provide manipulative materials whenever possible to make mathematics and science lessons meaningful.
7. Do not call on the student for a lengthy response. Elicit one-word or gestural answers when appropriate.
8. Avoid correcting errors of pronunciation, structure, or vocabulary. Accept the student's effort or, if necessary, state the response correctly without comment.
9. Do not expect mastery of language or the accuracy of a native-English speaker. Enjoy the flavor of the nonnative speech, especially when pronunciation does not interfere with comprehension.
10. Assign a dependable classmate to assist whenever additional directions are needed to follow through on assignments or seatwork.
11. Allow time for *silence* for taking in the new melody, rhythm, and rhyme of English.
12. Provide a climate of warmth and caring that nurtures a sense of comfort and ease for students who are coping with the demands of a new language. (p. 112)

Friendships between immigrant and American students create stimulating learning environments inside and outside school.

Interactions and Writing

According to Britton (cited in Romero, Mercado, & Vazquez-Faria, 1987), "In good conversation, participants profit from their own talking, . . . from what others contribute and above all from the interaction—that is, from the enabling effect of each upon the other" (p. 357). Vygotsky (1978) also stresses the need for social interaction in negotiating meaning. If middle-grades students are to feel good about their interactions and their ability to express themselves, the conversations they engage in, whether verbally or written, must be genuine in terms of topic, purpose, and audience.

The results of a recent study (Peyton, Staton, Richardson, & Wolfram, 1990) of the influence of writing tasks on LEP students in the middle grades clearly bore this out. In the study, sixth-grade LEP students demonstrated a wide range of writing abilities when they were free to write on a topic of their own choice for the purpose of communicating with their teacher as their audience in a dialogue journal. When the same students wrote on an assigned topic for a specific purpose and audience, their writing samples reflected less complex linguistic structures and lower-level thinking. Although Peyton and colleagues refrained from recommending that only unassigned writing be given to LEP students, they did make a strong argument for teachers of LEP students to encourage interaction and writing in a wide variety of contexts.

Adaptive Instruction

Teachers make decisions before, during, and after they teach that are designed to adapt their instruction to the needs of individual students. This need to individualize instruction is greater today than perhaps any other time in recent history because of the federal and state emphasis on providing equal educational opportunities for all students. The concept of *adaptive teaching* has been defined by Corno and Snow (1986) as

> Teaching that arranges environmental conditions to fit learners' individual differences. As learners gain in aptitude through experience with respect to the instructional goals at hand, such teaching adapts by becoming less intrusive. Less intrusion, less teacher or instructional mediation, increases the learner's information processing and/or behavioral burdens, and with this the need for more learner self-regulation. As the learner adapts, so also must the teacher. (p. 621)

This dynamic transaction between teaching and learning is especially visible in gifted and special education. *Inquiry teaching,* or teaching in which students are helped to discover abstract concepts from concrete instances with little teacher direction, is an example of adaptive instruction that works for the more able student but not as well for the less able student. Conversely, cognitive strategy instruction is more effective when used to teach the mentally handicapped than when used to teach the gifted. Cognitive strategy instruction may actually interfere with the more able students' learning (Corno & Snow, 1986).

Adaptive instruction has been the object of study since the early 1960s. Generally, whether such instruction has been used with the handicapped, the gifted, or the LEP student, research shows:

1. Each student should receive instruction based on his/her assessed capabilities.
2. Materials and methods should be selected on the basis of their flexibility in pacing and their appeal to individual students' interests.

3. Individual students should be kept informed of the progress they are making toward mastery of the content that is taught.
4. Students should play an active role in setting goals, pursuing activities to reach those goals, and evaluating the outcomes of their individual education plans.
5. Alternative activities and materials should be provided for students who need additional assistance.
6. Cooperation rather than competition should be stressed in individual and group learning. (Strother, 1985)

In addition to these six principles of adaptive instruction, research conducted and reviewed by Wang and Walberg (1983) suggests that differences among exceptional students are best characterized in relation to how they process information, not on how well they perform on traditional evaluation measures. Similarly, instruction that builds on each student's basic competencies and is responsive to individual interests and personal learning styles is preferable to conventional large-group instruction.

Multicultural Influences on Adolescent Learning

Many cultures within one society is a simple but fairly accurate description of the United States. It is a pluralistic society, or one in which "members of ethnic minority groups are permitted to retain many of their cultural ways, as long as they conform to those practices deemed necessary for harmonious coexistence within the society" (Bennett, 1990, p. 11). This is a different view of our society from the one presented in social studies textbooks of little more than three decades ago. Then, it was common to refer to the United States as a "melting pot," or a society in which ethnic minorities were "expected to give up their traditions and blend in or be absorbed by the host society or predominant culture" (p. 11).

Multicultural education is expanding to include global issues, such as world peace and hunger. However, in this part of the chapter on individual differences, we focus more narrowly on multiculturalism and its influence on young adolescents in the United States. Specifically, we describe how physical characteristics, peer relations, and teacher expectations that are linked to cultural differences tend to influence young adolescents' thinking and learning.

Physical Characteristics

Individual differences among young adolescents often make a difference in how they learn, particularly if these differences are physically noticeable and affect self-perception or acceptance by others. When these differences are associated with ethnic or racial minorities who are in their early teen years, the impact on learning can be especially dramatic. For example, consider the impact of the label *culturally disadvantaged*. Frequently, this label carries with it the false assumption that students who physically look, act, and speak differently from the majority culture are in some way limited in their capacity to learn. When credence is given to this false assumption, culturally different students end up in the remedial or lower academic track of their school classes in numbers out of proportion to their representation in the general population.

According to Casanova (1987), "It is very difficult for students to have high expectations for themselves when those around them assume that they are limited in their capacity to learn" (p. 375). This becomes a particularly difficult situation for the young adolescent who is already keenly sensitive to how he or she is perceived.

Peer Relations

Since the 1965 Immigration Act was passed, a large number of immigrants have come to the United States from Southeast Asia (Vietnam, Cambodia, Laos) and Central America, most for political asylum. Immigrants from Mexico, the Philippines, and East Asia (China, Korea, and Japan) have come primarily for economic reasons and to join family members already in the United States. With the exception of immigrants from the Caribbean area, the largest share of all immigrant groups have settled in California (Center for Research on Effective Schooling for Disadvantaged Students, 1990).

According to a study conducted by Rumbaut (Center for Research on Effective Schooling for Disadvantaged Students, 1990), "In 1989, more than 29% of California's K–12 public school children spoke a primary language other than English at home—thus almost a third of the children in California schools are either immigrants or native-born children of immigrants" (p. 11). Nearly all of the students in Rumbaut's study reported a sense of isolation from American students. For example, very few immigrant students reported having American friends with whom to study, and nearly all of the students said that they had encountered problems with American students, largely over racial and ethnic matters.

Classroom climate in the middle grades plays a large role in influencing how young adolescents think and learn. In a study of black adolescents, Fordham and Ogbu (1986) found that peer pressure among blacks to avoid "acting white" (see figure 3.2) is a major reason black students fail to achieve academically up to their potential. According to Fordham and Ogbu, this aversion to "acting white" is shared by members of other minority groups such as those "American Indians and Mexican Americans [who] perceive the public schools as an agent of assimilation into the white American or Anglo frame of reference [and as] detrimental to the integrity of their cultures, languages, and identities" (p. 177).

Peer pressure exerted by the members of some culture groups is only one of the reasons young adolescents fail to achieve in school. Earlier sections of this chapter addressed other reasons such as handicapping conditions and limited English proficiency. Underlying all of these potential threats to young adolescent achievement is the danger that students will fail to recognize the connection between school achievement and their futures.

For example, in focus-group discussions with 139 black middle-grades students, only a few students linked success in school with future success (Southeastern Educational Improvement Laboratory, 1989). Although most of the middle-

FIGURE 3.2   Attitudes and Behaviors Identified as "Acting White"

- Speaking standard English
- Listening to White music and White radio stations
- Going to the opera or ballet
- Spending a lot of time in the library studying
- Working hard to get good grades in school
- Getting good grades in school (those who get good grades are labeled "brainiacs")
- Going to the Smithsonian
- Going to a Rolling Stones concert at the Capital Center
- Doing volunteer work
- Going camping, hiking, or mountain climbing
- Having cocktails or a cocktail party
- Going to a symphony orchestra concert
- Having a party with no music
- Listening to classical music
- Being on time
- Reading and writing poetry
- Putting on airs

Source: From Christine I. Bennett, *Comprehensive Multicultural Education: Theory and Practice,* Second Edition. Copyright © 1990 by Allyn and Bacon. Reprinted with permission.

graders in the discussion groups aspired to jobs that required college educations, few distinguished between remedial and college preparatory track classes. Only a few of the students understood the importance of doing well in courses as a prerequisite to achieving their career plans. Clearly, pressures among young adolescents to conform to their peers' standards in thinking and learning may bear a particularly high cost to some culture groups.

Teacher Expectations

A trend that does not bode well for positive multicultural influences on young adolescent learning is what Sleeter (1990) refers to as the "whitening of the teaching force" (p. 37). Reasons for the declining number of people of color who are entering the teaching profession are interesting in themselves, but it is the *impact* of this decline, not the reasons for it, that are of importance here. Irvine (cited in Sleeter, 1990) has synthesized research on the impact of teachers of color on student achievement:

> They represent positive role models for all children, white and African-American; they are more likely to share and understand the cultural background of children of color than are white teachers; they are aware of the barriers of discrimination that children of color face; their expectations of children tend to be higher than those of white teachers; they interact with children of color in the classroom in more positive ways than white teachers; and they help motivate white colleagues to question their own racial stereotypes. (p. 37)

Open communication between a teacher and a parent enhances opportunities for home-school cooperation.

Teacher expectations that conflict with parental values or jargon that confuses parents who have recently immigrated to this country are barriers to home-school cooperation. According to Johnston (1990), certain practices make it possible for the school to maintain cooperation between itself and the parents of the children it serves. For example, when teachers' expectations are communicated in a way that invites responses from parents, a trust level is built. Johnston (1990), for example, describes middle-grades schools that use "Good News Grams" to communicate positive news about a student's progress. In turn, the child's parents are asked to comment on the "Good News Gram."

Differences in teacher expectations affect the academic achievement of middle-grades students in general, and cultural minorities in particular. For example, areas of cultural conflict between urban black students and their teachers include, among other things, differences in speaking and listening styles (Gilbert & Gay, 1985). Among blacks, the primary mode of communicating is oral; in the middle grades, the emphasis is placed on written communication. Moreover, it is written communication minus what Gilbert and Gay call the "artistic, dramatic talking" (p. 135) of blacks, or talk "in which nonverbal nuances, the placement of words, and the rhythm of speech are as important to the meaning as the words themselves" (p. 135).

When teachers' expectations are such that they value directness, preciseness, and conciseness in communication, it is typically the case that the teachers' expectations will prevail. As the teaching profession "whitens" (Sleeter, 1990) even more, it will become increasingly important to consider ways for lessening this conflict in communication styles.

Motivational Goals and Student Outcomes

Current interest in teacher and school effectiveness, public concern over falling test scores, reform movement reports, and social problems besetting the schools (e.g., drugs, lack of discipline, and early dropouts) have combined to focus more attention on the need for classrooms to become more motivating places in which to learn. The purposes of this chapter section are to describe the motivational processes that affect learning, to relate achievement motivation to young adolescents' needs, and to consider the importance of self-regulated learning strategies in motivating middle-grades students.

Motivational Processes Affecting Learning

Psychologists generally describe the study of motivation as focusing on how individuals reach their goals. In this section of the chapter, we focus more narrowly on achievement motivation as it pertains to the processes that affect middle-grades students' learning. To do this, we begin with a description of the two main classes of goals related to competence: performance goals and learning goals.

Performance Goals

According to Dweck (1986), performance goals are goals "in which individuals seek to gain favorable judgments of their competence or avoid negative judgments of their competence" (p. 1040). When middle-grades students pursue performance goals, they risk being compared with "normative" others. With performance goals, if a student is highly confident in his or her ability to reach a goal, the pursuit of that goal will be seen as challenging, and the student will exhibit a high degree of persistence. On the other, if the student is doubtful of his or her ability to achieve a goal, a sense of helplessness may set in. Subsequently, behaviors such as task avoidance and low persistence may result in failure to reach the goal.

Learning Goals

Dweck's (1986) definition of learning goals are goals "in which individuals seek to increase their competence, to understand or master something new" (p. 1040). Unlike with performance goals, middle-grades students who pursue learning goals do not concern themselves with questions such as: Am I smart enough to accomplish this goal? Instead, the student who pursues a learning goal will "focus on progress and mastery through effort [and thus will create] a tendency to seek and be energized by challenge" (p. 1041). For an example of how research findings support the use of learning goals, see the earlier section in this chapter entitled Findings from Research on "At-Risk" Students.

Achievement Motivation and Young Adolescents

Research on achievement goals (performance versus learning) conducted with middle-grades students has shown that students who perceive their classrooms to be learning-goal oriented report "using more effective strategies, [prefer] challenging tasks, [have] a more positive attitude toward the class, and [have] a stronger belief that success follows from one's effort" (Ames & Archer, 1988, p. 260). In comparison, middle-grades students who perceived their classrooms to be performance-goal oriented "tend to focus on their ability, evaluating their ability negatively and attributing failure to lack of ability" (p. 260).

The self-worth theory of achievement motivation is supported by the belief that a major focus of all classroom achievement is the need for students "to protect their sense of worth or personal value'' (Covington, 1984, p. 5). Young adolescents, as you learned in Chapter 2, have a high need for acceptance and approval, especially among peers. Consequently, the self-worth theory of achievement motivation predicts that middle-grades students will attempt various forms of subterfuge (e.g., procrastination, excuses, misbehavior) to avoid being targeted as incompetent. Such behaviors, of course, put students in direct conflict with the work-ethic orientation that prevails among most teachers. Some researchers are beginning to collect evidence that suggests self-regulated learning strategies may be an alternative to the task-avoidance behaviors described earlier.

Self-Regulated Learning Strategies

In a correlational study involving 173 seventh-graders from eight science and seven English classes, Pintrich and DeGroot (1990) found evidence for the importance of involving students in self-regulated learning. Students who reported using cognitive learning strategies were more likely to persist in a task and to believe they were capable of meeting their goals. Pintrich and DeGroot concluded that motivation, or the *will* to learn, must be complemented by the *skill* (self-regulated learning, in this case) to learn.

Slavin's (1984) work with cooperative learning methods has encouraged students in the middle grades to motivate their peers to succeed. According to Slavin, "The principal idea behind the cooperative learning methods is that by rewarding groups as well as individuals for their academic achievement, peer norms will come to favor rather than oppose high achievement" (p. 54). Consider for a moment how this might influence black students who shy away from excelling academically because such behavior is perceived as "acting white" (Fordham & Ogbu, 1986). It should be noted also that researchers have found cooperative learning methods to affect positively a wide range of social and emotional outcomes, such as improved cooperation among different racial and ethnic groups, acceptance of handicapped peers, and higher levels of self-esteem.

Summary

In this chapter, our goal has been to develop an awareness of the need for middle-grades educators to be responsive to a broad range of differences in young adolescents' ability, cultural background, and motivation. Developing an understanding of, and an appreciation for, diversity among middle-grades students will enhance your chance of becoming an effective teacher. Most importantly, we hope this chapter has demonstrated how the typical stresses and strains of growing up "in the middle" are further compounded by the individual differences described here.

REFERENCES

Ames, C., & Archer, J. (1988). Achievement goals in the classroom: Students' learning strategies and motivation processes. *Journal of Educational Psychology, 80,* 260–267.

Banks, J. A., & Banks, C. A. M. (Eds.). (1989). *Multicultural education: Issues and perspectives.* Boston, MA: Allyn and Bacon.

Bennett, C. I. (1990). *Comprehensive multi-*

cultural education: Theory and practice (2nd ed.). Boston, MA: Allyn and Bacon.

Casanova, U. (1987). Ethnic and cultural differences. In V. Richardson-Koehler (Ed.), *Educators' handbook: A research perspective* (pp. 370–393). New York: Longman.

Center for Research on Effective Schooling for Disadvantaged Students (CDS). (1990, November). Progress grades and written comments linked to less retention and estimated dropouts. *CDS Report*, p. 10. Baltimore, MD: Johns Hopkins University.

Corno, L., & Snow, R. E. (1986). Adapting teaching to individual differences among learners. In M. C. Wittrock (Ed.), *Handbook of research on teaching* (3rd ed., pp. 605–629). New York: Macmillan.

Covington, M. V. (1984). The self-worth theory of achievement motivation: Findings and implications. *The Elementary School Journal, 85,* 5–20.

Cuban, L. (1989). The "at-risk" label and the problem of urban school reform. *Phi Delta Kappan, 70,* 780–784, 799–801.

Dark, V. J., & Benbow, C. P. (1990). Enhanced problem translation and short-term memory: Components of mathematical talent. *Journal of Educational Psychology, 82,* 420–429.

Dweck, C. S. (1986). Motivational processes affecting learning. *American Psychologist, 41,* 1040–1048.

Ferguson, D. L., Ferguson, P. M., & Bogdan, R. C. (1987). If mainstreaming is the answer, what is the question? In V. Richardson-Koehler (Ed.), *Educators' handbook: A research perspective* (pp. 394–419). New York: Longman.

Fillmore, L. W., & Valadez, C. (1986). Teaching bilingual learners. In M. C. Wittrock (Ed.), *Handbook of research on teaching* (3rd ed., pp. 648–685). New York: Macmillan.

Fleming, W. E. (1990). The program for disadvantaged youth: Reform efforts in the middle grades. *Educational Horizons, 68,* 82–87.

Fordham, S., & Ogbu, J. (1986). Black students' school success: Coping with the "burden of acting white." *The Urban Review, 18,* 176–206.

Gilbert, W. E., II, & Gay, G. (1985). Improving the success in school of poor black children. *Phi Delta Kappan, 67,* 133–137.

Guilford, J. P. (1967). *The nature of human intelligence.* New York: McGraw-Hill.

Hanline, M. F., & Murray, C. (1984). Integrating severely handicapped children into regular public schools. *Phi Delta Kappan, 66,* 273–276.

Ingersoll, G. M. (1989). *Adolescents* (2nd ed.). Englewood Cliffs, NJ: Prentice Hall.

Johnston, J. H. (1990). *The new American family and the school.* Columbus, OH: National Middle School Association.

Maker, C. J. (1987). Gifted and talented. In V. Richardson-Koehler (Ed.), *Educators' handbook: A research perspective* (pp. 420–456). New York: Longman.

Passow, A. H., Goldberg, M. L., & Link, F. (1961). Enriched mathematics for gifted junior high school students. *Educational Leadership, 18,* 442–448.

Peyton, J. K., Staton, J., Richardson, G., & Wolfram, W. (1990). The influence of writing task on ESL students' written production. *Research in the Teaching of English, 24,* 142–171.

Pintrich, P. R., & DeGroot, E. V. (1990). Motivational and self-regulated learning components of classroom academic performance. *Journal of Educational Psychology, 82,* 33–40.

Ralph, J. (1989). Improving education for the disadvantaged: Do we know whom to help? *Phi Delta Kappan, 70,* 395–401.

Romero, M., Mercado, C., & Vazquez-Faria, J. (1987). Students of limited English proficiency. In V. Richardson-Koehler (Ed.), *Educators' handbook: A research perspective* (pp. 348–369). New York: Longman.

Rothman, R. (1990, August 1). Study of 8th graders finds 20% at high risk of failure. *Education Week,* p. 11.

Slavin, R. E. (1984). Students motivating students to excel: Cooperative incentives, cooperative tasks, and student achievement. *The Elementary School Journal, 85,* 53–63.

Sleeter, C. E. (1990). Staff development for desegregated schooling. *Phi Delta Kappan, 72,* 33–40.

Southeastern Educational Improvement Laboratory. (1989). Many black middle schoolers fail to recognize connection between schooling and careers. *Looking to the future: Focus-group discussions about college and careers with minority middle school students and parents.* Research Triangle Park, NC: Author.

Strother, D. B. (1985). Adapting instruction to individual needs: An eclectic approach. *Phi Delta Kappan, 67,* 308–311.

Thonis, E. (1989). Bilingual students: Reading and learning. In D. Lapp, J. Flood, & N. Farnan (Eds.), *Content area reading and learning* (pp. 105–113). Englewood Cliffs, NJ: Prentice Hall.

Torrance, E. P. (1966). *Torrance Tests of Creative Thinking: Directions manual.* Princeton, NJ: Personnel Press.

U.S. Department of Education. (1990, August). *National Education Longitudinal Study of 1988: A profile of the American eighth grader.* Washington, DC: Author.

Vygotsky, L. S. (1978). *Mind in society: The development of higher psychological processes.* Cambridge, MA: Harvard University Press.

Wang, M. C., & Walberg, H. J. (1983). Adaptive instruction and classroom time. *American Educational Research Journal, 20,* 601–627.

Zirkel, P. A. (1990). "Backlash" threatens special education. *Education Week, 9*(40), 64.

4

The Middle-Grades Curriculum

The middle-grades curriculum includes a variety of programs (academic, advisory, exploratory, field trips, even the culture of the educational environment), but this chapter is limited to a discussion of the knowledge and learning experiences generally associated with either the traditional subject-centered approach or an alternative to this approach.

Is there a curriculum—that is, a specified body of knowledge and learning experiences—that is unique and most appropriate for students in the middle grades? For the past three decades, broad curriculum questions such as this one were virtually nonexistent in the middle-grades movement. Instead, attention focused on the characteristics of young adolescents and how schools organized for middle-grades instruction. Recently, however, the content of the curriculum has fast become a focal point of national debate among educational theorists, state departments of education, and local school people. The reason for this sudden change in attention is thought to result largely from the pressures that are being exerted both inside and outside the middle-grades movement (Beane, 1990a; Cawelti, 1988).

We begin this chapter with a brief overview of the source of some of those pressures. Next, in describing what typically is called the traditional middle-grades curriculum, we point out the problems associated with its largely academic-centered subject approach. After that, we present an alternative approach to curriculum planning in the middle grades. Finally, the chapter concludes with a discussion of the issues surrounding curriculum reform and implementation.

Pressures Exerted on the Middle-Grades Curriculum

The decade of the 80s was known for the many school reform movements in the United States. The reform movements evolved from documents such as *A Nation at Risk* (National Commission on Excellence in Education, 1983) and a series of nationally administered tests that showed elementary, middle, and secondary school students were lacking in their ability to read, write, solve word problems, and identify well-known figures and events from our nation's history.

The reform movements, which came from private as well as public sectors of the population, were often accompanied by reports that received considerable attention from the media. Although not all of the reports resulted in mandates for curriculum reform from state departments of education, those that did generally affected the curriculum content of the middle grades. This is understandable, given that the middle grades serve as a link between elementary and secondary schooling and therefore cannot set their curriculum independently from the grades immediately preceding and following them. According to a survey conducted by the Association for Supervision and Curriculum Development and drawn from a national sample of 672 middle grades, "72 percent of the schools reported that students are required to pass a general competency test before entering high school" (Cawelti, 1988, p. 11).

Pressures have also been exerted on the content of the middle-grades curriculum from educational task forces formed within private and professional organizations. For example, the report of the Task Force on the Carnegie Council on Adolescent Development (Carnegie Council, 1989) has recommended that the middle grades teach a core of common knowledge: "Every student in the middle grades should learn to think critically through mastery of an appropriate body of knowledge, lead a healthy life, behave ethically and lawfully, and assume the responsibilities of citizenship in a pluralistic society" (p. 42). The report further asserts that middle-grades educators should design a curriculum that integrates the core subjects (e.g., English, mathematics, science, social studies) with the fine arts and foreign languages.

A leading scientific society, the American Association for the Advancement of

Science (AAAS), has made specific recommendations through its Project 2061 about the knowledge, skills, and attitudes that students in grades K–12 should achieve by the year 2061. Begun in 1985, this three-phase plan for reforming science, mathematics, and technology education advocates that subject matter be integrated in one of several ways: through organizing subject matter around the conceptual framework of a discipline, around problems and issues, or around themes (American Association for the Advancement of Science, 1990).

The National Science Foundation has funded eight "Troika" projects since 1985 in hopes of influencing the curriculum in grades K–8. The projects include scientists, educators, and publishers, all of whom are working cooperatively "to assure high-quality curriculum content and pedagogy" (McCormick, 1989, p. 6).

Even individuals have attempted to assert pressure on the middle-grades curriculum. For instance, E. D. Hirsch, a professor of English at the University of Virginia, has published a book, *Cultural Literacy: What Every American Needs to Know*, in which he lists approximately 5,000 items "intended to illustrate the character and range of the knowledge literate Americans tend to share" (Hirsch, 1987, p. 146). Critics of this book have pointed out that Hirsch "provides no indication that he has surveyed either curriculum guides or instructional practices that determine what is taught in school" (Estes, Gutman, & Harrison, 1988, p. 15). In addition, Hirsch has come under attack for implying that the foundation of literacy can be acquired by memorizing lists of facts assumed to be in the literate person's knowledge base.

In response to his critics, Hirsch (1988) stated that he wrote the book in an attempt to solve the practical problem of having no national core curriculum in the United States. This, too, has brought on a strong wave of protest from individuals who are opposed to instituting a national core curriculum.

In his resolve to be known as the Education President, George Bush announced on April 18, 1991, a strategy for reforming schools in the United States during the remaining years of this decade. The President's strategy, known as America 2000, is backed by the nation's governors and appears to mark a definite shift in the government's interest in a national curriculum. According to Smith, O'Day, and Cohen (1991), two of the goals spelled out in the America 2000 proposal may accelerate the speed with which the United States moves toward a national curriculum:

> Goal III calls for all students to have "demonstrated competency in challenging subject matter including English, mathematics, science, history, and geography" by the year 2000; Goal IV declares that "by the year 2000, U.S. students will be first in the world in science and mathematics achievement." The goals emphasize "challenging subject matter" in specified disciplines; discuss the need for students to "demonstrate the ability to reason, solve problems, apply knowledge, and write and communicate effectively"; and call for the nation to "substantially increase the percentage of students who are competent in more than one language." Such objectives begin to sound like the seeds of curriculum specification. (p. 74)

The President's America 2000 proposal is thought to have the potential to influence far more than the standardization of curriculum in this country, however. Many educators see it as the precursor of a new assessment system, one which would undoubtedly have major implications for publishers, teacher education, teacher assessment, and grouping practices like tracking. These are but a few of the many challenges a national curriculum would present.

Pressures to revise the content of the middle-grades curriculum have come from individuals within the middle-grades movement itself. According to Beane (1990b), a well-known authority on the affective dimensions of young adolescent learning,

> Attention should be given to moral and value exploration, since early adolescence is a stage where serious questions about life emerge. Here, middle level educators need to place a greater premium on critical examination of issues, such as racism, environmental destruction, poverty, homelessness, and nuclear destruction as both problems and issues of morality. The curriculum in an effective middle school cannot be sterile, simply sticking to the facts and cleaning the controversy out of real life. (p. 111)

To accomplish this goal of curriculum reform, Beane advocates involving young adolescents in curriculum-development groups and in school governance decisions so that they may experience the responsibility that goes with ownership in the curriculum.

Finally, pressures to reform the middle-grades curriculum have come from state boards of education. A good example is the California board's decision to adopt a new history-social science curriculum for the public schools and to mandate its implementation through in-depth staff-development opportunities, more appropriate instructional materials, better assessment measures, and long-term planning at the school and district levels. The new California *framework*, which the revised curriculum is being labeled, calls for an increase in the number of years that students will study United States and world history. Students in grades 5, 8, and 11 will study U.S. history, and those in grades 6, 7, and 10 will study world history. Figure 4.1 illustrates the staggered sequence of U.S. and world history courses.

> Its year-to-year continuity is *chronological*, with U.S. history each time presented within the global context of world history established the year before. Thus, the 8th grade study of the founding of the nation grows out of the 7th grade study of the Protestant Reformation and the European Enlightenment. Similarly, the 11th grade course in 20th century U.S. history grows out of the 10th grade course in 19th and 20th century world history. (Alexander & Crabtree, 1988, p. 12)

According to Alexander and Crabtree (1988), two individuals who had considerable input into the California framework, the staggered sequence allows students to study in depth, over time, a particular period in history. It also enables teachers

FIGURE 4.1   Chronological Emphases for Courses in World and United States History

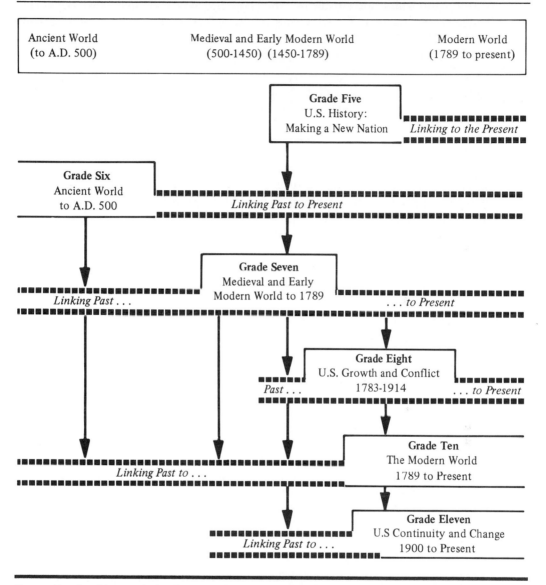

Source: Reprinted by permission from the *History-Social Science Framework for California Public Schools, Kindergarten Through Grade Twelve,* Copyright © 1988, California Department of Education, P.O. Box 271, Sacramento, CA 95802–0271.

to incorporate the literature, art, and primary documents that enliven a particular historical period. In short, the California framework represents the thinking of the task force report from the National Commission on Social Studies in the Schools (see O'Neil, 1989a).

In summary, the 1980s were indeed years in which pressures for curriculum reform from within and outside the middle-grades movement made themselves felt. The latter half of the 1990s will see the full implementation and assessment of many of the recommended changes. But what does the content of the middle-grades curriculum look like as it exists today?

The Traditional Middle-Grades Curriculum

This section of the chapter focuses on the courses traditionally offered in the middle grades and includes a discussion of their content and the practices used in teaching and learning that content. Because the information presented here comes primarily from data gathered in a large, national survey of education in the middle grades, we begin with an overview of that survey. We look at the findings from the survey and then discuss some of those findings in light of the current thinking on the middle-grades curriculum.

Background on the National Survey

In 1988, researchers at the Effective Middle Grades Program at the Johns Hopkins University Center for Research on Elementary and Middle Schools (CREMS) conducted a national survey to provide an overview of the types of courses and educational experiences available to young adolescents in the United States. The principals from 2,400 of the 25,000 public schools that enrolled seventh-graders (in grade spans covering K–8, 6–8, 7–9, or 7–12) received a copy of the survey.

Some 73 percent of the principals responded to questions that tapped information on a number of topics related to middle-grades education, including school size, grade span, grouping practices, advisory groups, team teaching, remediation, the content of the curriculum, and the teaching and learning practices that support the curriculum. Questions about the curriculum asked principals to describe the courses by type (core academic subjects, subjects in the practical and fine arts, and exploratory minicourses), to give the number of students enrolled in those courses, and to estimate how often the typical seventh-grade teacher engaged in a certain practice related to the curriculum (e.g., group projects in social studies).

Findings from the Survey

According to a report written by the researchers at CREMS (CREMS Report, 1990), the results of the survey showed that the middle-grades curriculum and its related classroom practices vary according to the size of the school, the grade span, the student/teacher ratio, and the type of community in which students live. Further, the researchers noted:

> In general, the schools serving middle grades students provide mainly basic or core courses and one or two other subjects, paying little attention to creating learning opportunities that are more responsive to the characteristics of young adolescents.

Schools primarily use a six-period day . . . which limits course periods and flexible scheduling. There is a general conservative emphasis on basic skills. (pp. 3–4)

Following is a description of the three different types of courses that principals reported were available to seventh-grade students in their schools: academic subjects, practical and fine arts, and exploratory courses. The five representative courses in the *academic subjects* area include reading, algebra, science, social studies and foreign languages. The six courses from the *practical and fine arts* area include physical education, art, industrial arts, home economics, computer education, and typing (or keyboarding). *Exploratory courses*, or *minicourses*, include electives such as cartooning, calligraphy, minority cultures, and robotics.

Academic Subjects

Reading is a course taken separately (but concurrently) with a course in English. In the national survey of middle grades, 85 percent of the principals reported that their schools offer supplemental reading instruction because so many of the students read below grade level. In fact, it is estimated that between 55 and 60 percent of all middle-grades students are required to take at least one course in reading during either their seventh- or eighth-grade year.

The emphasis given to supplementary reading instruction in the middle grades seems appropriate, given a recent report from the National Assessment of Educational Progress (NAEP) (Rothman, 1990), which found that the amount of classroom reading engaged in by fourth-, eighth-, and twelfth-grade students is directly related to their level of reading proficiency. The downside of this finding, however, is that "most of the reading instruction that takes place . . . is at a relatively low level . . . [and] few students reported discussing, analyzing, or writing about what they read" (p. 1).

Moreover, the principals' responses on the national survey of middle-grades education, which specifically relate to reading and writing in English classes, corroborate the NAEP finding that low-level, routine instruction in skills is emphasized over all other types of literacy activities.

Fifty-two percent of the principals reported that their "typical" English teachers assign drill-and-practice activities in almost every lesson, while only 1% give daily writing assignments of at least a page in length. . . . Overall, drill-and-practice activities were about twice as frequent as reading and discussion. (Becker, 1990, p. 453)

Algebra is offered in 63 percent of the middle-grades schools studied in the national survey of principals. However, unlike the other academic subjects, algebra is offered only to a selective group of students, with the great majority of students in the seventh and eighth grades taking mathematics courses that either repeat or review concepts taught in the lower grades. According to the survey results, "In all, only about one-sixth of all students will have taken an algebra course by the time they complete eighth grade" (Becker, 1990, p. 451).

The Second International Mathematics Study identified reteaching the content of the mathematics curriculum across several years of schooling (and treating it as if it were new information) as one of the characteristics that sets the United States mathematics curriculum apart from other countries' curricula. Moreover, according to this same international study, "Japan seems clearly to have a more 'algebra driven' curriculum while the U.S. has a more 'arithmetic driven' curriculum" (McKnight, 1990, p. 126).

In corroboration with the U.S. emphasis on an "arithmetic driven" curriculum, nearly half of the principals in the middle-grades survey noted that mathematics teachers rarely or never require students to use calculators to solve word problems; instead, they place the major emphasis on teaching students to do by hand the computations that are required to solve mathematical word problems.

As was the case in reading and English courses, the instruction in middle-grades mathematics is also comprised largely of drill and other low-level memorization tasks. In fact, drill-and-practice activities were more prevalent in mathematics than in reading and English: "Seventy-eight percent of the principals reported that math teachers give daily drills on computation, but only 25% reported that math teachers emphasize problem solving and applications each day" (Becker, 1990, p. 453).

Science courses are taken by approximately 80 percent of all seventh- and eighth-graders in more than 90 percent of the schools that were represented in the national survey of middle-grades education. Just as impressive is the fact that in 90 percent of the schools surveyed, students had the opportunity to take two full years of science. However, according to the principals who responded to the survey, rote learning again took precedence over any other approach to teaching the curriculum.

> Memorizing the "facts" that scientific investigation has discovered consumes much more instructional time in science than does engaging in any learning activities that would teach students how to think and learn as scientists do. A majority of principals (57%) reported that their typical science teachers teach basic science facts every day, but only 33% said that discussions of scientific methods are part of nearly every lesson. Fewer teachers (10%) have students do hands-on laboratory work daily, and fewer still (3% daily) use computer or video technology to provide scientific explanations. (Becker, 1990, p. 453)

Social studies is an area of the middle-grades curriculum in which daily drill-and-practice activities do not appear to dominate to the extent that they do in other curricular areas. For example, only 29 percent of the principals who responded to the national survey reported that teachers used daily drills over important historical facts. However, on a weekly basis, 80 percent of the principals reported that teachers use drill-type activities to teach the curriculum, as compared to 68 percent who said teachers use discussion. A surprisingly low number of principals (roughly one-third) said that teachers require students to complete writing or project assignments on a weekly basis. Another third said such assignments occur monthly, and the final third said they occur rarely or never.

Foreign language offerings are not a substantial part of the middle-grades curriculum. According to the principals who responded to the national survey, less than a majority of the schools offer students a full year of foreign language instruction.

> However, nearly 25% of schools do provide at least one-fourth of their seventh- and eighth-grade students with foreign language instruction. Overall, between 15% and 20% of all students take a year of foreign language in the middle grades. (Becker, 1990, p. 452)

Despite the still relatively small number of students who take advantage of foreign language instruction in the middle grades, there has been a decided upswing in interest in this part of the curriculum, possibly as a result of increased interest at the high school level. According to the executive director of the American Council on the Teaching of Foreign Languages (ACTFL), the United States is "enjoying a boom cycle now—and hoping it's not just a cycle" (O'Neil, 1990a, p. 2). According to the ACTFL, the three-year period between 1982 and 1985 witnessed a huge jump (more than a million) in foreign language enrollment for students in grades 7 through 12.

The growing interest in foreign language instruction is thought to be the result of several factors, including: (1) greater diversity in the population of the United States, (2) increasing concern for economic health and national security, (3) stiffer foreign language requirements for graduation from college, and (4) a tendency toward "proficiency-oriented" instruction (O'Neil, 1990a).

The latter factor, proficiency-oriented instruction, focuses on teaching students how to use a foreign language to communicate (e.g., how to order in French from a French menu) rather than merely teaching them how to recognize nouns from adjectives. This new approach to foreign language instruction is not without its critics, of course. Some worry that a foreign language curriculum that does not stress grammatical accuracy over the ability to communicate may short-change

A school's attention to art appreciation leads to a well-balanced middle-grades curriculum.

students in the long run. Others believe that as students become proficient in a language and need to use it in increasingly complex situations, they will be motivated to strive for greater accuracy. Of more immediate concern for middle-grades students, however, is the popular practice of requiring those who have studied a foreign language in elementary school to begin at the first level of instruction in that language when they reach the middle grades (Rhodes & Oxford, 1988).

Practical and Fine Arts

Physical education courses comprise a substantial offering in the middle-grades curriculum. More than 80 percent of the principals in the national survey reported that their schools offered practically all seventh- and eighth-grade students two full years of physical education for at least three days a week.

Art is offered in roughly 87 percent of the schools, and in a majority of these schools it is mandatory for seventh- or eighth-grade students to take at least 30 or more class periods of art. However, in schools where it is not mandatory, the principals estimated that between 35 and 40 percent of middle-grades students opt not to take art as part of their coursework.

Industrial arts, home economics, and *computer education* make up a significant part of the practical and fine arts curriculum. Approximately two-thirds of all middle-grades principals reported that their schools offer each of these subjects during either the seventh- or eighth-grade years. In 40 percent of the reporting schools, students receive 30 or more hours of classroom instruction in these three subjects, although the majority of students who exit eighth grade will have taken only one of the three.

Typing or *keyboarding* is offered in only 40 percent of the middle-grades schools that took part in the national survey. As few as 25 percent of all students exit the eighth grade with 30 or more hours of instruction in either of these two subjects. Even so, this is a considerable change from a few years ago when typing was firmly entrenched in high school business courses.

Exploratory Courses

Frequently, exploratory courses are offered as electives in the middle-grades curriculum. They typically focus on special topics (e.g., the stock market, outdoor education) and provide students simply with an awareness level of learning in these areas. Sometimes they are offered throughout the year during the part of the school day known as the activity period, or they may be offered for only part of the school year. By far, exploratory courses represent the least well-developed area of the middle-grades curriculum. Only 39 percent of the principals in the national survey reported that their schools offer these courses. Even then, roughly 30 percent or fewer of the students will actually enroll in such a course during their seventh- or eighth-grade years (Becker, 1990).

A Discussion of the Survey Findings

Findings from the CREMS national survey of middle grades education clearly characterize the typical middle-grades curriculum as being academic centered and discipline based. Although in the last decade middle-grades theorists (e.g., Arnold,

1985; Brazee, 1987; Vars, 1987) have called for a broader, more conceptually based curriculum that is responsive to young adolescents' developmental needs, the reality is that the current curriculum is more narrowly focused on knowledge-level learning of discrete subjects.

Nonetheless, as evidenced in several recent issues of *Update*, a newsletter published by the Association for Supervision and Curriculum Development, a few school systems are "attempting to tackle one of the thorniest issues facing curriculum developers—how to foster greater integration among the subject areas" (Association for Supervision and Curriculum Development, 1990, p. 1). As the writers of these newsletters suggest, the issue of curriculum integration is particularly relevant in today's world where the knowledge explosion taking place in all disciplines threatens to fragment the middle-grades curriculum even further, thus making it virtually impossible for teachers to approach the curriculum in ways that are developmentally appropriate for the young adolescent learner.

Understandably, even those middle grades that are making progress in developing an integrated curriculum (e.g., see Maeroff, 1990) continue to experience difficulty fitting in interdisciplinary courses within the existing organizational structure of a school. "I can't tell you how many times I've been in a school and seen good intentions gone astray," says Heidi Jacobs of Teachers College, Columbia University, on the topic of implementing an interdisciplinary curriculum.

> What Jacobs terms the "potpourri" problem results when interdisciplinary curriculum units represent merely a "sampling" from each of the disciplines rather than a well-articulated design. Proponents of a strong disciplinary approach have derided such efforts at curriculum integration by arguing the practice contributes to a lack of curricular focus and bypasses key disciplinary concepts. Conflict between the two camps contributes to a "polarity" problem, in which curriculum design is viewed as being either interdisciplinary or discipline-based perspectives. (Association for Supervision and Curriculum Development, 1990)

Finally, the results of the national survey on middle-grades education suggest that the curriculum, at least as it is typically described by the representative group of principals responding to the survey, fosters a subject-centered approach to teaching and learning. Beane (1990a) and others have argued that this approach is inappropriate to use with young adolescents, yet it lingers on and is supported by the typical middle-grades curriculum that was described in the national survey of principals. Some possible reasons for the popularity of the subject-centered approach are the following:

1. The subject approach to curriculum development has traditionally enjoyed the support of educators steeped in the notion of classical humanism, which is the belief that what is important to know can be learned from the study of certain subjects that have been handed down for generations. Traditionally, the academic subjects of English, history, science, and mathematics form the core of such a curriculum, with the fine arts added on.
2. The subject approach has also enjoyed the support of educators who subscribe to the concept of faculty psychology (or mental discipline), which is a theory

that holds the mind is divided into tiny compartments, each compartment being the repository of distinctly different kinds of information.

3. The subject approach to curriculum design has been the hallmark of university education. Consequently, it has been assumed, rightly or wrongly, that a subject approach to middle-grades curriculum will prepare students to enter the university at some appropriate future time.

One of the arguments against retaining the traditional subject-centered approach as the mainstay of the middle-grades curriculum is that it fragments the curriculum and inhibits the probability that teachers and students will see links across the curriculum. Another argument against this approach is that it creates the myth that cognition and affect are separate entities in the curriculum. The third, and perhaps most compelling, argument is that it limits teachers' and students' ability to integrate information from different subjects within themes that are developmentally appropriate for young adolescents.

An Alternative Middle-Grades Curriculum

In this portion of the chapter we examine in detail a very different kind of middle-grades curriculum than the one described by nearly 2,000 principals who responded to the CREMS survey. First, we present a rationale for an alternative curriculum, which takes into account the personal concerns of young adolescents and the social issues that have an impact on their lives. Next, we explore several curriculum themes that emerge from the overlap between young adolescents' personal concerns and the social issues that impact their everyday life. We also consider some developmentally appropriate skills that students would need to apply if they are to understand the curriculum themes that emerge from the overlap between young adolescents' personal and social concerns. Three broad concepts are then described that are thought to permeate almost any curriculum designed to teach students how to live and prosper in a democratic society. In conclusion, we illustrate what an alternative middle-grades curriculum might look like if it were built on curriculum themes that are pulled from the overlap between young adolescents' personal and social concerns.

Rationale for an Alternative Curriculum

In his book, *A Middle School Curriculum: From Rhetoric to Reality*, James A. Beane (1990a) challenges leaders in the middle-grades movement to find an answer to the question, What should be the curriculum of the middle school? In defining what he believes some of the criteria should be for answering that question, Beane (1990b) writes,

> Work in this area will require that reforming middle school curriculum be more than simply correlating traditional subject areas within an interdisciplinary team. Instead, middle school educators will have to rethink what they mean by the "core" of the curriculum and imagine the possibility of thematic units developed around compelling

personal and social issues without regard for subject area lines—themes that engage young adolescents in direct and critical study and action. (pp. 111–112)

The time for rethinking the core of the middle-grades curriculum seems particularly ripe. As pointed out earlier in this chapter, concern about the content of what students are learning has resulted in a variety of commissioned reports by organizations within the private and public sectors of the country, as well as by individuals who have an interest in studying curriculum reform. Yet, as Lewis (1990) has noted, "After almost seven years of serious, wide-ranging efforts to reform schools, students don't seem to be learning much more" (p. 534).

Perhaps, as Beane has argued, it *is* time to call a halt to looking for changes in student performance by tinkering and making adjustments within the existing middle-grades curriculum. Maybe a more productive approach to effecting change in students' learning would be to overhaul the curriculum completely—to allow the overlap between young adolescents' personal and social concerns to dictate the content of the curriculum.

Personal Concerns of Young Adolescents

Chapter 2 presented a thorough overview of the various physical, socioemotional, and cognitive changes that characterize young adolescence. Equally important to reviewing the information presented in Chapter 2 is the careful consideration of what Arnold (1985) points out in his article on a responsive curriculum for young adolescents:

> Young adolescents are asking some of the most profound questions human beings can ever ask: Who am I? What can I be? What should I be? What should I do? To respond to them effectively, we must forge a curriculum that frequently deals with their own questions. (p. 14)

Young adolescents' own questions and concerns, Beane (1990a) contends, should not be thought of as simply self-centered in nature; instead, they should be thought of as "issues that help to form the collective culture of young adolescents and to connect these young people to others of all ages who share similar concerns about their place in and relation to the larger society" (p. 38). Put in the context of the middle-grades curriculum, young adolescents' questions and concerns can form the basis of a meaningful curriculum. They also can provide students with the motivation or the will to follow their own lines of higher-order thinking in learning the content of the curriculum rather than memorizing endless lines of other people's thinking.

Social Issues that Affect Young Adolescents' Lives

The young adolescents of today are living in a vastly more complex technological society than ever experienced in the history of this country. It is a society in which even mature adults are sometimes left confused and frustrated. Social problems such as drug abuse, the spread of AIDS, poverty, homelessness, organized crime, environmental pollution, and racism are more than abstract concepts. These are

Young adolescents' own questions and concerns can form the basis of a meaningful curriculum.

real issues and everyday realities for far too many of the students enrolled in our middle grades. Yet, as Beane (1990a) has pointed out, "These issues are 'marginalized' by the typical academic-centered, subject area curriculum both in terms of the narrow view of what it presents and by what it leaves out" (p. 39).

Beane (1990a) has suggested that the following issues, or others like them, be considered for inclusion in the framework of an alternative middle-grades curriculum. As you read the list, try to think how each item might overlap with a personal concern of young adolescents.

1. Interdependence among peoples in multiple layers from the immediate network of relationships to the global level;
2. The diversity of cultures that are present within each of those layers, formed by race, ethnicity, gender, geographic region, and other factors;
3. Problems in the environment that range from diminishing resources to disposal of waste and that come together in the question of whether we can sustain a livable planet;
4. Political processes and structures, including their contradictions, that have simultaneously liberated and oppressed particular groups of people;
5. Economic problems ranging from securing personal economic security to increasing commercialization of interests to the issue of inequitable distribution of wealth and related power;
6. The place of technology as it enters into various aspects of life, and the moral issues it presents;
7. The increasing incidence of self-destructive behaviors including substance abuse, crime, adolescent pregnancies, participation in street gangs, and attempted and actual suicides. (p. 39)

Curriculum Themes

In Beane's (1990a) conception of an alternative middle-grades curriculum, the overlap between young adolescents' personal concerns and the social issues that surround them as "real people living out real lives in a very real world" (p. 39) is the domain from which curriculum themes are drawn. Earlier we asked you to think about what some of the personal concerns students might have that would overlap with the list of social issues that you were asked to read. In Figure 4.2, we present Beane's conception of what that intersection might look like.

Notice that the two outside columns list the personal and social concerns of young adolescents and that the center column lists possible themes that might be drawn from the overlap or intersection between the two types of concerns. Beane (1990a) argues that it is themes like these that should provide the framework for a middle-grades curriculum.

> If we look carefully at the personal concerns of young adolescents and the larger issues that face our world, it is readily apparent that there is a good deal of a particular kind of overlap between them. As it turns out, concerns in one or the other category are frequently micro or macro versions of each other. Such, for example, is the relationship between developing personal self-esteem and the search for collective efficacy among cultures [IDENTITIES], between forming peer group connections and pursuing global

FIGURE 4.2 Intersections of Personal and Social Concerns

EARLY ADOLESCENT CONCERNS	CURRICULUM THEMES	SOCIAL CONCERNS
Understanding personal changes	TRANSITIONS	Living in a changing world
Developing a personal identity	IDENTITIES	Cultural diversity
Finding a place in the group	INTERDEPENDENCE	Global interdependence
Personal fitness	WELLNESS	Environmental protection
Social status	SOCIAL STRUCTURES	Class systems
Dealing with adults	INDEPENDENCE	Human rights
Peer conflict and gangs	CONFLICT RESOLUTION	Global conflict
Commercial pressures	COMMERCIALISM	Effects of media
Questioning authority	JUSTICE	Laws and social customs
Personal friendships	CARING	Social welfare
Living in the school	INSTITUTIONS	Social institutions

Source: From J. A. Beane, *A Middle School Curriculum: From Rhetoric to Reality,* 1990, Columbus, OH: National Middle School Association, p. 41. Reprinted by permission of the National Middle School Association, February 1991.

interdependence [INTERDEPENDENCE], between the status differentiations among peers and the defining conditions of socioeconomic class distinctions [SOCIAL STRUCTURES], between personal fitness and environmental improvement [WELL-NESS], between understanding personal developmental changes and conceptualizing a society and world in transition [TRANSITIONS], and between frustration over adult authority and struggles for human and civil rights [INDEPENDENCE]. (p. 40)

The six themes (or others like them) identified in the preceding brackets provide examples of how the content of an alternative curriculum might be conceptualized. Consider for a moment how such a curriculum addresses the personal and social concerns of young adolescents, yet loses none of the academic rigor attributed to the subject-centered approach. It is clear that English, mathematics, social studies, and the sciences would all figure into the alternative middle-grades curriculum. The only difference would be on the focus. In the present-day middle-grades curriculum, the separate subjects receive the spotlight; in the proposed alternative curriculum, themes built around students' personal and social concerns would receive the spotlight.

Developmentally Appropriate Skills

In referring to his proposed alternative middle-grades curriculum as a "living" curriculum, Beane (1990a) reminds us that the skills we select to help students learn and apply the content of this curriculum must of necessity include such higher-order skills as the following:

1. *Reflective thinking*, both critical and creative, about the meanings and consequences of ideas and behaviors.
2. Identifying and judging the morality in problem situations; that is, *critical ethics*.
3. *Problem solving*, including problem finding and analysis.
4. Identifying and clarifying personal beliefs and standards upon which decisions and behaviors are based; this is *valuing*.
5. Describing and evaluating personal aspirations, interests, and other characteristics; that is, *self-concepting* and *self-esteeming*.
6. Acting upon problem situations both individually and collectively; that is, *social action skills*.
7. *Searching for completeness and meaning* in such areas as cultural diversity. (pp. 40–41)

At first glance it might appear that these skills are extremely high level and perhaps out of reach of most students at the middle-grades level. We would agree that this might be the case if teachers attempted to present such skills in an isolated fashion or in connection with content that had little or no relevance to the students. However, based on the premise that a "living" curriculum, such as the one proposed here, will involve students in a meaningful engagement with the content, it is reasonable to expect that they will be able to apply higher-order skills because they will have the need to and the interest in doing so.

The authenticity of the curriculum, coupled with the teaching of higher-order skills in a functional manner, should also compensate nicely for any difficulty in skill level. "In other words, the learning and valuing of skills are most likely assured if they are placed in a functional context where their application is immediate and compelling" (Beane, 1990a, p. 42).

Broad and Enduring Concepts

Two dimensions being proposed for an alternative middle-grades curriculum are (1) curriculum themes that emerge from the intersection of personal and social concerns and (2) the higher-order skills that students need to explore such themes. A third dimension has to do with the notion that broad and enduring concepts should permeate the content of any curriculum, particularly if one of the goals of that curriculum is to have a lasting and influential impact on the lives of the students for whom it is intended. Democracy, human dignity, and cultural diversity are the broad and enduring concepts that Beane proposes should permeate the content of his alternative middle-grades curriculum.

Democracy

A primary reason for pinpointing democracy as one of the three concepts that should permeate the middle-grades curriculum in the United States is to make certain that past inequities, in which content was selectively chosen, are not perpetuated. For example, too often the traditional middle-grades curriculum has reflected the interests and concerns of the dominant white majority at the expense of others who have contributed to this country's historical, intellectual, social, and economic development. Beane (1990a) notes, "Rather than extend this status quo, the middle schools have a moral obligation, rooted in democracy, to open it up for critical examination and broader understanding" (p. 44).

Human Dignity

Teaching about human dignity through themes that are a natural outgrowth of young adolescents' personal and social concerns is a vast improvement over the current practice of teaching about self-esteem, justice, caring, and equality as topics within discrete subject areas. The latter approach provides students with little or no opportunity to make connections between their own world and that of the larger world surrounding them. On the other hand, the proposed alternative middle-grades program, with its emphasis on personally and socially relevant themes, has the potential to interest students in a world of broader human struggles and efforts.

Cultural Diversity

An alternative curriculum built on the personal and social concerns of young adolescents provides the perfect opportunity to highlight some of the cultures that are obscured or missing in the traditional middle-grades curriculum. In making this observation, Beane (1990a) points out that he is referring not only to the culture of the non-European immigrant but also to the culture of young adolescents themselves. He also makes it clear that an alternative middle-grades program should involve young adolescents in the decision-making process that accompanies curriculum reform.

With the possible exception of his views on including young adolescents in the process, Beane (1990a) acknowledges that his ideas on curriculum reform are not that different from others working in the area to improve the lot of the students enrolled in today's middle grades.

> No doubt these concepts are somewhere behind some of the efforts to reform the climate and institutional structures of middle schools, but they ought to be more visible in our talk and action. Again, it is only in this way that the middle schools can find a place in the larger society and fulfill their broadest purpose. And it is only by articulating these concepts that the intersecting themes of personal and social living may eventually lead toward an improved quality of life for young adolescents now and in their futures. (p. 45)

What an Alternative Curriculum Might Look Like

Figure 4.3 illustrates the framework of the alternative middle-grades curriculum that Beane has proposed. Curriculum themes are generated in the area where the two circles denoting young adolescents' personal and social concerns overlap. Thematic units, whose contents are drawn from the overlapping area of the two circles, are taught, learned, and applied through the incorporation of the skills and concepts described earlier.

Following are four brief descriptions of thematic units that Beane (1990a) suggests might be developed from the framework presented in Figure 4.3. As you read the descriptions, see if you can identify the content or subject matter that is presently taught through the traditional middle-grades program but in separate subject areas. For example, in the thematic unit on independence, can you identify some of the past and present national revolutions that might be included in this unit?

1. We can picture a unit on *independence* that involves examining conflicts between young adolescents and authority figures in the community and school, identifying the causes of past and present national revolutions, analyzing the pressure from commercial media to conform, reflecting on the dependent conditions caused by substance abuse, exploring the tension between the dependence and independence in gang customs and behaviors, and studying past and present movements for human and civil rights.

2. We can begin to imagine young adolescents engaged in a unit on *human relationships* studying the peer group structure in their own school and community, investigating how societies and cultures are formed, exploring ways of promoting global interdependence, participating in community service projects, and interviewing people about how technology has changed their relationship with others.

3. We can picture a unit on *wellness* in which young adolescents develop a school recycling project, learn about the scientific aspects of pollution, investigate environmental regulations and their relationship to business practices, explore approaches to environmental problems, plot correlations between pollution and health problems in various regions, identify the effects of pollution on their own health, practice the many ways of maintaining physical fitness, and investigate nutrition (including in the school cafeteria).

FIGURE 4.3   A Middle-School Curriculum

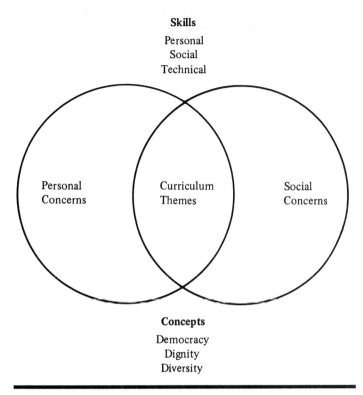

Skills
Personal
Social
Technical

Personal
Concerns

Curriculum
Themes

Social
Concerns

Concepts
Democracy
Dignity
Diversity

Source: From J. A. Beane, *A Middle School Curriculum: From Rhetoric to Reality,* 1990, Columbus, OH: National Middle School Association, p. 46. Reprinted by permission of the National Middle School Association, February 1991.

4. We can imagine a unit on *living in the future* in which young adolescents develop scenarios on what they consider to be desirable personal and social futures, recommend ideas for improving their communities, learn about biotechnical developments, investigate work trends and forecasts, and debate the moral issues of advancing technology. (pp. 45–46)

Issues in Curriculum Reform

The belief that current conceptions of curriculum in the schools of this country are fundamentally flawed is gaining widespread support as one report after another from the Association for the Advancement of Science (AAAS), the National Council of Teachers of Mathematics (NCTM), the National Commission on Social Studies (NCSS), and so on call for curriculum reform. Specifically, the AAAS,

NCTM, and NCSS reports "support curriculums that enable students to think critically, to ask questions and solve problems, and to see the links among issues and content within and across subject area boundaries" (O'Neil, 1990b, p. 4). In short, the emphasis for this decade promises to be on developing curriculums that engage students in their learning by fostering thoughtful, not rote, behaviors.

It is interesting to note, however, that few if any of these calls for reform have advocated a curriculum as genuinely different as the one proposed by Beane (1990a). By advocating that the present middle-grades curriculum be replaced by a curriculum more developmentally appropriate to young adolescents' interests and concerns, Beane has set an agenda for reform that he acknowledges may be difficult, if not impossible, to achieve. The issues that he sees as central to the implementation of his proposed middle-grades curriculum are described here.

1. The implementation process must proceed slowly but systematically, with sufficient time given to collaborative planning that involves teachers and young adolescents.
2. Labeling students as gifted or slow learners would carry little meaning in the proposed alternative curriculum. As members of heterogeneously grouped classrooms engaged in common thematic study, young adolescents would have opportunities to experience a wide range of views and to benefit from a curriculum permeated with a concern for human dignity and cultural diversity.
3. Scheduling must be flexible to accommodate a broad spectrum of variations in how students and teachers group to work on particular themes. The length of various themes and the manner in which teachers choose to work with a particular group must be free to vary.
4. Moving away from the academic-centered, separate-subject curriculum that is common today invariably means moving away from the usual ways of assessing and reporting the progress of young adolescents' work. Standardized tests and letter grades must be supplemented or replaced by thick descriptions of students' work, such as learning logs, portfolios, teachers' anecdotal records, and journals.

Without a doubt there are many more issues at stake in rethinking the middle-grades curriculum than these four items would suggest. Also, there are undoubtedly as many or more reasons for maintaining the status quo in the middle-grades curriculum as there are for changing it. What is important, however, is the need to challenge our own complacency and that of others when it comes to questions about the best environment for student learning. Riner (1989) reminds us in his essay on John Dewey's legacy to education that Dewey's challenge to his fellow educators nearly a century ago, on their complacency toward a subject-centered curriculum, "is as poignant today as it was to his contemporaries. It continues to haunt the essentialist curriculum reformers in their efforts to confine curriculum to traditional subject matters, as well as the defenders of the status quo" (pp. 183–184).

Summary

Pressures to reform the curriculum in almost every major subject area are also reflected in the middle-grades movement. The results of a national survey on middle-grades education conducted by the Center for Research on Elementary and Middle Schools at Johns Hopkins University characterize the content of the middle-grades curriculum as being narrowly focused on knowledge-level learning of discrete subject matter. Although a few middle grades are attempting to address the thorny issue of curriculum integration, even the most successful ones continue to experience difficulty fitting in interdisciplinary courses within the existing organizational structure.

The suggestion has been made that middle-grades educators need to place curriculum questions at the top of their priorities. Specifically, the call has gone out for a radically different middle-grades curriculum—one that would derive its content from the themes that emerge from the overlap in young adolescents' personal and social concerns. Whether or not this alternative middle-grades curriculum will gain the support it needs to be implemented as *the* middle-grades curriculum remains to be seen. What is more important is that the call for curriculum reform promises to keep each of us from becoming too complacent in our thinking on the topic of young adolescent education.

REFERENCES

Alexander, F., & Crabtree, C. (1988). California's new history—Social science curriculum promises richness and depth. *Educational Leadership, 46*, 10–13.

American Association for the Advancement of Science. (1990). *The liberal art of science: Agenda for action*. Washington, DC: Author.

Arnold, J. (1985). A responsive curriculum for early adolescents. *Middle Schools Journal, 16*(3), 14–18.

Association for Supervision and Curriculum Development. (1990). Curriculum integration: Modest efforts to link disciplines gain support. *Update, 32*, 1–2.

Beane, J. A. (1990a). *A middle school curriculum: From rhetoric to reality*. Columbus, OH: National Middle School Association.

Beane, J. A. (1990b). Affective dimensions of effective middle schools. *Educational Horizons, 68*, 109–112.

Becker, H. J. (1990). Curriculum and instruction in middle-grade schools. *Phi Delta Kappan, 71*, 450–457.

Brazee, E. (1987). Exploration in the "regular" curriculum. In E. Brazee (Ed.), *Exploratory curriculum for the middle level*. Rowley, MA: New England League of Middle Schools.

Carnegie Council on Adolescent Development. (1989). *Turning points: Preparing American youth for the 21st century*. Washington, DC: Carnegie Council on Adolescent Development.

Cawelti, G. (1988). Middle schools a better match with early adolescent needs, ASCD survey finds. *Curriculum Update*, November, 1–12.

Center for Research on Elementary and Middle Schools (1990). Implementation and effects of middle grades practices. *CREMS Report* (March, pp. 3–4). Baltimore, MD: Johns Hopkins University Center for Research on Elementary and Middle Schools.

Epstein, J. L., & McPartland, J. M. (1988). *Education in the middle grades: A national survey of practices and trends*. Baltimore, MD: Johns Hopkins University Center for Research on Elementary and Middle Schools.

Estes, T. H., Gutman, C. J., & Harrison, E. K. (1988). Cultural literacy: What every educator needs to know. *Educational Leadership, 46,* 14–17.

Hirsch, E. D., Jr. (1988). Hirsch responds: The best answer to a caricature is a practical program. *Educational Leadership, 46,* 18–19.

Hirsch, E. D., Jr. (1987). *Cultural literacy: What every American needs to know.* Boston: Houghton Mifflin.

Lewis, A. C. (1990). Getting unstuck: Curriculum as a tool of reform. *Phi Delta Kappan, 71,* 534–538.

Lounsbury, J. H. (1990). Middle level education: Perspectives, problems, and prospects. *Educational Horizons, 68,* 63–68.

Maeroff, G. I. (1990). Getting to know a good middle school: Shoreham-Wading River. *Phi Delta Kappan, 71,* 505–511.

McCormick, K. (1989). Battling scientific illiteracy: Educators seek consensus, action on needed reforms. *Curriculum Update,* June, 1–6.

McKnight, C. C. (1990). The organization of curricula in mathematics. *International Journal of Educational Research, 14,* 121–137.

National Assessment of Educational Progress. (1990). *Learning to read in our nation's schools.* Princeton, NJ: Educational Testing Service.

National Commission on Excellence in Education. (1983). *A nation at risk: The imperative for educational reform.* Washington, DC: U.S. Government Printing Office.

O'Neil, J. (1989a). Social studies: Charting a course for a field adrift. *Curriculum Update,* November, 1–3, 5–7.

O'Neil, J. (1989b). Global education: Controversy remains, but support growing. *Curriculum Update,* January, 1–6.

O'Neil, J. (1990a). Foreign languages: As enrollments climb, a new focus on 'proficiency.' *Curriculum Update,* January, 1–3, 6–7.

O'Neil, J. (1990b). Experts examine roadblocks to curriculum reform. *Update, 32,* 4.

Rhodes, N. C., & Oxford, R. L. (1988). Foreign languages in elementary and secondary schools: Results from a national survey. *Foreign Language Annals, 21,* 51–61.

Riner, P. S. (1989). Dewey's legacy to education. *The Educational Forum, 53,* 183–190.

Rothman, R. (1990). Students spend little time reading or writing in school, NAEP finds. *Education Week, 9*(38), 1–2.

Smith, M. S., O'Day, J. A., & Cohen, D. K. (1991). A national curriculum in the United States? *Educational Leadership, 49,* 74–81.

Vars, G. F. (1987). *Interdisciplinary teaching in the middle grades.* Columbus, OH: National Middle School Association.

_5_

Middle-Grades
Academic Core Content

Welcome to Neptune

Science
Mrs. Carey
Mr. Caskey

Language Arts
Mrs. McKenna
Mrs. Weaver

Mathematics
Mrs. Smith

Reading
Mr. Simpson

Social Studies
Mr. MacMillan

How is the content of the traditional middle-grades curriculum made available to teachers and students? What content typically is taught to middle-grades students in their academic core classes (English/language arts, social studies, science, and mathematics)? What does the research on the content of these core classes have to say to teachers? You will learn the answer to each of these questions in this chapter.

Recalling as much as you can about your own middle-grades schooling will help you make some interesting comparisons as you read the chapter. For example, remembering what content your teachers taught you, the materials they used, and what you liked and disliked about your young adolescent years will enable you to get some sense of the way things have changed, or stayed the same, over the years. Trying to make connections between then and now will also enable you to appreciate the degree to which research in the various subject areas has affected classroom practice.

Making the Content Available

The primary vehicle for delivering the content of the middle-grades curriculum is the textbook. Apple (1986) noted, "Whether we like it or not, the curriculum in most American schools is not defined by courses of study or suggested programs, but by . . . [the] grade-level-specific text in mathematics, reading, social studies, science, . . . and so on" (p. 85). The prevalence of textbook use in the middle grades and some of the criticisms leveled against present-day textbooks are the first two topics addressed in this chapter. Next, there is a brief section on teachers' reactions to the criticisms leveled against textbooks. Finally, some alternatives to textbook use are considered.

Prevalence of Textbook Use

Textbooks head the list of instructional materials in the middle grades, as they do at the elementary and secondary school levels. By some estimates, between 67 to 90 percent of all types of classroom instruction at all levels is dominated by textbooks (Tyson & Woodward, 1989; Woodward & Elliott, 1990). In *Report of the 1985–86 National Survey of Science and Mathematics Education*, Weiss (1987) described a 90 percent user rate among science and mathematics classrooms at each grade level. Commenting on the fact that newer forms of technology appear to pose no real threat to the textbook's dominance in U.S. schools, Cannon and Sewall (1989) wrote, "Despite the growing use of computers, textbooks remain the foundation for as much as 90% of classroom learning" (p. 7).

As far back as the early 1900s, researchers have recorded the pervasive presence of the textbook in U.S. school life (Woodward & Elliott, 1990). And, as the figures cited here and elsewhere (e.g., Cole & Sticht, 1981) would suggest, dependency on the textbook as the conveyor of course content shows no sign of abating. In fact, first among the five main conclusions drawn by Elliott and Woodward (1990) as a result of their extensive research on textbooks and schooling was this one:

> *Commercially published multigrade textbook programs constitute a virtual national curriculum in the basic subjects for public elementary and junior high schools.* . . . In contrast to the situation sixty years ago, contemporary student textbooks contain not only narrative text but section and chapter exercises and they are accompanied by arrays of workbooks, and worksheets, and (often) supplementary booklets for student use. In addition, teacher's editions of the student textbooks contain background information, detailed teaching plans, and achievement tests. (p. 222)

Given the wide availability of textbooks, plus research that shows that they dominate middle-grades instruction, it might be reasonable to assume that teachers rely too much on the textbook to teach the content of the curriculum. A useful distinction, it seems to us, is the difference between widespread use and dependence. Perhaps even more important is an understanding of the factors that may explain why some teachers depend heavily on textbooks whereas others use them selectively or hardly at all.

Use versus Dependence

According to Woodward and Elliott (1990), "Dependence on textbooks as opposed to use of textbooks is an issue at the core of professional practice" (p. 180). As with most issues, there is no clear dividing line that separates the teacher who uses textbooks from the one who is dependent on them. However, teachers who stay close to the textbook's organizational plan and rely almost exclusively on the material contained within its two covers to teach the content of the curriculum would tend to fall near the *dependent* end of whatever continuum might separate the two extremes. Unlike users of textbooks, teachers whose instruction is dependent on textbooks would seldom make adjustments in the way they use textbooks (e.g., skipping parts of the text, eliminating some exercises and/or substituting others).

Although researchers have produced well-documented studies that show that teachers vary widely in their use of textbooks, Woodward and Elliott's (1990) review of the literature suggests that, "in general, teachers tend to teach the core elements of the textbook and the teacher's guide" (p. 181). Other researchers (e.g., Applebee, Langer, & Mullis, 1987; Goodlad, 1984; Stake & Easley, 1978) have reported that the textbook, not the teacher, is viewed as the legitimate source of knowledge in the classroom. That is, teachers rely on textbooks to specify the content and amount of time they allot to covering specific topics rather than on their own professional judgments about the relevancy of content and the pacing of instruction.

At the same time, there is a growing body of research that suggests teachers, not textbooks, are the primary source of knowledge when it comes to imparting

Textbooks play an important role in young adolescents' learning of academic core content.

information about the content. For example, in some classrooms, teachers appear to use the textbook more as a safety net—something to fall back on—and less as a basis for their lectures or discussions (Davey, 1988; Ratekin, Simpson, Alvermann, & Dishner, 1985). In other classrooms, teachers may perceive the textbook as the major source of information, but their students' perceptions may be totally different (Smith & Feathers, 1983a, 1983b).

The question of which group of researchers is right is not the important issue. What is important is an understanding of why some teachers may teach strictly from the text whereas others may use it selectively. Here, there appears to be some agreement in the research literature. In at least three recent reviews of the literature on teachers' use of textbooks, the reviewers (Alvermann & Moore, 1991; Stodolsky, 1989; Woodward & Elliott, 1990) conclude that a number of factors probably interact to influence teachers' decisions about the use of textbooks. Several of these factors are discussed next.

Possible Explanations for Variations in Textbook Use

The degree to which teachers rely on textbooks to teach the content of the curriculum is influenced by their level of experience, the expertise they possess in a particular subject, the materials they use, and the time they are given to teach certain units of study.

1. Teachers with five years or more of teaching experience use textbooks about one-third as often as teachers who are in their first year of teaching.
2. In terms of subject matter expertise, it appears that high-knowledge teachers exhibit less dependence on textbooks than low-knowledge teachers. High-knowledge teachers also show greater dissatisfaction with the instructional caliber of their texts than do low-knowledge teachers.
3. The limited availability of appropriate supplementary materials influences the degree to which teachers depend on the textbook to teach the content of the curriculum. When supplementary materials are difficult to obtain or are written too far above or below the students' reading level, the chances for over-reliance on textbooks increases.
4. Time is a factor. Teachers tend to rely on textbooks less when they are given what they perceive to be inadequate time to cover the contents. Apparently having insufficient time to teach their subject matter encourages teachers to seek alternative methods of conveying the information to students (Woodward & Elliott, 1990).

Although common sense might have told us that factors like experiential level, subject matter expertise, availability of materials, and time constraints would influence textbook dependency, we include them here as reminders that generalizations about textbook use must be examined in light of different situations that may exist in each teacher's classroom and school. Awareness of these various situations makes it possible to predict with more accuracy where textbooks will tend to dominate the teacher's instruction.

Criticisms Leveled Against Textbooks

Despite the popularity of textbooks, they have come under sharp criticism during recent years.

> Chief among the shortcomings researchers have identified are "mentioning," or shallow coverage of a wide range of topics; "inconsiderateness," or poor writing; emphasis on lower-level memorizing of facts and generalizations to the exclusion of problem solving and other higher-order cognitive processes; the avoidance of important topics because some consider them too controversial; and failure to promote adequate understanding of the real nature of the knowledge fields, such as science and history, that are the bases of school subjects. (Elliott & Woodward, 1990, p. 223)

Mentioning

A good example of what is meant by shallow coverage, or *mentioning*, of important information comes to us from the research that was conducted by the Educational Products Information Exchange (Bernstein, 1985).

> Information about recent American presidents is usually limited to a sentence or two. The impossibility of making sense out of a presidency in so short a space is painfully illustrated by one book's treatment of former president Richard M. Nixon. In a chapter entitled "Conflict and Compromise," . . . the book says, "President Nixon tried to help his friends." Later in the text, the student learns that "laws were passed to increase honesty in government." Even if the two sentences had been together, it would have been hard for a fifth grader to make the connection between helping friends and laws about honesty in government. (p. 28)

In other content areas, such as mathematics, critics point to similar problems caused by mentioning; for example, "a lack of richness in content and a slow pace that puts American students behind their Asian and European counterparts" (Stodolsky, 198° p. 162).

Control o' *r* matters of content and pacing and the textbook's relative insensitivity to stu *ents'* common-sense experiences are some of the criticisms Torbe (1988) has l' eled against textbook publishers. Another of Torbe's criticisms has to do with th' fact that teachers who are already familiar with the content of their textbook' are less likely to appreciate or predict the difficulties students may have in learr g from text. Herber (1978) refers to this phenomenon as one of the proble s encountered in assumptive teaching.

"I' nsiderate" Writing

I' pointing out the problems caused by inconsiderate, or poor, writing, Bernstein 985) offers this short paragraph taken from a middle-grades social studies textbook:

> People worked hard to rebuild and unify America after the Civil War. It was time to move ahead. In 1790, the first census of the United States was taken. A census is an official count of people. Every ten years, a census is taken in the United States. In 1790,

there were 4 million Americans. Most of them were living in small settlements or on farms. Today, the United States has 220 million people. Most of these people live and work in or near cities. (p. 26)

The paragraph has several problems, but the primary one is a lack of unity. That is, all of the ideas do not relate to the main topic, which we are led to believe will be about some of the events following the Civil War. Paragraphs like this are frequently referred to as *inconsiderate* texts (Kantor, Anderson, & Armbruster, 1983); they create a sense of frustration for the reader.

Unrelated Illustrations

A textbook's aesthetic qualities play a large role in state adoptions of textbooks. When illustrations clarify the written text or personalize it in a way that makes a student want to read on, they are effective. Research has shown that illustrations, including photographs, can occupy as much as 50 percent of a book's pages. Although it would be senseless to argue for pictureless books, it is appropriate to insist that illustrations that are not explicitly related to the text be judged for what they are—fillers taking up space that could be put to better use.

When textbooks treat important topics superficially, when the quality of writing is poor, or when illustrations are unrelated to the text, criticism comes from all corners. Educators tend to blame publishers for trying to serve too many different needs by packing into one book all of the states' requests for topic coverage. Publishers, on the other hand, say they are only responding to market needs.

Theorists whose expertise lies in the area of curriculum reform say that the problem lies with the U.S. school system and the way it is presently structured. They believe that the curriculum of the future will require teachers to choose from a wide variety of print and nonprint media. When this happens, they say, textbooks will no longer dominate classroom instruction, and teachers won't expect to find a year's worth of the curriculum in textbooks of up to 400 pages or more in length (Elliott & Woodward, 1990).

Teachers' Reactions to Criticisms of Textbooks

At least one group of educators—the classroom teachers—do not share the general public's impression that textbooks are poorly written and illustrated. Based on a survey of 800 social studies teachers, who are part of a network that is affiliated with the National Commission on Social Studies in the Schools, it is clear that the teachers believe textbooks have improved over the past several years and that they value the exercises and review materials included in the books (Metcalf, 1988).

Similar results were obtained from a survey of 100 teachers who taught in either an urban or a suburban setting. The sample consisted of both elementary and secondary students and thus included the middle grades. Six of the teachers participated in an in-depth personal interview as a follow-up to the survey. As noted by Rogers (1988), the researcher who conducted the survey, teachers viewed textbooks as being primarily realistic, relevant to students' lives, and fair in their presentation of sensitive material.

> For example, 88 percent of [the] surveyed teachers either disagreed or strongly disagreed with the notion that the quality of textbooks has been "declining dramatically" during the past 10 years. Seventy-five percent disagreed strongly with criticisms labeling modern texts as "flat and/or unimaginative," written in a "choppy and stilted" style, "lacking in continuity," saturated with "pointless" workbook exercises. . . . [They] did not believe that texts try to "remold the character and values of children" or that they give a "one-sided view of the world." (p. 39)

Portions of excerpts from the six interviews indicate that teachers view textbooks as the core of the curriculum, as a means for conducting discussions, and as valuable orientation tools. Like the 800 social studies teachers in the previous study, teachers in the Rogers (1988) study wanted more of a say in textbook selection procedures. Finally, although they "agreed that textbooks exert a powerful influence on what is taught in school and how it is taught" (p. 39), teachers in the Rogers study also said that they frequently supplemented the textbook by choosing materials that were related to current events and their students' lives.

Alternatives to Textbook Use

A hallmark of professionalism in almost any field is the ability to make decisions based on one's knowledge of the field and the needs of the individuals who are in the professional's care. Teachers, like most other professionals, carry out their responsibilities in a variety of settings, some more conducive to decision making than others. At Shoreham-Wading River Middle School, on the eastern half of Long Island, teachers share in the decision-making process and are free to adapt the curriculum as they see fit. It is the type of setting that gives teachers the flexibility to move beyond the textbook, which they do often in the name of *experiential learning* (Maeroff, 1990).

> For instance, Irwin Zaretsky and Joan Ouellett, a core team of seventh-grade teachers, spend at least four weeks with their students at locales on the seashore and in the mountains. . . . Interdisciplinary lessons are adapted to the locale and specialists visit frequently. For example, the art teacher might demonstrate how to paint watercolors of the sand dunes. (p. 510)

Parents characterize such outings as educational experiences that prepare children to cooperate with others and to respect the environment in which they live—two admirable outcomes that no textbook assignment could come close to duplicating.

Another form of experiential learning that supplements the book knowledge that students get in their academic core programs is community service. Students at Shoreham-Wading River Middle School are out of the school building for a double period, one time a week, for six to eight weeks, doing volunteer work with the elderly, handicapped children, and others in need of community support.

Other forms of experiential learning that supplement what students learn in their textbooks include Project Adventure, similar to Outward Bound, but conducted as part of the physical education program on the school grounds. For the less physically daring, there is the school farm, which is a vital part of the school's science program. Students raise small animals, grow food in the garden, and conduct experiments with plants in the greenhouse. Also available as alternatives to the standard textbook way of learning are weekly field trips that last for two periods and are spread out over a month. Recently, students learned firsthand about sewage treatment in their town by interviewing some of the officers working in toxic control. And, if none of these opportunities to learn experientially are appealing to students, they may enjoy running the school's store. There, they learn to order merchandise, keep books, and do calculations by hand.

Experiential learning is not the only alternative to textbook-dominated instruction. Teachers in the middle grades can build classroom libraries of magazines obtained through a number of publishers who aim their materials at a young adolescent population. A handy and inexpensive resource for building a classroom library is Donald Stoll's (1990) *Magazines for Children*. This 47-page paperback contains an annotated list of magazines, a subject index, and an age/grade index. A list describing 13 of the titles recommended for middle-grades students is included in Appendix 5.1.

Finally, films, videos, audiocassettes, VCRs, slides, games, and computers provide a rich source of alternatives to the textbook. Chapter 10 is devoted to suggestions for using technology to supplement textbook information.

In summary, textbooks convey the content of the middle-grades curriculum, though clearly they have their faults. Despite stiff criticisms of textbook-dominated instruction, teachers generally see value in using the textbook and appear unconvinced of its decline. Nonetheless, a number of viable alternatives to the textbook exist. Exploring these alternatives will be viewed as a positive sign that middle-grades educators are interested in providing young adolescents with a wide range of learning experiences. As Gross (1987) has noted, "By carefully selecting instructional materials to fit the curriculum and the characteristics of the students to be taught, . . . teachers are freed to spend their time and energy in practices that enrich the content" (p. 3).

English/Language Arts

What do students learn in middle-grades English/language arts classes? The answer varies from one school system to another, but generally, literature, grammar, spelling, reading, and writing are the major components. Variation occurs more in the instructional approach used to teach each of these components than in the content itself. For example, a literature-based reading program would include a study of literature and reading, as its name implies, but this approach might also include instruction in grammar, spelling, and writing, particularly as these components relate to the literature being read.

As a consequence of the interrelatedness of the English/language arts content, it makes sense to organize this chapter section around the different instructional approaches to reading and writing. Within reading, we will discuss basal reading programs, literature-based programs, Chapter I/remedial programs, and reading to learn in content area classes. Within writing, we will look at grammar or skill-based instruction, writing process instruction, and writing to learn in content area classes. Finally, we will include a brief overview of what the research tells us about reading and writing instruction within the English/language arts core.

Reading

Middle-grades students are intensely interested in who they are and how they relate to their peers. Their interest in acting in socially acceptable ways presents opportunities and challenges in terms of reading instruction. Opportunities abound for putting young adolescents in touch with books and magazines that feature stories and information about teens; challenges also abound (e.g., how middle-grades students are grouped for reading instruction and whether they see themselves as reading above or below their peer group can make a difference in how they apply themselves). As you read about four common approaches to teaching reading in the middle grades, try to think about the impact each approach will have on young adolescents' social development.

Basal Reading Programs

Traditionally, basal reading programs have included a series of graded readers (books that are developmentally appropriate for different ability levels), workbooks, end-of-unit tests, and a variety of ancillary materials, all of which are aimed at developing students' word identification skills, comprehension, vocabulary, and study strategies. Beginning in the mid-1980s, a growing number of middle-grades schools began to require reading courses for students in seventh and eighth grades. As a result, most basal reading programs now extend from kindergarten through eighth grade.

Critics of basal reading programs at the middle-grades level object to the emphasis on stories and other forms of narrative text at the expense of content, or expository, text (Peters, 1990). The quality of the literature in basal reading programs has also come under criticism. Presently, most publishers of basal reading programs have tried to make the literature included in the readers as authentic as possible. That is, when stories and nonfiction pieces have been excerpted, an attempt has been made to retain the vocabulary and syntax of the originals as much as possible.

Some basal reading programs are more skills oriented than others. When skills are taught in isolation of the actual content in which students must apply them, there is always a problem with transfer. Other basal reading programs attempt to control for this problem by placing a greater emphasis on literature. In these programs, the literature drives the skills (e.g., if students are expected to read a mystery story in which following an author's sequence is important to comprehending the story, then the skill of sequencing will be taught).

Literature-Based Programs

In literature-based programs, students read "real" books as opposed to stories and pieces of exposition that have been collected and placed in basal readers. These so-called real books of literature-based programs are sometimes called *tradebooks*. Tradebooks are what you buy from bookstores or borrow from libraries. To be successful, literature-based programs must offer students a wide variety of trade-books from which to choose. Successful programs also create a literate environment in which students are given plenty of time to read, write, and talk about the books they choose (Atwell, 1987; Hancock & Hill, 1987).

Critics of literature-based programs are concerned that students will not receive adequate teacher guidance. For example, they cite the problem of scheduling individual reading conferences with 25 students or more. They also question the practice of unstructured reading time and the effects this will have on students' performance on standardized tests of reading achievement. According to Graham (1987), addressing problems like those raised by critics of literature-based programs is what provides the challenge for teachers who are dedicated to helping students take responsibility for their own learning and make their own choices in reading materials.

A more structured literature-based program used by some middle-grades teachers is the *Junior Great Books* program (Dennis & Moldof, 1975). This program, which contains stories from well-known authors such as Kurt Vonnegut, features whole-class discussions of stories that students have read. Discussions are structured so that students respond to students rather than to the teacher only.

Theme studies, which involve students in group research on a classwide basis, are another example of how literature-based programs can be structured. Students choose a theme that they are interested in exploring in depth—one that is broad enough to yield subtopics yet is not historically or geographically constrained. Unlike the other literature-based approaches described, theme studies extend beyond print and classroom walls. Films, the community, and concrete objects are all part of the resources students use in their world-as-a-laboratory research process (Gamberg, Kwak, Hutchings, & Altheim, 1988).

Chapter I/Remedial Programs

Federal money funded under Chapter I goes to more than 90 percent of the nation's school districts to pay for remedial reading and mathematics teachers. Chapter I was formerly known as Title I, which was part of the Elementary and Secondary Education Act created in 1965 as part of President Lyndon Johnson's war on poverty. Although Chapter I teachers are found primarily in elementary schools, some districts have enough funds to place Chapter I teachers in the middle schools as well. Sometimes local funding is used to supplement the federal money spent on remedial instruction for students who are falling behind in reading.

Regardless of whether the remedial reading program in a middle school is federally or locally funded, it is more than likely a pull-out program. That is, approximately 8 to 10 students will be taken from their regular classrooms for small-group tutoring in a separate room by a teacher who is qualified to instruct them in skills that they have either missed or have not learned in their regular reading group. At the middle-grades level, skill instruction typically focuses on comprehension and vocabulary development.

Critics of pull-out remedial reading programs charge that, "among other things, these programs [have] tended to segregate slow learners . . . and to stigmatize [them]" (Savage, 1987, p. 583). Others claim that, based on large-scale evaluations of Chapter I programs, any gains disadvantaged readers make in the early grades tend to disappear by the time students reach middle school. A further problem is the fragmentation of instruction that occurs when the content of the remedial reading teacher's instruction and that of the core curriculum teacher's instruction are not coordinated (Allington, Boxer, & Broikou, 1987).

Reading to Learn in Content Area Classes

As pointed out earlier in this chapter, textbooks play an important role in middle-grades instruction. Students are expected to learn the contents of their textbooks, either by reading the texts themselves or by listening as their teachers lecture on the contents. Content area teachers have typically rejected the notion of teaching students how to learn from their textbooks, assuming perhaps that students have the necessary skills from their elementary reading instruction.

When students read to learn, they must apply the appropriate strategies for comprehending and retaining the information they are assigned to read. Prereading, during-reading, and after-reading strategies can aid students in this process. However, for the most part, middle-grades students are not equipped for this kind of reading. Many do not see a connection between the reading they do in their English/language arts classes and the reading that is expected of them in social studies or science classes. In English/language arts classes, students are exposed primarily to narrative forms of writing; in their other classes, they are exposed to informational or expository writing. Strategies that are effective for learning from one type of text structure do not necessarily transfer.

Recent reform efforts to teach more content and to worry less about the strategies students may or may not have for learning the content have been criticized by individuals who believe that teachers should "avoid separating the acquisition of knowledge from the process or strategy" (Peters, 1990, p. 67) needed for acquiring such knowledge. Others (e.g., Herber, 1978) have called for this same integration of content and process, with content determining the process or strategy that should be used.

Writing

Think back to a paper you have written for one of your college classes. You probably wrote several drafts of that paper before it was ready to turn into the instructor. If you had set realistic goals for yourself at the start of the writing project, you probably had sufficient time to get the paper finished by the due date. Setting realistic goals can minimize the chances of gaps occurring between one's idealized self and one's actual performance.

The ability to set realistic goals is something most middle-grades students need help in developing. This skill is essential to gaining a sense of achievement and self-worth. As you read about each of the different approaches to writing instruction, try to imagine how each one would present opportunities for helping students set realistic goals for themselves as writers.

Grammar or Skill-Based Instruction

In Florio-Ruane and Dunn's (1987) review of the literature, they point out that grammar or skill-based instruction has traditionally placed great value in having students practice isolated parts of the writing process until they have become routinized. The rationale behind this approach is that mastery of correct grammatical constructions, spelling, punctuation, and syntax must occur prior to the time students engage in writing for meaningful communication. Those who favor grammar or skill-based instruction point to the complexity of the writing process. They argue that a process as multifaceted as writing "offers too many new bits of information for the beginner to hold in consciousness at one time . . . [thus they] recommend that the process be divided into constituent parts for teaching and learning" (p. 58).

Critics of grammar or skill-based instruction say that it results in too fragmented a picture of writing. Others argue that this approach to writing instruction lacks an authentic context in which to teach the various skills. For example, students are asked to practice grammatical constructions, punctuation, and spelling words using context-free textbook exercises or worksheets rather than to apply their knowledge of these skills to their own writing.

Writing Process Instruction

Seldom do writers go from ideas in their heads to finished papers in one giant step. Although some teachers break writing process instruction into three stages (prewriting, writing, and postwriting), the majority probably view the process as having at least five stages.

Part of the writing process calls for students to identify an appropriate audience for their ideas.

First, teachers encourage students to engage in brainstorming activities aimed at finding a topic, considering the "author's voice," and identifying the audience. Second, students write a first draft in which they get their ideas down on paper without regard for spelling, grammar, and punctuation. They then share these drafts with others to get ideas about what is and is not working. Third, students revise their writing based on the feedback they receive from individuals who have read the first draft. Sometimes these revisions require organizing what they have written in a different way, elaborating on key ideas, or deleting large chunks of extraneous information. Fourth, students go through their final drafts to correct any mechanical problems that exist; this is the editing phase. Finally, students publish their work for others to enjoy.

Although these stages in the writing process may appear to occur in a simple, linear fashion, in reality they are recursive and overlapping (Florio-Ruane & Dunn, 1987). For example, midway through a third or fourth draft of a paper, the writer may decide to return to the brainstorming stage to rethink a portion of the plot.

Drawbacks to writing process instruction have been pointed out by critics who view this approach to writing as theoretically sound but practically unmanageable. One drawback is the time that it takes a teacher to coach a student through the various phases of process writing, especially because of its recursive nature. Another is that teachers need special training in the process approach to writing if they are going to be successful in implementing this approach; many learned to write through the more traditional grammar or skill-based instruction and do not use process writing themselves.

Writing to Learn in Content Area Classes

In this approach, writing is a tool for encouraging students to think about and reflect on the content that they are expected to learn. Treating writing as a means, not an end, implies that students will not necessarily go through the various stages described in the process approach to writing. For instance, students who keep a learning log—a running account of what they are learning, any problems they are experiencing, and so on—will have no need to revise and edit their writing for publication; neither will students who use dialogue or buddy journals to record personal responses to something they have read or experienced in one of their content classes.

Writing to learn may also include summaries, fact sheets, cartoons, lab reports, and numerous other forms of written discourse that are tools for comprehending and remembering content material. The real potential in each of these activities lies in students' active engagement in the learning process (Vacca & Vacca, 1986).

This approach to writing, like any approach, is not without its critics. Some claim that although student-initiated content learning is to be applauded, problems may develop if teachers do not have time to monitor the quality of learning that is taking place. Problems also exist with maintaining a high level of commitment and motivation on the students' part. If teachers do not intervene at instructionally appropriate times, students may resort to shortcuts that actually undermine the value of writing to learn in their content area classes.

Overview of the Research

A fairly large body of research exists in the area of instructional approaches to reading and writing in the middle grades. In attempting to summarize this research, we have looked at three different levels of evaluation: large-scale assessment projects, such as the recurrent reading and writing studies conducted by the National Assessment of Educational Progress; smaller assessment projects that have focused directly on literacy instruction at the middle-grades level; and individual programs of research and evaluation in the area of English/language arts instruction.

Large-Scale Assessment Projects

Results from the 1988 National Assessment of Educational Progress (NAEP) in reading achievement and instruction (Langer, Applebee, Mullis, & Foertsch, 1990) are based on a sample of 13,000 students in grades 4, 8, and 12 in the nation's public and private schools. The research reported here is limited to information that was obtained on the eighth-grade students only. Some 61 percent of the eighth-graders reported reading a total of 10 or fewer pages a day across all their subject areas. In general, these students had difficulty in explaining or elaborating on what they had read.

The 1988 NAEP in writing achievement and instruction (Applebee, Langer, Jenkins, Mullis, & Foertsch, 1990) was conducted using a nationally representative sample of approximately 20,000 students in grades 4, 8, and 12. In addition, 756 eighth-grade teachers were asked to fill out questionnaires on the instruction they had provided to the students who were part of the sample. As before, only the results pertaining to the eighth-grade students are reported here. According to their teachers, 75 percent of the eighth-grade students received one hour or less of writing instruction per week. Only 14 percent of these students reported being asked to write a paper of three or more pages per week in their English classes. Across three different kinds of writing tasks (informative, persuasive, and narrative), the percentage of "adequate or better" responses among eighth-graders ranged from a low of 14 percent to a high of 51 percent. Over half of the teachers reported emphasizing both grammar or skill-based instruction *and* the process approach to writing. However, only 23 percent of the teachers said they emphasized writing to learn.

Smaller Assessment Projects

In a survey of middle-school reading instruction that involved 247 schools nationwide (with a response rate of approximately 70 percent), Irvin and Connors (1989) found that 14 percent or fewer of the schools indicated that reading to learn in the content areas was an important part of their programs. In contrast, no less than two-thirds of the schools reported offering a course in remedial reading. The most popular approach to reading instruction was the developmental reading course, which over two-thirds of the sixth-grade students (but only half of the seventh- and eighth-grade students) were required to take. Schools offering developmental reading courses reported that basal readers and skill-related materials were used most frequently.

In 1985, the Center for Early Adolescence at the University of North Carolina conducted an on-site study of 32 middle schools that had been designated as having successful literacy programs. Spending a high proportion of time on reading and writing, teaching content and process skills concurrently, and modeling effective comprehension strategies were among the characteristics that defined successful literacy instruction in the middle grades (Moore & Stefanich, 1990).

Individual Programs of Research and Evaluation

Time spent on reading during school hours has been shown to contribute significantly to gains in fifth- and sixth-grade students' reading achievement (Taylor, Frye, & Maruyama, 1990). This finding is of particular interest here because of the importance given to a high proportion of time being spent on reading in the successful schools visited by researchers in the Center for Early Adolescence study. It is also of interest because of the relatively small amount of reading that students in the NAEP study reported doing (less than 10 pages a day).

Finally, despite the fact that few middle-grades schools have reported giving attention to reading and writing to learn in the content areas, there is evidence to suggest that such programs do work (Monahan, 1990; Roehler, Foley, Lud, & Power, 1990). However, the development of these programs requires commitment on the part of all concerned, careful planning, and gradual implementation.

Social Studies

There is widespread disagreement about what content *should be* and actually *is* taught in middle-school social studies. According to one account, citizenship transmission and a combination of social science and reflective inquiry define the content of the social studies field (Armento, 1986). Others would add women's issues, teenage life, law in society, and global education (Newmann, 1986). Interestingly, the question of whether and where global education fits into this mix has been a source of disagreement for the past 25 years (O'Neil, 1989).

Disagreement also exists about the approaches that should be emphasized in teaching social studies to middle-grades students. Although most teachers rely on lecturing from single textbooks, punctuated from time to time with discussion (Armento, 1986; Shaver, 1987; Voss, 1986), there are some individuals (mostly researchers and teacher educators) who advocate using alternative approaches such as multilevel textbook programs (Memory & McGowan, 1985) and tradebooks (McGowan & Sutton, 1988).

Disagreements in the field make it difficult, if not impossible, to present a picture of the so-called typical middle-grades social studies program. Other than the widespread use of single textbooks to teach the content of the curriculum, there are no common threads. Consequently, in this section of the chapter on middle-grades content, we will focus on some of the approaches used in commercially published textbooks to present content. First, however, we will provide a brief overview of the research on student disinterest in social studies content and then make some suggestions for engaging students in that content.

Student Disinterest

According to Newmann (1986), "Lack of student engagement in social studies is the problem that most teachers at all levels struggle with day after day" (p. 242). Newmann separates disengagement from simple boredom, saying,

> Boredom . . . is only a symptom of the more fundamental condition: disengagement. As the sole diagnosis, boredom can lead to false remedies: gimmicks to interest and entertain students, strategies merely for capturing attention. . . . Some of these may be necessary occasionally, but the more serious problem is to engage students. (p. 242)

Why are students so disinterested in social studies content? Why is it that, over the years, researchers have consistently found that students in *all* grades, not just the middle grades, rate social studies as one of their least interesting subjects? Answers to these questions are not easy to find. However, one thing we know is that teachers do not seem to be at the root of students' disinterest. According to the research, students generally like their social studies teachers and find them enthusiastic, well-prepared, and caring (Shaver, 1987).

A more likely place to look for the root of student disinterest seems to be the *way* social studies is taught. In the middle grades, social studies instruction places importance on two things: (1) students being able to recall information from their textbooks for classroom discussions or tests and (2) students being able to complete the questions at the ends of chapters. Researchers who worked on Goodlad's (1984) nationwide study of schools noted that the way social studies content was taught seemed sterile and preoccupied with lower-level thinking. Topics that had the potential to spark some human interest were often watered down and made "safe." According to Shaver's (1987) review of the research, these conditions, coupled with "the low-level demands of textbook information recall" (p. 127) are the primary reasons for students' disinterest in social studies.

Suggestions for Engaging Students in the Content

Given the circumstances just described, how can teachers deal with the problem of student disengagement? Research suggests that to engage students in schoolwork, the following general conditions must be met:

1. Student expectation that a task can be completed successfully, but also that it will challenge the student;
2. The opportunity to produce a concrete product or to take actions that have some impact in one's environment;
3. The opportunity to work cooperatively with others as well as alone;
4. The perception that the task involves solving a problem considered personally significant to the student;
5. Sustained, uninterrupted time to work on the task;
6. The availability of supportive assistance in working on the task;
7. The opportunity for some control over the planning, execution and evaluation of results of the work. (Newmann, 1986, p. 244)

As you may have guessed, meeting these conditions would maximize student engagement in most courses, not just social studies. They are also conditions of schooling over which teachers have little or no control. For example, the pressure to cover large amounts of prescribed content works against conditions 4 and 5. The emphasis on the textbook as the major instructional tool presents a challenge for teachers who would like to meet condition 2. Is it hopeless, then, to expect teachers to meet any of the conditions for maximizing student engagement? We think not, but it will take perseverance and creativity on the teachers' part.

We turn now to focus on how the authors of two social studies textbooks have approached the content that middle-grades students are expected to learn. Our purpose will be to see if teachers might expand on these approaches and, in doing so, begin to meet some of the conditions just described.

A Textbook Approach to Presenting Content

Garraty, Singer, and Gallagher's (1986) *American History* has been praised by reviewers for "creating an engaging narrative of the national past . . . [and for its willingness] to raise moral questions on controversial issues" (Sewall, 1987, pp. 36–37). For example:

> To whites who knew him, [Nat] Turner had seemed the last person who might be expected to resort to violence. He was mild mannered and deeply religious. Yet in 1831 he and his followers murdered 57 people before they were captured. Historians still argue about whether or not Turner was insane. The point is that nearly every slave hated bondage. Nearly all were eager to see something done to destroy the system. (Sewall, 1987, p. 37)

Hands-on manipulatives make subject-matter learning come alive.

In this brief passage, the authors did more than put minority group issues into historical context; they also told *why* the event occurred, not just *what* occurred. According to Beck and McKeown (1988), "To the extent that history is narrative, a key to understanding lies in the learner's appreciation of a *causal chain* of events" (p. 33).

Teachers might use narrative histories as springboards to group research projects. For example, students might work cooperatively in groups of four or five to evaluate how primary and secondary sources differ in their characterization of Nat Turner. Students might also be engaged in planning what kind of research product their group will produce and how they want that product evaluated. By building on a piece of well-written prose in this way, teachers will be working toward creating the kinds of conditions suggested in conditions 2, 3, and 7. To do less than this consigns students to the routine drudgery of reading their textbooks and answering the questions at the end of the chapter sections.

Science

True or false: An astronaut in space is not affected by gravity. A tightrope walker holds a balance pole because it lowers her center of gravity. Mosquitoes sting with their rear ends. (Begley, 1990, p. 71)

If you said false to all of these, you pass! However, according to the journalist (Begley, 1990) who posed these three questions at the start of a *Newsweek* article, you would have flunked if you had depended on some science textbooks for the correct answers. Charging that textbooks contain simplistic explanations for complex phenomena, Begley concludes that "many popular misconceptions about science may be dutiful recitations of 'facts' learned from books" (p. 71). Some science textbook authors defend the use of simplified explanations on the grounds that presenting all of the facts before students are developmentally able to comprehend them will only cause confusion and result in the loss of student interest.

In this section of the chapter, you will learn more about what makes science so hard to learn for students who hold misconceptions, or naive concepts, about the natural world and how it works. Just as importantly, you will learn how you can teach for conceptual change. We begin with an overview of the research on science misconceptions, especially as it relates to the content of the middle-grades curriculum. We then describe the approaches teachers use to teach science content, focusing on one in particular—conceptual-change teaching.

Overview of the Research on Science Misconceptions

The textbook's dominance of the middle-grades science curriculum is not unlike that found in the other curriculum areas. However, in middle-grades science, textbook "facts" that lead to student misconceptions are only part of the problem. The other part is developmentally related. Students have spent their lives observing everyday phenomena that seem to defy scientific reasoning. These phenomena involve concepts of mass, weight, motion, gravity, velocity, and heat—all part of the general science content found in the middle-grades curriculum. When students are asked to give up their naive concepts, or misconceptions, about the natural world in which they live, they sometimes resist and cling stubbornly to their own theories of why things happen. As Watson and Konicek (1990) have so aptly stated the problem, "The substitution of one theory for another is not as easy as erasing the chalkboard" (p. 682).

Generally, the research on science misconceptions has supported the notion that students are resistant to changing their naive theories despite conflicting information in science textbooks and even despite good instruction and first-hand experimental evidence (e.g., Alvermann, Smith, & Readence, 1985; Champagne, Klopfer, & Anderson, 1980; Eaton, Anderson, & Smith, 1984; Maria, 1987; Swafford, 1989). Research findings have also demonstrated that the depth of a teacher's content knowledge will influence the degree to which he or she is capable of bringing about conceptual-change learning in his or her students (Dole & Smith, 1989; Guzzetti & Taylor, 1988). What these and other related studies have shown is that

> as misconceptions gradually become incorporated into one's mental model of the natural world, problem solving in science can be inhibited . . . [thus making it] important for the teacher to become aware of common misconceptions held by students so that attempts to remedy the situation can be made. (Good & Shymansky, 1987)

Approaches to Teaching Science

Following are four different approaches to teaching science in the middle grades. Although some are used more frequently than others, only the first approach— teaching for conceptual change—is thought to have the elements necessary for helping students correct their misconceptions about science content.

Conceptual-Change Teaching

One way of attempting to bring about conceptual change in students is to make them aware of any inconsistencies between their thinking and conventional scientific thinking. The conceptual-change teaching approach is thought to bring about this awareness by helping students to (1) become dissatisfied with their naive conceptions, (2) achieve minimal understanding of the scientific conception, (3) see the scientific conception as plausible, and (4) apply the scientific conception in a new situation (Posner, Strike, Hewson, & Gertzog, 1982).

Activity-Driven Teaching

According to Anderson and Smith (1987) in their review of the literature on teaching science, activity-driven teaching is an orientation that is more common among elementary teachers who are uncomfortable teaching science than among middle-grades science teachers. We include this orientation, however, because middle schools typically include upper elementary teachers who may or may not have majored in one of the sciences.

In activity-driven teaching, the focus is generally on textbook reading, demonstrations, question-answer sessions, and so on. Although teachers who subscribe to this approach attempt to make science learning meaningful for students, quite often their lack of content knowledge causes them to leave out crucial parts of a lesson.

Discovery Learning

Teachers who do not like to tell students the answers but prefer to have students derive their own answers from observation and experimentation are likely to favor discovery learning over any of the other approaches.

In discovery learning, procedural learning is valued over conceptual learning. That is, teachers would prefer students learn *how* to make observations, predictions, measurements, and interpretations rather than remember facts about an experiment's outcome per se. As Anderson and Smith (1987) point out, however, the problem with assuming that students will eventually discover appropriate scientific concepts on their own is that along the way they may find plenty of opportunities to reinforce their misconceptions.

Didactic Teaching

This orientation to teaching science is the most prevalent of all approaches in the middle-grades. The focus of didactic teaching is on the presentation of content rather than on the encouragement of student thinking. Because of the emphasis on presentation of content, didactic teachers are seldom aware of the misconceptions students may have. Nor do the questions they ask students allow for the type of response that might signal the presence of a misconception.

Anderson and Smith (1987) point out that "recall questions (e.g., 'What is the chemical formula for photosynthesis?') provide teachers with no hint about the existence or the nature of their students' misconceptions" (p. 100). Thus, didactic teaching, on top of being the most prevalent approach to middle-grades science, may mask valuable opportunities to teach for conceptual change.

Mathematics

There is much activity in the field of middle-grades mathematics. A new set of standards (National Council of Teachers of Mathematics, 1989) promises to make mathematics "a useful, exciting, and creative area of study that can be appreciated and enjoyed by all students in grades 5-8" (p. 65). Critics have been vocal in their claim that for too long a time the content of the mathematics curriculum was whatever was in the mathematics textbook (Nicely, 1985). Now, with the new standards in place, it does appear as though a new day is dawning.

In this section of the chapter, you will have an opportunity to compare the changes in mathematics content and emphases in grades 5 through 8 and the effect these changes will have on teachers' instructional approaches. First, however, you will learn why researchers believe that the developmental changes young adolescents go through are important determiners of how well (or how poorly) they will do in mathematics.

Young Adolescent Development and Mathematics Achievement

During young adolescence, students begin to develop more mature reasoning abilities. Where once they depended almost exclusively on concrete experiences to learn mathematical concepts, in young adolescence this dependence lessens considerably. However, as stressed in the new mathematics standards, concrete experiences should still be viewed as the means by which students learn to abstract more complex understandings of number concepts.

Growth of Students' Competence with Number Concepts

In the middle grades, students' competence with number concepts is typically viewed from two perspectives: "as growth from simpler forms of arithmetic to more complex forms of mathematics and as growth from intuitive, informal concepts and strategies to more formal methods" (Hiebert & Behr, 1988, p. 11). When students are ready to move from thinking about arithmetic to thinking about mathematics, this period of growth is marked by what Hiebert and Behr refer to as "a significant reconceptualization of number and operations on number" (p. 11).

There is a definite break in students' line of reasoning. The growth from informal to formal methods, however, is not marked by such a break; instead, it appears to be more continuous. Presently, too little is known about the function of informal strategies as precursors for more formal methods to make any definitive statement about how this second type of growth occurs.

Affect and Mathematics Achievement

As important as young adolescents' cognitive development is to their growth in mathematics, the feelings they have about their ability to learn new concepts may be the final determinant in how well they do. For example, the results of a longitudinal study of over 1,300 students and the teachers they had for mathematics (before and after they entered the middle grades) showed that low-achieving students valued mathematics less when they moved from more supportive to less supportive teachers (Midgley, Feldlaufer, & Eccles, 1989).

As pointed out by the authors of the new mathematics standards (National Council of Teachers of Mathematics, 1989), "Students will perform better and learn more in a caring environment in which they feel free to explore mathematical ideas, ask questions, discuss their ideas, and make mistakes" (p. 69).

Changes in Mathematics Content and Emphases in Grades 5 Though 8

The new standards will result in a broadening of the content that is taught in middle-grades mathematics classes. Instead of studying the same topics year after year, as they have in the past, students will now be introduced to new material, even if they have not mastered certain basic computational skills. To get an overview of the changes in content and emphases in grades 5 through 8, you will need to study carefully the information provided in Appendix 5.2.

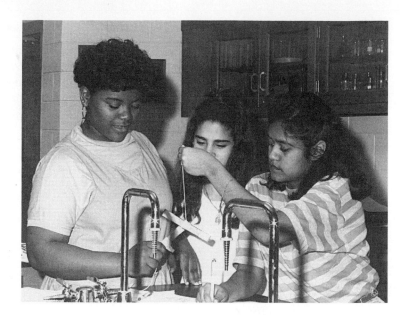

Hands-on and learner-directed activities are necessary for striking a balance in textbook-dominated classrooms.

Effects of Changes on Instructional Approaches

Although researchers do not agree on whether teachers are overly dependent on their textbooks (Stodolsky, 1989), the issue may be a moot point at this time, given the impact the new mathematics standards are expected to have on instruction. According to Hiebert and Behr (1988), interest in studying middle-grades students' growth in understanding mathematical concepts is a relatively new development. Consequently, since an understanding of how students grow in mathematics competency must precede any attempts to prescribe the kinds of instructional approaches teachers need to use, only broad parameters related to instruction can be discussed here.

Some Observations about Instruction

In too many middle schools, conventional mathematics instruction has resulted in students acquiring simplistic conceptions, or even misconceptions (Confrey, 1987), of number operations and routinized methods for solving problems. Students have not developed meaningful strategies for dealing with mathematics problems and therefore do not "own" the strategies they do use. Based on these observations, Hiebert and Behr (1988) see the following two roles for middle-grades mathematics instruction:

> First, instruction should facilitate students' constructions of meaning for written mathematical symbols. This is foundational because without appropriate meanings for symbols, students have no chance of developing . . . generalizable methods of solution. Second, instruction should identify and support the development of central conceptual strategies, from their first appearance in an incomplete or intuitive form to more formal procedures that generalize to all structurally similar problems. Of course, within the

bounds of these two suggested roles, there is a great deal of latitude. The precise nature of appropriate instruction still is an open question. (p. 15)

Suggested Activities Based on the New Standards

The activities suggested by the authors of the new mathematics standards are decidedly learner directed and aimed at engaging the learner both intellectually and physically. For example, small-group as well as whole-class and individual-type activities call for students to be actively involved in discussing, listening, and critiquing strategies for solving problems that stem from the students' interests, not solely from the pages of a textbook. Arguing that "middle grade students are especially responsive to hands-on activities in tactile, auditory, and visual instructional modes" (p. 67), the new standards (National Council of Teachers of Mathematics, 1989) emphasize using calculators and computers for computation and exploration of mathematics concepts. At the same time, the standards call for decreased attention to computational drilling, paper-and-pencil tasks that stress memorization, and teaching concepts in isolation.

Summary

Presently, textbooks are the conveyors of content in the academic core subjects of the middle-grades curriculum. Although there are clear indicators that dependency on textbooks may decrease in some curriculum areas in the future, it is also likely that their use will remain widespread. The difference will be in the way they are used. Teachers will be encouraged to draw from a variety of instructional materials to meet the diverse needs of middle-grades students.

The content and the approaches used to teach it vary from one core subject to the next. In English/language arts, the major components are literature, grammar, spelling, reading, and writing. The most prevalent instructional approaches include a focus on skill development and teacher presentation of content, although a process orientation is gaining acceptance in the area of writing. In social studies, there is widespread disagreement about what content should be taught and how it should be taught. Everyone agrees, however, a major hurdle that must be overcome is students' disinterest in social studies. In science, the content includes a mix of general science topics, and teachers are increasingly being asked to teach for conceptual change. Finally, in the area of mathematics, new directions in content emphases promise to broaden the curriculum and have an impact on the way teachers instruct middle-grades students in number concepts and problem solving.

REFERENCES

Allington, R. L., Boxer, N., & Broikou, K. (1987). Jeremy, remedial reading, and subject area classes. *Journal of Reading, 30,* 643–645.

Alvermann, D. E., & Moore, D. W. (1991). Secondary school reading. In R. Barr, M. Ka-mil, P. Mosenthal, & P. D. Pearson (Eds.), *Handbook of reading research, Volume II.* (pp. 951–983). New York: Longman.

Alvermann, D. E., Smith, L. C., & Readence, J. E., (1985). Prior knowledge activation and the comprehension of compatible and incompatible text. *Reading Research Quarterly, 20,* 420–436.

Anderson, C. W., & Smith, E. L. (1987). Teaching science. In V. Richardson-Koehler (Ed.), *Educators' handbook: A research perspective* (pp. 84–111). New York: Longman.

Apple, M. W. (1986). *Teachers and texts: A political economy of class and gender relations in education.* New York: Routledge & Kegan Paul.

Applebee, A. N., Langer, J. A., Jenkins, L. B., Mullis, I. V. S., & Foertsch, M. A. (1990). *Learning to write in our nation's schools: Instruction and achievement in 1988 at grades 4, 8, and 12.* Princeton, NJ: National Assessment of Educational Progress, Educational Testing Service.

Applebee, A. N., Langer, J. A, & Mullis, I. V. S. (1987). *The nation's report card: Learning to be literate in America.* (Report No. 15-RW-01). Princeton, NJ: National Assessment of Educational Progress, Educational Testing Service.

Armento, B. J. (1986). Research on teaching social studies. In M. C. Wittrock (Ed.), *Handbook of research on teaching* (3rd ed., pp. 942–951). New York: Macmillan.

Atwell, N. (1987). *In the middle: Writing, reading, and learning.* Upper Montclair, NJ: Boynton/Cook.

Beck, I. L., & McKeown, M. G. (1988). Toward meaningful accounts in history texts for young learners. *Educational Researcher, 17*(6), 31–39.

Begley, S. (1990, August 6). Don't believe what you read: Scholars tote up the errors in science textbooks. *Newsweek,* p. 71.

Bernstein, H. T. (1985). When more is less: The 'mentioning' problem in textbooks. *American Educator, 9*(2), 26–29, 44.

Cannon, P., & Sewall, G. T. (1989). Textbook consolidation: How big a menace? *Social Studies Review,* Fall, (2), 6–8.

Champagne, A. B., Klopfer, L. E., & Anderson, J. H. (1980). Factors influencing the learning of classical mechanics. *American Journal of Physics, 48,* 1074–1079.

Cole, J. Y., & Sticht, T. G. (1981). *The textbook in American society.* Washington, DC: Library of Congress.

Confrey, J. (1987). Mathematics learning and teaching. In V. Richardson-Koehler (Ed.), *Educators' handbook: A research perspective* (pp. 3–25). New York: Longman.

Davey, B. (1988). How do classroom teachers use their textbooks? *Journal of Reading, 31,* 340–345.

Dennis, R. P., & Moldof, E. P. (Eds.). (1975). *Junior great books.* Chicago: Great Books Foundation.

Dole, J. A., & Smith, E. L. (1989). Prior knowledge and learning from science text: An instructional study. In S. McCormick & J. Zutell (Eds.), *Cognitive and social perspectives for literacy research and instruction* (pp. 345–352). Chicago: National Reading Conference.

Eaton, J. F., Anderson, C. W., & Smith, E. L. (1984). Students' misconceptions interfere with science learning: Case studies of fifth grade students. *The Elementary School Journal, 84,* 365–379.

Elliott, D. L., & Woodward, A. (1990). Textbooks, curriculum, and school improvement. In D. L. Elliott & A. Woodward (Eds.), *Textbooks and schooling in the United States.* Eighty-ninth yearbook of the National Society for the Study of Education, Part I (pp. 222–232). Chicago: University of Chicago Press.

Florio-Ruane, S., & Dunn, S. (1987). Teaching writing: Some perennial questions and some possible answers. In V. Richardson-Koehler (Ed.), *Educator's handbook: A research perspective* (pp. 50–83). New York: Longman.

Gamberg, R., Kwak, W., Hutchings, M., & Altheim, J. (1988). *Learning and loving it.* Portsmouth, NH: Heinemann.

Garraty, J. A., Singer, A., & Gallagher, M. J. (1986). *American history.* Orlando, FL: Harcourt Brace Jovanovich.

Good, R., & Shymansky, J. (1987, April). *Issues regarding the establishment of criteria for the analysis and selection of science textbooks.* Paper presented at the annual meeting of the American Educational Research Association, Washington, DC.

Goodlad, J. I. (1984). *A place called school.* New York: McGraw-Hill.

Graham, K. (1987). Converting to a literature-based reading program. In J. Hancock & S. Hill (Eds.), *Literature-based reading programs at work* (pp. 42–52). Portsmouth, NH: Heinemann.

Gross, S. (Ed.). (1987). Research update. *Notes and News, 14*(10), 3.

Guzzetti, B. J., & Taylor, J. C. (1988, December). *From prior experience to prior knowledge: Effects of text and reader-based manipulations.* Paper presented at the annual meeting of the National Reading Conference, Tucson, AZ.

Hancock, J., & Hill, S. (Eds.). (1987). *Literature-based reading programs at work.* Portsmouth, NH: Heinemann.

Herber, H. L. (1978). *Teaching reading in content areas* (2nd ed.). Englewood Cliffs, NJ: Prentice-Hall.

Hiebert, J., & Behr, M. (1988). Introduction: Capturing the major themes. In J. Hiebert & M. Behr (Eds.), *Number concepts and operations in the middle grades* (Volume 2, pp. 1–8). Reston, VA: National Council of Teachers of Mathematics and Lawrence Erlbaum Associates.

Irvin, J. L., & Connors, N. A. (1989). Reading instruction in middle level schools: Results of a U.S. survey. *Journal of Reading, 32,* 306–311.

Kantor, R. N., Anderson, T. H., & Armbruster, B. B. (1983). How inconsiderate are children's textbooks? *Journal of Curriculum Studies, 15,* 61–72.

Langer, J. A., Applebee, A. N., Mullis, I. V. S., & Foertsch, M. A. (1990). *Learning to read in our nation's schools: Instruction and achievement in 1988 at grades 4, 8, and 12.* Princeton, NJ: National Assessment of Educational Progress, Educational Testing Service.

Maeroff, G. I. (1990). Getting to know a good middle school: Shoreham-Wading River. *Phi Delta Kappan, 71,* 504–511.

Maria, K. (1987, December). *Overcoming misconceptions in science: A replication study at the fifth grade level.* Paper presented at the annual meeting of the National Reading Conference, St. Petersburg, FL.

McGowan, T. M., & Sutton, A. M. (1988). Exploring a persistent association: Tradebooks and social studies teaching. *Journal of Social Studies Research, 12*(1), 8–13.

Memory, D. M., & McGowan, T. M. (1985). Using multilevel textbooks in social studies classes. *The Social Studies, 76,* 174–179.

Metcalf, F. (1988, September 7). Evaluating teachers' outlook on textbooks. *Education Week,* p. 48.

Midgley, C., Feldlaufer, H., & Eccles, J. S. (1989). Student/teacher relations and attitudes toward mathematics before and after the transition to junior high school. *Child Development, 60,* 981–992.

Monahan, J. N. (1990). Developing a strategic reading program. In G. G. Duffy (Ed.), *Reading in the middle school* (2nd ed., pp. 171–183). Newark, DE: International Reading Association.

Moore, D. W., & Stefanich, G. P. (1990). Middle school reading: A historical perspective. In G. G. Duffy (Ed.), *Reading in the middle school* (2nd ed., pp. 3–15). Newark, DE: International Reading Association.

National Council of Teachers of Mathematics. (1989). *Curriculum and evaluation standards for school mathematics.* Reston, VA: Author.

Newmann, F. M. (1986). Priorities for the future: Toward a common agenda. *Social Education, 50,* 240–250.

Nicely, R. F., Jr. (1985). Higher-order thinking skills in mathematics textbooks. *Educational Leadership, 42*(7), 26–30.

O'Neil, J. (1989, January). Global education: Controversy remains, but support growing. *ASCD Curriculum Update,* pp. 1–4, 6–8.

Peters, C. W. (1990). Content knowledge in reading: Creating a new framework. In G. G. Duffy (Ed.), *Reading in the middle school* (2nd ed., pp. 63–80). Newark, DE: International Reading Association.

Posner, G. J., Strike, K. A., Hewson, P. W., & Gertzog, W. A. (1982). Accommodation of a scientific conception: Toward a theory of conceptual change. *Science Education, 66,* 211–227.

Ratekin, N., Simpson, M. L., Alvermann, D. E., & Dishner, E. K. (1985). Why content teachers resist reading instruction. *Journal of Reading, 28,* 432–437.

Roehler, L. R., Foley, K. U., Lud, M. T., & Power, C. A. (1990). Developing integrated programs. In G. G. Duffy (Ed.), *Reading in the middle school* (2nd ed., pp. 184–199). Newark, DE: International Reading Association.

Rogers, V. (1988, August 3). School texts: The outlook of teachers. *Education Week,* p. 39.

Savage, D. G. (1987). Why Chapter I hasn't made much difference. *Phi Delta Kappan, 68,* 581–584.

Sewall, G. T. (1987). *American history textbooks: An assessment of quality.* New York: Teachers College, Columbia University.

Shaver, J. P. (1987). Implications from research: What should be taught in social studies? In V. Richardson-Koehler (Ed.), *Educators' handbook: A research perspective* (pp. 112–138). New York: Longman.

Smith, F. R., & Feathers, K. M. (1983a). Teacher and student perceptions of content area reading. *Journal of Reading, 26,* 348–354.

Smith, F. R., & Feathers, K. M. (1983b). The role of reading in content classrooms: Assumption vs. reality. *Journal of Reading, 27,* 262–267.

Stake, R. E., & Easley, J. A. (1978). *Case studies in science education (Vol. 2: Design, overview, and general findings).* Washington, DC: U.S. Government Printing Office.

Stodolsky, S. S. (1989). Is teaching really by the book? In P. W. Jackson & S. Haroutunian-Gordon (Eds.), *From Socrates to software: The teacher as text and the text as teacher.* Eighty-eighth yearbook of the National Society for the Study of Education, Part I (pp. 159–184). Chicago: University of Chicago Press.

Stoll, D. R. (Ed.). (1990). *Magazines for chil-dren.* Newark, DE: International Reading Association and Educational Press Association of America.

Swafford, J. (1989). *The effects of a science text and demonstration on conceptual change of high school students.* Unpublished doctoral dissertation, University of Georgia, Athens.

Taylor, B. M., Frye, B. J., & Maruyama, G. (1990). Time spent reading and reading growth. *American Educational Research Journal, 27,* 351–362.

Torbe, M. (1988, July). *Reading meanings: A discussion of the social definition of literacy in relation to school and its approaches to reading for meaning.* Paper presented at the Post-World Reading Congress Symposium, Queensland University, Brisbane, Australia.

Tyson, H., & Woodward, A. (1989). Why students aren't learning very much from textbooks. *Educational Leadership, 47*(3), 14–17.

Vacca, R. T., & Vacca, J. L. (1986). *Content area reading* (2nd ed.). Boston: Little, Brown.

Voss, J. V. (1986). Social studies. In R. E. Dillon & R. J. Sternberg (Eds.), *Cognition and instruction* (pp. 205–239). New York: Academic Press.

Watson, B., & Konicek, R. (1990). Teaching for conceptual change: Confronting children's experience. *Phi Delta Kappan, 71,* 680–685.

Weiss, I. R. (1987). *Report of the 1985–86 national survey of science and mathematics education.* Research Triangle Park, NC: National Science Foundation.

Woodward, A., & Elliott, D. L. (1990). Textbook use and teacher professionalism. In D. L. Elliott & A. Woodward (Eds.), *Textbooks and schooling in the United States.* Eighty-ninth yearbook of the National Society for the Study of Education, Part I (pp. 178–193). Chicago: University of Chicago Press.

APPENDIX 5.1

ANNOTATED LIST OF RECOMMENDED MAGAZINES
FOR MIDDLE GRADES

Cobblestone: The History Magazine for Young People is an American history magazine for children ages 8–14. Historical accuracy and original approaches to the issue theme (each issue is devoted to a different theme) are the primary concerns of the magazine. Each 48-page issue contains articles and historical photographs as well as recipes, games, activities, maps, mazes, kids' letters and art, a list of films to rent and places to visit, all tied into the theme.

Editorial Address
Cobblestone Publishing
30 Grove Street
Peterborough, NH 03458
603–924–7209

Ordering Address
Cobblestone
Cobblestone Publishing
30 Grove Street
Peterborough, NH 03458

Target Audience M/F, Ages 8–14, Grades 4–9

Subject American History

How Distributed Home and School

Editor-in-Chief Carolyn P. Yoder

Publisher Lyell C. Dawes

Cost $21.95 per year (12 issues); cumulative index, $5.95

Sample $3.95 with SAE and $1.05 postage

Dynamite is a 32 page, four-color entertainment magazine offered to young people through the Scholastic in-school book clubs. Written for students ages 8–12, it features interviews with popular entertainment figures, jokes, contests, puzzles, and posters.

Editorial Address
Dynamite
Scholastic
730 Broadway
New York, NY 10003
212–505–3000

Ordering Address
Can be ordered only through Scholastic in-school book clubs

Target Audience M/F, Ages 8–12

Subject Entertainment

How Distributed Through Scholastic in-school book clubs

Editor Sonia Black

Publisher Scholastic

Cost $1.50 per copy

Sample Teachers can participate in Scholastic Book Clubs by calling 314–636–8890 for information

---

Dolphin Log is a 16-page magazine published bimonthly by the Cousteau Society. It brings together science, history, and the arts as they relate to our global water system, including marine biology, ecology, the environment, natural history and water-related stories. The goal is to teach environmental ethics and an understanding of the interconnectedness of living organisms, including people.

Editorial Address
The Cousteau Society
8440 Santa Monica Blvd.
Los Angeles, CA 90069
213–656–4422

Ordering Address
The Cousteau Society
930 W. 21 Street
Norfolk, VA 23517
804–627–1144

Target Audience M/F, Ages 7–15

Subjects Educational Biology and Ecology

How Distributed Home and School

Editor Pamela Stacey

Publisher The Cousteau Society

Cost $10 per year

Sample Send SAE and 65¢ postage to editor

Free Spirit: News & Views on Growing Up is an issues-oriented publication for bright, talented, and creative youth. Making friends, setting goals, dealing with school, understanding tests, getting along with parents, and coping with pressure are just a few of the concerns facing young people today. *Free Spirit* attempts to air opinions, asks questions, and offers sound suggestions for readers to consider. This bimonthly magazine welcomes student submissions.

Editorial Address
Free Spirit Publishing
123 N. Third Street
Minneapolis, MN 55401
612–338–2068

Ordering Address
Pamela Espeland
123 N. Third Street
Minneapolis, MN 55401

Target Audience   M/F, Ages 11 and up

Subject   Issues-Oriented

How Distributed   Home and School

Editors   Judy Galbraith and Pamela Espeland

Publisher   Free Spirit Publishing

Cost $10 per year

The Goldfinch is a history magazine for children ages 9–13. Each 32-page issue studies Iowa's history. *The Goldfinch* offers plays, games, puzzles, and contests to aid in understanding local, state, and natural history. It also publishes readers' poetry, stories, and artwork.

Editorial Address
State Historical Society of Iowa
402 Iowa Avenue
Iowa City, IA 52240
319–335–3916

Ordering Address
The Goldfinch
State Historical Society of Iowa
402 Iowa Avenue
Iowa City, IA 52240

Target Audience   M/F, Ages 9–13

Subject   Iowa History

How Distributed   Home

Editor   Carolyn Hardesty

Publisher   State Historical Society of Iowa

Cost $10 per year (4 issues)

Images of Excellence is a four-color Social Studies series that strives to encourage middle and junior high school students to gain a deeper understanding of the efforts and character of significant historical and contemporary figures from world culture. It is hoped that this understanding will serve to stimulate readers to emulate these real-life persons. Published in a series of six, each 20-page publication includes a narrative description of the major events in the "hero's" life and a number of related background stories.

Editorial Address
Images of Excellence Foundation
PO Box 1131
Boiling Springs, NC 28017
704–434–2786

Ordering Address
Images of Excellence
Images of Excellence Foundation
PO Box 1131
Boiling Springs, NC 28017

Target Audience   M/F, Grades 5–8

Subject   Social Studies

How Distributed   School

Editor   Robert Detjen

Publisher   Images of Excellence Foundation

Cost $5 per series (10 or more $4), plus $1 shipping

Sample   Contact editor

Listen deals with drug prevention. Through stories, clear and factual information, personality profiles, positive alternative activities, and self-help features, *Listen* seeks to offer its readers positive reasons for avoiding drug use of all kinds, including alcohol and tobacco. This 32-page magazine, published since 1948, is read by 80,000 teenagers each month.

Editorial Address
Narcotics Education
12501 Old Columbia Pike
Silver Spring, MD 20904
301–680–6726

Ordering Address
Leilani Proctor
Listen
12501 Old Columbia Pike
Silver Spring, MD 20904

Target Audience   M/F, Ages 13–18, Grades 7–12

Subject   Drug Prevention

How Distributed   Home and School

Editor   Gary B. Swanson

Publisher   Narcotics Education

Cost $14.95 per year

Free Sample   Write to editorial address

Merlyn's Pen, The National Magazine of Student Writing This 32-page magazine is devoted entirely to publishing distinguished stories, poems, plays, and essays by some of the nation's best young writers. Every writer receives a personal response within 11 weeks.

Editorial Address
Merlyn's Pen
PO Box 1058
East Greenwich, RI 02818
401–885–5175

Ordering Address
Department CML
PO Box 1058
East Greenwich, RI 02818
1–800–247–2027

Target Audience   M/F, Grades 7–10

Subjects   Fiction, Poetry, and Essays

How Distributed   Home and School

Editor   R. Jim Stahl

Publisher   Merlyn's Pen

Cost $5.95 per school year (over 20 orders); single subscriptions, $14.95 (4 issues)

Odyssey is a space exploration and astronomy magazine. Articles range from backyard stargazing to black holes and the Space Shuttle to interstellar flight. Experiments and projects are regular features. *Odyssey* also publishes reader art, projects, and puzzles. The 40-page magazine was established in January 1979 and now reaches 100,743 readers.

Editorial Address
Kalmbach Publishing
21027 Crossroads Circle
PO Box 1612
Waukesha, WI 53187
414–796–8776

Ordering Address
Nancy Mack
Odyssey
1027 N. Seventh Street
Milwaukee, WI 53233
414–272–2060

Target Audience   M/F, Ages 8–14, Grades 3–8

Subjects   Space Exploration and Astronomy

How Distributed   Home

Editor   Nancy Mack

Publisher   Kalmbach Publishing

Cost $19.95 per year (12 issues)

Sample   Send SAE and four first class stamps

Penny Power is intended to help 8–14-year-olds recognize and make informed decisions in the growing world of consumerism surrounding them. This bimonthly magazine evaluates products marketed to kids including books, movies, and TV programs; it pokes fun at advertising; and it explores earning money, allowances, money management, and other ways kids can attain financial know-how. It also discusses peer pressure, problems with school and friends, and other issues of concern to young people.

Editorial Address
Consumers Union
of the United States
256 Washington Street
Mt. Vernon, NY 10553
914–667–9400

Ordering Address
Penny Power
Consumers Union
of the United States
256 Washington Street
Mt. Vernon, NY 10553

Target Audience M/F, Ages 8–14

Subject Consumer Education

How Distributed Home

Editor Charlotte M. Baecher

Publisher Consumers Union of the United States

Cost $11.95 per year (6 issues)

Scholastic Dynamath is a 16-page classroom magazine used as a supplement for math programs. It presents in a humorous format activities such as word problems, computation, measurement, and test preparation.

Editorial Address
Scholastic
730 Broadway
New York, NY 10003
212–505–3000

Ordering Address
Scholastic
2931 E. McCarty Street
PO Box 3710
Jefferson City, MO 65102
–9957
314–636–8890

Target Audience M/F, Grades 5–6

Subject Math

How Distributed School

Editor Jackie Glasthal

Publisher Scholastic

Cost $5.95 per student for 10 or more (10 issues)

Sample Available to teachers and librarians

Shoe Tree, the literary magazine by and for young writers, presents stories, poems, book reviews, and personal narratives contributed by writers and illustrators ages 6–14 in the belief that young artists need encouragement. The 6" by 9", 64-page book is published by the National Association for Young Writers, a non-profit group of writers and teachers dedicated to the development of good writing.

Editorial Address
National Association for
Young Writers
215 Valle del Sol Drive
Santa Fe, NM 87501
505–982–8596

Ordering Address
Shoe Tree
Membership Services
Department yw
PO Box 3000
Denville, NJ 07834

Target Audience M/F, Ages 6–14

Subject Literary Magazine

How Distributed Home

Editor Shelia Cowing

Publisher National Association for Young Writers

Cost $15 per year (3 issues)

Sample For submission guide and contest rules, send sase to editor

Stone Soup: The Magazine by Children is a bimonthly literary magazine publishing fiction, poetry, book reviews, and art by children through age 13. Each 48-page issue contains writing on a variety of topics relevant to children's lives, art from around the world, photos of their young authors, and an activity guide. Submissions to *Stone Soup* are welcome.

Editorial Address
Children's Art Foundation
PO Box 83
Santa Cruz, CA 95063
408–426–5557

Ordering Address
Stone Soup
PO Box 83
Santa Cruz, CA 95063

Target Audience M/F, Ages 6–13

Subject Literature

How Distributed Home and School

Editor Gerry Mandel

Publisher Children's Art Foundation

Cost $20 per year

Sample Write to editor

APPENDIX 5.2

SUMMARY OF CHANGES IN CONTENT AND EMPHASIS IN 5–8 MATHEMATICS

Increased Attention

Problem Solving
- Pursuing open-ended problems and extended problem-solving projects
- Investigating and formulating questions from problem situations
- Representing situations verbally, numerically, graphically, geometrically, or symbolically

Communication
- Discussing, writing, reading, and listening to mathematical ideas

Reasoning
- Reasoning in spatial contexts
- Reasoning with proportions
- Reasoning from graphs
- Reasoning inductively and deductively

Connections
- Connecting mathematics to other subjects and to the world outside the classroom
- Connecting topics within mathematics
- Applying mathematics

Decreased Attention

Problem Solving
- Practicing routine, one-step problems
- Practicing problems categorized by types (e.g., coin problems, age problems)

Communication
- Doing fill-in-the-blank worksheets
- Answering questions that require only yes, no, or a number as responses

Reasoning
- Relying on outside authority (teacher or an answer key)

Connections
- Learning isolated topics
- Developing skills out of context

Number/Operations/Computation
- Developing number sense
- Developing operation sense
- Creating algorithms and procedures
- Using estimation both in solving problems and in checking the reasonableness of results
- Exploring relationships among representations of, and operations on, whole numbers, fractions, decimals, integers, and rational numbers
- Developing an understanding of ratio, proportion, and percent

Number/Operations/Computation
- Memorizing rules and algorithms
- Practicing tedious paper-and-pencil computations
- Finding exact forms of answers
- Memorizing procedures, such as cross-multiplication, without understanding
- Practicing rounding numbers out of context

Patterns and Functions
- Identifying and using functional relationships
- Developing and using tables, graphs, and rules to describe situations
- Interpreting among different mathematical representations

Patterns and Functions
- Topics seldom in the current curriculum

Algebra
- Developing an understanding of variables, expressions, and equations
- Using a variety of methods to solve linear equations and informally investigate inequalities and nonlinear equations

Algebra
- Manipulating symbols
- Memorizing procedures and drilling on equation solving

Statistics
- Using statistical methods to describe, analyze, evaluate, and make decisions

Statistics
- Memorizing formulas

Probability
- Creating experimental and theoretical models of situations involving probabilities

Probability
- Memorizing formulas

Geometry
- Developing an understanding of geometric objects and relationships
- Using geometry in solving problems

Geometry
- Memorizing geometric vocabulary
- Memorizing facts and relationships

Measurement
- Estimating and using measurement to solve problems

Measurement
- Memorizing and manipulating formulas
- Converting within and between measurement systems

Instructional practices

- Actively involving students individually and in groups in exploring, conjecturing, analyzing, and applying mathematics in both a mathematical and a real-world context
- Using appropriate technology for computation and exploration
- Using concrete materials
- Being a facilitator of learning
- Assessing learning as an integral part of instruction

Instructional Practices

- Teaching computations out of context
- Drilling on paper-and-pencil algorithms
- Teaching topics in isolation
- Stressing memorization
- Being the dispenser of knowledge
- Testing for the sole purpose of assigning grades

6

Teachers as
Decision Makers

Teaching is a demanding profession. Research has shown that during their interactions with students, teachers, on the average, make one decision every two minutes (Clark & Peterson, 1986). This finding is even more remarkable when one considers the complexity of the decision making that teachers of young adolescents face.

In this chapter, you will learn about the underlying thought processes that enable teachers to make appropriate decisions as they go about their daily instructional routines. Specifically, you will discover the reciprocal relationship that exists between teachers' thought processes and teachers' actions. You will also learn what constitutes teachers' interactive thoughts and decisions. Finally, you will learn how teachers' implicit theories and beliefs influence their decision making. Within each of these three broad chapter divisions, you will find plenty of practical ideas on how to develop and reflect on your own thinking and decision-making processes.

Teachers' Thought Processes and Actions

In 1974, a group of educators who were interested in improving the image of teaching assembled at a week-long National Conference on Studies in Teaching. One of the major outcomes of the conference was a position paper that sought to elevate teaching to a level that was on par with other professions such as medicine, law, and architecture. This position paper, which became known as the Panel 6 report (National Institute of Education, 1975), carried several recommendations aimed at eliminating the view of teachers as technicians in favor of teachers as decision makers.

By 1976, the National Institute of Education had established the Institute for Research on Teaching (IRT) at Michigan State University. Soon after the establishment of the IRT, a host of researchers from all over the United States began to focus on the nature of teachers' thought processes and how they relate to teachers' actions.

To help you visualize the relationship between teachers' thought processes and teachers' actions, we have included in Figure 6.1 a model that can also serve as an advance organizer for the information presented in the remainder of this chapter. The model, which was developed by Clark and Peterson (1986), illustrates two important domains of teaching: teachers' thought processes and teachers' actions and their observable effects. Each domain is represented by a circle, and each circle is joined by a double-headed arrow. In short, there is a reciprocal relationship between teachers' thinking and doing.

As shown in Figure 6.1, teachers' thought processes can be categorized as (1) teacher planning (both before and after a lesson, (2) teachers' interactive thoughts and decisions, and (3) teachers' theories and beliefs. Teacher planning, which occurs before and after actual classroom interaction, is dealt with extensively in the next two chapters of this book. Hence, in the present chapter, we will focus on only the two latter categories. Before we turn our attention to these two categories, however, it is important to take one last look at the model depicted in Figure 6.1.

A Closer Look at the Model

Note that two-headed arrows form the circumferences of the circle labeled "Teachers' Thought Processes." These bidirectional arrows are to remind us that the developers of the model (Clark & Peterson, 1986) perceive the three different thought processes as simultaneously affecting and being affected by each other. The same is true for teachers' actions. For example, imagine you are a language arts teacher who believes that young adolescents do their best work in peer-editing

FIGURE 6.1   Clark and Peterson's (1986) Model of Teachers' Thought and Action

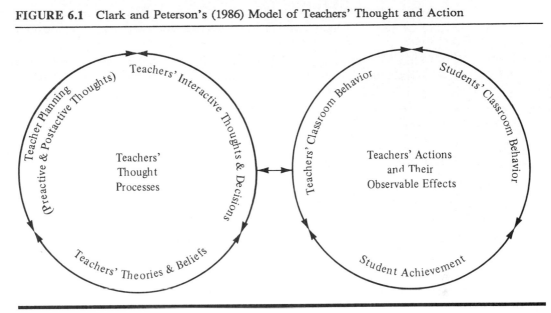

Source: From "A Model of Teacher Thought and Action" by Christopher M. Clark and Penelope L. Peterson. Reprinted with permission of Macmillan Publishing Company from *Handbook of Research on Teaching,* Third Edition, edited by Merlin C. Wittrock. Copyright © 1986 by the American Educational Research Association.

groups when they are allowed to choose who will be in those groups. This belief will influence how you structure your peer-editing sessions.

Next, imagine that three of the six groups (all of whom have chosen their own members) demonstrate that they are incapable of working together productively. They engage in loud arguments, name calling, and other disruptive behaviors. Your first inclination is to reassign the most rowdy students to groups of your own choosing, which you do, and the noise abates, though the students do no better in their roles as peer editors. They appear to lack a strategy for making suggestions to their peers.

You reflect on this dilemma as you sit at your desk after the last student has left for the day. You remember that 50 percent of the class worked well in their self-selected, peer-editing groups. Their participation in class and their written work convinced you that at least *some* young adolescents do well when they choose their own groups.

You decide to alter your theory about young adolescents doing better in self-selected groups. From now on, you promise yourself that you will operate on the belief that young adolescents who have had sufficient experience in group process skills do well in self-selected, peer-editing groups. With that in mind, you begin to plan activities for those who need experiences in small-group processing. You resolve to weave these activities into your regularly scheduled classes so that students do not feel as though they are being singled out. After the first six-week marking period, you notice a decided increase in the number of students who are capable of selecting their own peer-editing partners and working together successfully.

This scenario serves as an example of Clark and Peterson's (1986) model; that is, the relationships within and between domains are reciprocal. This point is important and in direct contradiction to earlier models of teacher thought and action (e.g., Dunkin & Biddle, 1974), which assumed that causality was linear rather than cyclical and circular in nature.

Interactive Thoughts and Decisions

We begin this section of the chapter by describing a common method for studying teachers' interactive thoughts and decisions. We report on the content of teachers' interactive thoughts and then focus at length on the nature of teachers' interactive decision making. In particular, we look for evidence of relationships between teachers' interactive decision making and teacher effectiveness.

Method for Studying Teachers' Interactive Thought Processes

Finding ways to study the thinking and decision-making processes that go on inside teachers' heads has provided quite a challenge to researchers. Unlike teacher actions, teachers' interactive thoughts and decisions are not readily available for observation and measurement. The difficulty lies primarily with finding methodologies that are sensitive to the changes in teachers' instructional moves as a result of the cues they pick up from students' responses (or lack of responses) to their teaching.

One technique that researchers have used to study teachers' thought processes has been to videotape teachers as they teach. Then, using stimulated recall interviews, the researchers would sit with teachers as they reviewed their videotapes. The idea was to stimulate teachers' recall of their interactive thoughts during the time they were teaching. Open-ended interview questions were interspersed between videotaped teaching segments to capture the essence of teachers' thinking.

Several weaknesses exist for this self-reporting type of methodology. First, there is no guarantee that teachers were recalling accurately their interactive thoughts that occurred as they taught. Also, there is the distinct possibility that teachers were answering as they thought the researchers would have them answer. And third, even if the teachers could accurately recall their interactive thoughts while teaching, the open-ended questions on the interview schedule may have reflected more of the researchers' interests and biases than the teachers' concerns.

Nonetheless, despite these shortcomings, videotaping followed by stimulated recalls and interviews remains one of the few viable options for studying teachers' interactive thoughts and decisions. So that you may form your own opinion about the worth of this type of methodology, we provide excerpts from two middle-grades science teachers' classes. The teachers were representative of 22 other middle-grades teachers who participated in the study (Alvermann, O'Brien, & Dillon, 1990). First, read each excerpt in its entirety. Next, read the videotaped teachers' stimulated recall of what she was doing (and why). Then, decide for yourself whether you think the teachers' accounts of their interactive thoughts and decisions are plausible.

Mrs. Matthews's Class

Mrs. Matthews taught earth science to average-ability eighth-grade students enrolled in a medium-size school that is located in a small town in rural northeast Georgia. On the day of this particular videotaped excerpt, Mrs. Matthews was going over students' homework (a set of assigned questions) with them.

> TEACHER: What is chemistry? Remember how we always do this now. All right, Annette?
>
> ANNETTE: Composition of matter.
>
> TEACHER: Composition of matter. What does that mean? I mean that sounds kind of interesting.
>
> KEVIN: It's the history of, um, things that take up space. What minerals are, uh . . .
>
> TEACHER: (interrupting) Composition of things that take up space, okay. What were you going to say, Kevin?
>
> KEVIN: Like what minerals are broken down into matter and what forms of matter and different types of rock.
>
> TEACHER: Okay. I agree with what has been said. Chemistry *is* the study of physical things in the earth, and we've talked about those physical things that we can put our hands on. *Matter*—that's another word. That was one on your definitions list. What about that word? Okay, Tony?
>
> TONY: Anything that takes up space.
>
> MELANIE: It has mass.
>
> TEACHER: It has mass. What does that mean to you, Cory?

Mrs. Matthews's Stimulated Recall

[What students] need to know is how to go about learning. That's what I try to teach them. Don't regurgitate it back to me. Now there *are* things that you regurgitate— formulas, for instance. I try to distinguish with them [students] the things that they have to know verbatim and the things that they need to have a general knowledge of, to gain understanding. [I tell students] learn it [information], know how to use it . . . just as long as you understand . . . and then hand it [tell it] back to me.

Mrs. Gustafson's Class

Mrs. Gustafson taught general science to seventh-grade students. Her students were also average in ability. On the day of the videotaped excerpt that appears below, Mrs. Gustafson was going over a worksheet assignment based on the previous day's reading.

> TEACHER: Okay, we've read pages 396 to 403. We're going to go ahead and discuss it and see what kinds of information we got from it. First question: Ancient reptiles lived in various environments—mainly environments that

they inhabited—and there is one reptile that inhabited each. Name me some environments, Freeman?

FREEMAN: Um, the ponds and they have lobe-finned fish in them, and on the edges of ponds, crocodilelike reptiles, and the forest contained insect-eating lizardlike reptiles.

TEACHER: Okay, good. Uh, number 2: What did the primitive bird look like that may have evolved from reptiles. Okay, Amy?

AMY: It would have teeth as reptiles do and a long, bony tail with joints as reptiles do—and feathers.

TEACHER: Okay, and feathers. Why do they think that this is probably listed as bird and not a reptile?

DIANE: Because it had feathers?

TEACHER: Because it had feathers, right, okay. Number 3: Which reptiles that live today look most like the ancient reptiles? Janice? [*Note:* This pattern of checking students' worksheets continued through the last question, number 10. Then Mrs. Gustafson gave students their next day's assignment.]

TEACHER: Okay, for the rest of class time, you should put those questions away. You're going to be reading in your books, and you have a sheet to answer questions on about vertebrates in general.

Mrs. Gustafson's Stimulated Recall

It absolutely doesn't matter who it [the student] is. They will not read if they don't have [a] paper and pencil [task to do]. They won't discuss without writing the answers first. I see a difference in students these days. I don't see the enthusiasm coming from the children. [I never hear from students], "Oh, I know the answer," or "I've got something to add," or [students] coming up with any questions to add or ask in a little more depth. It [the discussion] is strictly one-sided. The enthusiasm to delve deeper, to do a little more for the sake of knowledge, I don't see [from students]. That disturbs me.

Reflecting on decisions made during teaching informs future decision making.

Commentary on Stimulated Recalls

It appears that both Mrs. Matthews and Mrs. Gustafson were able to give plausible accounts of what they were thinking about (and why they made the decisions they did) on the day of the videotaping. Mrs. Matthews was intent upon communicating to students her concern that they know how to distinguish between information that is appropriately memorized versus that which must be understood. She wanted students to be able to make this distinction because she felt that it was essential for them to learn how to learn.

Mrs. Gustafson also was able to articulate what she was thinking about when she assigned students paper-and-pencil tasks as part of their reading assignment. She stated she used worksheets to ensure that students would have something to contribute toward class discussion. Ironically, the worksheets may have contributed further to what Mrs. Gustafson cited as students' lack of enthusiasm for learning.

In the next section of this chapter, you will discover what a variety of teachers reported thinking as they interacted with students in their classrooms. As you read some examples from these teachers' stimulated recall interviews, try to imagine what the full transcript of their classroom dialogues must have looked like. Your earlier reading of the transcribed excerpts from Mrs. Matthews's and Mrs. Gustafson's classroom interactions will help you in this task.

Content of Teachers' Interactive Thoughts

How much of the time, if any, do teachers spend thinking about objectives, subject matter, instructional strategies, and students' learning as they simultaneously try to teach and manage the normal type of classroom disruptions? Clark and Peterson (1986) reviewed a number of studies that looked at teachers' responses to these types of questions and other similarly related ones. The studies, which involved teachers in grades 1 through 8, all used some form of stimulated recall as the method for collecting data on the teachers' interactive thoughts. According to Clark and Peterson's review of the literature, the following four major findings emerged:

1. Between 39 and 50 percent of the teachers' interactive thoughts were concerned with the learner. This was by far the largest reported category of teachers' thinking. Examples of teachers' interactive thoughts about learners (as reported in their stimulated recall interviews) include: "I was thinking that they don't understand what they are doing." "I was also thinking, 'Tricia's kind of silly right now. If I ask her, I probably won't get a straight answer' " (p. 269).
2. The next largest category (between 20 and 30 percent of teachers' reported interactive thoughts) dealt with instructional procedures and strategies. Examples include: "I thought after I explained it to her, 'I didn't make that very clear.' " "I was thinking that they needed some sort of positive reinforcement" (p. 269).
3. Only a small percentage of the teachers' comments were concerned with subject matter. An example taken from one teacher's stimulated recall interview follows: "At this point here, I wanted to focus in on the idea of Japan being today an industrial nation, rather than an agricultural nation" (p. 269).

4. The smallest category of teachers' interactive thoughts were concerned with instructional objectives. An example follows: "I wanted them to identify the senses that they were using" (p. 269).

Interactive Decision Making and Teachers' Thoughts

It is clear from these examples that teachers do report thinking about a number of instructional factors and, most importantly, the learner, as they simultaneously try to teach and manage the routine disruptions of normal classroom life. What is not clear at this point is what teachers *do* with their thoughts. That is, what decisions do they make in response to the thoughts they are interactively generating?

According to Wodlinger (1980), for a decision to qualify as an interactive decision, the teacher's thoughts must be focused on the student and/or the instructional materials involved in teaching the student. In addition, the teacher must have demonstrated an awareness of options. Wodlinger provided this example:

> They weren't too sure yesterday, and they had problems with this stuff, so I thought I would go back and ask those particular people [who] were having problems yesterday. So with Laura and Steve, you know, I specifically asked them a question just to see if they were able to understand them from yesterday. (p. 282)

Shavelson and Stern's (1981) model of interactive decision making is based on their observation that teachers form mental images of what lessons should look like. Once a lesson begins, these mental images become routinized so that little conscious decision making needs to occur. Instead, an activity flow is set in motion that makes handling students' behaviors and instruction fairly automatic. Only when something occurs that disrupts the routinized activity flow must a teacher make a conscious decision about an alternative form of action.

Studies of interactive decision making among beginning versus experienced teachers (Calderhead, 1981) show that beginning teachers do not have the rich cognitive structures that allow them to react to critical incidents in the same way that experienced teachers react. For example, experienced teachers' thoughts on what middle-grades students are like and their past experiences in dealing with students at this age level make it possible for them to predict in advance the most appropriate ways to handle instructional and classroom management problems.

Nature of Interactive Decision Making

Classroom teaching involves decision making. As stated at the beginning of this chapter, we now have evidence that teachers make, on the average, one decision every two minutes. This fact would seem to call for extraordinary expertise on the part of teachers. The complexity of the task seems even more compounded when one considers the broad range of developmental growth present in middle-grades classrooms (see Chapter 2). What is the nature of interactive decision making? How do teachers master the required knowledge and expertise to deal with interactive decision making? Is there a relationship between teachers' interactive decision making and teacher effectiveness? How can teachers learn to be more effective at making decisions interactively?

A good way to begin thinking about the nature of interactive decision making is to contemplate what Harker and Green (1985) have to say on the topic.

> In every classroom, the teacher makes a continuing series of decisions about what, when, and how to communicate with children. These decisions grow out of the teacher's evaluation of the nature and quality of the communication that is taking place: "Are they going to understand this? Should I rephrase this question? How can I get Antonio or Kathleen to participate? Who should have the next turn?" This decision making, consciously or unconsciously, is an integral part of every interaction. The roots of this decision making are the teacher's goals, the teacher's knowledge about the nature of teaching-learning processes as communicative processes, and the teacher's ability to assess and understand the student's communications and reactions to the teacher. (p. 221)

According to Harker and Green, the decisions teachers make interactively are conditioned in part by the responses students make. This notion is not new. Earlier models of interactive teacher decision making (e.g., Marland, 1977; Peterson & Clark, 1978; Shavelson & Stern, 1981) all acknowledged the large role student behavioral cues played in teachers' interactive decision making. For example, Marland (1977) reported that 44 percent of teachers' interactive decisions were in response to student behavioral cues. More recently, however, there has been a move to consider other antecedents to teacher decision making that extend beyond student restlessness, inattentiveness, and incomplete or incorrect responses. Working toward a new model of teacher interactive decision making, Clark and Peterson (1986) have stressed the need to consider antecedents such as "judgments about the environment, the teacher's state of mind, or the appropriateness of a particular teaching strategy" (p. 277).

Required Knowledge and Expertise

Where do teachers acquire the extensive practical knowledge and expertise necessary for making interactive decisions? One interesting approach to this question was a study conducted in Sweden by Dahllof and Lundgren (1970). They were interested in looking at the organizational constraints under which teachers work and how those constraints influence the teaching process. These researchers uncovered a phenomenon that they named the "steering group," which consisted of those students in a class who fell within the bottom range of percentiles (10th to 25th) on achievement.

Teachers used steering groups to help them pace their lessons. Dahllof and Lundgren reported that when students in the steering group grasped a concept, the teacher moved the entire class on to a new concept; similarly, when they had difficulty grasping a concept, the teacher slowed the instructional pace of the whole class until the steering-group students caught on.

One might conclude from the Dahllof and Lundgren study that teachers acquire practical knowledge about interactive decision making by observing what the slowest group can do instructionally and then pacing the rest of the class accordingly. Fortunately, the answer is not quite that simple. Although students' ability level may contribute to teachers' decisions concerning whole-class instructional pacing, it is only part of what has become known as teachers' situated knowledge and expertise in teaching.

Traditionally, teachers' situated knowledge has been viewed as craft knowledge or conventional wisdom—something that teachers acquire after a lifetime of classroom teaching (Zeichner, Tabachnick, & Densmore, 1987). This rather negative view of situated knowledge seems to be changing as educators discover the importance of taking into account a variety of classroom factors that have an effect on teachers' ability to teach and students' ability to learn. For example, we know that no two classrooms are ever exactly the same. The make-up of the student body, the "chemistry" that occurs between the student body and the teacher, the time of year, physical surroundings, the methods the teacher uses to teach, choice of textbooks, and many other factors all figure into the picture.

Teachers who take into account these various factors and use them to solve problems that arise as a result of the factors themselves are said to have *situated knowledge* and *expertise in teaching*. Many times this situated knowledge allows teachers to act as though they were on "automatic pilot." That is, they are so tuned in to the multifaceted nature of their students' lives, the constraints and opportunities afforded by the local school setting, and their own personal and professional goals that they are able to make complex decisions in a fairly routine fashion.

To get a feel for how situated knowledge might help a middle-grades language arts teacher make an interactive decision about the course of action to take when three-fourths of the class fails to turn in a major assignment on the last day of a 10-week marking period, pretend that you *are* the teacher. Figure 6.2 provides some

Developing expertise in making instructional decisions comes from attending to students' interests and needs.

FIGURE 6.2   Simulation Activity

Facts about the Teacher:

You are in your first year of teaching at a predominantly middle-class school in what is known as the Silicon Valley of California. You enjoy the support of your principal and fellow teachers. You have met most of the students' parents at one time or another during the school year, either informally at PTO functions or formally at open-house sessions and the like.

You have read several reports about the influence of homework on student achievement. You know, for example, that structured homework assignments can have a positive effect on student achievement (Keith & Page, 1985), but you also know that this conclusion has been challenged by others (e.g., Levine, 1988).

In addition, you know that a recent study by Guthrie and Kirst (1988) showed that California students in grades 6, 8, and 12 reported that they spend approximately 80 minutes per school night doing homework. Finally, you are aware that the most frequently made assignment is one that involves either textbook questions or worksheets, rather than essays and independent projects (Murphy & Decker, 1989), which you are prone to give.

Facts about the Students:

Your seventh-grade class consists of 28 students (16 females and 12 males). The majority of the students are Anglos, but there is a fair mix of Hispanics, Blacks, Pacific Islanders, and Vietnamese. The school principal has told you that the students are capable of doing above-average work and your own estimation of their ability agrees with the principal's assessment.

Up to now (the third 10-week marking period of the school year), your students have been fairly consistent in turning in their homework, although they have expressed a dislike for doing essays and independent projects. The assignment in question is a 750-word essay on the school's new policy regarding a "no-pass, no-play" ruling recently handed down by the local school board.

Facts about the Middle School:

The school is organized according to interdisciplinary teams. You are a member of a team that plans together one hour daily. As a team, you observe consistent guidelines and procedures for making assignments and for setting up classroom expectations for completing the assignments. The team encourages interdisciplinary assignments and encourages giving students several options to choose from a variety of assignments.

The school has an advisor/advisee program. Some of the students in the particular class are also in your advisee class in the morning. Because your school has a "no-pass, no-play" policy, you realize that students who do not turn in assignments may get failing grades and be barred from playing sports.

facts that you will need to consider as you complete this simulation activity. After you have read the facts about the teacher, students, and school, follow the directions provided in Figure 6.3.

Relationship between Decision Making and Teacher Effectiveness

With all of the research on teacher effectiveness that is available to practitioners through staff-development programs, journal articles, and professional meetings, it would be easy to assume that we must know a great deal about the type of

FIGURE 6.3   Directions for Completing the Simulation

1. Select from the information given to you about the teacher, the students, and the school those factors that seem most relevant in making your decision about the homework assignment. List those factors in the chart provided below:

	TEACHER	STUDENTS	SCHOOL
Factor 1			
Factor 2			
Factor 3			
Factor 4			

2. With a partner, compare your lists of relevant factors. Where differences occur, discuss these, and try to arrive at one list.

3. Write that list in the space provided below:

TEACHER   **STUDENTS**   **SCHOOL**

4. Use the factors you identified to derive a rationale for your stance on turning in major assignments on time. Discuss your rationale with your partner.

5. Now, imagine you are in the classroom and discover that three-fourths of the class fails to turn in the assignment. Take out a sheet of notebook paper and with your partner, construct what might be the interactions that would occur between you and the class. (Use the excerpts presented earlier from Mrs. Matthews's and Mrs. Gustafson's classes as a guide for your imaginary interactions.)

6. Identify in the margins of your interaction sheet the thoughts that passed through your mind as you said different things. Also, describe the options that were available to you. Finally, state your decision at the bottom of your interaction sheet. Be sure to identify your decision by drawing a red line under it.

interactive decision making effective teachers engage in. Actually, this is not the case.

As Clark and Peterson (1986) point out in their comprehensive review of the literature on interactive decision making, relatively few empirical studies have been conducted on the relationship between teachers' interactive decision making and effective teaching. The three studies that they identify used either student scores on a standardized achievement test (Morine & Vallance, 1975; Peterson & Clark, 1978) or high levels of student involvement in classroom tasks (Doyle, 1977) as the criteria for defining effective teaching. Two general findings from these studies included the following:

1. Early intervention that neutralizes student misbehavior is associated with effective classroom management and, hence, effective teaching.
2. The effective teacher is one who differentiates relevant from irrelevant information as he or she interacts with students and then "chunks" that information when it comes time to make a decision. The less effective teacher, on the other hand, does not use differentiation and chunking in interactive decision making. Rather, he or she tends to take into account a large number of factors, with little or no attention to selecting the most relevant ones.

You may want to rate the effectiveness of your interactive decision making in the homework assignment case against these two standards. For example, did you intervene early? Did you focus on a limited number of relevant factors and then analyze those factors before coming to your decision? If you did one or neither of these things, what extenuating circumstances may have accounted for your actions?

Learning to Be More Effective Interactive Decision Makers

How do novice teachers learn to be effective interactive decision makers? Lacking years of classroom experience, how can they hope to use the available situated knowledge in ways that will develop their expertise in making decisions? These are questions for which researchers have no answers, at least no answers based on experimental studies. In Clark and Peterson's (1986) words, "We do not have a clear idea . . . of what constitutes *effective* interactive decision making by a teacher" (p. 281). Their suggestion that teachers not be instructed in interactive decision making per se, but rather in ways that will enable them "to perceive, analyze, and transform their perceptions of the classroom in ways similar to those used by effective teachers" (p. 281) is echoed by Berliner (1987) in his work with expert and novice teachers.

The rationale for studying expert and novice teachers rests on the assumption that, through an understanding of their developing belief systems and practices, an improved knowledge base can be derived from which to draw implications for teacher education. According to Shulman (1987), codifying the emerging knowledge and actions of experienced and inexperienced teachers can lead to a knowledge base that is grounded in what he calls the "wisdom of practice." In Shulman's (1987) words, the focus is on attempting "to make the implied more explicit so that it can be shared and deliberated upon" (p. 480).

Teachers' Implicit Theories and Beliefs

To this point in the chapter, we have been examining teachers' interactive decision making from primarily a cognitive perspective. However, as Wagner (1987) has pointed out, "In everyday school life, teachers' thought processes tend to be much more descriptive, more emotional, more contradictory and less straightforward than many current studies of teachers' thinking have led us to believe" (p. 161). As a result of her in-depth study that employed stimulated recall methodology to investigate what teachers and students in seven sixth-grade German classrooms reported actually thinking about during class lessons, Wagner found:

1. Teachers' thinking quite often seemed to go around in circles, posing questions without resolving them, "jumping" from one issue to another, considering goals and strategies without ever putting them into practice, with no apparent realization of the many contradictions in the content of teachers' thought.
2. Some of [the teachers'] thought processes also revealed considerable emotional involvement—teachers got angry about students, were over-awed by their colleagues, sometimes identified with one of the students or had a strong desire to reach certain goals and were disappointed when they were not achieved. (p. 161)

Although Wagner's study was conducted in German classrooms, what she found out about the interrelationship between teachers' cognitive and affective processing of critical classroom events would seem to bear some resemblance to the internal conflicts that middle-grades teachers in the United States may experience when they engage in interactive decision making. Unfortunately, there is little in the research literature on the relationship between cognitive and affective processing as it relates to teachers' interactive decision making. The closest body of literature is that which deals with teachers' implicit theories and beliefs about teaching and learning. It is to this topic that we turn our attention for the remainder of the chapter. Specifically, we will examine the results of two studies that focused on the thoughts of 15 elementary teachers (5 of whom taught sixth-graders) during the interactive decision-making process. We will conclude with a look at a relatively new system for studying teachers' language to determine what that language can tell us about the meaning teachers of young adolescents attach to their instructional activities.

Two Studies of Teachers' Thoughts during Interactive Teaching
The first study (Marland, 1977) involved six elementary teachers, two of whom taught sixth-grade language arts lessons. Based on his analyses of data obtained through stimulated recall interviews, Marland identified five principles of practice. These are reported in Clark and Peterson's (1986) review of the literature on teachers' thought processes and are included in Figure 6.4. As Clark and Peterson (1986) were quick to point out, Marland did not find any evidence in his analysis that would suggest the teachers in his study used their knowledge of subject matter to guide their interactive decision making.

The second study (Conners, 1978) was a replication of Marland's work and involved nine elementary teachers, three of whom were sixth-grade teachers in different schools. Like Marland, Conners employed the stimulated recall method to obtain interview data from the teachers in his study. As reported by Clark and Peterson (1986), all nine teachers in the Conners study used the principles of suppressing emotions, teacher authenticity, and self-monitoring to guide their interactions with students (see Figure 6.5).

Before leaving this section of the chapter, you may want to try to connect the principles of practice derived by Marland and Conners to what you have learned about the developmental characteristics of young adolescents. One way to make these connections is to consider which of the physical, intellectual, and socioemotional characteristics of young adolescents (see Chapter 2) would have to be in place for the principles of practice to apply.

FIGURE 6.4   Marland's Five Principles of Practice

1. *The principle of compensation* represented an attempt on the part of the teacher to discriminate in favor of the shy, the introverted, the low-ability group, and the culturally impoverished. . . . This principle figured less prominently in the explanations of teachers of higher grades.
2. *The principle of strategic leniency* was a variation of the principle of compensation. Strategic leniency referred to a teacher's tendency to ignore infractions of classroom rules by children who the teacher regarded as needing special attention.
3. *The principle of power sharing* involved the teacher using the informal peer power structure to influence students. In this way, the teacher was seen as sharing both responsibility and authority with certain students. That is, the teacher would selectively reinforce the good behavior of students who she perceived as class leaders to use their influence on their peers as an instrument for classroom management.
4. *The principle of progressive checking* involved periodically checking progress, indentification of problems, and providing encouragement for low-ability-group students during seatwork. In addition to the direct assistance provided during this checking, the teacher who utilized this principle also reasoned that she was providing stimulus variation for students with short attention spans.
5. *The principle of suppressing emotions* was derived from teacher reports that they consciously suppressed the emotional feelings that they were experiencing while teaching. This principle was invoked because of the belief that, if they expressed their feelings and emotions, it might overly excite the students and encourage them to express their own feelings and emotions, thus creating a management problem. (p. 289)

Source: From "Teachers' Thought Processes" by Christopher M. Clark and Penelope L. Peterson. Excerpted with permission of Macmillan Publishing Company from *Handbook of Research on Teaching,* Third Edition, edited by Merlin C. Wittrock. Copyright © 1986 by the American Educational Research Association.

For example, if middle-grades teachers are to share power with class leaders, students would have to be at a stage in their physical development where peer approval and the desire to belong to peer groups are uppermost in their minds. Or, if teachers are to engage in the principle of progressive checking (e.g., providing encouragement for low-ability groups), students would have to be at a stage in their intellectual development where they are capable of deciding how to allocate their attention so that they might benefit from a teacher's differentiated instruction. Finally, if teachers are to present themselves as open, honest, and fallible human beings, students would have to be at a stage in their socioemotional development where they are capable of showing support, friendship, and trust toward authority figures.

Teachers' Language and What It Reveals about Their Theories and Beliefs

Developing expertise in interactive decision making calls for more than simply applying rules of practice. If you are to become an effective decision maker, you will also want to engage in reflective practices such as examining your own implicit theories and beliefs about teaching and learning.

FIGURE 6.5   Conners's Principles of Practice

1. *The principle of suppressing emotions* was similar to that described by Marland. But in addition to its use as a disruption-prevention strategy, Conners's teachers reported using what could be called "visible suppression of emotions" (e.g., remaining silent and stern-faced until the class quiets down), and also intentionally violating this principle by occasionally expressing anger or frustration to make a powerful impression on their students.
2. *The principle of teacher authenticity* involved teacher presentation of self in such a way that good personal relationships with students and a socially constructive classroom atmosphere would result. This principle was expressed as a desire to behave in ways that were open, sincere, honest, and fallible.
3. *The principle of self-monitoring* was defined as the need for teachers to remain aware of their behavior and the estimated effects of their behavior on their students. For the teachers interviewed by Conners, this principle seemed to be acted upon at a global and intuitive level of judgment, for example, by asking oneself "How am I doing?" regularly during teaching. (p. 290)
4. *The principle of cognitive linking* indicated that new information should be explicitly related by the teacher to past and future student learning experiences.
5. *The principle of integration* called for opportunities for students to practice and apply skills and concepts learned in one subject area in other subjects and contexts.
6. *The principle of closure* involved teacher commitment to the importance of summarizing, reviewing, and tying together main points at the end of a lesson or unit.
7. *The principle of general involvement* was expressed as the desire to have all students participate fully in class activities, to minimize student isolation (self-selected or otherwise), and to help shy or withdrawn students to overcome their reluctance to participate.
8. *The principle of equality of treatment* called for fair and consistent treatment of each student.

Source: From "Teachers' Thought Processes" by Christopher M. Clark and Penelope L. Peterson. Excerpted with permission of Macmillan Publishing Company from *Handbook of Research on Teaching,* Third Edition, edited by Merlin C. Wittrock. Copyright © 1986 by the American Educational Research Association.

Recently, a group of researchers in Canada (Russell, Munby, Spafford, & Johnston, 1988) developed a method for engaging teachers in conversation about their practical, or craft, knowledge. As a group of middle-grades teachers talked, Munby (1983) discovered in an earlier study that they used metaphors to describe what they did as they taught. When these metaphors were subjected to closer scrutiny, Munby and his associates found they could convey quite accurately what it was that teachers believed was most significant about their practical knowledge.

Teachers' rich metaphorical language can be used to help them reflect on their own implicit theories and beliefs. For example, in the case of one teacher named Alice, Munby and his associates (Russell et al., 1988) were able to show how her use of figurative language depicted lessons as moving objects. The following is but a partial listing of the figures of speech Alice used: "I just went ahead," "They're always a step ahead of the other classes because everything goes so smoothly," "We move along faster," "We'll probably even back up a little bit," "These kids need a push in every direction," "In that particular class, uh, we go very slow," "If he's lost . . . he's just going to get further behind," "I'm pushing and backing up as far as I can," and "I finally got to the point" (p. 68).

For fun, you might also want to try your hand at self-reflection through language. Find a friend who will record your voice as you talk for approximately 10 minutes on the topic of becoming a middle-grades teacher. Describe what you believe it will be like to teach young adolescents. What problems do you anticipate? How has reading this chapter made you more aware of your own implicit theories and beliefs about teaching and learning? What are some of these theories and beliefs?

Transcribe the recording and pick out the figurative language. Are there any clues in your figures of speech that would give you a window on how you are thinking about teaching young adolescents? Share these with the friend who agreed to record your talk. You may also want to record the figures of speech you used in a journal or diary so that you can compare them to a new set of metaphors at some later time.

Summary

Decision making is a complex activity, whatever the situation or setting. When teachers make decisions about instruction, there is a seemingly endless number of variables that must be considered. Moreover, teachers' thought processes and their actions are so intertwined with students' classroom behaviors and achievements that one action can set in motion a series of cyclical reactions, which eventually feed back into teachers' thinking and decision making.

Knowing how students' responses to instruction influence teachers' interactive thoughts and decisions is vital to becoming an effective middle-grades teacher. If you participated in the various activities designed to simulate the decision-making process, you will have undoubtedly gained some idea of the complexity of tasks teachers face. Successfully meeting the challenges that each decision-making opportunity presents can be quite satisfying. Learning to make good instructional decisions interactively is the mark of a good teacher and a true professional.

REFERENCES

Alvermann, D. E., O'Brien, D. G., & Dillon, D. R. (1990). What teachers do when they say they're having discussions following content reading assignments: A qualitative analysis. *Reading Research Quarterly*, 25, 296–322.

Berliner, D. C. (1987). Ways of thinking about students and classrooms by more and less experienced teachers. In J. Calderhead (Ed.), *Exploring teachers' thinking* (pp. 60–83). London: Cassell Educational.

Calderhead, J. (1981). A psychological approach to research on teachers' classroom decision making. *British Educational Research Journal*, 7, 51–57.

Clark, C. M., & Peterson, P. L. (1986). Teachers' thought processes. In M. C. Wittrock (Ed.), *Handbook of research on teaching* (3rd ed., pp. 255–296). New York: Macmillan.

Conners, R. D. (1978). *An analysis of teacher thought processes, beliefs, and principles during instruction*. Unpublished doctoral dissertation, University of Alberta, Edmonton, Canada.

Dahllof, U., & Lundgren, U. P. (1970). *Macro- and micro approaches combined for curriculum processes analysis: A Swedish educational field project*. Goteborg, Sweden: University of Goteborg, Institute of Education.

Doyle, W. (1977). Learning the classroom environment: An ecological analysis. *Journal of Teacher Education, 28,* 51–55.

Dunkin, M. J., & Biddle, B. J. (1974). *The study of teaching*. New York: Holt, Rinehart & Winston.

Guthrie, J. W., & Kirst, M. W. (1988, March). *Conditions of education in California 1988.* Berkeley: Policy Analysis for California Education. (Policy Paper No. 88-3-2).

Harker, J. O., & Green, J. L. (1985). When you get the right answer to the wrong question: Observing and understanding communication in classrooms. In A. Jaggar & M. T. Smith-Burke (Eds.), *Observing the language learner* (pp. 221–231). Newark, DE: International Reading Association.

Keith, T., & Page, E. (1985). Homework works at school: National evidence for policy changes. *School Psychology Review, 14*(3), 351–359.

Levine, D. V. (1988, April). *Homework and reading achievement in NAEP data on thirteen-year-olds.* Paper presented at the annual meeting of the American Educational Research Association, New Orleans.

Marland, P. W. (1977). *A study of teachers' interactive thoughts.* Unpublished doctoral dissertation, University of Alberta, Edmonton, Canada.

Morine, G., & Vallance, E. (1975). *Special study B: A study of teacher and pupil perceptions of classroom interaction.* (Tech. Rep. No. 75-11-6). San Francisco: Far West Laboratory.

Munby, H. (1983, April). *A qualitative study of teachers' beliefs and principles.* Paper presented at the annual meeting of the American Educational Research Association, Montreal.

Murphy, J., & Decker, K. (1989). Teachers' use of homework in high school. *Journal of Educational Research, 82,* 261–269.

National Institute of Education. (1975). *Teaching as clinical information processing* (Report of Panel 6, National Conference on Studies in Teaching). Washington, DC: National Institute of Education.

Peterson, P. L., & Clark, C. M. (1978). Teachers' reports of their cognitive processes during teaching. *American Educational Research Journal, 15,* 555–565.

Russell, T., Munby, H., Spafford, C., & Johnston, P. (1988). Learning the professional knowledge of teaching: Metaphors, puzzles, and the theory-practice relationship. In P. Grimmets & G. L. Erickson (Eds.), *Reflection in teacher education* (pp. 67–89). New York: Teachers College Press, Columbia University.

Shavelson, R. J., & Stern, P. (1981). Research on teachers' pedagogical thoughts, judgments, decisions, and behavior. *Review of Educational Research, 51,* 455–498.

Shulman, L. (1987). Knowledge and teaching: Foundations of the new reform. *Harvard Educational Review, 57*(1), 1–22.

Wagner, A. C. (1987). 'Knots' in teachers' thinking. In J. Calderhead (Ed.), *Exploring teachers' thinking* (pp. 161–178). London: Cassell Educational.

Wodlinger, M. G. (1980). *A study of teacher interactive decision making.* Unpublished doctoral dissertation, University of Alberta, Edmonton, Canada.

Zeichner, K. M., & Tabachnick, B. R., & Densmore, K. (1987). Individual, institutional, and cultural influences on the development of teachers' craft knowledge. In J. Calderhead (Ed.), *Exploring teachers' thinking* (pp. 21–59). London: Cassell.

_7

Instructional Planning: Yearly, Unit, Weekly, and Daily Planning

Teacher planning plays a critical role in effective instruction in the middle grades. As we described in Chapter 1, many middle-grades schools are organized around interdisciplinary teams of teachers who plan together. Before considering the role of team planning in the middle grades, it would be beneficial to discuss planning in general and what research says about teacher planning. Specifically, we will address questions such as: What is teacher planning? Why do teachers plan? What factors affect teachers' plans? How do teachers' plans affect instruction? How do teachers plan? and What does the research say about teacher planning? After answering these questions, we will describe and discuss team planning in the middle grades.

The last part of the chapter will be devoted to four major types of planning that most middle-grades teachers engage in: yearly, unit, weekly, and daily planning. This chapter deals primarily with how teachers plan and organize the content they will be teaching. Two other equally important components of teacher planning are how teachers decide on the strategies they will use to teach the content and what learning strategies they want to weave into their lessons. We discuss these two components of planning in Chapters 8, 11, and 12.

What Is Teacher Planning?

Clark and Yinger (1987) define *planning* as "a basic psychological process in which a person visualizes the future, lists means and ends, and constructs a framework to guide his or her future action" (p. 345). This definition implies that teachers must first decide where they want to go and then devise a way to get there. The definition also implies that teachers' mental activities play a major role in the planning process.

Teachers think about and visualize their plans in many different places, in numerous ways, and at various times. For example, while washing dishes, a teacher may decide to introduce a unit on electricity by comparing an electric circuit to a water circuit. Similarly, a teacher may mentally "walk through" a lesson ahead of time to make sure he or she has assembled all the materials necessary for the lesson. Much of the time and effort that teachers spend planning and revising never actually appear in the final written plans.

Nevertheless, the visualization component of planning appears to be widespread. Research (e.g., Livingston & Borko, 1989) indicates that both expert and novice teachers engage in some type of mental planning. The end product of planning can take many forms. Some teachers end up with very detailed and elaborate plans, other teachers have a list of activities, and still others have only sketchy outlines. However, on the whole, most teachers do end up with something in writing.

Why Do Teachers Plan?

As you may expect, teachers plan for a variety of reasons. Clark and Yinger (1979) and McCutcheon (1980) identified five categories of reasons why teachers plan. These categories are presented in Figure 7.1.

FIGURE 7.1   Reasons Teachers Plan

1. Teachers plan to satisfy their own psychological needs such as increasing their confidence and reducing their anxiety. Imagine how nervous you would be standing in front of a class of young adolescents with absolutely no plan in mind!

2. Teachers plan in order to be ready to instruct their students. This reason includes tasks such as learning the content and selecting materials.

3. Teachers plan in order to be prepared to interact with their students. For example, by planning questioning strategies and discussion activities, teachers are better prepared to interact with their students.

4. Teachers plan to fulfill administrative requirements. Many teachers are required to turn in weekly plans to their principals. In many cases, these weekly plans are recorded in small boxes in planbooks. Some teachers may have other detailed plans for themselves in addition to planbooks that they turn in. For some teachers, however, these planbooks constitute the extent of their written plans.

5. Teachers plan for substitute teachers. When a teacher is absent, a substitute must carry on classroom instruction according to the plans that the teacher has provided.

What Factors Affect Teachers' Plans?

Borko and Niles (1987) have identified four categories of factors that teachers take into account when they plan: (1) student characteristics, (2) instructional task characteristics, (3) instructional context characteristics, and (4) teacher characteristics.

Student Characteristics

Student ability level is especially critical in the middle grades when students are in transition from the concrete operational stage to the formal operational stage of cognitive development. Teachers have many sources available to them to assess the ability level of their students. Considering these various student abilities is probably the most influential factor in teacher planning.

Other student characteristics that play a role in teacher planning include student interest, motivation, prior knowledge, participation, behavior, and the ability to cooperate with others. Thus, a seventh-grade teacher may teach the same content to six classes during the day but may actually have six different plans, each based on the characteristics of the students in the class. For example, a class composed of students who are highly motivated and work well together may work in small groups for the entire period. On the other hand, a class composed primarily of hard-to-manage students may be engaged in a highly structured, teacher-directed lesson for the entire period.

Instructional Task Characteristics

The instructional task itself has several characteristics that can affect teachers' plans. According to Shavelson and Stern (1981), the instructional task is composed of the subject matter, the activities used to teach the subject matter, and the materials the teacher and students use. Thus, a teacher would probably plan a lesson on dividing fractions quite differently from a lesson on poetry. A teacher would also probably plan a science lesson on acids and bases in one way if litmus paper, test tubes, and a variety of chemicals were available and in quite a different way if no materials were available. Despite the variety of resources available, research shows that the textbook serves as the major source of content and ideas for activities for teachers and as the predominant material that students are exposed to during instruction.

Instructional Context Characteristics

The instructional context includes characteristics of the classroom as well as any characteristics of the school and the community that may affect teachers' plans. For example, a science lesson conducted in a well-equipped lab could be quite different from a science lesson conducted in a long, narrow, trailer. Similarly, a unit on values clarification or a discussion of Judy Blume's (1973) book *Deenie* might be encouraged in one community but frowned upon in another.

Teacher Characteristics

Each teacher brings to the classroom a different set of experiences, personality traits, beliefs about teaching, and ideas about students and how they learn. Each of these factors affects the types of plans that a teacher develops. For example, a teacher who has low tolerance for noise and movement in the classroom may plan lessons where students work primarily alone without much interaction with each other. On the other hand, a teacher who believes that students learn best by talking about their ideas with each other and the teacher may design lessons where students are involved in active discussions and cooperative groups.

As you can see, not only do the factors within each of these four categories affect teachers' plans but all four categories also interact with each other. It is because of this interaction that you can walk into five different classrooms and see five entirely different types of lessons in progress. It is this variation that makes schools and classrooms exciting places.

How Do Teachers' Plans Affect Instruction?

Research shows that teacher planning has a direct influence on what takes place in the classroom during instruction. Researchers such as Peterson, Marx, and Clark (1978), Carnahan (1980), and Brown (1988) have identified several ways that middle-grades teachers' plans affect instruction. First, teacher planning at the beginning of the school years helps to establish classroom routines. Routines enhance classroom management and help ensure a smooth flow from one activity to another. (The role of classroom routines is discussed in detail in Chapter 15.)

Second, teacher planning plays a significant role in the selection and sequence of topics to be taught. Using textbooks, state curriculum requirements, and state-mandated criterion-referenced tests, teachers make decisions about the topics they are going to teach and the order in which they will teach them. In the middle grades, these types of decisions can be made during team planning to capitalize on inter-disciplinary aspects of the content. Decisions about topic selection and sequence are usually made during a stage of planning referred to as *yearly planning,* which we discuss later in this chapter.

Next, teacher planning affects the amount of time spent on a particular topic. Teachers who have a thorough knowledge of their students' abilities, interests, and prior knowledge about a topic are in the best position to decide how much time to allocate to each topic. Ungraded pretests, administered before a particular unit is fully developed, are excellent measures for determining the students' prior knowledge about a topic. Results of such tests can be used to determine how much time to spend on various dimensions of the topic.

Fourth, teacher planning affects the ways in which teachers group their students for instruction. Depending on the topic and the purpose of the lesson, students can be grouped according to a variety of factors, such as ability, interest, interpersonal skills, work habits, and leadership qualities. Teachers who plan effectively take all of these factors into account when they group students.

Last, effective teacher planning affects the structure of classroom instruction and the flow from one activity to another, but not the exact verbal interactions between the teacher and the students and among the students themselves. Clark and Yinger (1987) point out, "Once interactive teaching begins, the teacher's plans move to the background and interactive decision making becomes more important" (p. 357).

Considering all the ways that teacher planning affects instruction, Borko and Niles (1987) ask an important question: "Is it possible to plan too much?" (p. 178). Their answer, based on research, is yes. It appears that teachers who plan too much, down to the last detail and question, have a tendency to be overly rigid and lack spontaneity. Their plans turn into scripts and they are almost afraid to deviate from them. As a result, such teachers tend to focus almost entirely on the content and neglect to consider the students and their needs.

How Do Teachers Plan?

There are several models of teacher planning and we will briefly describe three of them: the Tyler model, the Yinger model, and the Leinhardt model.

The Tyler Model

Tyler's (1950) *rational model* is linear in nature and focuses on behavioral objectives and daily lesson plans. According to this model, planning should occur in four steps carried out in a specific sequence. First, teachers should specify the objectives that they want their students to accomplish. For example, an objective in a unit on Africa might be for students to be able to compare and contrast the climate in South Africa with the climate in North Africa.

Second, teachers should select the activities that are most appropriate for teaching the objectives. Activities for our sample objective in the Africa unit might include having students watch a video or film on African climate or having students read the international weather report in the newspaper and record temperatures of a South Africa and North Africa city on a chart over a period of several weeks.

Third, teachers should organize and sequence the learning activities. Activities should be sequenced in such a way so as to lead students from the known to the unknown, building on any prior knowledge that the students might have about the content being taught. As such, activities should go from simple to complex and from concrete to abstract.

Fourth, teachers should select the evaluation procedures to be used to determine if students have accomplished the objective. In our Africa example, a teacher might evaluate the objective by having students write a short story in which they describe the types of clothing a student might wear as he or she travels from South Africa to North Africa. (Writing objectives, selecting the activities to teach the objectives, and evaluating objectives are all discussed in detail in the next chapter.)

The Yinger Model

Yinger's (1980) process model is cyclic in nature and looks at planning in terms of problem solving or decision making. According to this model, the planning cycle has three stages: problem finding, problem design, and problem implementation and evaluation. During the problem-finding stage, the teacher takes a very general planning problem and moves it toward a more specific planning problem. For example, a mathematics teacher may have a very general planning problem, such as

Teacher planning plays an important role in effective instruction.

"My students do not understand negative numbers." During the problem-finding stage, the teacher would translate this general problem into a more specific problem, such as "I need a better representation for negative numbers. I've been comparing negative numbers to a multistory building with floors above and below ground level. Maybe I should try another representation."

During the problem-design stage, the teacher refines and elaborates on the ideas generated during the previous stage. For example, using our negative number problem, the teacher may decide to use another representation for negative numbers, such as having versus owing money. Then, the teacher will plan the details of the activity and maybe actually rehearse it mentally in order to anticipate questions or problems that students might have.

At the last stage, problem implementation and evaluation, the teacher actually implements the activity with the students and makes a decision about how effective it is at solving the problem. If it is not effective, then the first two stages are repeated. If it is effective, the teacher can move on with instruction. If it is an activity that will be used frequently (e.g., a specific procedure for correcting homework), then it may become a routine. (We discuss classroom routines in detail in Chapter 15.)

The planning cycle suggested by the Yinger model is a continuous process in which ideas are constantly planned, implemented, evaluated, and revised. Thus, depending on the nature of the problem, the cycle could be completed in either a very short or very long period of time. Each cycle of the planning model affects the next cycle, almost to the point where planning and teaching become one.

The Leinhardt Model

Leinhardt's (1983) model of planning revolves around activity structures and routines. *Activity structures* are frameworks for the various segments or components of a lesson. For example, seatwork and discussion are activity structures because they serve as frameworks for parts of a lesson. *Routines* are scripts of expected teacher and student behaviors that support the activity structures. For example, in the activity structure of seatwork, a teacher may have an established routine for how the students should head their papers, record their answers, and turn in their papers, as well as a routine for how the papers are graded and returned.

Leinhardt's model adheres to the notion that because teachers (especially expert teachers) are so familiar with the various activity structures that they use and because they have taught their students the routines necessary to support the activity structures, teachers do not have to go into great detail describing and elaborating on activity structures and routines during planning. As such, the words *small-group work* written in a planbook may conjure up an elaborate mental picture for a teacher who uses this activity structure frequently. If students are familiar with the routine for small-group work, a teacher may only have to say, "Okay, you have the next 15 minutes for small-group work" in order to have students get in their groups, do the expected work, and be ready to proceed with the next activity in 15 minutes.

What Does the Research Say about Teacher Planning?

Now that we have described these three very different models of teacher planning, we will next discuss what the research says about how teachers actually plan. Despite the fact that many teacher-preparation programs focus on the Tyler model, research (e.g., Brown, 1988; McCutcheon, 1982; Yinger, 1980) suggests that most teachers, especially expert teachers, do not begin planning by identifying and stating objectives. On the whole, teachers begin by planning or selecting activities that will fit into the time slots that are available for the lesson. These activities are then refined to take into account the student, instructional task, instructional context, and teacher characteristics that we discussed in the beginning of this chapter.

Research by Clark and Elmore (1981) and McCutcheon (1980) indicates that the most frequently used source of ideas for activities is the teacher's guide, followed by the teacher's editions of student texts, and then the student texts themselves. Additional research (e.g., Peterson, Marx, & Clark, 1978) suggests that teachers spend the greatest percentage of their planning time on content—learning the content and deciding on the strategies and activities to teach it best. Teachers spend the smallest percentage of their planning time on objectives.

However, as Kauchak and Eggen (1989) point out, the findings about planning objectives may be misleading for several reasons. First, just because many teachers report that they do not begin the planning process by writing objectives does not imply that they do not think about objectives at some stage of their planning. Second, many of the textbooks and curriculum guides that teachers use already provide objectives. McCutcheon's (1982) research suggests that many teachers feel that it is pointless and a poor use of time for them to rewrite these objectives in their own planbooks. Third, teachers may not write objectives for each lesson because it is time consuming and, in some cases, difficult. To attend to content and all of the other factors that teachers attend to at the beginning of the planning process is cognitively demanding.

Does this mean that preservice teachers should not be taught how to write objectives? As Kauchak and Eggen (1989) point out, the answer is no. Most likely, at some time or another during the planning process, teachers think about and sometimes write down objectives. Just because they do not do it as the first step in the planning process, as the Tyler model suggests, does not mean that objectives are unimportant. (In the next chapter we talk more about the importance of objectives and how to write them and use them in the planning process.)

Obviously, no two teachers plan in exactly the same way. One important factor that seems to determine how teachers plan is experience: expert and novice teachers appear to plan differently. Research (e.g., Brown, 1988) suggests that the Tyler model is followed primarily by preservice and beginning teachers, whereas the Yinger and the Leinhardt models are followed primarily by expert teachers. This finding may be due to the fact that experienced teachers know the content better and have taught it more frequently than novice teachers and hence do not have to think about objectives at the beginning of the planning process. This finding may also be because many preservice teachers are taught to plan according to the Tyler model and, as a result, tend to use this model during their first year or two of teaching.

Team Planning in the Middle Grades

As we discussed in Chapter 1, team planning plays an important role in effective instruction in the middle grades. Planning in many middle-grades schools is centered around interdisciplinary teams of teachers. In fact, interdisciplinary teams of teachers are frequently cited as the "keystone for effective education in the middle school" (Mac Iver, 1990, p. 460). Such teams usually consist of a mathematics teacher, a language arts teacher, a science teacher, and a social studies teacher. In some schools, a reading teacher and a special education teacher may also be part of a team. These teachers plan together for a common group of students. Team members should share the same part of the school building as well as a common planning time. In addition to team planning time, some schools also provide additional planning time for team members to do their own individual planning.

Advantages of Interdisciplinary Teams

The concept of interdisciplinary teams in the middle grades has several advantages. First, all teachers have personal talents as well as individual strengths and weaknesses. From this aspect, teams are helpful because "within well-functioning groups, members can use their personal talents and the complimentary talents of others—a possibility that could give groups an advantage over solitary decision makers" (Lalik & Niles, 1990, p. 320). Through team planning, teachers can "regularly discuss teaching practices, observe others teach, and collaboratively design and evaluate instructional materials" (Lalik & Niles, p. 320).

Second, team planning can help teachers address the interdisciplinary nature of the content they teach. In the real world, there are very few instances of things or events that can readily be categorized as, for example, solely science or solely language arts. Much of what exists and happens in our world is an integration of many disciplines. Through team planning, teachers can more easily plan interdisciplinary units and lessons that allow students to see how the various disciplines overlap and influence each other.

Next, interdisciplinary teams benefit the students on the team because students, in a sense, "join a small community in which people—students and adults—get to know each other well to create a climate for intellectual development" (Carnegie Council on Adolescent Development, 1989, p. 37). In addition to creating a climate for intellectual development, effective teams can also create a climate for social, emotional, and physical development. All team members work with and get to know a common group of students. As a result, at least four teachers, who work and plan together, become aware of each student's strengths and weaknesses as well as any short- or long-term problems that may affect a student's performance. Four teachers working effectively together with students, especially students who have problems, can accomplish much more than any one individual teacher.

Fourth, team planning can enhance classroom management. Teams can plan common rules and routines that are consistently implemented and enforced by all team members. Such consistency increases the odds that students will do what is expected of them because the expectations will be the same from all of their teachers.

Last, teams can help to establish collegiality among teachers. Having a group of team members who lend support and encouragement enhances a teacher's sense of belonging. This is especially important for new teachers who, without a supporting team, can sometimes get the feeling that they are all alone.

Research on Interdisciplinary Teams

How prevalent is the concept of teams and team planning in schools for young adolescents across the nation? Recent surveys conducted by the *Center for Research on Elementary and Middle Schools* (CREMS) at Johns Hopkins University (1990) reveal that the answer to that question depends on the grade organization of the schools. Among schools that encompass grades 6–8, approximately 40 percent use interdisciplinary teams. Among schools with other grade organizations (e.g., K–8, K–12, and 7–12), only about 25 percent use interdisciplinary teams.

How often do the teachers on these teams actually plan together? Again, the answer depends on the grade organization of the schools. The CREMS (1990) survey reports that teams in 6–8 and 7–8 schools are more likely to be allotted at least two or more hours per week of common planning time than teams in schools with other grade organizations.

One of the most common complaints among interdisciplinary teams is that they do not have enough planning time (Mac Iver, 1990). Obtaining additional common planning time should be a high priority for interdisciplinary teams serving young adolescents. As one middle-grades schools proponent, Paul George, points out, "Teachers are skillful at interpersonal communication and will work diligently to get things done if they're given the extra time" (McKenna, 1989, p. 16).

Research indicates that organizing middle-grades schools around interdisciplinary teams has a number of advantages. In their study comparing middle-grades teachers on interdisciplinary teams with junior high school teachers using a departmental organization, Ashton and Webb (1986) found that the middle-grades teachers had a higher sense of efficacy, were more satisfied with teaching, and felt teaching was more important than their junior high counterparts.

Additionally, the middle-grades teachers felt that establishing personal relationships with their students and acting as role models were major components of their jobs. None of the junior high teachers expressed these views about their jobs. The researchers speculated that the team organization created a sense of community among the middle-grades teachers that was lacking in the junior high teachers.

Unfortunately, despite the research cited on the effectiveness of teams, there has been little research on *how* middle-grades teachers actually *plan* on interdisciplinary teams. Lalik and Niles (1990) investigated the collaborative planning of

Interdisciplinary teams create a sense of community among teachers.

a reading lesson by two groups of student teachers. The researchers found that both groups began their planning task in the same way: Each group had a leader and began by defining its task.

However, from there, the two groups proceeded differently. One group generated a list of possible activities and spent the remainder of its time selecting and sequencing the activities the group decided to use. The other group spent little time on activities but instead spent a great deal of time developing a test for the lesson. One group spent 45 minutes planning the lesson, whereas the other group spent over two hours. The results of this study indicate that, given the same task, teams of teachers plan different lessons and spend different amounts of time doing so. Additional research is clearly needed to determine how expert teachers on interdisciplinary teams actually plan.

Types of Planning in the Middle Grades

Research (e.g., Brown, 1988) conducted on how middle-grades teachers plan indicates that planning occurs in a *nested* fashion. That is, middle-grades teachers appear to plan in the following sequence: (1) yearly planning, (2) unit planning, (3) weekly planning, and (4) daily planning. When teachers plan, they rely "increasingly on plans set at the previous (and more general) level as they move from yearly and unit to more detailed and specific weekly and daily planning" (Brown, 1988, p. 74). Yinger's (1980) model is followed for yearly, unit, and weekly planning, whereas Leinhardt's (1983) model is followed for daily planning.

One type of planning that research suggests does not occur as frequently as was once thought is the objectives-first type of lesson planning proposed by the Tyler

(1950) model. For example, in a study conducted by Clark and Yinger (1979), only 7 percent of the teachers surveyed reported that lesson planning was important to them. However, as pointed out previously in this chapter, objectives do serve a purpose and play a role in planning. In the next chapter we will discuss objectives and lesson planning in detail. The remainder of this chapter will be devoted to yearly, unit, weekly, and daily planning in the middle-grades schools.

Yearly Planning

Yearly planning is long term in nature and involves organizing and scheduling the content to be taught during the entire year. Yearly planning is one of the most important types of planning that teachers engage in because it provides an overall framework for all of the content that will be taught during the year. Unfortunately, yearly planning is frequently overlooked by new or inexperienced teachers. Teachers who fail to do any type of yearly planning lack a sense of where they are going with their instruction. They tend to miss the overall picture and, as a result, fail to provide their students with any notion of how one topic relates to another throughout the year.

In a study of expert and novice teachers, Livingston and Borko (1989) found that the novice teachers "rarely linked related concepts, either within or across the curriculum" (p. 38). This may be as much a result of inexperience at planning as unfamiliarity with the content. Effective teachers, on the other hand, know where they are going not only "in the linear sense of one topic following another, but in the global sense of a network of big ideas and the relationships among these ideas" (Lampert, 1988, p. 163).

Purposes of Yearly Planning

Research (e.g., Brown, 1988) indicates that teachers usually engage in yearly planning for at least six reasons:

1. To become familiar with the content to be taught
2. To determine the sequence in which the content will be taught
3. To incorporate any changes in materials, textbooks, or content that may have been made since the last time they taught a particular topic
4. To develop a rough schedule of when various topics will be taught during the year
5. To make additions, deletions, and adaptations to the curriculum, taking into account their own particular circumstances and the needs of their students
6. To plan classroom routines

Materials and Factors that Influence Yearly Planning

Brown's (1988) research shows that middle-grades teachers use a variety of materials during yearly planning. For example, unit file folders were used by 92 percent of the middle-grades teachers in Brown's study. Unit file folders generally consist of "lecture notes, handouts, worksheets, audiovisual aids, quizzes, and tests used in previous years" (Brown, p. 77). Teachers usually keep a unit file folder for each unit that they teach during the year. As you can see, experienced teachers have a clear advantage over inexperienced teachers when it comes to yearly planning. In addition to unit file folders, teachers also use the textbook, the school calendar, the district curriculum guide, and the state competency objectives when they do their yearly planning.

Brown's (1988) research also shows that middle-grades teachers take various factors into account during yearly planning. Factors that appear to be quite influential include the previous year's successes and failures, the content in the district curriculum guide and in the textbook, the school calendar, student interest, and classroom management.

Sample Outline Developed during Yearly Planning

Let's take a look at how a seventh-grade science teacher, Mr. Hart, develops a sketchy outline during yearly planning. Suppose the textbook that Mr. Hart uses is *General Science: A Voyage of Discovery* (Prentice Hall, 1989). Gathering the textbook and other resources such as unit file folders, the state curriculum guide, the school calendar, and sample textbooks from several other publishing companies, Mr. Hart begins to plan for the upcoming year. The textbook covers the following topics in the order given:

A VOYAGE OF DISCOVERY

UNIT 1   ASTRONOMY

1   Exploring the Universe

2   Stars and Galaxies

3   The Solar System

4   Earth and Its Moons

UNIT 2   THE CHANGING EARTH

5   History of the Earth

6   Surface Changes on the Earth

7   Subsurface Changes on the Earth

UNIT 3   HUMAN BIOLOGY

8   Skeletal and Muscular Systems

9   Digestive System

10   Circulatory System

11   Respiratory and Excretory Systems

12   Nervous System

13   Endocrine System

14   Reproduction and Development

UNIT 4   HUMAN HEALTH

15   Nutrition and Health

16	Infectious Diseases
17	Chronic Disorders
18	Drugs, Alcohol, and Tobacco

UNIT 5	CHEMISTRY OF MATTER
19	Atoms and Bonding
20	The Periodic Table
21	Chemical Reactions

UNIT 6	MECHANICS
22	Force and Work
23	Motion and Gravity

Looking over the state curriculum guide, Mr. Hart notices that, as was the case last year, Unit 6 on Mechanics is not included in the seventh grade curriculum for the upcoming year. But Mr. Hart recalls that he taught it anyway last year in some of his classes because the students finished all of the other material before the end of the year. While going through his file folder on Mechanics, Mr. Hart also remembers that his students did not enjoy or do well on the chapter on force and work but they got very excited and interested in the chapter on motion and gravity.

Mr. Hart also finds a note in the file folder that he wrote to himself last year reminding him to think about teaching some of the concepts in the chapter on motion and gravity while he teaches the chapter on the solar system in the unit on astronomy. Therefore, he decides to eliminate the chapter on force and work, and move some of the concepts on motion and gravity to the chapter on the solar system.

After talking with the teachers who taught sixth-grade science last year, Mr. Hart also decides to move Unit 3 on Human Biology and Unit 4 on Human Health to the beginning of the year. The sixth-grade teachers told him that they ended the year with a chapter on mammals, which would serve as a nice introduction to the units on humans.

Finally, Mr. Hart decides to move Unit 1 on Astronomy to the end of the year. His students always enjoy the chapters covered in that particular unit. He finds that it is very hard to keep the students interested during the last few weeks of school, so he tries to schedule an exciting topic to conclude the school year.

Now, Mr. Hart's outline looks like this:

A VOYAGE OF DISCOVERY

UNIT 3	HUMAN BIOLOGY
8	Skeletal and Muscular Systems
9	Digestive System
10	Circulatory System
11	Respiratory and Excretory Systems

12	Nervous System
13	Endocrine System
14	Reproduction and Development

UNIT 4 HUMAN HEALTH

15	Nutrition and Health
16	Infectious Diseases
17	Chronic Disorders
18	Drugs, Alcohol, and Tobacco

UNIT 2 THE CHANGING EARTH

5	History of the Earth
6	Surface Changes on the Earth
7	Subsurface Changes on the Earth

UNIT 5 CHEMISTRY OF MATTER

19	Atoms and Bonding
20	The Periodic Table
21	Chemical Reactions

UNIT 1 ASTRONOMY

1	Exploring the Universe
2	Stars and Galaxies
23	Motion and Gravity
3	The Solar System
4	Earth and Its Moons

Keep in mind that in some middle-grades schools, especially schools that are departmentalized, all of the seventh-grade science teachers may plan together to decide on the sequence of topics for the upcoming year. If this were the case, Mr. Hart's outline could look quite different at this stage. On the other hand, if Mr. Hart were a member of an interdisciplinary team of seventh-grade teachers who planned together, the outline could also look different.

For example, Mr. Hart might schedule the unit on astronomy to be taught at the same time that the language arts teacher is teaching a unit on science fiction. Mr. Hart and the language arts teacher could then plan their units together so that each of them could reinforce facts and concepts that the other is teaching. Joint activities, readings, and field trips could be planned for the students.

Now that Mr. Hart has sequenced the topics for the coming year, he begins to work on a rough schedule of when each unit will be taught. His unit file folders and past experience provide him with a sense of how much time he should allocate for the various units and chapters. Mr. Hart also pays close attention to the school calendar for the coming year so he can plan around events such as vacations and several days in a row of testing. Now, Mr. Hart's outline looks like this:

A VOYAGE OF DISCOVERY

UNIT 3   HUMAN BIOLOGY

Sept., Oct., beginning of Nov.

- 8   Skeletal and Muscular Systems
- 9   Digestive System
- 10   Circulatory System
- 11   Respiratory and Excretory Systems
- 12   Nervous System
- 13   Endocrine System
- 14   Reproduction and Development

UNIT 4   HUMAN HEALTH

Nov. (minus Thanksgiving break)
Dec. (minus Christmas break)

- 15   Nutrition and Health
- 16   Infectious Diseases
- 17   Chronic Disorders
- 18   Drugs, Alcohol, and Tobacco

UNIT 2   THE CHANGING EARTH

Jan.

- 5   History of the Earth
- 6   Surface Changes on the Earth
- 7   Subsurface Changes on the Earth

UNIT 5   CHEMISTRY OF MATTER

Feb., March (minus spring break)

- 19   Atoms and Bonding
- 20   The Periodic Table
- 21   Chemical Reactions

UNIT 1   ASTRONOMY

April, May, early June

- 1   Exploring the Universe
- 2   Stars and Galaxies
- 23   Motion and Gravity
- 3   The Solar System
- 4   Earth and Its Moons

At this stage of yearly planning, Mr. Hart will also begin to think about activities and materials that should be planned in advance. For example, at the beginning of the school year, Mr. Hart's principal requires that teachers submit a list of field trips they have planned for the entire year so that funds can be allocated in advance. Mr. Hart always takes his students to the planetarium during the unit on astronomy, so he writes this on his outline. He is also aware of an excellent two-day program conducted by the city police department on drug and alcohol prevention. He makes a note of this program on his outline so that he remembers to call as soon as possible to schedule them to come to his classroom on two afternoons while he is teaching the chapter on drugs, alcohol, and tobacco. Notice some of the other activities that Mr. Hart has listed on his outline at this stage of yearly planning:

A VOYAGE OF DISCOVERY

UNIT 3 HUMAN BIOLOGY

Sept., Oct., beginning of Nov.

8   Skeletal and Muscular Systems – *movement experiments*
9   Digestive System
10   Circulatory System
11   Respiratory and Excretory Systems
12   Nervous System – *Video: "Functions of the Nervous System"*
13   Endocrine System
14   Reproduction and Development – *district sex ed. prog. (3 days, guest speaker)*

UNIT 4 HUMAN HEALTH

Nov. (minus Thanksgiving break)
Dec. (minus christmas break)

15   Nutrition and Health – *guest speaker, Dr. Jarrett, Adolescent Physician*
16   Infectious Diseases
17   Chronic Disorders
18   Drugs, Alcohol, and Tobacco – *police drug and alcohol program*

UNIT 2 THE CHANGING EARTH

Jan.

5   History of the Earth – *film: "History Layer by Layer"*
6   Surface Changes on the Earth
7   Subsurface Changes on the Earth

UNIT 5 CHEMISTRY OF MATTER

Feb, march (minus spring break)

19   Atoms and Bonding
20   The Periodic Table – *chemical formula bulletin board*
21   Chemical Reactions – *Mini-experiments on chemical changes*

UNIT 1 ASTRONOMY

April, May, June early

1   Exploring the Universe
2   Stars and Galaxies – *field trip to Planetarium*
23   Motion and Gravity
3   The Solar System
4   Earth and Its Moons – *video: "Eclipses of the Sun and Moon"*

At this point in yearly planning, Mr. Hart may even begin to plan some of the routines he wants his students to follow during the coming year. He will probably spend time during the first few days of school teaching these routines to his students. For example, Mr. Hart may have a specific routine for how he wants students to keep notes during their lab work, a specific routine for how students should distribute and collect materials that will be used during labs, and a specific routine for how students should complete and correct their homework. During yearly planning, Mr. Hart decides on the specific routines that his students need to know and plans how he will teach the routines to his students.

Notice that at the end of his yearly planning, Mr. Hart does not end up with a schedule of exactly what will happen on every day during the coming year. In fact, Mr. Hart has not yet planned many of the activities and procedures that he will use to teach the content. At this point, Mr. Hart only has a tentative framework for what will be taught and when it will be taught. More detailed planning occurs when he begins his unit planning.

Suggestions for Yearly Planning

Before we begin our discussion on unit planning, we propose several suggestions that will help you as you engage in yearly planning. Since Mr. Hart has taught seventh-grade science from this particular textbook before, he has several advantages over a first-year teacher. In addition to knowing the content and the ways that the textbook presents the material, he has several years of previous successes and failures to draw on. When you begin your first attempt at yearly planning, you will lack the experience that helps Mr. Hart, so Figure 7.2 provides you with some suggestions on how to get started.

Unit Planning

Unit planning involves developing a "series of interconnected lessons focusing on a general topic" (Kauchak & Eggen, 1989, p. 215). Unit planning, like yearly planning, is long term in the sense that it involves more than planning for just a day or two. Middle-grades teachers' unit plans generally include about two to three weeks' of lessons. Knowing exactly how to "chunk" the content into units takes experience and also depends on a thorough knowledge of the content to be taught and the prior knowledge the students have of the content. For example, Mr. Hart might decide to plan a three-week unit on chemistry, composed of lessons on atoms and bonding, the periodic table, and chemical reactions. Or he may decide to plan a short one-week unit on atoms and bonding and another two-week unit on the periodic table and chemical reactions.

Teachers usually begin planning their units several weeks before they intend to teach them. You can begin planning your first two or three units during the summer before school starts. Beginning unit planning early provides you with ample time to collect materials and resources and to schedule exact dates and times for field trips, guest speakers, and other events that must be planned ahead.

Brown's (1988) research tells us that middle-grades teachers' unit plans usually consist of lists or notes outlining the topics that will be covered in the unit as well as activities that will be used to teach the content. In some cases, accompanying textbook pages are also listed. Despite the fact that experienced teachers rarely write objectives during unit planning, Brown reports that the teachers in her study "thought about objectives and reviewed behavioral objectives stated in curriculum guides, texts, and competency lists. It appears that as teachers plan they seek connections between these objectives and their own repertoire of activities, materials, and evaluation procedures" (p. 79).

FIGURE 7.2 Suggestions for Yearly Planning

1. Spend time familiarizing yourself with the textbook and all other materials (e.g., workbooks, transparencies) that accompany it. We suggest that you sit down and read the entire textbook from beginning to end. Pay particular attention to the preface and introduction to the textbook. You will gain a sense of the philosophy of the authors and how the topics relate to one another and to the overall theme of the book. This will also give you a sense of how free you are to move chapters around to meet your own and your students' needs. Many times, especially in mathematics, the content in one chapter will draw heavily on the content in a previous chapter, so the sequence of chapters may not be as flexible as you would like.
2. In addition to familiarizing yourself with the textbook, it is equally important to become familiar with your state and/or district curriculum guide. Curriculum guides will provide you will a list of the content you are required to teach as well as some excellent ideas for activities and sample units for teaching the content.
3. Seek advice from experienced teachers, especially those teachers who worked with your particular students last year. These teachers can give you a good idea of the overall strengths and weaknesses of your students as well as some sense of the material that was covered in the previous year. Also plan to talk with those teachers who will be teaching the same subject(s) and grade level(s) as you. Preplanning time scheduled in the beginning of the school year is an excellent opportunity to meet with these teachers. Many principals schedule departmental and/or team meetings during preplanning time.
4. Begin your yearly planning as soon as possible. Many teachers begin at the end of the previous year by going through their unit file folders and organizing them for the coming year. If you are beginning your first year of the teaching, try to start your yearly planning during the summer by going through textbooks and curriculum guides and by contacting other teachers for suggestions.

Purposes of Unit Planning

Middle-grades teachers engage in unit planning for several reasons. First, teachers plan units so that they can organize and sequence a related body of material into daily lessons. If teachers were to plan only from one day to the next, the result would probably be a series of unrelated lessons, which would fail to give students a sense of how the facts and concepts taught are related. But by planning units, teachers are more able to convey the overall picture to their students by ensuring that each daily lesson builds on the previous lessons and leads into the next day's lesson.

Second, teachers engage in unit planning in order to decide on the activities they will use to teach the content. Experienced teachers have a wealth of successful activities at their fingertips. They know which activities work best for teaching the content and, during unit planning, they select those that are most appropriate for their students' particular needs.

Third, teachers engage in unit planning in order to gather or make the materials that are needed for the various activities throughout the unit. For example, a sixth-grade teacher who is planning a unit on mythology might begin to check out mythology books from the library and might also visit curriculum centers to gather other materials such as videos or films on mythological characters. Similarly, supplemental textbooks and workbooks contain alternative ideas and suggestions for activities that can be used during the unit.

Materials and Factors that Influence Unit Planning

As was the case with yearly planning, middle-grades teachers also use unit file folders, the textbook, the school calendar, the district curriculum guide, and the state competency objectives during unit planning (Brown, 1988). In addition, middle-grades teachers also use audiovisual aids and supplemental textbooks when planning units. Since teachers are planning and selecting activities during unit planning, audiovisual aids such as videos, films, filmstrips, and pictures play a large role at this stage of planning.

When middle-grades teachers plan units, they take into account many of the same factors that were important to them during yearly planning. For example, past experience, the textbook content, student interest, and the school calendar all affect teachers' unit plans. However, two factors that teachers do not appear to consider during yearly planning play a role in unit planning. First, the nature of the subject matter is taken into account at the unit-planning stage. In order to decide how to organize and sequence the content and then select activities and materials to teach the content, teachers must consider the nature of the subject matter.

Second, as teachers plan and select activities, the availability of materials is an important factor that they take into account when they are planning units. For example, a science teacher can quickly disregard a suggested activity if he or she knows that the required materials are unavailable.

Sample Unit Plan

Let's follow Ms. Janet Lewis, a former middle-grades teacher in Oglethorpe County, Georgia, as she plans a unit on insects for her sixth-grade science classes. Using a variety of materials such as the textbook, the district curriculum guide, and supplemental textbooks, Ms. Lewis decides to teach the following topics in the order given:

INSECTS

A. Classification
B. Characteristics
C. Structure
D. Survival Behaviors
E. Insect Control

Next, Ms. Lewis adds some detail to her outline by filling in the key facts and concepts that she wants her students to learn.

INSECTS

A. Classification
   1. history of classification system (C. Linneaus)

2. structure of classification system (kingdom, phylum, class, order, family, genus, species)

B. Characteristics
1. insects vs. other arthropods
2. types of mouth parts, types of legs, behaviors, wing shape, etc.

C. Structure
1. body parts
a. head (antennae, eyes, mouth parts)
b. thorax (segments, legs, wings, eardrum)
c. abdomen (anu, spiracles, egg-laying structure)
2. physiological functions of body parts (sensory, respiratory, locomotion, reproductive, feeding)

D. Survival Behaviors
1. metamorphosis (complete and incomplete)
2. symbiosis
3. weapons
4. mimicry
5. chemical defenses
6. migration

E. Insect Control
1. pesticides
2. predators, parasites, pathogens
3. pest-management programs

Next, Ms. Lewis decides on the materials and activities she will use to teach the various facts and concepts. In some instances, she may even list the teaching strategy that she will use. (We discuss teaching strategies in detail in Chapter 12.) Now her outline looks like this:

INSECTS

—small discussion groups
— classification chart activity

A. Classification
1. history of classification system (C. Linneaus)
2. Structure of classification system (kingdom, phylum, class, order, family, genus, species)

Circle the Insect" game —
"Observe an Insect"— activity (outdoors)

B. Characteristics
   1. insects vs. other arthropods
   2. types of mouth parts, types of legs, behaviors, wing shape, etc.

C. Structure

-group discussion (insect overheads)

-insect specimen observations in groups

   1. body parts
     a. head (antennae, eyes, mouth parts)
     b. thorax (segments, legs, wings, eardrum)
     c. abdomen (anu, spiracles, egg-laying structure)

-grasshopper coding activity

   2. physiological functions of body parts (sensory, respiratory, loco-motion, reproductive, feeding)

D. Survival Behaviors

-video:"Success Story: How Insects Survive"
-survival experiment

   1. metamorphosis (complete and in-complete)
   2. symbiosis
   3. weapons
   4. mimicry
   5. chemical defenses
   6. migration

→in depth Lesson
-insect specimens
- metamorphosis worksheet
-bee colony video: "Life of a Honeybee"

E. Insect Control

-"Fighting Pests with Pests" (Ranger Rick Magazine)
-"Natural Insect Control" activity

   1. pesticides
   2. predators, parasites, pathogens
   3. pest-management programs

At this point, Ms. Lewis may begin to make decisions about how much material she should cover each day. She may also plan her introduction to the unit and some type of closing or summary activity for the students to do at the end of the unit. Her final version of her outline looks like this:

INSECTS

Introduction

Day 1
- Videotape: "Insects—The Lovely and the Lethal"
- Small groups: "Connect the Insect Ideas" game
- discussion and explanation of classroom materials and projects (classroom display of insect books, preserved specimens, killing jar, group insect collection project for bulletin board, etc.)

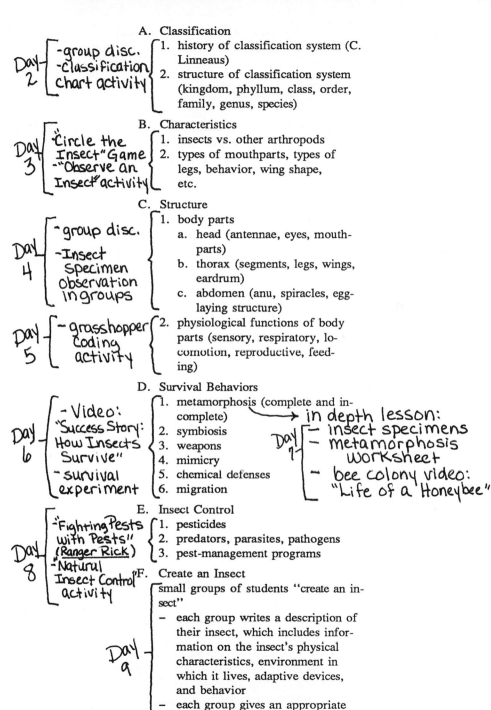

A. Classification

Day 2 — -group disc. -classification chart activity

1. history of classification system (C. Linneaus)
2. structure of classification system (kingdom, phyllum, class, order, family, genus, species)

B. Characteristics

Day 3 — "Circle the Insect" Game -"Observe an Insect" activity

1. insects vs. other arthropods
2. types of mouthparts, types of legs, behavior, wing shape, etc.

C. Structure

Day 4 — -group disc. -Insect Specimen Observation in groups

1. body parts
   a. head (antennae, eyes, mouthparts)
   b. thorax (segments, legs, wings, eardrum)
   c. abdomen (anu, spiracles, egg-laying structure)

Day 5 — -grasshopper Coding activity

2. physiological functions of body parts (sensory, respiratory, locomotion, reproductive, feeding)

D. Survival Behaviors

Day 6 — -Video: "Success Story: How Insects Survive" -survival experiment

1. metamorphosis (complete and incomplete)
2. symbiosis
3. weapons
4. mimicry
5. chemical defenses
6. migration

Day 7 — in depth lesson:
- insect specimens
- metamorphosis worksheet
- bee colony video: "Life of a Honeybee"

E. Insect Control

Day 8 — -"Fighting Pests with Pests" (Ranger Rick) -"Natural Insect Control" activity

1. pesticides
2. predators, parasites, pathogens
3. pest-management programs

F. Create an Insect

small groups of students "create an insect"

Day 9 —
- each group writes a description of their insect, which includes information on the insect's physical characteristics, environment in which it lives, adaptive devices, and behavior
- each group gives an appropriate name to their insect

Day 10 —
- each group draws a picture of their insect

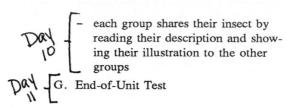

Day 10 { – each group shares their insect by reading their description and showing their illustration to the other groups

Day 11 { G. End-of-Unit Test

Ms. Lewis will probably make a list of all of the materials she will need for the unit and begin to collect them in one place in her room so they are ready on the first day of her unit. She may also construct an end-of-unit test or revise an old one. At this time, an experienced teacher like Ms. Lewis has just about finished her unit plan on insects. She has planned the content that she will teach, she has planned the sequence in which she will teach it, she has planned the activities she will use to teach it, and she is beginning to assemble the materials she will need throughout the unit.

However, at this point, an inexperienced teacher may not be finished with all of the details of the unit. An inexperienced teacher may not be able to look at the words *history of the classification system* or *symbiosis* and teach a lesson without any other preparation. For this reason, many new teachers will plan more details for each lesson in their unit. This type of planning is called *lesson planning* and we will discuss it in detail in the next chapter.

Sample Interdisciplinary Unit
Recall from Chapter 3 Beane's (1990) middle-grades curriculum that "focuses on the common needs, problems, interests, and concerns of young people and the society" (p. 35). One curriculum theme suggested by Beane is transitions, revolving around young adolescents' concerns about their own personal changes as well as society's concerns about a changing world. Figure 7.3 illustrates a list of topics that might be developed into an interdisciplinary unit by a team of teachers. Many of the topics listed under young adolescents' concerns are drawn from Vars (1987). What other possible topics can you add to the list?

Suggestions for Unit Planning
The process of planning units can be greatly enhanced, particularly if you are a novice teacher, by implementing the following suggestions when appropriate:

1. Before you develop a unit, administer a short pretest on the topic of the unit to your students. A pretest gives you an idea of what the students already know about the topic. You can use the results of the pretest to help you develop the unit. For example, you may find that all of your students already know something that you were planning to spend two days on, so you can adjust your plans accordingly. A pretest does not count in the students' grades for the course.

2. Skim textbooks other than the one your particular school is using. Such textbooks contain a wealth of suggestions on alternative ways of teaching the content as well as various activities that you can use in your classroom. You can frequently borrow textbooks from your school or district resource center or from a curriculum library at a nearby college or university.

FIGURE 7.3 Topics for an Interdisciplinary Unit on Transitions

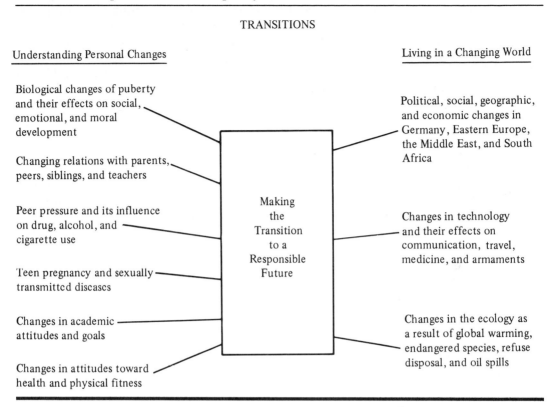

TRANSITIONS

Understanding Personal Changes

Living in a Changing World

Biological changes of puberty and their effects on social, emotional, and moral development

Changing relations with parents, peers, siblings, and teachers

Peer pressure and its influence on drug, alcohol, and cigarette use

Teen pregnancy and sexually transmitted diseases

Changes in academic attitudes and goals

Changes in attitudes toward health and physical fitness

Making the Transition to a Responsible Future

Political, social, geographic, and economic changes in Germany, Eastern Europe, the Middle East, and South Africa

Changes in technology and their effects on communication, travel, medicine, and armaments

Changes in the ecology as a result of global warming, endangered species, refuse disposal, and oil spills

3. Visit your school or district library and curriculum center for resources before you develop your plans. You may find videos, films, filmstrips, books, and other materials that you can plan lessons around.

Weekly Planning

For most middle-grades teachers, weekly planning is a finetuning of their unit plans. Teachers usually engage in weekly planning at the end of the previous week or during the weekend for the coming week. Middle-grades teachers' weekly plans are generally written in planbooks and consist of a list of activities to be done on each day of the week. Frequently, textbook page numbers and student assignments are also included (Brown, 1988).

Purposes of Weekly Planning

Teachers engage in weekly planning for several reasons. First, weekly plans help teachers make adjustments in their unit plans to coincide with the school schedule for the week.

Second, teachers engage in weekly planning in order to plan the final details of their unit plans. For example, Ms. Lewis may have planned her unit on insects three weeks before she actually planned to teach it. Now, during the weekend before she plans to start the unit, she can look over the unit, make sure all of the materials are ready, and plan all of the fine details for the various activities.

Third, teachers engage in weekly planning because, in many cases, they are required to do so by their principal or supervisor. In many schools, teachers are required to turn in (sometimes a week ahead) weekly plans. These plans are used for a variety of purposes such as providing for substitute teachers.

Materials and Factors that Influence Weekly Planning

When teachers prepare their weekly plans, they use all of the materials that they used during unit planning, such as the textbook, unit file folders, and the school calendar. In addition, they use the actual unit plan itself.

During weekly planning, teachers are influenced by many of the same factors that influenced them during unit planning. For example, availability of materials, textbook content, and classroom management are still important to teachers during weekly planning. In addition, the students' performance during the previous week plays a role in weekly planning (Brown, 1988). For example, if students do not understand the material that was taught the previous week, a teacher will most likely revise his or her plans for the coming week. Keep in mind that a unit does not always have to start on a Monday. In fact, many teachers end a unit on Friday so the students can study over the weekend and take the unit test on Monday. Then, depending on the school schedule, the teacher may start a new unit on Tuesday.

Sample Weekly Plan

Let's take a look at Ms. Lewis's planbook for the week she is beginning her unit on insects, as shown in Figure 7.4.

Suggestions for Weekly Planning

Weekly plans are important because they help teachers bridge the gap between unit plans and daily plans. Following these suggestions during your weekly planning will make your lessons go more smoothly.

1. At the end of the week, before you start on your plans for the next week, go back over the previous week's plans and note any changes you would make if you were to teach that week's lessons again. Many teachers put each week's plans into their unit file folders for the next year. Writing changes and suggestions while they are fresh in your mind will be a great help next year when you begin to plan again.

2. As you implement your weekly plans in the classroom, make daily notes to yourself regarding aspects of the next week's plan that you may want to adjust. For example, Ms. Lewis may plan for her students to collect insect samples twice during the unit, once during the first week and again during the second week. Suppose the procedure she has her students use does not work very well the first time and she makes some changes in it. She will probably also make a note on next week's plans

FIGURE 7.4   Ms. Lewis's Planbook for the Week of October 14–18

Week of: <u>October 14–18</u>

MONDAY	TUESDAY	WEDNESDAY	THURSDAY	FRIDAY
<u>Characteristics Of Insects</u>	<u>Structure Of Insects</u>	<u>Functions of Insect Body Parts</u>	<u>Survival Behavior</u>	<u>Metamorphosis</u>
-Introduction to various characteristics -"Circle the Insect" game -"Observe an Insect" activity (outdoors)	-small-group observations of specimens - groups' reports	- discuss textbook examples & illustrations pp. 235–239 - grasshopper coding activity	-Video: "Sucess Story..." - discussion and examples of 6 behaviors	- examine specimens -metamorphosis worksheet - Video: "Life of a Honeybee"
<u>Homework:</u> bring in 3 specimens	<u>Homework:</u> specimen completion chart	<u>Homework:</u> diagram labeling activity	<u>Homework:</u> insect behavior list	

Source: Adapted with permission from Janet Lewis.

reminding herself about the changes so her students do better the second time they collect insect samples.

Daily Planning

Regardless of how well you have done your yearly, unit, and weekly plans, it is your daily plans that really affect how well your lesson will go. The fine details that you plan on a daily basis determine whether your lesson will be a success or a disaster. Recall from the beginning of this chapter that daily plans of experienced teachers usually follow Leinhardt's (1983) model in which teachers plan around familiar activities and routines. For example, an experienced teacher may need to write no more than "Seatwork, pp. 213–214" on his or her daily plan, but a novice teacher may need to write out explicit step-by-step-directions in order to carry out that part of a lesson.

Accordingly, the daily plans of experienced teachers usually resemble weekly plans with notes and changes marked on them. Sometimes, rather than writing on their weekly plans, teachers' daily plans will consist of a sheet of paper listing activities, page numbers, and students' assignments. Teachers frequently make adjustments in the daily plans right up to the point when their students enter the classroom.

Purposes of Daily Planning

Middle-grades teachers engage in daily planning for at least four reasons (Brown, 1988). First, daily plans help teachers make decisions about how to incorporate the previous day's lesson into the new lesson. Beginning a lesson by referring to aspects of a previous lesson helps students tie together the material and see how the lessons are related.

Second, daily planning enables teachers to get materials ready and to set up the classroom for the next lesson. For example, a teacher who is planning to teach circumference may get out 24 protractors from the supply closet the night before the lesson.

Third, daily planning allows teachers time to plan the exact procedures and details of the coming lesson. For example, at the end of her unit on insects, Ms. Lewis has planned a group activity in which the students create their own insect. The night before, Ms. Lewis will probably sit down and sketch out exactly how she will explain the activity to the students. She may also decide on which students are going to be in each group. Some teachers may plan group memberships during unit or weekly planning. Other teachers may wait until the night before the activity and determine group membership according to how the students worked throughout the other lessons of the unit.

Fourth, teachers engage in daily planning in order to assign homework. Teachers generally plan tentative homework assignments during weekly planning, but these assignments frequently have to be adjusted based on the results of the previous lesson.

Materials and Factors that Influence Daily Planning

Middle-grades teachers use their unit plans, their weekly plans, the textbook, and audiovisual aids to plan their daily lessons. They also use their students' homework assignments for the previous day's lesson to adjust their daily plans. Student performance on homework assignments provides teachers with excellent information about how well their students understood the material in the previous day's lesson. Teachers can use this information to decide whether to spend additional time reviewing the material or whether to proceed with new material.

In addition to the factors that affected weekly planning, two other factors also affect the daily plans of middle-grades teachers (Brown, 1988). First, daily plans are affected by student interest in the previous lesson. For example, if, at the end of the day, Ms. Lewis is aware that her students had no interest at all in the lesson, and she had planned to build on it the next day, she would most likely make some sort of adjustment in the next day's plans.

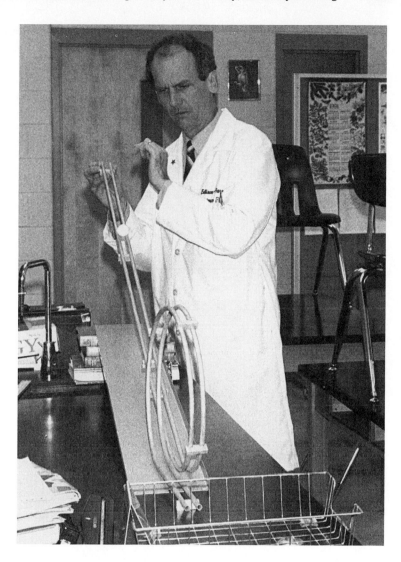

Part of daily planning involves getting materials ready for the next day's lesson.

Second, middle-grades teachers report that the disposition of their students as they enter the classroom can affect the plans for the coming lesson. For example, students who enter a classroom upset about a fight in the hallway or hot and tired from a strenuous game during P.E. may be unable to carry out the particular lesson planned. Experienced teachers will immediately recognize the situation and adjust their plans accordingly.

Sample Daily Plan

Depending on how the lesson on Tuesday, October 15, went (Figure 7.4), Ms. Lewis's plan for Wednesday, October 16, may look like that shown in Figure 7.5.

FIGURE 7.5   Notes Ms. Lewis Wrote in Her Planbook for Wednesday's Lesson

WEDNESDAY

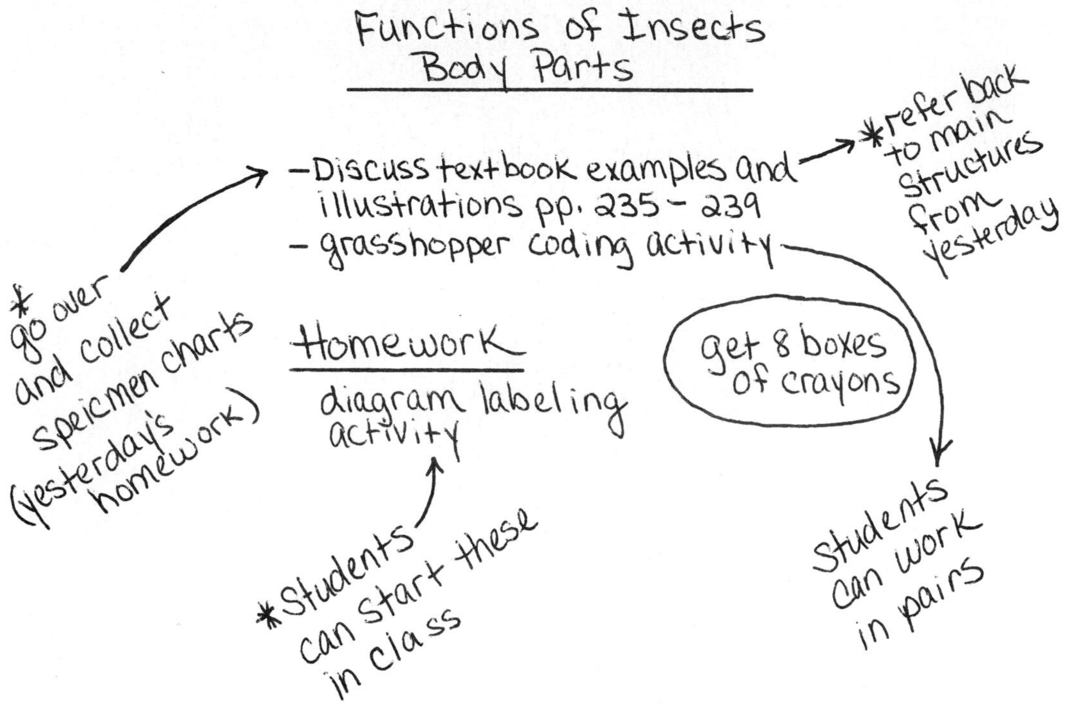

Functions of Insects
Body Parts

—Discuss textbook examples and
illustrations pp. 235 – 239
— grasshopper coding activity

*refer back to main structures from yesterday

*go over and collect speicmen charts (yesterday's homework)

Homework
diagram labeling activity

get 8 boxes of crayons

*Students can start these in class

Students can work in pairs

Source: Adapted with permission from Janet Lewis.

Suggestions for Daily Planning

As a beginning teacher, there are several things you can do to make daily planning more effective:

1. Keep all notes and daily plans and include them in your unit file folders for the next year. Regardless of whether or not you actually teach each lesson that you plan, keep the plans for the next year. They will be an excellent source of ideas for you as you plan new units each year.
2. Seek help from other teachers and team members when a plan does not go as expected. Experienced teachers are particularly adept at salvaging a failed lesson and turning it into a learning experience for themselves and their students.
3. Whenever possible, have backup plans for emergency situations. A guest speaker who fails to show up or an outdoor activity canceled because of rain can leave an unprepared teacher with nothing to do. Experienced teachers have a wealth of alternative plans to fall back on in situations like these.

Summary

Planning is a critical component of effective classroom instruction. Middle-grades teachers plan for a variety of reasons and their plans affect their actions in the classroom. Research indicates that experts and novices plan in different ways but, on the whole, most teachers engage in yearly, unit, weekly, and daily planning. Planning is not a guarantee that a lesson will go perfectly, but teachers who plan appropriately increase the odds that they will be successful in the classroom.

REFERENCES

Ashton, P. T., & Webb, R. V. (1986). *Making a difference: Teachers' sense of efficacy and student achievement.* New York: Longman.

Beane, J. A. (1990). *A middle school curriculum: from rhetoric to reality.* Columbus, OH: National Middle School Association.

Blume, J. (1973). *Deenie.* Scarsdale, NY: Bradbury Press.

Borko, H., & Niles, J. A. (1987). Descriptions of teacher planning: Ideas for teachers and researchers. In V. Richardson-Koehler (Ed.), *Educators' handbook: A research perspective* (pp. 167–187). New York: Longman.

Brown, D. S. (1988). Twelve middle-school teachers' planning. *The Elementary School Journal, 89,* 69–87.

Carnahan, R. S. (1980). *The effects of teacher planning on classroom processes.* (Technical Report No. 541). Madison: Wisconsin Research and Development Center for Individualized Schooling.

Carnegie Council on Adolescent Development. (1989). *Turning points: Preparing American youth for the 21st century.* Washington, DC: Carnegie Council on Adolescent Development.

Center for Research on Elementary and Middle Schools. (1990, March). *Implementation and effects of middle grades practices.* Baltimore: The Johns Hopkins University.

Clark, C. M., & Elmore, J. L. (1981). *Transforming curriculum in mathematics, science, and writing: A case study of teacher yearly planning.* (Research Series No. 99). East Lansing: Michigan State University, Institute for Research on Teaching.

Clark, C. M., & Yinger, R. J. (1979). *Three studies of teacher planning.* (Research Series No. 55). East Lansing: Michigan State University, Institute for Research on Teaching.

Clark, C. M., & Yinger, R. J. (1987). Teacher planning. In D. C. Berliner & B. V. Rosenshine (Eds.), *Talks to teachers* (pp. 342–365). New York: Random House.

Kauchak, D. P., & Eggen, P. D. (1989). *Learning and teaching.* Boston: Allyn and Bacon.

Lalik, R. V., & Niles, J. A. (1990). Collaborative planning by two groups of student teachers. *The Elementary School Journal, 90,* 319–336.

Lampert, M. (1988). What can research on teacher education tell us about improving quality in mathematics education? *Teaching and Teacher Education, 4,* 157–170.

Leinhardt, G. (1983, April). *Routines in expert math teachers' thoughts and actions.* Paper presented at the annual meeting of the American Educational Research Association, Montreal.

Livingston, C., & Borko, H. (1989). Expert-novice differences in teaching: A cognitive analysis and implications for teacher education. *Journal of Teacher Education, 40*(4), 36–42.

Mac Iver, D. J. (1990). Meeting the needs of young adolescents: Advisory groups, interdisciplinary teaching teams, and school transition programs. *Phi Delta Kappan, 71*(6), 458–464.

McCutcheon, G. (1980). How do elementary school teachers plan? The nature of planning and influences on it. *The Elementary School Journal, 81,* 4–23.

McCutcheon, G. (1982). How do elementary

school teachers plan? The nature of planning and influences on it. In W. Doyle & T. Good (Eds.), *Focus on teaching* (pp. 260–279). Chicago: University of Chicago Press.

McKenna, B. (1989). Whatever happened to team teaching? *American Educator, 13*(2), 15–19.

Peterson, P. L., Marx, R. W., & Clark, C. M. (1978). Teacher planning, teacher behavior, and student achievement. *American Educational Research Journal, 15,* 417–432.

Shavelson, R. J., & Stern, P. (1981). Research on teachers' pedagogical thoughts, judgments, decisions, and behavior. *Review of Educational Research, 51,* 455–498.

Tyler, R. W. (1950). *Basic principles of curriculum and instruction.* Chicago: University of Chicago Press.

Vars, G. F. (1987). *Interdisciplinary teaching in the middle grades.* Columbus, OH: National Middle School Association.

Yinger, R. J. (1980). A study of teacher planning. *The Elementary School Journal, 80,* 107–127.

_8_

Instructional Planning: Lesson Planning

After reading the previous chapter, you probably have a pretty good idea of the types of activities teachers perform when they engage in yearly, unit, weekly, and daily planning. But the one type of planning that we have not discussed yet is lesson planning. That is, how do teachers actually plan a lesson? For example, how does Mr. Pomante go about planning a 48-minute lesson on haiku as part of a unit on poetry? Or how does Ms. Canton decide how to structure a 55-minute lesson designed to introduce her students to the concept of circumference?

Our goal in this chapter is to provide you with the background you will need to construct effective lessons. The remainder of this chapter is divided into three sections. In the first section, we describe the characteristics of a lesson. Next, we identify the components of an effective lesson and provide an example of each component. In the third section, we present the basic format for a lesson plan, along with sample lesson plans from various content areas.

Characteristics of a Lesson

Research conducted by Weade and Evertson (1988) in seventh-, eighth-, and ninth-grade classrooms provides us with an excellent description of the characteristics of a lesson. Through a variety of methods, including classroom observation, Weade and Evertson found that most lessons are composed of a series of activities. Recall from the previous chapter that Leinhardt's (1983) model of planning revolved around activities and the routines that support them. Tests, discussions, seatwork, small-group work, and whole-class presentations are examples of activities that can comprise a lesson. The time between activities is usually referred to as a *transition*. As you probably guessed, activities and transitions that are well planned and carried out enhance classroom management. (In Chapter 15, we discuss the management aspect of activities and transitions in detail.)

As the teacher moves from one activity to another, the social and academic task demands placed on the students change (Doyle, 1986; Erickson, 1982, 1986; Green & Weade, 1987). Examples of **social task demands** include knowing when you are allowed to talk and whether or not you have to raise your hand. For example, students may be permitted to talk when working in small groups but may be required to do individual seatwork in silence. Examples of **academic task demands** include knowing what you will be expected to have learned at the end of a lesson and knowing what product, if any, you are expected to turn in at the end of a lesson. For example, students may be expected to have their own individual detailed notes at the end of a lecture but may be expected to have only one project per group at the end of small group work.

In Weade and Evertson's (1988) research, the less effective teachers had more transitions throughout their lessons than the more effective teachers. As a result, students in the less effective classrooms were required to reassess the social and academic task demands of the lessons more often than the students in the more effective classrooms. In addition, the less effective teachers tended to change social task demands more often than they changed activities. Effective teachers, on the other hand, made changes in social task demands during the transition from one activity to another.

In order to increase the likelihood of a lesson being successful, Weade and Evertson (1988) recommend that you identify the social and academic task demands for all of the activities that comprise the lesson. You should then make sure that you and your students are prepared for these demands. Figure 8.1 lists some questions that will help you identify the social and academic task demands of the activities in your lessons.

FIGURE 8.1 Identifying Social and Academic Demands

For *each activity or event (e.g., reviewing a quiz, introducing new content, giving oral reports, doing problems at the board) that will take place in the lesson:*

1. What is the *social task demand,* for example, who can talk to whom, about what, where, when, in what ways and for what purpose?
   - How will groups (whole group, pairs, task-related groups) be organized?
   - Will a turn-taking system be needed? If so, how will it be organized (by the structure of the materials, by student initiative, by teacher designation of responder)?
   - What materials (papers, workbooks, textbooks, writing implements) will be needed, and what will be necessary for students to assemble these?
   - What prior experiences do teacher and students share in doing the social task (e.g., the way we did this the last time)? To what extent was it successful the last time? What adjustments may be needed?
2. What is the *academic task demand,* for example, what must be known, understood, and produced to reach the instructional objective?
   - What prior knowledge will students need and use in accomplishing the task?
   - What are the sources of knowledge students will need to accomplish the task (e.g., concepts taught yesterday, "rules" given in the workbook)?
   - What is the new knowledge students will be acquiring?
   - What reasoning is required for students to accomplish the task?
   - How can strategies be made available to help students accomplish the task?
   - How will students demonstrate accomplishment of the task?
   - How can relationships between reasoning and task accomplishment be made visible?
   - How will errors in understanding be recognized and corrected?
3. What is the match between the social task demand and the academic task demand of *each* planned event? Will the social expectations facilitate and support academic participation?

Source: Reprinted with permission from *Teaching and Teacher Education, 4,* R. Weade and C. M. Evertson, "The Construction of Lessons in Effective and Less Effective Classrooms," Copyright 1988, Pergamon Press plc. Used with permission of the author.

Components of an Effective Lesson

There are three important components of an effective lesson: the introduction, the presentation, and the closing. We will not go into too much detail here because the specifics of these three components will be presented in depth in Chapters 11 and 12. However, it is essential that you keep in mind the general characteristics of these three components of effective lessons as you read the next section on lesson planning.

The Introduction

Every good lesson has an introduction that sets the tone for the rest of the lesson. The introduction is often called *set induction* or *anticipatory set.* Regardless of what it is called, effective teachers achieve two purposes in their introduction. First, they capture the attention, interest, and curiosity of their students. In short, they increase students' motivation to learn. Imagine how interested your students would be if you began a lesson by saying, "Open your books to page 251 and begin reading silently." Certainly, it is difficult to plan an exciting introduction for every single lesson, but it should be a goal of yours to do so. Stimulating introductions are especially important at the beginning of units since these introductions will set the tone for a series of lessons.

Second, effective teachers provide an introductory overview of the lesson for their students. This overview serves as a framework to help students understand what they will be doing during the lesson, how the lesson is related to previous lessons, and how the lesson fits into the larger picture. A brief review of the previous day's lesson is frequently incorporated into the introductions of effective teachers. Effective teachers also communicate their goals, objectives, and expectations to their students during their introductions. As Berliner (1987) points out, "Telling students in advance what they are going to learn, what the key points to be mastered are, and what they should know at the end of an instructional episode has been positively related to student achievement" (p. 260).

The Presentation

During the actual lesson presentation, effective teachers usually do at least seven things.

1. They maintain the attention and interest of their students during the entire lesson.
2. They conduct the lesson at a brisk pace.
3. They make effective and frequent use of established routines.
4. They provide their students with opportunities to learn new information or practice new skills.
5. They monitor the progress of their students through informal and formal assessment procedures.
6. They provide their students with appropriate feedback about their performance and progress.
7. They maintain a pleasant, relaxed yet task-oriented atmosphere in their classrooms.

Since all seven of these characteristics of effective lesson presentations are discussed in detail elsewhere in the book, we will not elaborate on them here. But keep them in mind during the rest of this chapter as you read about lesson planning.

The Closing

Effective teachers close their lesson appropriately. You probably remember classes in which the teacher was always in the middle of a sentence when the bell rang. You gathered your things, turned in assignments, scribbled down your homework, ran out the door, and never really got a sense of what the lesson was all about. And, to make matters worse, you were frequently late for your next class! Effective teachers time their lessons carefully so they have a few minutes at the end for the closing. Think of an effective closing as one that occurs in two phases: a content closing and a procedural closing.

The *content closing* of a lesson can be brief and to the point so long as it achieves its purpose. It should provide a summary of the main points of the lesson. It should also help students identify the relationships among past, present, and future lessons. In essence, a good content closing helps students pull the lesson together.

The *procedural closing* of a lesson ensures that students are ready to move on to the next subject or class at the appropriate time. For example, it provides students with ample time to copy down homework assignments, turn papers in, get desks back in place, put equipment and supplies in their appropriate place, and be ready to leave on schedule. In many middle-grades schools, students have very little time to get to their next class and they should not have to use several minutes of that time on procedural tasks that could be done in the last minute or two of class.

Lesson Planning

Now that you know what a lesson is and some of the important components of an effective lesson, let's talk about how to plan a lesson. The words *lesson planning* usually conjure up a variety of images among teachers. Some teachers picture themselves filling in small boxes in planbooks, others visualize themselves jotting notes and outlines on sheets of paper. Regardless of the format, lesson plans usually focus on "specific instructional sessions" (Kauchak & Eggen, 1989, p. 220). In middle-grades schools, the instructional session is usually one class period. For example, Ms. Sweeney may write a specific lesson plan for her 50-minute, third-period language arts class. Or Mr. White may write a lesson plan for his 45-minute, eighth-period mathematics class.

In some schools, writing lesson plans is optional; in other schools, teachers are required to write and turn in their lesson plans weekly. In the last chapter, we showed you some sample weekly plans. On the whole, these weekly plans merely listed activities that would occur during the lesson each day. As we mentioned in the last chapter, some teachers, especially experienced teachers, are able to teach from these sketchy weekly plans because they are familiar with the content and, over the years, have developed sophisticated activities and routines to teach the content.

Research by McCutcheon (1980) and Morine-Dershimer (1979) indicates that lesson planning for experienced teachers is usually a mental activity. That is, instead of writing down their plans, experienced teachers create mental pictures of lesson plans that usually guide their classroom instruction. However, novice teachers and experienced teachers who are teaching new content for the first time tend to engage in more detailed lesson planning.

In fact, Sardo (1982) found that it is the least experienced teachers who plan according to the detailed Tyler (1950) objectives-first model. It may be that inexperienced teachers follow this model initially because it is the way they were trained and it suits their purposes for the first few years of teaching. However, as they gain experience, become more familiar with the content, and build a repertoire of activities and routines, their planning becomes more of a mental activity. Even though experienced teachers tend not to engage in detailed lesson planning, many of them report that this type of planning served as an important foundation for them as beginning teachers (Clark & Peterson, 1986).

In the remainder of this section, we will take you through the process of writing a lesson plan. There are a variety of lesson plan formats, but most include the following components: instructional objectives, procedures, materials, and evaluation.

Instructional Objectives

Ever since instructional objectives, sometimes referred to as *behavioral objectives*, became popular in the 1960s, their use has been controversial.

Advantages of Instructional Objectives

Perhaps the most compelling argument for the use of instructional objectives is that they can guide the instructional process and lead to more effective lessons. In order to teach effectively, proponents of objectives argue, teachers have to know what the outcome of their teaching should be and whether or not their students have achieved that outcome. For example, Cooley and Leinhardt (1980) found that the degree to which students were successful on mathematics and reading tests was related to whether or not the skills that were tested were actually taught. This result reflects the notion that effective teachers have clear goals and objectives in mind when they teach.

In addition, teachers can use instructional objectives to communicate the purposes of their lessons to their students. Instructional objectives can also be used by teachers to explain what is going on in their classrooms to parents, administrators, and the general public.

Disadvantages of Instructional Objectives

Some critics of instructional objectives argue that they do not really affect learning, and there is some research evidence to support this notion (e.g., Duchastel & Merrill, 1973). However, such research is limited in that very little, if any, of it has been conducted with students in the middle grades or elementary grades.

Some critics of instructional objectives believe that many important goals cannot be measured. Hence, the use of objectives often limits teachers to trivial outcomes. Critics also argue that because objectives focus on small, specific behaviors, teachers must write a great many of them in order to convey adequately the intended outcomes of their lessons. An additional criticism of objectives is that they can lead to a lack of spontaneity in teaching. If teachers are concerned with covering all the objectives they planned for a certain lesson, they are less likely to deviate from their plans when serendipitous, but important, events occur in the classroom.

Despite the criticisms of instructional objectives, many educators agree that they do have value if used in moderation. Teachers who use the[...] not allow them to limit their instruction or dictate the curricul[...]

There are a variety of approaches to writing instructional [...] eral, however, most approaches focus on learner outcomes. Th[...] student be expected to do as a result of your instruction? Two p[...] to writing objective are those of Mager (1962) and Gronlund (197[...]. As a preservice or a beginning teacher, you may be required to write objectives according to one of these two approaches. If not, you should use the approach that works best for you.

Mager's Approach

Building on the Tyler model, Mager's (1962) approach to writing instructional objectives focuses on very specific student behaviors and on how the student will demonstrate those behaviors. Mager's objectives have three components:

1. Performance (what the learner is to be able to do)
2. Conditions (important conditions under which the performance is expected to occur)
3. Criterion (the quality or level of performance that will be considered acceptable) (Mager, 1962, p. 23)

Consider the following objective:

Given a list of 20 words, the student will list a synonym for 18 of the 20 words.

The performance is "will list"; the condition is "given a list of 20 words"; the criterion is "18 of the 20 words." The intent of this objective is to determine if the student can supply synonyms for certain words. The performance, in this case, "will list," must be written in measurable terms. Thus, verbs such as *will understand, will appreciate,* and *will learn* are not appropriate performances.

Consider a slightly different objective:

Given a thesaurus and a list of 20 words, the student will list a synonym for 18 of the 20 words.

In this objective, the performance and the criterion are the same as in the previous objective but the condition is "given a thesaurus and a list of 20 words." The intent of this objective is to determine if the student can use a thesaurus.

Gronlund's Approach

Gronlund's (1978) approach differs from Mager's (1962) approach in that Gronlund first states a general objective, which is then followed by some specific objectives that might accompany the general objective. In addition, Gronlund's objectives do not include a criterion or condition. Using our two previous sample objectives, Gronlund's objectives might read as follows:

General Objective:	understands the concept of synonyms
Specific Objectives:	defines synonym
	chooses synonyms
	supplies synonyms

General Objective:	knows how to use a thesaurus
Specific Objectives:	defines thesaurus
	identifies a thesaurus
	locates synonyms in a thesaurus

As you can see, objectives can range from very general to very specific. Figure 8.2 illustrates just how specific you can be when you write objectives.

The sample objectives in Figure 8.2 focus primarily on the cognitive development of students. However, recall from Chapter 2, our discussion of the cognitive, social, emotional, and physical changes that young adolescents are going through. Accordingly, it is important for middle-grades teachers to plan lessons that focus not only on students' cognitive development but also on their affective and psychomotor development. Instructional objectives can be written for each of these three domains.

Cognitive Objectives

Objectives in the cognitive domain "deal with the recall or recognition of learned material and the development of intellectual abilities and skills" (Hopkins, Stanley, & Hopkins, 1990, p. 170). Bloom, Engelhart, Furst, Hill, and Krathwohl (1956) developed a six-level taxonomy for classifying objectives in the cognitive domain: knowledge, comprehension, application, analysis, synthesis, and evaluation. Presumably, the taxonomy is hierarchical because the cognitive demands placed on a student increase from one level to the next. That is, the levels of the hierarchy move from simple to complex and from concrete to abstract.

Woolfolk (1990) provides an excellent description of the six levels of the taxonomy:

1. *Knowledge:* Remembering or recognizing something previously encountered without necessarily understanding, using, or changing it.
2. *Comprehension:* Understanding the material being communicated without necessarily relating it to anything else.
3. *Application:* Using a general concept to solve a specific problem.
4. *Analysis:* Breaking something down into its parts.
5. *Synthesis:* Creating something new by combining new ideas.
6. *Evaluation:* Judging the value of materials or methods as they might be applied in a particular situation. (p. 402)

In order to ensure that their students are provided with opportunities to go beyond rote memorization, middle-grades teachers are encouraged to plan appropriate lessons from a wide range of levels. As a result, students will be increasingly challenged to use their higher-order thinking skills. Teachers should also ensure that their instructional objectives are at the appropriate level of difficulty based on their students' background knowledge and previous learning experiences. The following examples illustrate instructional objectives written for each level of the cognitive domain:

FIGURE 8.2 Levels of Specificity in Instructional Objectives

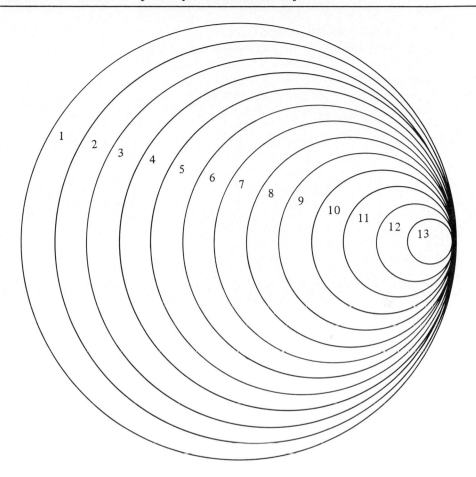

1. The student will be able to achieve personal goals and fulfill his or her obligations to society.
2. The student will be able to demonstrate functional literacy.
3. The student will be able to perform mathematical operations.
4. The student will be able to perform simple addition, subtraction, multiplication, and division operations.
5. The student will be able to perform simple addition operations.
6. The student will be able to add any two single-digit numbers.
7. The student will be able to add 3 and 2.
8. The student will be able to add 3 objects and 2 objects.
9. The student will be able to add 3 apples and 2 apples.
10. The student will be able to add 3 apples and 2 apples when words (not objects) are used.
11. The student will be able to add 3 apples and 2 apples when words are present in writing.
12. The student will be able to add 3 apples and 2 apples 90% of the time, when the problem is posed in written form.
13. The student will be able to add 3 apples and 2 apples 90% of the time when the problem is phrased, "If you had 3 apples and I gave you 2 more, how many would you have?"

Source: From Kennith D. Hopkins, Julian C. Stanley, and B. R. Hopkins, *Educational and Psychological Measurement and Evaluation,* Seventh Edition. Copyright © 1990. Reprinted with permission of Allyn and Bacon. The authors are indebted to Cecil Clark for providing the basis for this example.

1. *Knowledge:* Define free verse.
2. *Comprehension:* Summarize the main idea of a given story.
3. *Application:* Diagram a compound sentence.
4. *Analysis:* Distinguish between a metaphor and a simile.
5. *Synthesis:* Write a poem containing alliteration.
6. *Evaluation:* Assess the merits of a given essay.

As mentioned in the previous chapter, many textbook authors provide instructional objectives that identify what the students should learn from the lessons. Most textbook authors are extremely diligent in ensuring that these objectives cover a variety of cognitive levels. Here is a sample of some of the objectives listed in *General Science: A Voyage of Exploration* published by Prentice Hall (1989):

1. Describe the scientific method.
2. Name the three principal subatomic particles.
3. Distinguish between a compression and rarefaction of a wave.
4. Contrast alpha, beta, and gamma decay.
5. Determine the half-life of a sample of sugar cubes.
6. Evaluate the use of artificial satellites.
7. Demonstrate Newton's Third Law of Motion.

In addition to planning lessons that cover a range of levels, it is also important for middle-grades teachers to make sure that test items and classroom questions also reflect a variety of cognitive levels. We discuss the role of Bloom's taxonomy in planning test items in Chapter 9 and in planning classroom questions in Chapter 13.

Affective Objectives

Objectives in the affective domain deal with "interests, attitudes, and values and the development of appreciations" (Hopkins, Stanley, & Hopkins, 1990, p. 170). In comparison to the cognitive domain, which is concerned with whether or not a student *can* do a certain task, the affective domain is concerned with whether or not the student *will* do it at appropriate times after learning how to do it. Krathwohl, Bloom, and Masia (1964) developed a taxonomy for the affective domain that is composed of the following levels: receiving, responding, valuing, organization, and characterization by a value. A description of each of the five levels follows:

1. *Receiving:* Being sensitive to or attending to the presence of a certain stimulus in the environment
2. *Responding:* Seeking out and attaching significance to the stimulus
3. *Valuing:* Indicating that the stimulus has worth to someone
4. *Organization:* Reorganizing a current value system to include the new value
5. *Characterization by value:* Responding consistently with the new value in appropriate situations

The following examples illustrate behaviors that might occur at each level of the affective domain:

1. *Receiving:* Looks at the paintings during a field trip to an art museum
2. *Responding:* Discusses a certain painting on the bus ride back to school
3. *Valuing:* Prefers to go to an art museum rather than to a basketball game
4. *Organization:* Purchases a year's pass to the art museum
5. *Characterization by a value:* Shows appreciation of art openly; becomes known among peers as an art lover

Unfortunately, for a variety of reasons, the affective domain is frequently overlooked by many teachers. However, given the fact that many of today's young adolescents are being forced to make important decisions at very early ages, we cannot continue to ignore the affective domain. As the Carnegie Council on Adolescent Development (1989) points out, today's young adolescents should "embrace many virtues such as courage, acceptance of responsibility, honesty, integrity, tolerance, appreciation of individual differences, and caring about others" (p. 16). Additionally, the report states, young adolescents should "understand the importance of developing and maintaining close relationships with certain other people, including friends and family, relationships of the character that require great effort and even sacrifice, but without which life is filled with insecurity and loneliness" (p. 16).

Following is a list of suggestions for incorporating affective goals and objectives into your lessons:

1. Provide each student, perhaps on a rotating basis, with some type of responsibility in the classroom. For example, you can assign jobs such as cleaning the blackboard, collecting homework, and closing windows at the end of the day to your students. Over time, students should perform their jobs without reminders from you, and should be held responsible for carrying out their jobs. In addition, you can encourage parents to give their children increasingly more responsibility at home.

2. Provide your students with choices and alternatives as much as possible. For example, students can make their own selections from several books or from several activities or assignments. In appropriate situations, students can also select partners to work with or groups to work in. Exploratory programs provide students with excellent opportunities to make long-term choices among topics and activities.

3. When you provide students with choices, encourage them to make the choices and make them freely. Discuss the reasons for making choices so that students consider alternatives other than those their friends choose.

4. Help students weigh all alternatives thoughtfully. Provide guidance in thinking about the consequences of each alternative. As mentioned in Chapter 2, many young adolescents have difficulty determining the long-term consequences of their choices and actions. As a result, they fail to realize how their present choices and actions can affect their future.

5. Encourage your students to reflect on the abilities and people they prize and cherish the most so that they can learn to make appropriate commitments. For example, a student who is especially interested in and talented in music or a particular sport should be provided with guidance in developing that talent.

Similarly, students should be encouraged to make commitments to family and friends who are especially important to them. For example, many young adolescents are at an age when they do not want to be seen anywhere with their parents or families because of what their peers might think. Also, many young adolescents, especially girls, choose their friends based on membership in popular groups. Classroom discussions, especially during advisor/advisee time, can explore the issue of making commitments to family and friends regardless of what peers might think.

6. Provide students with opportunities to affirm their choices publicly. Defending choices in front of their peers is especially difficult for young adolescents and is a good indication of a deepening commitment. Help students act, behave, and live in accordance with their choices.

Psychomotor Objectives

Objectives in the psychomotor domain deal with "the development and use of the muscles and the body's ability to coordinate its movement" (Popham, 1988, p. 60). Unfortunately, developing the psychomotor domain is frequently associated only with the needs of very young children. However, in the middle grades, subjects such as art, music, industrial arts, and physical education are very much dependent on the psychomotor domain.

Additionally, skills such as constructing graphs and figures in mathematics, keyboard skills in computer classes, and carrying out laboratory activities in science also rely on the psychomotor domain. Skill in the psychomotor domain is crucial in careers such as surgery, carpentry, dentistry, hair styling, drafting, and tailoring. Harrow (1972) developed a taxonomy of psychomotor behaviors that has the following levels: reflex movements, basic-fundamental movements, perceptual abilities, physical abilities, skilled movements, and nondiscursive communication. A description of each level follows.

1. *Reflex movements:* Actions that are involuntary responses to a stimulus; developed without difficulty in most normal children
2. *Basic-fundamental movements:* Voluntary actions that combine reflex movements into patterns; usually developed without training
3. *Perceptual abilities:* Visual, auditory, kinesthetic, and tactile discrimination skills coordinated with movement patterns
4. *Physical abilities:* Endurance, strength, flexibility, and agility skills
5. *Skilled movements:* Skills that require some degree of efficiency; classified according to degree of difficulty and mastery level
6. *Nondiscursive communication:* Expressive and interpretive movements

Sample objectives for each level include:

1. *Reflex movement:* Not usually a concern in the classroom since these movements are involuntary.
2. *Basic-fundamental movements:* Jump and land on two feet.
3. *Perceptual abilities:* Catch a football.

4. *Physical abilities:* Execute fifty jumping jacks.

5. *Skilled movements:* Type 65 words per minute with no mistakes.

6. *Nondiscursive communication:* Choreograph a dance routine.

In the next section of this chapter, we provide a lesson plan that illustrates how psychomotor objectives can be incorporated into lessons for young adolescents.

In summary, the instructional value of each of these three taxonomies is their ability to guide teachers in structuring lessons that move from simple to complex and from concrete to abstract. The hierarchical nature of the taxonomies allows teachers to ensure that they cover a wide range of skills rather than just focusing, for example, on skills requiring rote memorization.

You should not be overly concerned with whether or not you can classify objectives in the appropriate level of a taxonomy with 100 percent accuracy. For example, it is more important for you to be able to look at a lesson plan (or a test) and realize that none of the activities (or items on the test) take students beyond the knowledge level than it is for you to be able to decide whether a certain objective is at the application level or the analysis level. In fact, Hopkins, Stanley, and Hopkins (1990) report that "judges frequently disagree on the taxonomy level represented by items at levels other than the knowledge level" (p. 175).

Procedures

After specifying the objectives, the next step in planning a lesson is to determine the procedures that you will use to teach the objectives most effectively. As we mentioned in the previous section, most lessons are composed of a series of activities. In essence, then, at this stage of lesson planning you have three tasks: (1) selecting the activities, (2) sequencing the activities, and (3) grouping students for the activities.

Selecting Activities

Some educators use the terms *activities* and *procedures* interchangeably when they talk about the components of a lesson plan. We prefer to make a distinction. When we talk about the activities themselves, we use the term *activities*. When we talk about writing down a description of the activities on the actual lesson plan, we use the term *procedures* because we feel it conveys more than just writing down a list of activities. As already discussed, experienced teachers are often capable of teaching from a list of activities, but preservice teachers, student teachers, and beginning teachers tend to write more detailed descriptions than experienced teachers. Thus, we feel the term *procedures* more accurately describes what novice teachers write down at this stage of lesson planning. Later in this section we will show you some sample descriptions of procedures that novice teachers wrote.

There are a number of factors that teachers take into consideration when they select activities for their lessons. In the beginning of the previous chapter, we discussed four categories of factors that teachers take into account when they plan: student characteristics, instructional task characteristics, instructional context characteristics, and teacher characteristics. The factors in each of these categories play an important role in selecting activities for your lessons. Accordingly, you may find it helpful to go back and review the descriptions of these four categories in the last chapter.

Doyle and Carter (1987) have identified four additional categories of factors that play a role in selecting activities: student engagement, physical arrangements, complexity, and time.

Student Engagement.   When planning activities for your lessons, you will want to ensure that the activities you select will hold your students' interest and keep them on task. Research suggests that students tend to be more engaged in some activities than in others. For example, disruptive behavior appears to be highest during individual work such as seatwork and silent reading (Silverstein, 1979). Engagement also is low during activities that proceed slowly and in which most students are inactive such as during student presentations (Gump, 1969).

During whole-class and small-group activities, however, students tend to be the most engaged and least disruptive (Silverstein, 1979). However, as Doyle and Carter (1987) point out, individual students and groups of students vary greatly in their degree of involvement and in their behavior during lessons. Accordingly, you should consider each class separately when you plan the activities for your lessons. You may find that you will have to plan two entirely different lessons to teach the same content to two different classes of students.

Physical Arrangements.   The physical arrangement of your classroom can play a large role in the effectiveness of your lessons. For example, activities that require a great deal of space for students to work and move about will not be very effective if students do not have the required space. Whole-class discussions will probably not be very effective if students are sitting in small groups in such a way that some students have their backs to you.

At the end of the day, rows of desks can quickly be changed into small groups for the next day's lessons.

When planning activities for your lessons, you should also consider whether or not the social task demands of the activity match the physical arrangement of your classroom. For example, when students are expected to work individually in silence, it is probably not a good idea to have them seated in small groups.

You may find that there are some activities that just will not work because of the way your classroom is arranged. Sometimes it will be impossible to rearrange your classroom to suit a particular activity. If this is the case, especially if you are a novice teacher, you are probably better off not attempting such activities. (In Chapter 15, we discuss physical arrangements of classrooms in detail.)

Complexity.   Pacing and signaling are two variables that can affect the complexity of activities (Doyle & Carter, 1987). *Pacing* refers to how fast or slow the activity moves. Activities such as lectures, discussions, and tests are generally externally paced by the teacher. Activities such as seatwork are most often internally paced by the students themselves. Research (e.g., Gump, 1969) suggests that student engagement is highest during activities that are externally paced ''because students are pulled along through the program of action, and momentum can be sustained'' (Doyle & Carter, 1987, p. 193).

Signaling refers to how and when students receive directions about their expected behavior during an activity. In a sense, then, signaling refers to how and when students learn the social task demands of an activity. Kounin and Gump (1974) found that student involvement is highest during activities such as teacher presentation when students continually receive information about the social task demands. Student involvement appears to be lowest during activities in which such information comes from multiple sources and is slow in coming such as during student presentations. As you can see, making students aware of the social task demands of activities can play a large role in the effectiveness of your lessons.

Time.   One of the most important factors to consider when planning activities for your lessons is how much time they will take to complete. Teachers who teach in middle-grades schools with inflexible periods must ensure that their lessons can fit into the amount of time they have available. Teachers who teach in self-contained classrooms have more flexibility because they can adjust their own schedules to make up for lessons that might go over or under the time planned.

Teachers who teach on teams using flexible block scheduling can arrange ahead of time with their team members for lessons that may require extra time. Even when lessons unexpectedly take longer than planned, teachers on teams with flexible block scheduling can usually arrange to keep their students longer than they originally planned.

Timing lessons is one of the most difficult parts of planning for novice teachers. It takes a great deal of experience to be able to judge how long a particular activity will take with a particular group of students. As the year progresses, teachers usually get a better idea of how fast or slow a particular group of students works. One student teacher recently remarked after teaching the same lesson to two different classes of students, 'I had 20 minutes left in first period but I only got halfway through in sixth period.''

The difficulty level of the material can also affect how long it takes students to complete certain activities. For example, Lyon and Gettinger (1985) found that for seventh- and eighth-grade students, tasks at the knowledge level of Bloom's taxonomy were learned faster than tasks at the comprehension or application levels.

Sample Activities.   Figure 8.3 provides an extensive list of some of the possible activities that you might use to construct your lessons. We discuss many of these activities later in this chapter and in other chapters in this book, especially in Chapters 11, 12, and 14.

Sequencing Activities

The order in which you sequence your activities plays an important role in the effectiveness of your lessons. Sometimes the sequence of your activities is obvious and you really will not have to make any decisions. For example, a teacher can hardly hold a discussion about a story until the students read the story or it is read to them. Other times, the nature of the content will dictate the sequence of your activities. For example, changing mixed numbers to improper fractions must be taught before multiplying mixed numbers.

Many times you will have to make decisions about the sequence of your activities. In order to help you make these decisions, we provide two guidelines. First, your activities should lead students from simple to complex and from concrete to abstract. The use of Bloom's, Krathwohl's, and Harrow's taxonomies can help ensure that you do not ask students to engage in activities that are too difficult for them or for which they do not have the prerequisite background. For example, students should not be expected to be able to create a limerick (synthesis level) until they understand what a limerick is (comprehension level).

Second, in general, students should not be asked to do something new and difficult for the first time on their own. Using our limerick example, it would not be a good idea to write a definition of a limerick on the board and then ask each student to write one of their own. When students are asked to do something new

FIGURE 8.3   Activities for Constructing Lessons

dramatizations	demonstrations	student-led discussions
seatwork	library work	sociodramas
guest speakers	debates	simulations
tests/quizzes	interviews	individualized instruction
games/contests	peer tutoring	group projects/discussions
roleplaying	creative writing	individual presentations
recitation	field trips	group presentations
lectures	panel discussions	watching videos/films/film-
brainstorming	blackboard work	strips
drills	reading groups/free reading	cooperative learning
experiments	teacher-led discussions	reciprocal teaching
learning centers		

and difficult for the first time, we suggest the following sequence of activities: whole class, small group, individual.

Again using our limerick example, the teacher might first read several examples of limericks and ask the students if they can determine a rule for writing a limerick. Together, the class can brainstorm the rule. Then the teacher can lead the *whole class* in composing a limerick. The teacher can write it on the board, the overhead projector, a bulletin board, or poster paper. Next, students can work in *small groups* to compose group limericks. Each group can read their limerick to the class. The group limericks could also be displayed on a bulletin board. Finally, students are now ready to write their own *individual* limerick. This can be done as a final activity or as a homework assignment.

Keep in mind, however, that there are occasions when it is perfectly appropriate to challenge students by asking them to try something new on their own. In these instances, students' creativity can be stimulated. However, if you think students will be frustrated by trying something new and difficult on their own, then we recommend the whole class, small group, individual sequence.

Grouping Students

For many of the activities that you use in your lessons, you will have to decide on the most effective way to group your students. Many activities can be conducted with the whole class, with small groups or pairs, or on an individual basis.

Whole-Class Instruction.   Presentations, recitations, and teacher-led discussions and demonstrations are examples of activities frequently conducted with the whole class. One advantage of using whole-class instruction is that student engagement is typically high because the teacher has control over the pace of the activity. An additional advantage of whole-class instruction is that students can be called on when necessary in order to hold their "attention and give the teacher feedback concerning understanding" (Doyle & Carter, 1987, p. 198).

Unfortunately, research suggests that teachers tend to call more often on high-ability students than low-ability students in order to keep discussions going (Good, 1981). Chapters 13 and 14 provide excellent suggestions for conducting lectures, presentations, demonstrations, recitations, and discussions with the whole class.

Small Groups or Pairs.   Peer tutoring, cooperative learning, reading groups, laboratory experiments, and learning centers are just a few of the activities that students can work on in small groups or pairs. Small-group and pair work is an excellent method of promoting positive social interaction and responsibility among the young adolescents in your classroom. Having students work in groups or pairs is also an effective way of dealing with limited supplies. The primary disadvantage associated with group work is that managing several groups or pairs simultaneously can be a difficult task. Chapter 15 provides you with suggestions for managing student groups and pairs in your classroom.

There are a number of methods that you can use to group students within your classroom. Students can be grouped or paired on a variety of variables such as interests and friendships. This type of grouping tends to result in high productivity because the students are motivated and tend to work well together. When groups are responsible for a joint product, students can be grouped according to leadership ability. Ensuring that each group has a leader who can organize the group and keep them on task increases the likelihood that they will complete their task. Students can even be grouped on a completely random basis for activities that call for a mix of interests, abilities, and friendships.

Students can also be grouped by ability. Grouping students by ability within your classroom appears to have some advantages over whole-class instruction. Ability grouping is a controversial topic among educators, and results of the research that has been conducted with middle-grades students is mixed. For example, in 1986, Slavin reviewed eight research studies conducted on the effects of within-class ability grouping of students. He found that all of the studies favored grouping. The effects were higher for low-ability students than for average- or high-ability students. However, since all of the studies focused on grouping for mathematics, we cannot generalize to other subject areas.

Having a small number of groups (e.g., 2 or 3) in your classroom is more effective than having a large number (e.g., 4 or 6). Many educators believe that ability grouping can have a detrimental effect on students, particularly low-ability students, by labeling them. However, if you change group membership frequently and do not allow groups to become stagnant, then labeling should not be a problem. Chapter 15 provides additional information on the various ways you can group the students within your classroom.

Individualized Activities.   Individual projects, seatwork, conferences, and individualized instruction are examples of activities usually conducted on an individual basis. The primary advantage of having students work on their own is that the work can be tailored to each student's individual needs. Also, individualized activities are

Peer tutoring promotes positive social interactions and responsibility among young adolescents.

often times more motivating at the early adolescent stage of development when individual interests are beginning to be defined. Another advantage of having students work on their own is that it provides the teachers with time to work with individuals or small groups of students.

A disadvantage of having students work on their own in the classroom is that, compared to whole-class instruction, student engagement is typically low (Gump, 1967). Additionally, preparing individual assignments and then providing some type of feedback to the student takes a great deal of teacher time.

Sample Procedures

As a summary to this section on the procedures component of a lesson plan, we will share with you the procedures for three lessons. The first two were developed and taught by student teachers and the third one was developed and taught by an expert teacher. The first sample is described in detail; the second and third samples are described briefly.

Student Teacher 1

This lesson was planned and taught by Dennis Rowley, a middle-grades student teacher at the University of Georgia. Figure 8.4 shows you what Dennis wrote down to describe the activities in his lesson. Dennis actually used this plan to guide himself as he taught the lesson to his fifth-grade students.

As Figure 8.4 indicates, this lesson was the first of several being devoted to the book *The Lion, the Witch and the Wardrobe* (Lewis, 1950). The purpose of the lesson was to introduce the students to the book in general and as an example of fantasy in particular. The lesson was composed of three activities, which Dennis labeled 1, 2, and 3. The first activity was a teacher-led discussion; the second activity was oral reading by the teacher; the third activity was individual seatwork during which the students drew a picture. Following is an analysis of each of the activities. And, since one of us actually observed Dennis teach this lesson, we describe to you what happened in terms of student engagement and timing.

Activity 1: Teacher-Led Discussion.   Dennis wrote a detailed description of the procedures he planned to use for the discussion in activity 1. In this discussion, Dennis wanted to set the stage for the lesson. His plans indicate that he will start with fiction, break it down into fantasy and realistic fiction, and then discuss fantasy with alternate worlds. On his lesson plan, Dennis wrote down some examples of fantasy, realistic fiction, and fantasy with alternate worlds with which he knew the students were familiar. As an analogy, he then planned to compare the real-world setting and the fantasy world setting of *The Lion, the Witch and the Wardrobe* with *Alice in Wonderland* and *The Wizard of Oz*. Dennis even drew a picture on his lesson plan, comparing the looking glass, the tornado, and the wardrobe as vehicles connecting the real world to the fantasy world. He also wrote some examples of things that can happen in the fantasy world.

If we compare what Dennis wrote down in the way of procedures for this activity to what an experienced teacher might have written down, Dennis probably

FIGURE 8.4 Dennis Rowley's Lesson Plan

Monday, May 7 '90, Reading

Introduction to <u>the Lion, Witch, and the Wardrobe</u> as fantasy.

<u>Activity</u> : ① TTW focus students by discussing fiction then distinguishing between fantasy and realistic fiction.

<u>fantasy</u>
Hobbitt
Charlotte's Web
Runaway Ralph

<u>realistic fiction</u>
War with Grandpa
Little House on Prairie

Discuss fantasy w/ alternate worlds - <u>Alice in Wonderland</u>, <u>Wizard of Oz</u>.

Compare to L,W,W - real world setting, during WW II, England, for parts; fantasy world (Narnia) for most.

Strange creatures

evil forces
good forces

magic potions

magic in general

In fantasy world, author can let anything happen to tell the story. <u>Imaginary</u> life very prominent, human-like animals (anthropomorphism)
② Read Chapter 1 outloud.
③ Students respond by drawing picture of a faun per description at end of chapter 1.

Source: Used with permission of Dennis M. Rowley.

wrote much more detail. An experienced teacher who had done this or a similar activity previously might only need to write down "Discuss *The Lion, the Witch and the Wardrobe* as fantasy" in order to do the same activity Dennis did. And, in another year or two, Dennis will probably be able to do this or a similar activity without writing down as much detail. But, as a novice teacher, the detail in this plan helped Dennis effectively carry out the activity. It served as an outline from which he taught and it reminded him of key points he wanted to make during the lesson.

This activity went pretty much as Dennis planned. Keep in mind that this activity was not a lecture during which Dennis *gave* the students information. It was a discussion during which both Dennis and his students talked and the students supplied much of the information.

For example, Dennis did not begin by defining *fiction*. He began by asking the students if they could tell him what fiction is and give him some examples. They were able to do this. Then, to make the information more concrete, he wrote the words *fantasy* and *realistic fiction* on the board and underlined them just as he did on his lesson plan. He then asked his students if they could explain the difference between the two and give him some examples. Again, they were able to do this and he wrote some of their examples under the headings on the board. When Dennis described fantasy worlds, he actually drew the pictures of the looking glass, the tornado, and the wardrobe on the board in order to make the idea more concrete to his students.

Dennis also did several things that he had not actually written down on his plans. He told the students that C. S. Lewis was the author of the book and then named some other books by Lewis. When describing the setting of the book, he told them it was during World War II and asked if they could give him an approximate year. He also showed them London on a map. And, to find out if the students understood the difference between the real world and the fantasy world in the books, he asked if they could name the real world and the fantasy world in each (i.e., England/Wonderland, Kansas/Oz, England/Narnia).

On the whole, most students were engaged during this activity. Since Dennis could control the pace of the discussion, he kept it moving at a rate that ensured having enough time to finish the other two activities he planned for the lesson. Unfortunately, the seating arrangement in the classroom was not ideal for conducting a discussion. Students were seated in groups of four (i.e., two pairs of students facing each other). Thus, it was difficult for all students to face Dennis and it was relatively easy for students to distract each other.

Dennis did a good job of moving around the room and calling on students who were not on task. At one point, without the other students knowing it, Dennis quietly took away some work that one student was doing while the discussion was going on. In short, Dennis effectively monitored student engagement during the discussion.

Activity 2: Oral Reading by Teacher.   This activity is relatively straightforward. Dennis read the first chapter of the book to the students. As you can see in Figure 8.4, Dennis wrote very little on his plan to describe this activity, probably because there wasn't much he wanted to remind himself of doing. Dennis's description of this activity is very similar to what an experienced teacher would write down.

During the oral reading, most students attended to the story. However, they were not as attentive as during the discussion, perhaps because they were not actively involved in the reading. The seating arrangement was fine because, not having to use the blackboard, Dennis was free to circulate around the room and monitor all of the students. The pace of this activity was controlled completely by Dennis and he appeared to know exactly how long it would take him to read the chapter.

Before he started to read, Dennis did something that he had not written down on his plan. He told the students several things to listen for as he read. In essence, he supplied them with a purpose for listening. In particular, he told them to listen carefully to the description of the faun so they had a good idea of what it looked like.

Activity 3: Individual Seatwork.   For this final activity, Dennis asked his students to draw a picture of the faun that he had read about in the first chapter (he deliberately had not shown them the picture in the book). Again, he wrote very little detail on his lesson plan.

Unfortunately, the transition from the oral reading to the drawing activity was not as smooth as it could have been. Dennis was clear in his directions and he quickly distributed drawing paper to the students. However, some students had crayons in their desks, others wanted to use markers instead and went to the closet to find them, and a few even wanted to use pencils and got up to sharpen them. Once they were up, several students wandered around and chatted with other students. Realizing that he had not done a good job of identifying and preparing students for the social task demands of this activity, Dennis did something that got everyone back on task. He quietly said that he would read the description of the faun again as soon as everyone was seated.

Once the students settled down and began their drawings, they were appropriately engaged in this activity. The seating arrangement was conducive for sharing crayons and for quiet talk among students. Since the students were working individually, Dennis had very little control over the pace of the activity. He knew how much time he had left for lesson, but he did not tell the students they had to be finished by the end of class. He wanted them to work at their own pace, so he told them if they didn't finish they could work on their drawings later in the day.

As expected, some students completed their drawings very quickly and Dennis held them up for the other students to see. For each one, he gave specific feedback on some particular aspect of the drawing that was well done (e.g., "Those green horns are really impressive, Erica"). Dennis also pointed out to the students that, because they all had their own interpretation of what was read, there was wide variation among the drawings.

Student Teacher 2

Our descriptions of this lesson will not be as detailed as the last one. But we would like to share with you another lesson planned by a student teacher so you can compare it with the next one, which was developed by an experienced teacher.

This lesson on adding fractions was planned and taught by Dianne Fincher, a student teacher at the University of Georgia. Figure 8.5 shows you what Dianne wrote down on her lesson plan to describe the activities in her lesson.

Dianne's lesson had three activities: drill (which Dianne labeled *opener*), demonstration, and small-group work. Dianne developed the lesson plan under the

FIGURE 8.5 Dianne Fincher's Lesson Plan

Opener: Ask students to respond to the following questions:
1. 3 apples + 4 apples is
2. 2 snakes + 6 snakes is
3. 4 Nintendo Cart. + 6 Nintendo Cart. is
4. 5 fourths + 3 fourths is
5. 2 eighths + 5 eighths is
6. 1 half + 3 halves is
7. 2 thirds + 3 thirds is
8. 1 fifth + 3 fifths is
9. 2 sevenths + 1 seventh is
10. 2 tenths + 5 tenths is

Ask: Do you know of any candy that is divided into fractional parts?
Use Kit Kat/Hershey bars and other candy to demonstrate adding fractions with like denominators. Also use some examples with mixed numbers.
Ask: Why do we keep the same denominator?
Group Practice: Divide class into groups. Give each group some Jelly Beans. Explain Handout. Put some addition problems on the board.
Ask groups for some of their fractions and additions. Go over with the class. Put some on the board.
Closure: Take two minutes to write about what you have learned today. Ask for volunteers to share.
Homework: Page 241 #7-21 odd and page 249 #11-23 odd

Source: Used with permission of Dianne Fincher.

supervision of Lola Bell, a middle-grades teacher in Oconee County, Georgia. They adapted some of the ideas suggested in resource books that accompanied their textbook. As you can see, Dianne's descriptions were detailed, especially for the first activity where she wrote down every question she would ask the students. As was the case with Dennis, Dianne was able to use this plan to guide herself during the lesson. She kept the plan nearby as she taught and she referred to it throughout the lesson to make sure she was covering the key points.

Expert Teacher. This lesson was planned and taught by Dera Weaver, a teacher in Clarke County, Georgia. Dera's lesson on paragraph types was taught to her eighth-grade students.

As Figure 8.6 indicates, Dera's lesson was composed of two activities: lecture/discussion on the four types of paragraphs, and small-group construction of paragraphs. Not unlike most expert teachers, Dera wrote down very little to describe these activities. As she taught, the lesson plan was on her desk, but Dera did not refer to it at all during the lesson. At the top of her lesson plan Dera wrote a note to herself to remind two students about their notebooks and to remind all students that letters were due today. Dera also wrote the homework assignment on her plan.

FIGURE 8.6 Dera Weaver's Lesson Plan

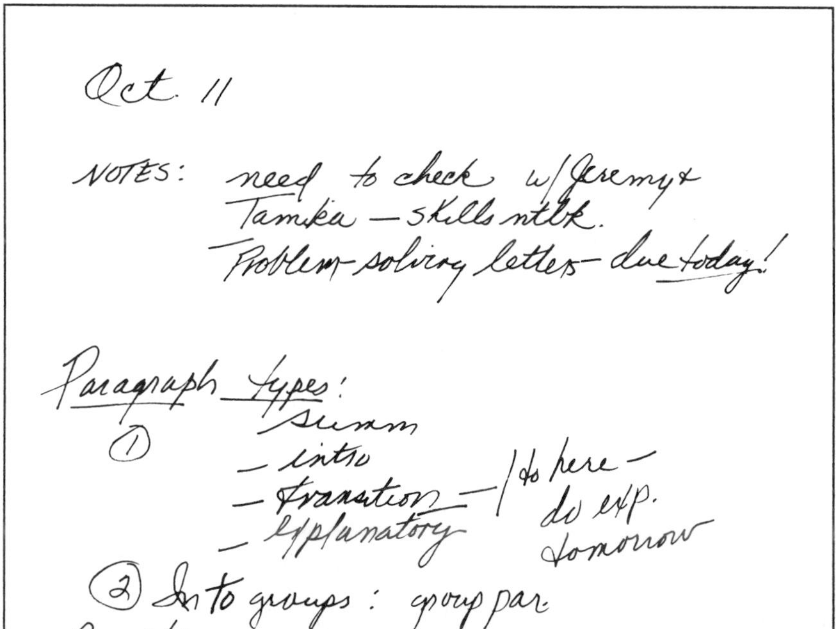
Oct. 11

NOTES: need to check w/Jeremy & Tamika — skills ntbk.
Problem-solving letters — due today!

Paragraph types:
① Summ
— intro
— transition — | do here —
— explanatory | do exp. tomorrow
② Into groups: group par.
Ass't: Read Whales; look for par. types

Source: Used with permission of Dera Weaver.

Although she did not write it on her lesson plan, Dera also had a short introduction to the lesson and a closing that summarized the lesson. As you can see on Figure 8.6, after the lesson was over, Dera drew a line under *transition,* indicating that she did not have time to discuss the explanatory paragraph. She wrote a note reminding herself to start there tomorrow.

Practice Exercise.   As a summary to this discussion of Dennis's, Dianne's, and Dera's lessons, you may want to work with a partner or a small group to see if you can identify the academic task demands and social task demands for each of the activities in the three lessons. You can use the questions supplied in Figure 8.1 to help you get started. When you finish, compare your list with that of another pair or group of students. Your list should give you a pretty good idea of the wide variety of things you have to plan for in each lesson.

Materials

The third component of a typical lesson plan is the materials component, which is usually a listing of the textbooks, supplemental reading materials, aids, supplies, and equipment that the teacher will need for each activity. For example, in Dennis's lesson, the materials needed were a copy of the book *The Lion, the Witch and the Wardrobe,* chalk, drawing paper, and crayons. Dianne needed Kit Kat or Hershey bars, a copy of the handout for each student, and jelly beans for each group.

The materials component of a lesson plan serves the important function of reminding yourself of all the materials that you should have ready for the lesson. Materials that are already in your classroom and are used on a regular basis are not usually written down on the lesson plan. The materials component also serves as a helpful reminder to preview films, filmstrips, videos, and tapes, and to make sure that equipment such as computers and projectors are in working order. (Incorporating technology into your lessons is discussed in detail in Chapter 10.)

As you plan and select the materials that you will use in your lessons, keep in mind the developmental nature of the young adolescents in your classroom. Recall from Chapter 2 that most of the middle-grades students will be at the concrete level of cognitive development. Therefore, any materials that you can use to make the content more concrete will help students understand it better. Materials such as pictures, bulletin boards, maps, globes, graphs, charts, films, videos, and records are especially useful when trying to make abstract content more concrete.

Evaluation

One of the most important components of a lesson plan is evaluation. The evaluation component identifies the procedures that the teacher will use to determine whether or not the students learned what they were supposed to learn. In general, each objective is evaluated and the evaluation should correspond to the behavior stated in the objective.

For example, the objective "plan ways individuals can reduce pollution" should be evaluated by asking students to plan ways that individuals can reduce pollution.

FIGURE 8.7 Taylor McKenna's Lesson Plan

Topic Playwriting   Day 1   Grade 8

OBJECTIVE(S)	PROCEDURES	MATERIALS	EVALUATION
	Present introduction to playwriting. Discuss plans for the unit, writing and dramatizing scripts for video production. Discuss the function of imagination and concentration in the creative process.		

1. Students maintain self-control and concentration when performing.	1. Concentration experiment. Students close their eyes and visualize a soldier. Teacher moves around the room and taps each student on the head. Teacher points out that concentration is fragile. Students describe their images. Teacher points out that both actors and playwrights must visualize characters and scenes.		Observation
			  ✔ for concentration
			  ✕ for none

	2. Mirror Game. Students choose partners. One student pretends he or she is getting ready for school while the partner, the "mirror," matches the movements and facial expressions. No talking is permitted. Teacher encourages simultaneous movement.		
2. Students can define characterization.	3. Kmart Cashier Game. Teacher defines characterization. Students discuss the activities that occur during a sales transaction at Kmart. Students move desks back and find a space of their own. Students then imagine they are cashier ringing up a purchase. Students speak aloud as if they have a customer. Repeat the game, changing personality of the cashiers from crabby to robotic to snobby.		Questions to class following activity. How were the characters created? What did you change?

3. Students can change their voices, body movements, and facial expressions to create a character in performance.	4. Read and discuss the story "Something Outrageous." Identify the setting, major groups of characters, the personalities of these characters, the conflict, and the resolution.	copy of "Something Outrageous"	Observation during performance
			  ✔ changes voice
			  ✔ changes movement
			  ✔ facial expression
			  ✕ no attempt at characterization

	5. Review the story "Something Outrageous." Assign parts and distribute costume pieces. Set up scenery and dramatize. Switch parts so that every student participates. Assign larger parts to students with high concentration and creativity.	costume pieces and scenery	

Source: Used with permission of Taylor McKenna.

Students should not be asked to define pollution, or to provide examples of pollution, or to plan ways that industries can reduce pollution. In short, there should be a match between your objectives, the activities you use to teach those objectives, and the procedures you use to evaluate student performance on those objectives. (We discuss evaluation in detail in Chapter 9.)

Sample Lesson Plan

As a summary exercise, we present a sample lesson plan that includes the four components we just discussed: objectives, procedures, materials, and evaluation. The lesson plan was developed and taught by Taylor McKenna, a University of Georgia student teacher. Take a few minutes and read through Taylor's lesson plan in Figure 8.7. Her lesson plan is for the first day in a unit on playwriting.

Think about each of the four components of Taylor's lesson plan in light of the information presented in this section. Specifically, are the objectives written in measurable terms? Do the objectives take the students beyond the knowledge level of the cognitive domain? Are the activities likely to engage young adolescents? Are the activities logically sequenced? Are a variety of materials used? Do the materials help make abstract concepts more concrete? Is each objective evaluated? Do the evaluation procedures reflect the objectives?

Summary

This chapter has provided you with a sense of what a lesson is and what its important components are. You should also have a good idea of the process involved in planning effective lessons for young adolescents. The type of lesson planning that we described in this chapter is typical of preservice and beginning teachers. Although many experienced teachers do not engage in detailed lesson planning, they do agree that they did it as beginning teachers and it helped them. They also report they do it to some extent when they teach new material for the first time. By planning this way as a student teacher and a beginning teacher, you should be able to create lessons that are both appropriate and engaging for young adolescents.

As you begin to plan lessons, keep in mind that all teachers plan differently. We encourage you to experiment and seek the advice and feedback of expert teachers as you develop your planning skills. Ultimately, the procedures you use to plan and the format you use to write down your plans will be effective only if they work for you.

REFERENCES _____

Berliner, D. C. (1987). But do they understand? In V. Richardson-Koehler (Ed.), *Educators' handbook: A research perspective* (pp. 259–293). New York: Longman.

Bloom, B. S., Engelhard, M. T., Furst, E. J.,

Hill, W. H., & Krathwohl, D. R. (1956). *Taxonomy of educational objectives: Handbook I: The cognitive domain*. New York: David McKay.

Carnegie Council on Adolescent Development.

(1989). *Turning points: Preparing American Youth for the 21st century*. Washington, DC: Carnegie Council of New York.

Clark, C. M., & Peterson, P. L. (1986). Teachers' thought processes. In M. C. Wittrock (Ed.), *Handbook of research on teaching* (3rd ed., pp. 255–296). New York: Macmillan.

Cooley, W. W., & Leinhardt, G. (1980). The instructional dimensions study. *Educational Evaluation and Policy Study, 2*, 7–26.

Doyle, W. (1986). Classroom organization and management. In M. C. Wittrock (Ed.), *Handbook of research on teaching* (3rd ed., pp. 392–431). New York: Macmillan.

Doyle, W., & Carter, K. (1987). Choosing the means of instruction. In V. Richardson-Koehler (Ed.), *Educators' handbook: A research perspective* (pp. 188–206). New York: Longman.

Duchastel, P. C., & Merrill, P. E. (1973). The effects of behavioral objectives on learning: A review of empirical studies. *Review of Educational Research, 43*, 53–69.

Erickson, F. (1982). Classroom discourse as improvisation: Relationships between academic task structure and social participation structure in lessons. In L. C. Wilkinson (Ed.), *Communicating in classrooms* (pp. 153–181). New York: Academic Press.

Erickson, F. (1986). Tasks in times: Objects of study in a natural history of teaching. In K. K. Zumwalt (Ed.), *Improving teaching* (pp. 121–148). Washington, DC: Association for Supervision and Curriculum Development.

Good, T. L. (1981). Teacher expectations and student perceptions: A decade of research. *Educational Leadership, 38*, 415–422.

Green, J. L., & Weade, R. (1987). In search of meaning: A sociolinguistic perspective. In D. Bloome (Ed.), *Literacy and schooling*. Norwood, NJ: Ablex.

Gronlund, N. E. (1978). *Stating behavioral objectives for classroom instruction* (2nd ed.). Toronto: Macmillan.

Gump, P. V. (1967). *The classroom behavior setting: Its nature and relation to student behavior* (final report). Washington, DC: Office of Education, Bureau of Research. (ERIC Document No. ED015515).

Gump, P. V. (1969). Intra-setting analysis: The third grade classroom as a special but instructive case. In E. Williams & H. Rausch (Eds.), *Naturalistic viewpoints in psychological research*. New York: Holt, Rinehart and Winston.

Harrow, A. J. (1972). *A taxonomy of the psychomotor domain: A guide for developing behavioral objectives*. New York: David McKay.

Hopkins, K. D., Stanley, J. C., & Hopkins, B. R. (1990). *Educational and psychological measurement and evaluation* (7th ed.). Englewood Cliffs, NJ: Prentice Hall.

Kauchak, D. P., & Eggen, P. D. (1989). *Learning and teaching*. Boston: Allyn and Bacon.

Kounin, J. S., & Gump, P. V. (1974). Signal systems of lesson settings and the task-related behavior of preschool children. *Journal of Educational Psychology, 66*, 554–562.

Krathwohl, D. R., Bloom, B. S., & Masia, B. B. (1964). *Taxonomy of educational objectives: Handbook II: Affective domain*. New York: David McKay.

Leinhardt, G. (1983, April). *Routines in expert math teachers' thoughts and actions*. Paper presented at the annual meeting of the American Educational Research Association, Montreal.

Lewis, C. S. (1950). *The lion, the witch and the wardrobe*. New York: Macmillan.

Lyon, M. A., & Gettinger, M. (1985). Differences in student performance on knowledge, comprehension, and application tasks: Implications for school learning. *Journal of Educational Psychology, 77*, 12–19.

Mager, R. F. (1962). *Preparing objectives for programmed instruction*. Belmont, CA: Pitman Learning, Inc.

McCutcheon, G. (1980). How do elementary school teachers plan? The nature of planning and influences on it. *The Elementary School Journal, 81*, 4–23.

Morine-Dershimer, G. (1979). *Teacher plans and classroom reality: The South Bay Study, part IV*. (Research Series No. 60). East Lansing: Michigan State University, Institute for Research on Teaching.

Popham, W. J. (1988). *Educational evaluation*

(2nd ed.). Englewood Cliffs, NJ: Prentice Hall.

Sardo, D. (1982, October). *Teacher planning styles in the middle school.* Paper presented at the meeting of the Eastern Educational Research Association, Ellenville, NY.

Silverstein, J. M. (1979). *Individual and environmental correlates of pupil problematic and nonproblematic classroom behavior.* Unpublished doctoral dissertation, New York University.

Slavin, R. E. (1986). *Ability grouping and student achievement: A best evidence synthesis.*

(Technical Report No. 1). Baltimore, MD: Johns Hopkins University, Center for Research on Elementary and Middle Schools.

Tyler, R. W. (1950). *Basic principles of curriculum and instruction.* Chicago: University of Chicago Press.

Weade, R., & Evertson, C. M. (1988). The construction of lessons in effective and less effective classrooms. *Teaching and Teacher Education, 4,* 189–213.

Woolfolk, A. E. (1990). *Educational psychology* (4th ed.). Englewood Cliffs, NJ: Prentice Hall.

_9_

Classroom Assessment

We have mentioned frequently that the primary responsibility of teachers is to instruct their students. But how do we know if students have learned what we taught? How do we know if our instruction was effective? Good teachers answer these questions through classroom assessment. It is often assumed, as Calfee and Hiebert (1988) point out, "that the knowledgeable teacher plays a critical role in valid classroom assessment, and that effective instruction requires informed professional judgment" (p. 45). Hence, a thorough knowledge of effective classroom assessment practices *can* have a significant impact on instruction. Unfortunately, it appears that many teachers renege on their responsibility to link instruction with assessment and, as a result, assessment has little bearing on how or what they teach (Wang, 1988).

One of the reasons why many teachers fail to link instruction with assessment may be that, on the whole, teachers do not receive much training in effective assessment practices. For example, Gullickson and Hopkins (1987) reported that in many teacher education programs, a course in educational assessment is optional and only about 25 percent of preservice students elect to take such a course. Students' reluctance to enroll in an optional educational assessment course may be due to their perception that the content of such a course may not be useful in the classroom.

Gullickson (1986) found that teachers and professors disagreed about the emphasis that statistics and nontest assessment procedures should receive in such a course. Not surprisingly, teachers felt that, relative to other topics, statistics should not be given as much emphasis in assessment courses. Professors, on the other hand, reported that they gave top priority in their courses to a number of statistical topics. Teachers also felt that nontest assessment procedures such as observation and rating scales should receive significant emphasis in assessment courses. Professors, however, reported giving such assessment procedures relatively little emphasis in their courses.

What should teachers know in order to carry out effective classroom assessment? In 1989, a committee composed of members of the American Association of Colleges of Teacher Education, the American Federation of Teachers, the National Council on Measurement in Education, and the National Education Association recommended seven competencies necessary for effective assessment of students. The committee stated that effective teachers should be able to:

1. Choose assessment methods appropriate for instructional decisions.
2. Develop assessment methods appropriate for instructional decisions.
3. Administer, score, and interpret the results of both commercially and teacher-prepared assessment methods.
4. Use assessment results to make decisions about individuals, instruction, curriculum, and school improvement.
5. Use pupil assessment to develop grading procedures.
6. Communicate assessment results to students, parents, and other interested individuals.
7. Recognize unethical, illegal, and inappropriate assessment methods.

It is our intent in this chapter to begin to build the foundation that you will eventually need in order to demonstrate these seven competencies. First, however, we will provide you with some definitions that will help you as you read through the rest of this chapter.

Definitions

Many people, including teachers, use the terms *assessment, evaluation, measurement,* and *test* interchangeably. However, in actual practice, there are fine distinctions among these words.

Assessment, the broadest and most inclusive of the terms, refers to the collection and evaluation of information and the use of that information to make a decision. To use an example outside of the field of education, suppose you are trying to decide whether or not to see a certain movie tonight. You would collect as much information as possible about the quality of the movie itself and any other factors, such as the cost of the movie, the distance you would have to drive to get to the movie, weather conditions during your drive, and so on. Then you would make your decision. This entire process, from beginning to end, is assessment.

Evaluation refers to the process of determining worth or value. It implies some type of judgment that eventually leads to a decision. In our movie example, after collecting all of your information, you may decide that the movie is probably excellent and you will go to see it. Notice that you did not make this decision randomly. You collected as much information as possible before you made your evaluation of the movie and your decision to see it. Some of this information may be quantitative and some may be qualitative. This is where measurement comes in.

Measurement refers to quantifying or assigning a numerical rating to collected information. Many different types of information can be collected and quantified. Again, using our movie example, a friend of yours has seen the movie and he rates it as a 9 out of 10. A well-respected movie critic gives it her highest endorsement of five stars. It has been nominated for seven academy awards. Audiences are standing in line for 45 minutes to get tickets.

In education, measurement is important because it provides teachers with the quantitative information they need to compare students to each other or to a predetermined criteria or standard. Keep in mind that not all information can be quantified. In our movie example, you may have seen a preview of the movie and thought it looked interesting. It may be hard for you to quantify this information but it is still likely to play a role in your final decision.

You have probably noticed by now that the more information you collect, and the more varied this information, the better your chance of making a good decision. This is especially true when making educational decisions where the stakes are much higher than they are in our movie example.

Testing refers to the systematic procedure of gathering information in order to make comparisons Thus, testing is one type of measurement. Generally, when testing is used as a type of measurement, individuals are aware that they are being tested and they are aware of the purpose of the test.

Two important types of tests that you will probably encounter as you begin your teaching career are norm-referenced tests and criterion-referenced tests. In **norm-referenced** testing, students are compared to others who have taken the test. Thus, results of norm-referenced tests will tell students how they performed relative to their peers (e.g., class, state, nation). However, results of norm-referenced tests will not tell you which items your students got right or wrong or their particular strengths and weaknesses within a specific area.

Norm-referenced tests are used primarily to measure general ability and to rank students for selection purposes. Thus, designers of norm-referenced tests aim for wide variation in scores so that differences among students are obvious. The Scholastic Aptitude Test (SAT) is an example of a norm-referenced test.

In contrast, **criterion-referenced** tests compare student performance to a predetermined or absolute standard or criterion related to a specific objective. Students' performance relative to their peers is not important in this type of testing. Thus, variation in scores is not a concern. Criterion-referenced tests are useful for measuring student and class mastery of specific objectives and for diagnosing students' strengths and weaknesses in specific areas. An example of a criterion-referenced test is the Red Cross Senior Lifesaving Test. In sum, it is the purpose of the test and the use of its results rather than the particular test itself that determines whether it is norm- or criterion-referenced.

As you can see from these definitions and examples, testing is only one method of collecting information. There are many other ways to collect information for the purpose of making decisions. In our movie example, information was collected in a variety of ways. The same is true when making decisions about young adolescents in classrooms. Observations, interviews, portfolios, questionnaires, checklists, rating scales, and a variety of other evaluation techniques can provide important information for classroom assessment.

In middle-grades classrooms, where students' physical, social, and emotional development can affect their classroom performance, it is important to collect as much and as varied information as possible when making educational decisions. Later in this chapter, we will discuss a variety of evaluation techniques and their particular relevance to middle-grades classrooms.

Purposes of Assessment

Why do we assess students? Given the number of tests that are administered in classrooms each year, this question is extremely significant. The primary purpose of assessing students is to improve learning. However, there are many other reasons why we assess students and these reasons have been categorized in a variety of ways. Borrowing from Airasian (1989), we will discuss internal and external assessment and the purposes of each.

Internal Assessment

Internal assessments "are the assessments individual teachers utilize daily to maintain order, to guide instruction, and to assign grades to their students" (Airasian, 1989, p. 333). Internal assessments are initiated by teachers, as opposed to being mandated by principals or school boards, and thus teachers have a great deal of control over this type of assessment. Internal assessments can be conducted through the use of *formal* assessment techniques, such as tests, or through the use of *informal* assessment techniques, such as observation or discussion.

Primarily, internal assessments help teachers plan appropriate instruction for their students and also let teachers know if their students have learned what was taught. This can be accomplished before, during, and after an instructional unit. Before beginning an instructional unit, a pretest can be administered to students. Given the wide range of development and the variety of abilities and interests among young adolescents, it is crucial for middle-grades teachers to assess their students in order to plan developmentally appropriate instruction. During an instructional unit, evaluation techniques such as observation, seatwork, homework, and short quizzes can be used daily. At the end of an instructional unit, a posttest or a summary project is frequently used.

The preinstructional and day-to-day evaluations that allow teachers and students to make decisions throughout the instructional unit is referred to as *formative evaluation*. The summary evaluation at the end of the instructional unit, usually for the purpose of assessing achievement, is referred to as *summative evaluation*.

Another purpose of internal assessment is that it provides teachers with information necessary for making decisions about individual students. Decisions about whether or not a student should be promoted to the next grade, be moved to another team, be assigned enrichment work, or be designated the group leader all depend on frequent and appropriate internal assessment.

Teachers' use of internal assessment also allows them to provide parents with appropriate feedback regarding their child's progress. Most parents will not be satisfied with general statements, such as, "Jack is not doing well in mathematics" or "Shawn is a good science student." Frequent and appropriate assessment will allow you to provide more specific and more helpful information, such as, "Jack has not turned in the last six homework assignments and he only solved 2 out of 12 problems correctly on a test involving area and perimeter" or "Shawn received 100 on the last three science tests and he has turned in all of the required lab reports."

Internal assessments also provide specific information that can be used to assign grades to students. Most middle-grades administrators require teachers to assign grades to students at the end of a marking period. The more appropriate information the teacher has collected during the marking period, the more meaningful the grades will be to students and to their parents. We will discuss grades in more detail later in this chapter.

Finally, internal assessments can be used to make decisions about grouping students for instruction. In middle-grades classrooms, students can be grouped for a variety of reasons and a variety of activities. Effective grouping of young adolescents depends on a thorough knowledge of factors such as students' ability and interest levels, background knowledge, work and behavior habits, and friendship groups within the class. Information concerning all of these factors can be obtained through appropriate internal assessments.

External Assessment

External assessment is "mandated by an authority external to the local school, usually the state school board or legislature" (Airasian, 1989, p. 333). Formal assessment techniques, such as standardized tests, are generally used for external assessments. With the recent trend toward more accountability in education, externally mandated assessment has become more prevalent in the last decade. Despite the fact that external assessments usually have little impact on day-to-day instructional decisions in the classroom, they do have several important purposes.

First, as just mentioned, external assessments provide accountability information to school boards, local and state educational administrators, politicians, and taxpayers. Second, external assessments can also provide general information necessary for making local, district, or state curriculum recommendations. For example, school district administrators may decide to revise their middle-grades science curriculum because, on the whole, their students' performance was extremely low on a recent state science assessment.

Also, if used appropriately, external assessments can alert the general public, national policymakers, and politicians to the problems surrounding education today. Issues such as teacher pay, parental support, and additional funds for educational research and development can all be addressed through external assessments of one kind or another.

Despite the appropriate uses of external assessment, there is a growing fear among educators that this type of assessment is also being used inappropriately for various reasons. For example, in some states, external assessment results are published in newspapers and inappropriate comparisons are made among districts, schools, and, in some cases, teachers. In addition, Shepard (1989) reports of real estate agents using the results of external assessments to "identify the 'best' schools as selling points for expensive housing" (p. 4).

One of the most effective things teachers can do to counteract the inappropriate uses of external assessments is to become as knowledgeable as possible about all aspects of the assessment process so that they can effectively discuss it with students, other teachers, principals, parents, and, if necessary, school board members and politicians. Teachers who can intelligently discuss assessment and point out its appropriate and inappropriate uses to other educators and laypeople can do much for the field of education.

The remainder of this chapter is devoted to three important topics that should help you become more knowledgeable about the assessment process: (1) classroom assessment techniques, (2) classroom assessment systems, and (3) standardized tests.

Classroom Assessment Techniques

Before going into detail about the various assessment techniques that are appropriate in middle-grades classrooms, it is beneficial to discuss seven characteristics of effective assessment in general. Regardless of the assessment techniques that teachers select, they should ensure that the overall assessment plan in their classrooms is: (1) continuous, (2) valid, (3) reliable, (4) comprehensive, (5) systematic, (6) objective, and (7) efficient.

As we discussed previously, effective assessment is **continuous;** that is, it occurs before, during, and after instructional units. It is an integral part of the instructional process, as opposed to an afterthought two weeks before grades are due. Good teachers do not depend entirely on one or two formal tests during a marking period to find out how well their students learned what was taught.

Assessment that is **valid** reflects goals, objectives, and instructional procedures. In short, valid assessment reflects what was taught. A synonym for *valid* in this context is *relevant*. For example, suppose an objective in a seventh-grade language arts class was that students would be able to compose an original haiku, and instructional activities revolved around that objective. Valid assessment of that objective would in some way involve students composing a haiku, as opposed to listing the characteristics of a haiku or identifying a haiku.

Reliable assessment provides a consistent measure of the ability or trait it is intended to assess. That is, you would expect to get about the same results on the assessment from one administration to the next and from one form to another, assuming the assessment was conducted under the same conditions both times.

Comprehensive assessment involves collecting a variety of relevant information about students. As you may remember from our movie example, the more varied and valid the information, the more accurate the decision. This is especially true when assessing young adolescents. With this age group, comprehensive assessment can involve not only information about their achievement but also information about their physical development, social-emotional development, work and study skills, interests, and attitudes. In some cases, information about home and community background may also play a role in the decisions you make about young adolescents.

Systematic assessment assures that information is collected and evaluated about *all* students. This type of assessment is not difficult when techniques such as tests, quizzes, and homework are used. But when teachers use informal techniques, such as observation or recitation, it is quite easy to make wrong decisions about what students know and understand during your lesson. For example, during recitation, several students may answer correctly, leading you to assume that all students understand. Good teachers develop strategies for soliciting answers from volunteers as well as nonvolunteers in order to get a more accurate picture of what is being learned.

Objective assessment means that two or more experts can follow the same assessment procedures and come up with the same results and interpretations. For example, two or more experts should be able to score your students' tests (including essay questions!) and come up with the same results. Similarly, two or more experts should be able to use your observational system and come up with the same results for each child. *Objectivity*, as it is used here, refers to the scoring of the assessment, not the form of the assessment.

Efficient assessment is both time and cost effective. Teachers should aim for getting the most information possible in the shortest amount of time possible for the least amount of money possible. In terms of efficiency, time is usually more of a factor than cost for teachers. (Cost usually plays more of a role in standardized testing, which we discuss later in the chapter.) Teachers should weigh the time involved in constructing, administering, scoring, and reporting information against the usefulness of the information obtained.

For example, if a writing test takes 12 hours to score but provides very little useful information, it is not very time efficient. On the other hand, a five-item, multiple-choice quiz may provide enough information to let you know how to adjust your plans for the next day. Of course, the opposite could also be true. A short writing sample could provide much more relevant information than a long multiple-choice test. In sum, it is not the form of the test or the type of items on the test that determine the efficiency of the test. Rather, it is the usefulness of the results of the test relative to the amount of time invested that determines efficiency.

Now that you know what characterizes effective assessment, we will discuss some of the various assessment techniques used in middle-grades classrooms. In particular, you will learn about teacher-made tests, curriculum-embedded tests, observation, portfolios, interviews and questionnaires, and sociometric devices. We will discuss the advantages and disadvantages of each of these techniques and present guidelines for constructing and using them in the classroom.

Teacher-Made Tests

Research shows that middle-grades teachers use teacher-made tests and they use them more often than elementary school teachers do (Airasian, 1989). When constructing their own tests, teachers rely most heavily on completion or short-answer items. It also appears that teachers use matching more often than true-false or multiple-choice items and they rarely use essays (Fleming & Chambers, 1983).

Despite the importance of challenging young adolescents to engage in more higher-level thinking, middle-grades teachers limit their test questions almost exclusively to the knowledge level. Fleming and Chambers (1983) found that almost 94 percent of middle-grades teachers' questions are on the knowledge level, significantly more than elementary teachers (69 percent) and high school teachers (69 percent). Surprisingly, students appear to be more concerned about teacher-made tests than standardized tests: they think teacher-made tests are harder and they get more nervous taking them (Stetz & Beck, 1979). Perhaps this is because students realize that teacher-made tests have more immediate classroom implications than standardized tests.

Teacher-made tests have several advantages, especially when compared to other forms of tests. First, teacher-made tests can be constructed to reflect the specific goals and objectives that teachers stressed during instruction. Second, teacher-made tests are less expensive and more readily available than standardized tests. Third, since teachers usually score their own tests, both teachers and students receive more immediate feedback from teacher-made tests than from standardized

Teacher-made tests should reflect the goals and objectives stressed during instruction.

tests. Finally, because of these three advantages, teacher-made tests usually provide much more useful information for classroom decisions than standardized tests do.

On the other hand, teacher-made tests also have several disadvantages. First, they are very time consuming and difficult to construct appropriately. Second, when constructing tests, teachers may not do an adequate job of sampling the test domain. For example, teachers may place too much emphasis on a topic that received relatively little emphasis during instruction. Third, teachers may weigh different items inappropriately. For example, a student may receive a low score because she answered one or two unimportant questions incorrectly despite the fact that she answered the important questions correctly. Last, since teachers know the exact items on the tests they construct, they may have a tendency to "teach to the test." When this occurs, the test is no longer a systematic sampling of what was taught and it provides little useful information for making instructional decisions.

As mentioned, middle-grades teachers use a variety of items when they construct their own tests. We will now discuss several of these item types in detail.

Completion

Completion items are also known as *fill-in-the-blank* or *supply* items. One advantage of completion items is that, compared to many other types of items, the effect

---

FIGURE 9.1   Guidelines for Construction Completion Items

---

1. *Require short, specific answers.*

2. *Avoid "multimutilated" statements.* Blanks should not be scattered haphazardly throughout a statement. Rather, they should reflect important information you are trying to elicit from your students.

   Poor

   _____ was born in _____ and wrote _____ in _____. (Technically, a student who answers "I was born in the hospital and wrote with a pen in my house" would be correct!)

   Improved

   Jane Austen was born in the city of _____ and wrote the novel _____ in the year _____.

3. *Be specific about the terms of the answer.*
   Poor

   What did Jane Austen write? _____. (A student who answers "a book" is correct!)

   Improved

   Name a novel that Jane Austen wrote. _____

4. *Give credit for all possible correct answers and let students know if they will lose credit for incorrect spellings.*

---

of guessing is virtually eliminated. A second advantage is that, in terms of efficiency, they are easy to construct and score. On the other hand, completion items have the disadvantage of being difficult to score objectively. Additionally, completion items are frequently limited to testing lower-level objectives. Figure 9.1 provides guidelines for constructing completion items.

True-False

True-false items have several advantages as well as disadvantages. They are extremely easy and quick to score. In addition, if constructed properly, they can be used to assess principles and generalities as well as misconceptions. However, the guessing factor can adversely affect the reliability of true-false tests. The effect of guessing can be diminished by lengthening the test. But it will take a considerably larger number of items to achieve a reliable test made up of true-false items than multiple-choice items. (For this reason, it is generally recommended that a test not be composed entirely of true-false items).

FIGURE 9.2   Guidelines for Constructing True-False Items

---

1. *Use statements that are absolutely true or absolutely false.*

2. *Ask students to correct any statements they mark false.*   This practice can help eliminate some of the guessing factor involved in true-false items.

3. *Avoid the use of irrelevant cues.*   Items that use words such as *always* and *never* tend to be false, whereas items that use words such as *can* and *may* tend to be true. Knowledgeable students know this and answer accordingly.

   Poor
   None of the people in Switzerland are engaged in farming.

   Improved
   The mountains of Switzerland prevent the Swiss people from raising grains extensively.

4. *Construct true statements approximately the same length as false statements.*   In their desire to make true statements "absolutely" true, many teachers tend to construct true statements longer than false statements.

5. *Use precise language that is not subject to a variety of interpretations.*

   Poor
   By 1861, a great many states had established universities.

   Improved
   By 1861, 20 states had established universities.

6. *Avoid double negatives and negatively stated items.*

   Poor
   Freezing weather is not frequently unknown in southern California.

   Improved
   Winter temperatures dip below freezing in some parts of southern California.

Also, true-false items tend to be used primarily to test facts and other lower-level information. They are also difficult and time consuming to construct properly. Guidelines for constructing true-false items are given in Figure 9.2.

Multiple Choice

Multiple-choice items are composed of a question or statement, referred to as the **stem,** and a list of responses. One of the responses is the correct answer and the others are referred to as **distractors.** Multiple-choice items have several advantages over other types of items. First, they are extremely reliable and flexible. Despite what many people think, multiple-choice items can be written to measure higher-level objectives. Second, with multiple-choice items, the effect of guessing is lower than with true-false items. Third, if the distractors are carefully constructed, multiple-choice items can provide important diagnostic information. Last, multiple-choice items are easier and quicker to score than other types of items such as completion and essay.

The major disadvantage of multiple-choice items is that they are extremely difficult and time consuming to construct properly. This is primarily because plausible distractors are sometimes difficult to provide. In addition, if not properly constructed, multiple-choice items can contain cues that lead students to the correct answers. Figure 9.3 identifies guidelines that you should keep in mind when constructing multiple-choice items.

FIGURE 9.3 Guidelines for Constructing Multiple-Choice Items

---

1. *State the stem as briefly as possible in the form of a direct question or incomplete statement.*

2. *State the stem to reflect one, clear problem.* Students should not have to read the responses to find out what the question is.

3. *State the stem to include all words that might otherwise be repeated in each response.*
   Poor
   The members of the board of directors of a corporation are usually chosen by which of these?
   a. the bondholders of the corporation
   b. the stockholders of the corporation
   c. the president of the corporation
   d. the employees of the corporation

   Improved
   Which persons associated with a corporation usually choose its board of directors?
   a. bondholders
   b. stockholders
   c. officials
   d. employees

4. *State the stem in positive form.* Negatively worded items are needlessly confusing. Students may get them wrong, not because they don't know the information but because they can't understand the question.

(continued)

FIGURE 9.3 *Continued*

5. *Avoid interrelated items.* An answer to one question should not depend on the answer to a previous question. Otherwise, students who miss the first question will most likely miss the second question, thereby being penalized twice. Alternatively, the stem of one question should not give away the answer to another question.

6. *State the responses in such a way that the correct answer is not systematically different from the distractors.* Students who do not know the correct answer frequently choose an answer that looks different from the others. For example, Carter (1986) found that many seventh-grade students who did not know the correct answer to a multiple-choice item reported choosing the longest answer because, as one student put it, "I figure my teacher doesn't have time to write all that unless it's the right one" (p. 21).

7. *State all distractors so they are plausible, thereby making them attractive to students who do not know the correct answer.*

   Poor
   Which of the following men was at one time vice-president of the United States?
   a. John Kennedy
   b. Richard Nixon
   c. Marco Polo
   d. Franklin Roosevelt

   Improved
   Which of the following men was at one time vice-president of the United States?
   a. John Kennedy
   b. Richard Nixon
   c. Ronald Reagan
   d. Franklin Roosevelt

8. *Avoid grammatical and other irrelevant cues.*

   Poor
   A large body of water is an
   a. ocean
   b. river
   c. creek
   d. stream

   Improved
   What is the name used to refer to a large body of water?
   a. ocean
   b. river
   c. creek
   d. stream

9. *If the response "None of the above" is used, it should not be the correct answer.* If "none of the above" is used as the correct answer, especially in mathematics problems, students who solve the problem incorrectly will most likely choose "none of the above" if their answer is not among the choices. As a result, these students will get the question correct without really knowing how to do the problem.

10. *Avoid the tendency to make "C" the correct answer.* For whatever reason, teachers overuse "C" as the correct answer. Test-wise students know this and select "C" when they don't know the correct answer (Carter, 1986). Carter also reports that test-wise seventh-grade students think their teachers never use "A" for the correct answer and "D" is always for the dumb answer.

FIGURE 9.4   Guidelines for Constructing Matching Tests

---

1. *Include a small number of stimuli as well as two or three extra responses.*

2. *Stimuli as well as responses should be drawn from the same domain.*   For example, if a matching test requires students to match explorers with countries they explored, then one column should consist *only* of explorers and the other column should consist *only* of countries.

3. *Directions should clearly state what is being matched.*

   The following example violates all three of the above guidelines.

   Match the words in the left column with the words in the right column.

____ 1.	Organized by crafts	a.	Taft-Hartley Act
____ 2.	Employees' refusal to work	b.	Industrial Revolution
____ 3.	First president of CIO	c.	AF of L
____ 4.	Resulted in a change of economic relationship between employer and employees	d.	Strike
____ 5.	Outlawed the closed shop	e.	John L. Lewis

Matching Tests

Matching tests usually consist of two columns—a stimulus column and a response column. Students match the stimulus with the correct response. Matching tests are ideal for asking students several questions about a body of related material. In a sense, matching tests are really composed of several multiple-choice items, all with the same list of responses. Matching tests arc casy to construct and score. Their only disadvantage is that they are difficult to use in testing for higher-level objectives. Guidelines for constructing matching tests are given in Figure 9.4.

You can see the results of violating the three guidelines given in Figure 9.4. First, it is hard to tell what is being matched because the directions are not specific. Second, it is very easy to answer all questions correctly without knowing very much about the topic. For example, since there is only one person listed among the responses, he must be the first president of the CIO. Similarly, since there is only one act listed, it must be the one that outlawed the closed shop. Third, students who know four of the answers will get the fifth one correct by process of elimination since there are no extra responses.

Example   The following example, constructed by two Gwinnett County, Georgia, middle-grades teachers, Diane Zieg and Suzanne Franks, illustrates correct implementation of the three guidelines:

Match the Civil War battle descriptions in Column A with the battle sites in Column B.

	A		*B*
____ 1.	First battle of the war	a.	Bull Run
____ 2.	Battle between ironclads	b.	Chancellorsville
		c.	Fort Sumter
____ 3.	Turning point of the war	d.	Gettysburg
____ 4.	Grant's victory in the west	e.	James River
		f.	Vicksburg

Essay

Essay questions are well suited for measuring higher-level objectives that require students to organize and integrate ideas. In addition, essay questions have the advantage of being easier to construct than some other item types. Essay questions are also ideal for evaluating affective objectives. The primary disadvantage of essay questions is that they are extremely difficult and time consuming to grade objectively. Also, since essay questions take longer to answer than other types of items, less material can usually be covered on tests composed entirely of essay questions.

When designing essay questions, keep the following guidelines in mind:

1. *State directions in such a way that students know exactly what information you expect them to include in their answers.* Directions such as "Discuss the process of photosynthesis" give students very little idea about the type of information they are expected to include in their answers.
2. *Let students know what role, if any, spelling, grammar, and punctuation will play in their grade.* Some teachers give two grades—one for content and one for mechanics.
3. *Let students know the total point value of each essay.*

Scoring essays is difficult and controversial. General recommendations that should help you score essays more objectively include:

1. *Do not let irrelevant factors affect the scoring of essays.* Chase (1986) found that irrelevant factors such as sex, race, penmanship, and the teacher's achievement expectations for the student interact to affect middle-grades teachers' scoring of students' essays. If possible, try to make scoring anonymous.
2. *When scoring more than one essay per student, score all students' answers to one essay. Continue this process until all essays have been scored.* By using this procedure, you will reduce the possibility that a student's performance on one essay will affect your scoring of that student's other essays.

Two popular methods used by teachers to score essays are holistic scoring and analytic scoring. Scores obtained by these two methods appear to be highly correlated when used by middle-grades teachers (Vacc, 1989). **Holistic** scoring involves a quick reading of a student's essay and assigning a score based on an overall impression rather than on a breakdown of specific criteria. Results of holistic scoring usually take into account factors other than content, such as expression, organization, and creativity. The chief advantage of this scoring method is that it is very time efficient; however, students may be at a disadvantage if they are not aware of the criteria their teacher will use to score their essays.

Analytic scoring involves assigning points to the various components of the essay. When this method is used, it is helpful to write out your own "model" essay, identify critical components, and decide how many points to give to each component. This scoring method is ideal when content is of primary importance. The obvious disadvantage of analytic scoring is that it is extremely time consuming. Figure 9.5 illustrates the analytic scoring method applied to a short essay question. Two University of Georgia students, Nancy Mizelle and Jody Beckman, designed

FIGURE 9.5   Analytic Scoring of Short Essay

Question

Using Newton's Law of Gravity, explain the origin of the solar system. (6 points)

Ideal Answer: Students' answers may include information beyond what is included in the ideal answer. But points are assigned according to the following scheme:

1 point: The force of gravity once pulled the solar system together.

1 point: Gravity pulled together gas and dust into a large cloud that began to spin slightly.

1 point: The cloud eventually collapsed, the spin speeded up, and the cloud became flat.

1 point: Gravity pulled smaller bits of gas and dust together, joining them to form larger clumps.

1 point: The largest clump became the sun.

1 point: The smaller clumps became the planets and other objects.

Source: Used with permission of Nancy Mizelle and Jody Beckman.

the essay and assigned points to their ideal answer. They included the essay on a test given at the end of a seventh-grade unit on the solar system.

Effective Testing Practices

Good teachers ensure that their students do their best on classroom tests by doing certain things before, during, and after the test is administered. Before students take a test, you can prepare them for it in several ways. First, specify the exact test coverage. This does not mean that you should tell students the exact questions that will be on the test, but you should let them know what topics or areas are important. It will also help your students if you tell them something about the types of items that will be on the test. Good students study differently for essay tests than they do for multiple-choice tests. You may want to give your students a practice test or sample items similar to those that will be on the test.

In addition Kauchak and Eggen (1989) also recommend letting your students know that you have positive expectations for their performance on the test. If students know that you think they are prepared and will do a good job, they will have more confidence going into the test. It is also a good practice to plan an independent assignment or activity that students can work on when they finish the test. This will help ensure that students who finish early do not get bored and distract others who may still be working on the test.

During the test you should make every effort to keep distractions to a minimum. A "Testing: Do Not Disturb" sign on your door will help keep out unnecessary visitors. If classroom windows look out on a busy playground or some other distracting scene, you may want to lower the shades during the test. You should also make sure that students are comfortable and have enough room to work. As mentioned previously, young adolescents vary tremendously in their physical development and frequently end up in seats that are too large or too small. It is also a good idea to circulate around the room periodically to ensure that students are on task and are actually working on the test.

After the test, grade it as quickly as possible so you can give students immediate feedback. The feedback that you give your students should let them know "what they have learned well or mastered and what they need to spend more time learning" (Guskey, 1989, p. 353). When giving back tests, you should take time to go over questions that were frequently missed and to answer general questions about the test. Students who performed poorly should be scheduled for additional time so you can go over their tests in detail with them.

Analyzing Test Results

Research indicates that, on the whole, teachers do not do a good job of analyzing the results of their tests (Gullickson & Ellwein, 1985). This is unfortunate because a thorough analysis of the test results can supply you with important pieces of information. By analyzing your students' test results, you can get a good idea of how well your class performed as a whole, as well as how individual students performed on each item. Also, you can examine the effectiveness of your test items.

Student Item Analysis.   A student item analysis will provide you with information about individual as well as group strengths and weaknesses. This information can help you make important instructional decisions, such as what material you should reteach, which students are ready for enrichment activities, and which students need remedial work. Table 9.1 illustrates a sample student analysis chart that can help you organize test results.

As Table 9.1 indicates, Laurie and Steve did not answer any questions correctly and will need extensive remedial work. Brent, on the other hand, answered all

TABLE 9.1   Analysis of Student Test Results

	TEST ITEMS									
STUDENT	*1*	*2*	*3*	*4*	*5*	*6*	*7*	*8*	*9*	*10*
Laurie	X	X	X	X	X	X	X	X	X	X
George				X		X		X		
Elizabeth				X	X	X				X
Steve	X	X	X	X	X	X	X	X	X	X
Brenda				X		X				
Brent										
Marilyn				X		X	X			
Jack	X			X		X			X	
Bill			X	X		X				
Judy	X	X				X				
Keith	X		X	X						
Tony			X	X	X	X				
Cy	X			X		X			X	X

X = incorrect

questions correctly and could probably benefit from some enrichment activities. The table also shows that item #4 was answered incorrectly by all students except Brent and Judy and item #6 was answered incorrectly by all students except Brent and Keith. These items should be examined to ensure that they were worded in such a way that their intent was clear to the students. If no problems are found with the items themselves, then you will probably want to go back and reteach this material. Reteaching should be done as soon as possible, especially if knowledge of the material is a prerequisite for lessons in the near future.

Item Profile. When multiple-choice items (and to some extent, matching items) are used on tests, it is also helpful to examine the pattern of responses on each item. By doing such an examination, you can determine the effectiveness of the distractors you used. This information will help you make important decisions concerning test revision. Table 9.2 illustrates a sample pattern of responses for items #1, 2, and 4 in Table 9.1.

The profile of item #1 shows that distractor D was not effective in attracting students who did not know the correct answer. If this test is used in the future, a more attractive distractor should be substituted for distractor D. The profile for item #2 indicates that all distractors were equally attractive to students. This item can probably be used again without revision. The profile for item #4 shows that serious problems exist either with the item itself or with students' understanding of the material tested by the item. It could be that the item is not clearly written. Alternatively, it could be that most of the students do not understand the material that this item tests. If the latter is the case, then reteaching the material tested in this item is clearly necessary.

Curriculum-Embedded Tests

Curriculum-embedded tests are tests commercially produced by publishing companies. These tests frequently "accompany a textbook series and some are produced as part of 'packaged' curricula that schools and school systems sometimes purchase" (Cangelosi, 1990, p. 26). In addition to assessing student achievement, these tests are used in a variety of ways by classroom teachers. For example, Kuhs, Porter, Floden, Freeman, Schmidt, & Schwille (1985) report that teachers use

TABLE 9.2 Item Profile

	RESPONSE ALTERNATIVES AND NUMBER OF STUDENTS WHO SELECTED EACH RESPONSE			
	A	*B*	*C*	*D*
Item #1	*7	3	3	0
Item #2	1	*10	1	1
Item #4	0	0	11	*2

* = correct answer

curriculum-embedded tests to make decisions about student placement and curriculum selection and pace. These tests can also be used for practice tests, extra worksheets, and homework assignments.

It appears that curriculum-embedded tests comprise a large portion of all the tests administered to students. For example, fourth- and sixth-grade mathematics teachers reported that almost 80 percent of their testing involved curriculum-embedded tests (Burry, Catterall, Choppin, & Dorr-Bremme, 1982). The clear advantage of curriculum-embedded tests is that they are directly applicable to the curriculum that is being taught in the classroom. Classroom teachers can pick and choose the particular items they want their students to answer. In addition, teachers who are knowledgeable about item construction can revise or eliminate items that they feel are poorly written.

Observation

Observation occurs routinely in all classrooms. For instance, as the students work, teachers frequently circulate among them and observe what they are doing. Teachers also observe how students answer questions during discussions. Student performance is often observed in art, music, and physical education classes. This casual observation of students is frequently used by teachers as a form of assessment. In fact, there is some evidence that observation may be the most prevalent form of assessment used by classroom teachers (Salmon-Cox, 1981). Elementary teachers rely more on observation than do high school teachers, and language arts teachers rely on it more than mathematics and science teachers (Stiggins & Bridgeford, 1985).

In any event, observation appears to be a powerful assessment technique that can provide important information to middle-grades teachers. Despite the wealth of information that can be obtained through observation, teachers receive very little training in how to use it as an effective assessment technique (Guerin & Maier, 1983).

Observation has the advantage of being able to assess students in their natural setting, as compared to the somewhat stressful setting of test taking. Observation can be integrated into the teaching process much easier than some other assessment techniques. Also, when compared to tests, observation can provide more varied information, especially qualitative information, about students.

Observation does have its disadvantages, however. Unless reliable instruments are used that clearly distinguish among behaviors, teachers can collect faulty information. Also, since there are no right or wrong answers, it is difficult for some teachers to remain objective when they collect observational data. And last, it is easy to overgeneralize from one, short observation.

It is beyond the scope of this chapter to make you proficient in using observational techniques to assess students in your classroom. Such proficiency requires a thorough knowledge of the various observational techniques and extensive practice using them. We would, however, like to at least acquaint you with a few observational techniques that are appropriate for use in middle-grades classrooms. We draw our definitions and descriptions from Guerin and Maier's 1983 book *Informal Assessment in Education.*

As defined by Guerin and Maier (1983), observational assessment techniques are usually categorized as either direct or indirect. **Direct observation** procedures involve systematically watching and recording behavior through the use of "a predetermined observational schema" (p. 81). An example of direct observation is counting how many times David hits another student during a 45-minute class period. In contrast, **indirect observation** procedures "rely heavily on memory and usually call for judgments" (p. 81). An example of indirect observation is filling out a rating scale on Anita's behavior during classroom discussion the previous quarter. Indirect observation usually takes place after the behavior has happened. As such, in most cases, it is more subjective than direct observation.

Portfolio Assessment

Portfolio assessment is a relatively new type of assessment that is especially appropriate for use with young adolescents. It involves all students in the class having a portfolio or file in which they place their best work during a given time period. Currently, portfolio assessment is used primarily in language arts classes to assess students' reading and writing. But this type of assessment can be used by all middle-grades teachers regardless of the subjects they teach. There are two important features that distinguish portfolio assessment from other types of assessment: students learn how to engage in self-assessment and teachers have a better sense of how their students' abilities have grown and improved over time.

Rief (1990) describes a type of portfolio assessment in which the teacher determines the external criteria and the students determine the internal criteria. *External criteria* refer to the number of pieces students must put in their portfolios and how often they get evaluated. *Internal criteria* refer to which pieces get placed in the portfolio and why. Students also keep working files, where they keep their work in progress and work they do not select to put in their portfolio. Rief also encourages teachers to keep and share their own portfolios with their students.

When selecting pieces to be put in their portfolios, Rief (1990) recommends students think about the following questions:

- What makes this your best piece?
- How did you go about writing it?
- What problems did you encounter?
- What makes your most effective piece different from your least effective piece?
- What goals did you set for yourself?
- How well did you accomplish them?
- What are your goals for the next 12 weeks? (p. 28)

If students are to be graded, their grades should be given according to the goals that they set and achieved for themselves.

In this classroom, portfolios are kept in a file drawer so students have easy access to their work.

Interviews and Questionnaires

Interviews and questionnaires involve the simple procedure of asking students what you want to know. Interviews are oral; questionnaires are written. A primary advantage of the interview is that teachers can adapt it to their own particular needs. An interview with a student can be restructured immediately, depending on the student's responses. Interviews are also useful because they provide immediate feedback to teachers. During advisor/advisee sessions when young adolescents' thoughts and opinions are sought on various issues, interviews are particularly appropriate. They can help establish rapport and trust among middle-grades teachers and their students.

Interviews also have their disadvantages, however. The primary disadvantages of interviews are that they are extremely time consuming and, because interviews are adaptable, they are susceptible to interviewer bias. For example, in an unstructured interview, teachers' preestablished beliefs and opinions can affect the structure of the interview and the types of questions that are asked during the interview. Figure 9.6 provides suggestions to help you conduct effective interviews with your students.

Questionnaires are also an excellent method of obtaining information about

FIGURE 9.6   Guidelines for Conducting Interviews

1. *Have a specific purpose for the interview and conduct the interview to achieve that purpose.*   All too often interviews result in idle chitchat because they do not have a focus. Preparing specific questions ahead of time can help get the interview started and keep it on track. Questions can be altered, added, or eliminated as needed as the interview progresses.
2. *Let the student talk.*   Avoid turning the interview into an interrogation. Solicit student input and encourage free talk.
3. *End the interview with a summary of the main points and a plan of action.*   Presumably, your interview had a purpose. At the end of the interview, it should be clear to both you and the student whether or not the purpose was accomplished. Summarize the main points of the interview and discuss with the student the outcome of the interview.

students' attitudes, interests, and opinions on a variety of issues. When compared to interviews, questionnaires are much less time consuming because they allow you to collect the same information from a number of students simultaneously. If conducted anonymously, questionnaires are sometimes less threatening to students than interviews and may result in more honest answers. On the other hand, questionnaires require more time to score and are not as immediately adaptable as interviews.

If you construct your own questionnaires, keep the following guidelines in mind:

1. *Provide clear directions.*   Students should know exactly what they are expected to do on the questionnaire as well as how the results of the questionnaire will be used.
2. *Avoid ambiguous and leading questions.* Questions that are confusing or that suggest students should answer in a certain way will be of little use to you in making classroom decisions.

Figure 9.7 illustrates a questionnaire administered by a Gwinnett County, Georgia, middle-grades teacher, Beth Kieffer, to her seventh-grade class at the end of a science unit on the atmosphere. The questionnaire provided her with information that helped her revise the unit for future use.

Sociometric Devices

Sociometric devices help teachers understand the interpersonal relationships among the students in their classrooms. As we discussed in Chapter 2, young adolescents' status among their peers can affect their social and emotional development as well as their academic performance in the classroom. Because of the influence of peers, as well as young adolescents' need to be a part of a group, knowledge of the interpersonal relationships among students is crucial for middle-grades teachers.

Sociometric devices can provide teachers with information such as what the established groups are in the class, which students seem to have no close friends,

FIGURE 9.7   Attitudinal Assessment

1. What did you like most about the unit on atmosphere? _____

   _____

   Why? _____

   _____

2. What did you dislike about the unit on atmosphere? _____

   _____

   Why? _____

   _____

3. Rank the following methods of learning from 1 to 6, with 1 being the most liked and 6 being the least liked:

   ____ activities   ____ lecture   ____ films

   ____ discussion   ____ notetaking   ____ worksheets

4. Of all the activities we did, which one was your favorite? _____

   _____

   Why? _____

   _____

5. Of all the activities we did, which one was your least favorite? _____

   _____

   Why? _____

   _____

6. What one thing, throughout the whole unit, helped you the most in learning about the

   atmosphere? _____

   _____

Source: Used with permission of Beth Kieffer.

and which students are leaders. Such information can be useful to teachers for a variety of purposes, including structuring advisor/advisee sessions, grouping students for classroom activities, and recommending students for counseling.

It is easy to construct and administer sociometric devices. Middle-grades teachers can use sociometric devices for a variety of purposes. For instance, sociometric devices usually ask students to list two or three classmates with whom they prefer to work or be with for certain activities (e.g., sit with on the bus, work with on a class project, study with for a test, sit with at lunch). The teacher then summarizes the information on a chart, table, or diagram, frequently referred to as a *sociogram*. Figures 9.8 and 9.9, which use a circle method of summarizing results, illustrate the same students' responses for two different questions.

FIGURE 9.8   Sociogram Showing With Whom Students Would Like to Study

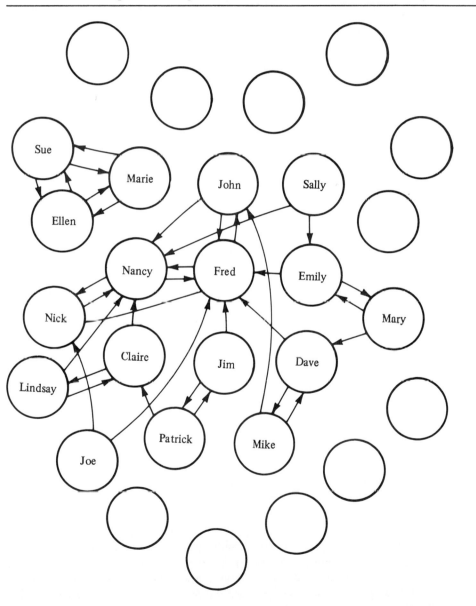

FIGURE 9.9 Sociogram Showing Whom Students Would Like to Sit with on the Bus

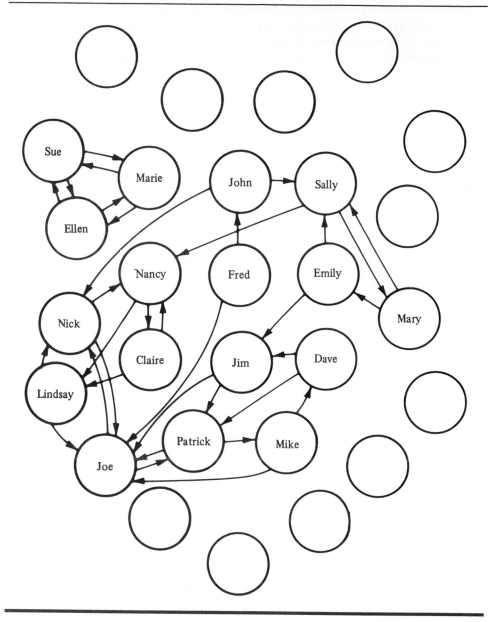

As you can see, when asked with whom they would like to study, Fred and Nancy were chosen most frequently. With the exception of Joe and Sally, who were not chosen at all, all students were chosen at least once. But the situation changed when students were asked whom they would like to sit with on the bus. Fred was not chosen by any student and Joe was chosen quite frequently. Despite Joe's popularity, he clearly was not perceived by his peers to be a good study partner. Fred, on the other hand, is not very popular but students probably realized that he is smart and they wanted to study with him. In addition to identifying "stars" and "isolates," both sociograms identify clearly formed cliques that stay together regardless of the activity.

Classroom Assessment Systems

Now that you are familiar with the various assessment techniques and how to construct your own tests, you should think about how to put it altogether in the classroom. In the beginning of the school year, or at the beginning of a new term, effective teachers usually sit down and make decisions about how many tests they will give, how they will integrate homework into their assessment, and how they will assign grades. Kauchak and Eggen (1989) define the end product of all of these decisions as a classroom assessment system.

Frequency of Testing

Before deciding how many tests to give during a certain term or marking period, it is probably a good idea to check with other teachers on your team or with your principal to find out if your school has any policies on testing. For example, are you required to give a midterm and a final? Is there a minimum number of tests that you are required to give? Are there certain days set aside for tests or exams? Answers to questions such as these will affect your own classroom assessment system. If you are working on a team, it is also a good idea to design a team assessment system. Such a system will help ensure that major tests are spaced appropriately throughout the term or marking period. (Most of us don't do our best when we have three exams on the same day!)

How often should you test students? You will most likely want to give some type of summative test at the end of every unit of material. In addition, you will probably be doing a great deal of informal observation throughout each unit. But how about short quizzes and other types of formative evaluation throughout each unit? Research suggests that a moderate amount of testing not only helps students learn the material better but is actually preferred by students (Crooks, 1988). Some students report that they feel more organized when frequent, short tests are given because this method of evaluation forces them to keep up with readings and assignments almost daily. This method of evaluation also helps students become familiar with the teacher's testing style.

You can also help your students by letting them know as far as possible in advance when their tests will be. As you are probably aware, most young adolescents are not noted for their long-range planning. Providing them with a schedule for the entire term or marking period can be especially useful for helping them organize their time and developing good study habits.

Role of Homework

Homework is a valuable source of immediate information on whether or not students are learning what you are teaching. In addition, evidence suggests that appropriately designed homework assignments increase achievement (Walberg, Pascal, & Weinstein, 1985). Additionally, Marshall (1982) found a positive relationship between the number of hours spent doing homework per week and achievement. Homework that is graded (Walberg, Pascal, & Weinstein, 1985) and commented on (Elawar & Corno, 1985) by the teacher increases achievement more than homework that is ungraded or not commented on.

Appropriately designed homework assignments are those that students can do independently in a reasonably short period of time. Thus, homework assignments should provide additional practice on class-related material. It is a good practice to let students get started on homework assignments during the last few minutes of class. In fact, doing the first few questions, problems, or exercises together, as a class, increases the probability that students will finish the assignment at home. After students complete their homework assignments, they should be provided with some type of feedback. Brophy and Good (1986) recommend that students should be held accountable for correctly completing homework assignments, that homework should be checked, and that errors should be corrected.

Perhaps one of the hardest decisions you will have to make about homework is what to do with it after students complete it. Will you check all of it yourself? Will you have students check their own or each other's work? Will you count it for a grade? If so, how will you count it? All of these are important questions that only you can answer. How will you decide what to do?

Kauchak and Eggen (1989) provide several helpful suggestions. First, check with your principal and other teachers to find out what the school policy is. It is very helpful if your team has a team policy on homework that is consistent from teacher to teacher. After that, experiment. Try different methods until you find just the right one for you and your students. Regardless of what you decide, keep in mind that doing and correcting homework should be a productive use of your time as well as students' time.

Assigning Grades

As we mentioned in Chapter 2, early adolescence is the time when students become more competitive and more grade conscious. Young adolescents tend to rate their own ability and that of their peers by the grades they receive. Remember also that young adolescents begin to compare report cards when they enter the middle grades. In short, grades are extremely important to most young adolescents and should be taken seriously by teachers.

Assigning grades is a difficult process for most beginning teachers. But if you plan ahead, at the beginning of the term or marking period, the process will be much easier. Decisions involving which assessment information to count and how to weigh such information in your grading system should be made before the term or marking period begins.

One of the first steps in deciding on a grading system is to find out if your school or team already has established criteria for assigning grades. For example, is it a school or team policy that 93 to 100 percent is equal to a grade of A, or can you decide that in your classes 90 to 100 percent is equal to an A? It is also a good idea to take a look at the actual report cards to find out if you are responsible only for an achievement grade or if you are also expected to grade students on other factors such as effort and management. Knowing the answers to these questions ahead of time can help you collect the appropriate information throughout the entire term or marking period.

Terwilliger (1989) lists several additional guidelines to keep in mind as you design your classroom grading system. First, your grading system should reflect the instructional goals and outcomes that you established for that term or marking period. Accordingly, the highest grades should "be assigned to those who achieve the most advanced outcomes" (p. 15).

Second, Terwilliger (1989) recommends that all assessment information you use in your grading system should be quantified by expressing it as scores or points. This practice helps to eliminate any subjective judgments that might affect the grades you assign. For example, information such as "Bob really contributed to class discussions this quarter" should not affect Bob's grade unless his contribution, as well as all other students' contributions, are quantified in some way.

Third, a failing grade should be assigned to a student only in the case where "that student does not possess a *minimal* level of competence independent of the student's performance relative to other students" (Terwilliger, 1989, p. 16). For example, you should assign Fred a failing grade only if he does not possess minimal competence. He should not receive a failing grade just because he happens to have

An effective grading system reflects instructional goals that are appropriate for young adolescents.

the lowest average in the class. We feel that it is part of each student's responsibility to demonstrate to you that he or she possesses a minimal level of competence. Students who do not carry out those tasks and assignments that contribute to their grade and do not perform at a minimal level on tests may indeed deserve a failing grade.

Fourth, students (and their parents) should be aware of your grading system as well as your overall classroom assessment system. In other words, students should know exactly where their grades come from. For instance, students should know when tests will be administered and how they will count in their grades, when assignments are due and how they will count in their grades, and conditions under which grades will be lowered (e.g., late assignments). It is a good practice to distribute a chart or diagram, as well as a schedule of due dates, to your students at the beginning of the term or marking period. Students can attach this information to their notebooks and check off assignments, record their grades, and actually compute their grades at the end of the term. This practice helps keep students organized and also provides them with a means of becoming more responsible for their own work.

Fifth, you should take a practical approach to grading. Realistic expectations should be set for your students as well as for yourself.

Standardized Tests

We did not include standardized tests in the previous section on classroom assessment techniques because, on the whole, standardized tests do not play a significant role in the day-to-day instructional decisions that are made in the classroom. For example, Schmidt (1981) reports that standardized tests are rarely used by classroom teachers to make decisions about placement, content, or grading. Despite their lack of use by classroom teachers, "nearly all major studies of testing in the schools have focused on the role of standardized tests" (Stiggins, Conklin, & Bridgeford, 1986, p. 5). Thus, while they may be an important assessment technique, we do not consider standardized tests an important *classroom* assessment technique.

Standardized tests are, however, administered at least once a year in a large majority of middle-grades classrooms throughout the country. In addition, they can provide you with some important information about your students' overall achievement in various areas. Therefore, you should be knowledgeable about the characteristics and purposes of standardized tests as well as the types of information that can be obtained from them. At some point in your teaching career, you will most likely be approached by a parent or another teacher with questions about a student's standardized test results. The more familiar you are with standardized testing practices, the more likely you will be to provide appropriate answers.

Characteristics of Standardized Tests

Payne (in press) defines a *standardized test* as "a systematic sample of performance obtained under prescribed conditions, scored according to definite rules, and capable of evaluation by reference to normative information." Each of the three components of the definition merits discussion. First, as you may recall from taking standardized tests (such as the Scholastic Aptitude Test or the admission test of the American College Testing Program you may have taken for admission into college), the test was administered under prescribed conditions. For example, a set of prescribed directions were read to you and you had a designated amount of time for the various parts of the test. Presumably, regardless of where you took the test, these conditions were the same.

Second, your test, as well as the tests of all other individuals, was scored according to a set of prescribed rules. You most likely used an answer sheet that was later scored by a computer. Since the items on the test had been field tested, each item had one clear-cut answer so the scoring was routine. The items on most standardized tests have been shown to have high reliability and validity.

Third, because you took the test under the same conditions as everyone else, and because your test was scored according to the same set of rules as everyone else, you can compare your performance to that of the norming group. Normative information is generally provided so that you can make these comparisons.

Purposes of Standardized Tests

Standardized tests are often used to provide information about what students have learned in a variety of areas. These standardized tests are known as **achievement** tests. For example, middle-grades students frequently take a standardized achievement test such as the California Achievement Tests or the Metropolitan Achievement Tests. Results of tests such as these provide information about students' overall achievement in areas such as reading comprehension, science, and mathematics problem solving.

Decisions about curriculum can also be made by using standardized tests. Results of such tests can help principals and curriculum specialists identify overall strengths and weaknesses in their instructional programs. For example, after examining the district results of a standardized achievement test, the mathematics coordinator may decide that the seventh-grade mathematics curriculum should be reorganized with more emphasis on problem solving and less emphasis on computation.

Standardized tests are frequently used to identify students' strengths and weaknesses in a particular area. Results of these types of standardized tests, referred to as **diagnostic** tests, can be helpful in planning enrichment and remedial instruction for students. An example of a diagnostic test is the Stanford Diagnostic Reading Test, which tests a variety of reading skills ranging from auditory discrimination to inferential comprehension.

There are certain advantages of standardized tests, especially when compared to teacher-made tests. First, because of the effort and expense that is put into the construction of standardized tests, they are usually highly reliable and valid. Second, because normative information is usually provided, standardized tests allow you to compare your students' results with the results of students in the norming group. Third, standardized tests are usually accompanied by a manual that specifies the conditions under which the test should be administered. This allows you to test all of your students under the same conditions and to avoid having to make decisions about time, directions, and other factors related to the administration of the test.

Standardized tests, however, also have several disadvantages when compared to teacher-made tests. First, standardized tests are more expensive than teacher-made tests. Second, standardized tests do not provide the immediate feedback that teacher-made tests do. Standardized tests are frequently sent elsewhere to be scored and it may be several months before teachers get the results. Third, because standardized tests are comprehensive, there is a possibility that there may be items or even entire topics on the test that your students have not yet learned. Last, despite all good intentions, the standard administration conditions can be violated relatively easily.

For example, Wodtke, Harper, Schommer, and Brunelli (1989) observed violations such as inadequate testing environment, frequent and lengthy interruptions during testing, variability in length of testing sessions, teacher coaching, and disruptive student behavior including calling out answers. As the researchers pointed out, violations such as these are "so nonstandardized as to render their scores incomparable and quite possibly unreliable as well" (p. 223).

Summarizing Test Scores

There are two important measures that are frequently used to summarize and interpret test data: measures of central tendency and measures of variability. We will discuss these two measures as well as two types of scores that are used to describe student performance on tests.

Measures of Central Tendency

As its name indicates, *central tendency* refers to the fact that scores tend to cluster near a certain score or sometimes two or three scores. There are three measures of central tendency that are significant when we talk about test scores.

The **mean** is an arithmetic average of all the scores. As you probably already know, the mean is obtained by adding all the scores and then dividing by the total number of scores. When all the scores are arranged in order from lowest to highest, the **median** is the middle score. Thus, in a group of scores, half of the scores are above the median and half of the scores are below it. The median is more representative of the average than the mean if a set of scores includes some extremely high or extremely low scores that could distort the mean. The most frequently occurring score is the **mode.** A set of scores that has two modes is referred to as **bimodal.**

Measures of Variability

Measures of central tendency give you some indication of what the representative score is in a set of scores, but measures of central tendency do not provide you with any information about how varied the scores are. Two measures of variability, the range and the standard deviation, can provide you with this information.

The **range** is the number of score points that a set of scores covers. You can compute the range for a set of scores by subtracting the lowest score from the highest score and adding one. The range does not tell you how varied the scores are between the highest and lowest score. The **standard deviation,** however, tells you the average of how spread out the scores are around the mean. The larger the standard deviation, the more variability among the scores. The smaller the standard deviation, the less variability among the scores.

Types of Scores

Two types of scores that you will most likely encounter when you examine your students' standardized test results are percentile ranks and grade equivalent scores. A **percentile rank** refers to the percentage of scores in a set of scores that are equal to or lower than the score in question. For example, suppose that Rosemary's percentile rank on the vocabulary section of the California Achievement Test is 81. This means that Rosemary scored as well as or better than 81 percent of the norming sample. Notice that Rosemary's percentile rank of 81 does not mean she got 81 percent of the items correct. A percentile rank does not provide information about how many items were answered correctly or incorrectly. It only provides information about how well a student performed relative to the norming group.

Grade-equivalent scores are more difficult to explain than percentile ranks and are frequently misinterpreted. So, instead of just defining them, we will work through an example. Suppose Rosemary's grade-equivalent score on the mathematics concepts section of the California Achievement Test is 8.3. This score is interpreted as the third month of the eighth year of school. This score means that Rosemary performed as well as the average eighth-grader in the third month of school would have performed if he or she had taken the same test that Rosemary did.

This score has different interpretations depending on what grade Rosemary is in. If Rosemary is in fifth grade, it means she is above average; if she is in the eighth grade, it means she is about average; and if she is in eleventh grade, it means she is below average. Suppose Rosemary is in fifth grade. Does this mean she understands concepts that are taught in eighth grade? No! She probably has never even been taught eighth-grade mathematics concepts. This score only means that Rosemary performed as an average eighth-grader in the third month of school would have performed on *his* or *her* test.

It is probably easy for you to see how students and parents can become confused about the interpretation of grade-equivalent scores. Hopefully, if Rosemary's parents want you to move her into an eighth-grade mathematics class, you will be able to explain to them why that would not be appropriate.

Summary

Assessment is an important responsibility of the middle-grades teacher. The entire assessment process has several components, including evaluation and measurement. A test is one form of measurement, but there are numerous other techniques, both formal and informal, that can be used in assessment. Assessment is conducted for a variety of reasons, some helpful and some not so helpful to the teacher. Teachers use numerous assessment procedures in their classroom, including teacher-made tests, curriculum-embedded tests, observation, portfolios, interviews and questionnaires, sociometric devices, and standardized tests. Each of these procedures plays an important role in educational assessment.

REFERENCES

Airasian, P. W. (1989). Classroom assessment and educational improvement. In L. W. Anderson (Ed.), *The effective teacher* (pp. 333–342). New York: Random House.

Brophy, J. E., & Good, T. L. (1986). Teacher behavior and student achievement. In M. C. Wittrock (Ed.), *Handbook of research on teaching* (3rd ed., pp. 328–375). New York: Macmillan.

Burry, J., Catterall, J., Choppin, B., & Dorr-Bremme, D. (1982). *Testing in the nation's schools and districts: How much? What kinds? To what ends? At what costs?* (CSE Report No. 194). Los Angeles: Center for the Study of Evaluation, University of California.

Calfee, R., & Hiebert, E. (1988). The teacher's role in using assessment to improve learning. *Proceedings of the 1987 ETS Invitational Conference* (pp. 45–61). Princeton, NJ: Educational Testing Service.

Cangelosi, J. S. (1990). *Designing tests for evaluating student achievement*. New York: Longman.

Carter, K. (1986). Test-wiseness for teachers and students. *Educational Measurement: Issues and Practice, 5*(4), 20–23.

Chase, C. I. (1986). Essay test scoring: Interaction of relevant variables. *Journal of Educational Measurement, 23,* 33–41.

Crooks, T. J. (1988). The impact of classroom evaluation practices on students. *Review of Educational Research, 58,* 438–481.

Elawar, M. C., & Corno, L. (1985). A factorial experiment in teachers' written feedback on student homework: Changing teacher behavior a little rather than a lot. *Journal of Educational Psychology, 77,* 162–173.

Fleming, M., & Chambers, B. (1983). Teacher-made tests: Windows on the classroom. In W. E. Hathaway (Ed.), *New directions for testing and measurement: Vol. 19, Testing in the schools* (pp. 29–38). San Francisco: Jossey-Bass.

Guerin, G. R., & Maier, A. S. (1983). *Informal assessment in education*. Palo Alto, CA: Mayfield.

Gullickson, A. R. (1986). Teacher education and teacher-perceived needs in educational measurement and evaluation. *Journal of Educational Measurement, 23,* 347–354.

Gullickson, A. R., & Ellwein, M. C. (1985). Post hoc analysis of teacher-made tests: The goodness-of-fit between prescription and practice. *Educational Measurement: Issues and Practice, 4*(1), 15–18.

Gullickson, A. R., & Hopkins, K. D. (1987). The context of educational measurement instruction for preservice teachers: Professor perspectives. *Educational Measurement: Issues and Practice, 6*(3), 12–16.

Guskey, T. R. (1989). Feedback, correctives, and enrichment. In L. W. Anderson (Ed.), *The effective teacher* (pp. 353–363). New York: Random House.

Kauchak, D. P., & Eggen, P. D. (1989). *Learning and teaching: Research-based methods*. Boston: Allyn and Bacon.

Kuhs, T., Porter, A., Floden, R., Freeman, D., Schmidt, W., & Schwille, J. (1985). Differences among teachers in their use of curriculum-embedded tests. *The Elementary School Journal, 86,* 141–153.

Marshall, P. M. (1982). *Homework and social facilitation theory in teaching elementary school mathematics*. Unpublished doctoral dissertation, Stanford University.

Payne, D. A. (in press). *Measuring and evaluating educational outcomes*. Columbus, OH: Charles Merrill.

Rief, L. (1990). Finding the value in evaluation: Self-assessment in a middle school classroom. *Educational Leadership, 47*(6), 24–29.

Salmon-Cox, L. (1981). Teachers and standardized achievement tests: What's really happening? *Phi Delta Kappan, 62,* 631–634.

Schmidt, W. H. (1981, April). *Teacher knowl-*

edge and use of standardized tests. Paper presented at the annual meeting of the American Educational Research Association, Los Angeles.

Shepard, L. A. (1989). Why we need better assessments. *Educational Leadership, 46*(7), 4–9.

Stetz, F., & Beck, M. (1979, April). *Comments from the classroom: Teachers' and students' opinions of achievement tests.* Paper presented at the meeting of the American Educational Research Association, San Francisco.

Stiggins, R. J., & Bridgeford, N. J. (1985). The ecology of classroom assessment. *Journal of Educational Measurement, 22,* 271–286.

Stiggins, R. J., Conklin, N. F., & Bridgeford, N. J. (1986). Classroom assessment: The key to effective education. *Educational Measurement: Issues and Practice, 5*(2), 5–17.

Terwilliger, J. S. (1989). Classroom standard set-ting and grading practices. *Educational Measurement: Issues and Practice, 8*(2), 15–19.

Vacc, N. N. (1989). Writing evaluations: Examining four teachers' holistic and analytic scores. *The Elementary School Journal, 90,* 87–95.

Walberg, H., Pascal, R., & Weinstein, T. (1985). Homework's powerful effects on learning. *Educational Leadership, 42,* 76–79.

Wang, M. C. (1988). The wedding of instruction and assessment in the classroom. *Proceedings of the 1987 ETS Invitational Conference* (pp. 63–79). Princeton, NJ: Educational Testing Service.

Wodtke, K. H., Harper, F., Schommer, M., & Brunelli, P. (1989). How standardized is school testing? An exploratory observational study of standardized group testing in kindergarten. *Educational Evaluation and Policy Analysis, 11,* 223–235.

__10__

Using Technology
to Improve Instruction

In its most recent report to the nation's schools, the National School Boards Association (NSBA) claimed that technology has the potential to transform education in the twenty-first century. Elaborating on this claim, a member of the NSBA, Mecklenburger (1988), wrote:

> We're not just talking about film projectors and a handful of micro-computers here. The NSBA broadly defines technology to include all manner of video, distance communications, curriculum management systems, administrative networks, and more—at home and in communities, as well as in school. (p. 18)

Similar claims were made for technology 30 years ago. Marshall McLuhan, a Canadian English professor during the 1960s, predicted the "death of the book" was imminent, but as Conran (1989) has pointed out, books and other print media are selling more widely than ever before. Although McLuhan's prediction that there would be a demise of the book has proven false, there is no denying that technology is a major force in our culture today.

Interestingly, at present, the trend is for print and nonprint media to mimic each other:

> There is a proliferation of print which takes its form and content from electronic media: *USA Today* mimes short bursts of information on the TV broadcast; . . . modern information layouts capture the information "flow" of TV commercials and programs; and novellas "based on" mini-series and TV programs are ubiquitous. Further, we encounter electronic media which resembles print (the mini-series, the USA Today TV program, PM Magazine formats). So electronic media hasn't so much displaced print media, as it has informed and reconstituted cultural genres and forms. (Luke, 1989, p. 10)

In this chapter you will learn how technology is beginning to make inroads into the way middle-grades students learn. Specifically, you will discover how the results of media-in-teaching studies of the past have helped to inform our current use of media, primarily the computer. Next, you will learn about one of the components of computer-based instruction: computer-assisted instruction. Finally, you will learn about other common forms of instructional media as well as some not-so-common forms like hypermedia.

Media-in-Teaching Studies

As far back as Plato's time, there was concern for the impact different media had on students' learning. Reportedly, Plato recommended that instruction be delivered orally, rather than in writing, when he discovered what he deemed to be the adverse effects of print on young students' learning (Saettler, 1968).

Historical Overview

Historically, there has been the expectation that the use of media in teaching will result in improved student motivation and performance. "At least since Thorndike suggested the use of pictures as labor-saving devices at the turn of the century, each new medium has created a wave of interest and positive enthusiasm on the part of educators," according to Clark and Salomon (1986, p. 464) in their review of the literature on media in teaching. A case in point is B. F. Skinner's teaching machine.

Programmed Instruction

Skinner (1986), a noted behaviorist who believed that students learned best through programmed instruction (or instruction designed to control their behavior with external stimuli), recalled the following about his invention, the teaching machine:

At a meeting at the University of Pittsburgh in 1954, I demonstrated a machine designed to teach arithmetic. . . . In that machine, a strip of paper passes from one side of the box to the other, exposing a square section on which a problem is printed. Small holes are punched in the paper, and the student causes numerals to show through these holes by moving sliders. The student then tests what he or she has done by turning a knob on the front of the box. If the student has solved the problem correctly, a new problem moves into place; if the answer is wrong, the student must reset the sliders. . . . Students came to my machine without having studied any special material beforehand; they were being taught, not tested. . . . The students composed their responses instead of choosing them. . . . In my machine the items were arranged in a special sequence, so that, after completing the material in frame 1, the students were better able to tackle frame 2, and their behavior became steadily more effective as they passed from frame to frame. I began to speak of "programmed instruction." . . . I was soon saying that, with the help of teaching machines and programmed instruction, students could learn twice as much in the same time and with the same effort as in a standard classroom. . . . Great numbers of programs were written. Most of them were published in workbook form, with correct answers hidden beneath a sliding mask or found on another page. (p. 104)

Despite Skinner's enthusiasm for what his machine could do, he found that the education establishment was largely unimpressed with programmed instruction. Then, with the Soviet Union's launch of Sputnik I, educators turned away from behaviorism and looked to Jerome Bruner for his ideas on education. Influenced by Bruner and other cognitivists, educators adopted a process approach to instruction. Behaviorists were out of favor and so was programmed instruction.

Educational Television

Enthusiasts who advocated the use of television in classrooms 30 years ago believed that this particular medium would revolutionize how teachers taught and students learned. How wrong they were! As Wagschal (1984) has noted:

> The television sets that still work are brought into the classroom only on very special occasions, most notably when the space shuttle goes into orbit or sets down again. Meanwhile, of course, my children—and children across the U.S.—are spending their out-of-school hours glued to the tube. Yet their typical school day proceeds as if television did not exist. (p. 252)

Wagschal's point is that what happened to educational television may happen to computer-based instruction if we do not learn from past mistakes. He argues that three parallels exist between the two media in terms of how they were implemented in schools. First, as with television 30 years ago, insufficient funds have been budgeted for maintenance and repair of the computer equipment presently in schools. Second, only a few school districts have invested in the large-scale staff development programs that are necessary if teachers are going to learn how to integrate computers into their regular classroom instruction. Third, and probably most serious of all, teachers generally are no more convinced that computer-based instruction has a place in the curriculum than they were three decades ago when revolutionary claims for television were being made.

Learning from Past Mistakes

According to Clark and Salomon's (1986) extensive review of the research on media-in-teaching, there have been over 500 studies alone conducted for the purpose of comparing computer-based instruction with more conventional modes of instruction. Their summary of this research shows that, as with earlier studies conducted on other media, "no medium enhances learning more than any other medium regardless of learning task, learner traits, symbolic elements, curriculum content, or setting" (p. 474).

What implications will educators draw from this finding? It is possible that some will assume an I-told-you-so posture and go about their business as usual. Others, however, may lean in the direction of an attitude expressed by Wagschal (1984):

> Whether we schoolpeople like computers or not, whether the available software meets our high standards or not, and whether computers fit easily into our curricula or not, these machines are going to play a major role in our daily lives—*just as commercial television now does.* The fact that public school personnel found commercial television too banal to be of any interest pedagogically did not prevent the full-scale invasion of that medium into Americans' daily lives. And the discomfort of school personnel with computers will be equally unlikely to halt the invasion of this new interactive electronic technology into our daily lives.
>
> What we should be doing with this new technolgoy—and what we failed to do with television—is to learn to incorporate it into classroom activities in ways that suit our goals for ourselves and our students. If this effort proved successful, we might well find ourselves guiding the development of computer hardware and software in directions that *we* had chosen. (p. 253)

If teachers are to become actively involved in incorporating computer-based instruction into their classrooms, the following conditions must be met (Kerr, 1990):

1. Recognition must be given to the fact that teachers work under certain constraints, such as 40-minute class periods and district-mandated curricula, neither of which may be particularly compatible with creative uses of the computer. But if flexible scheduling were made an option, even for only a portion of the school year, or if assessments were changed to include behavior-based competencies as well as paper-and-pencil tasks, teachers might be more willing to integrate computer-based instruction into their traditional routines.
2. Improved software, the development of models of teaching with computers, and in-depth staff development programs are all part of the conditions that must be met if large-scale implementation of computer-based instruction is to succeed.
3. Preservice teacher training institutions must integrate computer-based instruction into their own curricula. Opportunities for internalizing how to learn, think, and teach using

technology must be available to preservice teachers if they are to experience the " 'look and feel' of classrooms in which technology has been well integrated." (p. 213)

Computer-Based Instruction

Computer-based instruction is sometimes used synonymously with *computer-assisted instruction*. At other times, a distinction is made between the two terms, with computer-based instruction being more inclusive. We have adopted the latter stance and define *computer-based instruction* as including these four components: computer-managed instruction (e.g., database management, teacher utility programs), programming, computer-assisted instruction, and interactive computing.

In this section of the chapter, we focus exclusively on computer-assisted instruction, the extent to which it is used, criteria for evaluating it, and the degree to which it is effective. Computer-managed instruction and programming are two components of computer-based instruction that cannot be adequately described in a single chapter. Interactive computing will be included in the final section of this chapter.

Computer-Assisted Instruction

Traditionally, software for computer-assisted instruction (CAI) has been used for drill and practice, demonstrations or tutorials, simulations, and instructional games. Teachers use CAI software to provide remediation to students who require extra help as well as to challenge those who are above average and in need of expanded concept development. Teachers also use CAI software to reinforce a variety of skills in the content areas (Mathison & Lungren, 1989). Examples of some different types of CAI software used in social studies, science, mathematics, and English can be found in Figure 10.1.

Extent to Which CAI Is Used

In 1988, the Association for Supervision and Curriculum Development (ASCD) surveyed 672 middle-grades principals nationwide to determine characteristics of instruction in their schools for pupils aged 10 to 14. Among the many results reported from this study, one in particular is of importance to this chapter. That is, only 10 percent of the principals said teachers in their schools regularly integrated computers into their subject matter instruction (Cawelti, 1988).

Seventh-grade students, who were part of a large-scale study, seemed to corroborate the principals' observations. As shown in Figure 10.2 (Cawelti, 1988), a uniformly small percent of the students reported using computers to practice math, reading, and spelling; to do science problems; or to learn and make music. Using computers to play games took precedence over all other uses of the computer.

From Kerr's (1990) review of research on the instructional uses of computers, it is probably safe to conclude that middle-grades teachers rarely use CAI software in their content area classes. According to Kerr, "The first use of computers in most districts continues to be to teach about computers" (p. 204). Teaching about

FIGURE 10.1 Types of CAI Software Programs Available in Four Content Areas

Social Studies

1. *Drill and practice.* Drill and practice programs are available in many different areas of social studies. A multiple-choice drill and practice program focusing on pertinent questions of American history can help students prepare for unit tests and such standardized tests as the American History Achievement Test.
2. *Demonstration and tutorial.* There are many types of these programs available in social studies. In a geography unit you may be studying the various fifty United States in detail. Tutorial programs exist that teach size, place, and shape of the various fifty United States. These programs often can display the U.S. map for assistance and reinforce the correct spelling of state names.
3. *Simulation.* It might be helpful while teaching a unit on the passage of a bill through Congress to provide a simulation program in which students role-play members of Congress faced with options, obstacles, and choices. This type of simulation checks students' comprehension periodically with questions on Congress and the eight stages in a bill's passage.
4. *Instructional Game.* There are economic games in arcade format that require students to use marketing strategies to raise profits in an imaginary business. Using game format software such as this reinforces knowledge gained from classroom instruction.

Science

1. *Drill and practice.* A drill and practice program on chemistry properties can provide students with review or reinforcement.
2. *Demonstration and tutorial.* A program on light and optics gives practice problems as well as tutorial help for physics students. This can be a positive added dimension to a physics class studying reflection, refraction, and lenses.
3. *Simulation.* Simulations in science can provide opportunities for individual experiments that might otherwise be too expensive, too dangerous, or too impractical for the normal classroom. A simulation program on volcanoes can provide geologic data and information with students predicting volcanic activity based on the collected data.
4. *Instructional Game.* Instructional games for focusing on major systems and organs of the human body provide motivation for students studying anatomy or physiology.

Mathematics

1. *Drill and Practice* Using a program that drills students on positive and negative numbers, monomials and polynomials, and factoring polynomial and trinomial equations would certainly complement an algebra class.
2. *Demonstrations and tutorials.* A program on constructing a robot helps students learn about logic and circuit design as they take notes, test ideas, and learn to program robots. The tutorial would teach about robot anatomy, circuitry, logic, and computer chips.
3. *Simulation.* A simulation on running a business combines knowledge of mathematics and economics. Students learn about market surveys, expert help, bank loans, franchises, and operating decisions.
4. *Instructional Games.* Constructing and solving equations are necessary skills in mathematics. It might be helpful to provide a computer game that has students construct equations and receive points for using particular squares on the computer "game board."

English

1. *Drill and Practice.* There are many programs focusing on isolated English skills. If students have difficulty with punctuation, they might use a computer program that provides practice in punctuating dialogue, narrative, and poetry.
2. *Demonstration and tutorial.* A program on sentence structure teaches structure, presents specific concepts, quizzes to measure developing knowledge, and tests to measure mastery of objectives.
3. *Simulation.* It might be helpful to present a simulation program within a journalism class. Such a program could have students conduct interviews, follow up on new tips, and make judgments on information collected from several sources. These activities can motivate discussion and newswriting.
4. *Instructional Game.* There are software programs that use a board game format and a simulated newspaper office setting to review and practice punctuation, capitalization, subject-verb agreement, verb tense, adverb-adjective use, and homonyms.

Source: From Diane Lapp, James Flood, and Nancy Farnan, *Content Area Reading and Learning: Instructional Strategies.* Copyright © 1989 by Allyn and Bacon. Reprinted with permission.

FIGURE 10.2   Student-Reported Uses of Computers in Seventh Grade

	FREQUENCY—GRADE 7				
	Almost Every Day	*Several Times a Week*	*About Once a Week*	*Less than Once a Week*	*Never*
Practice Math	5.7%	4.7%	9.8%	17.5%	62.3%
Practice Reading	3.1%	3.8%	5.9%	8.8%	78.4%
Practice Spelling	2.8%	3.3%	7.8%	10.0%	76.1%
Do Science Problems	1.9%	2.9%	3.1%	6.8%	85.3%
Learn & Make Music	2.4%	3.0%	6.2%	10.3%	78.1%
Play Games	19.4%	15.4%	16.3%	24.6%	24.3%

Source: Reprinted with permission from G. Cawelti, "Middle Schools a Better Match with Early Adolescent Needs, ASCD Survey Finds," *ASCD Curriculum Update,* 1988, p. 9.

computers normally is the responsibility of someone other than the classroom teacher, typically someone who is teaching computer literacy as part of the practical curriculum strand or as an exploratory course. Chapter 4, as you will recall, discusses the placement of computer literacy, or computer education, courses in the overall curriculum of the middle grades.

Despite the fact that at present computers are rarely integrated into content area classrooms, those teachers who do use CAI view it as an integral part of classroom life, much like pencils, books, and the 3Rs, according to a study on what it means to develop a computer-literate school (Hunter, Dearborn, & Snyder, 1983). In the six schools in Maryland and Virginia where the year-long study was conducted, the following student behaviors were noted:

> Sixth-graders used computer programs to help analyze the results of their science experiments. They used word processors to experiment with and improve their compositions. . . . Eighth-graders relived the discovery of America vicariously with the help of a computer-aided simulation. (Hunter, Dearborn, & Snyder, 1983, p. 115)

If technology is to play a major role in transforming education in the twenty-first century, as some individuals predict it will, then it must become more widely acceptable and used by content area teachers in their regular classroom settings. Although some teachers are already exploring the possibilities of teaching with CAI, the majority are not.

Important determinants of whether teachers will use computers in their classrooms include the extent to which their districts provide technical support, and the opportunity to participate in the selection of CAI software programs. In the next section of this chapter, we present a set of guidelines that can be used in the selection of CAI programs. Because you will likely be asked to evaluate such programs in the future, we think it is important that you know what criteria determine whether software is of good or inferior quality.

Evaluation Criteria

Compared to the traditional textbook, electronic texts (e.g., computer programs, computer databases) are costly to produce and expensive to obtain for classroom use. The hardware needed to use electronic texts, the service and maintenance costs of the hardware, and the estimated "life" of electronic texts themselves are all factors to consider when selecting CAI software. The potential for teachers to make use of the software is another factor, but one that is not easily ascertained in advance (Kerr, 1989).

According to Mathison and Lungren (1989), "The central question when considering software is 'How can I utilize the computer to strengthen the instruction my students receive?' " (p. 313). With this as a focus, other questions that need to be addressed include:

1. Are there deficits in the curriculum materials that I am presently using?
2. Could these deficit areas be compensated for by CAI software?
3. Which topics do my students have trouble understanding, and are there suitable software programs on these topics?
4. Could I use CAI software to individualize my instruction?
5. Am I providing all students with the opportunity to think critically, or am I assuming that less-abled learners just need more drill-and-practice activities?

Once these questions have been addressed and you are aware of the ways computers can be used as instructional tools within the curriculum, you are ready to begin looking through software catalogs and speaking to representatives of the various software companies. As Mathison and Lungren (1989) wisely point out, it is imperative that you not buy programs without first previewing them or, better yet, seeing them demonstrated in your own classroom.

CAI software programs, like textbooks, differ greatly in the way they present

Self-selection of computer-assisted instruction (CAI) software enhances individualized learning.

topics. This becomes extremely important as you consider how you can make the best use of the programs that are available. For example, the manner in which directions are given, the readability of the electronic text, the completeness of the documentation that accompanies a program, the quality and quantity of practice provided, the use of examples, and the type of feedback given are all criteria that should be evaluated prior to selecting a specific program. In Figure 10.3, you will find that all of these criteria have been elaborated on and placed in a checklist format. Reading through the checklist now will provide you with an overview of what you will need to consider when it is time to use the checklist to evaluate CAI programs for use in your own classroom.

CAI: Is It Effective?

Although currently there is disagreement as to how effective CAI is compared to more traditional forms of supplementary instruction like peer tutoring (Levin & Meister, 1986; Niemiec, Blackwell, Walberg, 1986), studies carried out in the 1960s and 1970s found CAI was "generally *more effective* in raising students' scores on standardized achievement tests than were alternative approaches" (Center for Research on Elementary and Middle Schools, 1987, p. 17).

These earlier studies involved mostly drill-and-practice software used on centralized computer hardware systems. Although there is reportedly room for guarded optimism, the real impact of microcomputers and microsoftware on middle-grades students' achievement in the various content areas is virtually unknown at this time (Center for Research on Elementary and Middle Schools, 1987; Kerr, 1990; Lloyd, 1984).

According to Becker (cited in Center for Research on Elementary and Middle School, 1987), part of the reason for so little being known about the impact of CAI on student achievement is due to problems with research designs:

> And even if we were to consider all the . . . studies to be without damning flaws, together they do not come close to providing prescriptive data for deciding whether and how to use computers as adjuncts for instruction. Different hardware and software, different arrangements for using computers in the context of classroom and teacher-directed learning in school buildings, and different ways of integrating computer activities with the rest of the instruction in that subject may all affect student achievement.
>
> In addition, the use of computers for one set of skills (e.g., automaticity of algorithmic procedures) or concepts (e.g., pre-algebra mathematics) or one group of students (e.g., below-grade-level students) may say very little about their value in other situations. (pp. 18–19).

Impact on Special Populations

The impact of CAI used with students who are members of at-risk populations is equally unclear. On the one hand, there is research to show that CAI has had little overall effect when used with at-risk students beyond the third-grade level (Pogrow,

FIGURE 10.3   Checklist of Software Evaluation Criteria

Directions

1. Machine Operations
   a. Procedure for inputting responses (such procedure involves use of common keys and few strokes)
   b. Procedure for reentering or exiting program
   c. Opportunity to review directions
2. Specific content expectations
   a. Directions clear for each section of program
   b. Directions accompanied by examples
   c. Opportunity to review directions
   d. Opportunity to skip directions

Readability and Screen Design

1. Readability level
2. Punctuation, grammar, spelling
3. Screen format
   a. Uncluttered
   b. Conservative use of flashes, beeps, and inverse
   c. If in color, purposeful use
   d. Frequent screen clears
   e. Variation of letter style and size

Documentation

1. Specify hardware needed
2. Specify audience
3. Specify goals/objectives
4. Specify prerequisite skills
5. Pre/post tests included
6. Description of program organization
7. Description of overall strategy
8. Approximate length of program
9. Option to enter/exit program at different places
10. Suggestions for pre- or follow-up instruction
11. Suggestions for integration of program into instructional plan

Practice

1. Does practice match instruction?
2. Is amount of practice sufficient?
3. Does practice come in small enough chunks interspersed with instruction?
4. Can learner ask for more practice?
5. Can learner ask for no practice?
6. If appropriate, is practice sequenced from simple to more complex?
7. If appropriate, can learner request the level of difficulty desired?
8. Can learner return to practice if desired?

Use of Examples

1. Do examples parallel new material to be learned?
   a. Level of complexity
   b. Format
2. If rules or concepts are being presented, are they accompanied by examples and nonexamples?
3. Can the learner control the number of examples she or he receives?
4. Can learner review examples?
5. If learning involves a sequence of steps, are steps clearly indicated?

Feedback

1. Is feedback corrective or evaluative?
2. Is feedback specific enough to highlight particular errors made by different individuals?
3. Is feedback positive and encouraging?
4. Are the number of tries reasonable?
5. Are cues (hints) given if first response is incorrect? Are these cues sensitive to the type of error made?
6. Is feedback given for correct as well as incorrect answers?
7. Does feedback message for correct answer vary?

1990). It is believed the reason for this poor showing is that CAI has failed to take into account at-risk students' real educational needs; for example, the need to be strategic in their approach to learning:

> Beyond the primary grades, CAI (whether in the form of expensive integrated learning systems or computers as tools) has not lived up to its promises to help at-risk students, because [it is] predicated on an incorrect assumption: that at-risk students fail to internalize concepts because of insufficient practice or practice too boring to have an effect. The root cause of poor performance among at-risk students in grades 4–7, however, is not inadequate practice. . . . The primary cause is inadequate metacognitive skills. That is, at-risk students do not consciously apply and test mental strategies to deal with normal thinking activities like reading and problem solving. (Pogrow, 1990, pp. 61–62)

On the other hand, research exists that shows CAI used with Spanish-speaking children resulted in greater achievement gains for sixth-graders who were in the CAI program than for those enrolled in the regular classroom program (Saracho, 1982). Interestingly, however, students in the CAI program demonstrated less favorable attitudes toward their form of instruction than did students in the non-CAI program. Saracho hypothesized that students in the CAI program may have felt stigmatized if they viewed participation in this group as being remedial in nature.

Learner versus Computer Control

One of the most intriguing questions researchers have been asking about CAI is whether the learner or the computer should be given control over the instructional options that are available in most CAI programs. This question has special appeal to those who argue that students learn better and are more motivated when they are responsible for making their own instructional choices.

Research findings in the past have been mixed on this matter. However, in one of the few studies involving middle-grades students, researchers (Kinzie, Sullivan, & Berdel, 1988) found that eighth-grade students who were given limited control over CAI program options performed significantly better on a 25-item multiple-choice science test than did an equivalent group of students who depended on the computer to make the choices. Students who had control of the options were told by the computer each time they responded incorrectly to a test item. Then they were given an opportunity to review the material before attempting to answer the question a second time. Students in the computer-controlled group were also told when their answers were incorrect, but they had no choice in whether they wanted to see the material for review; the computer simply presented them with it.

Instructionally, this study is important because it suggests that computer-controlled instruction may be ineffective for middle-grades students if it limits their right to make a decision about whether they need to review the material. The study is also important because it suggests that requiring students to study bits of information that they already know may have a negative effect on what they learn, though Reinking and Schreiner's (1985) study of middle-grades students showed the reverse to be true. In a follow-up to his original study, Reinking (1988) attempted to clarify why the computer-controlled option benefited students. However, due to the complexity of the issue, much work remains to be done in this area before any conclusion can be drawn.

Impact on the Learning Environment

For many years, and continuing into the present, there has been the tendency to hail each new technological advance in education as having the potential to revolutionize the way teachers teach and students learn. Each time, however, technology's assumed potential has not lived up to expectations. A recent study by some researchers interested in exploring the effectiveness of QUILL, a software writing package (Michaels & Bruce, 1989), helps to explain why "innovations (whether new technology or new pedagogical methods) will not in and of themselves reorganize teaching and learning" (p. 40).

QUILL assists students in applying the process writing steps described in Chapter 5. It includes a text editor, a text storage and retrieval program, a program for helping students plan and organize their thoughts, and an electronic mail program. For two years Michaels and Bruce (1989) studied the effects of implementing QUILL into two urban sixth-grade classrooms, which differed with respect to the way they were organized (activity centered versus highly structured). They found that the use of computers was influenced by teacher attitude and patterns of social organization within the classroom.

For example, one teacher showed a keen interest in learning how to use the software package herself, whereas the other teacher did not, preferring instead to rely on student experts. Both teachers' attitudes about using QUILL fit naturally into their own style of classroom organization. The teacher who knew a great deal about QUILL by the end of the second year exerted much control over the amount and pacing of students' writing; the teacher who had not mastered QUILL permitted much more student-controlled writing.

As Michaels and Bruce (1989) point out, their goal was not to characterize one teacher as being more effective in implementing QUILL than the other. Instead, they "tried to show how [the teachers'] differences in computer use made a great deal of sense in light of their overall goals, styles, and attitudes" (p. 21). Most importantly, we think their study showed that CAI can be effective without revolutionizing the way teaching and learning occur in the classroom. Perhaps too much has been expected of technology in the past. Technology's potential is mediated by many classroom factors, most of which are culturally specific and difficult to alter.

Other Forms of Instructional Media

In this final section of the chapter, you will learn how to match different forms of instructional media to the learning outcomes you want your students to achieve. Specifically, you will find here examples of how common instructional media (other than computers), multimedia, and hypermedia can be used to enrich classroom learning.

Common Instructional Media

If you think back to what you learned in Chapter 2, you will recall that young adolescents are typically described in Piagetian terms as concrete operational or formal operational thinkers, depending on their individual stages of development. You will also recall that recent research suggests only 15 percent of young adolescents are formal thinkers by age 14. This means that approximately 85 percent of students in the middle grades need concrete examples and experiences if they are to comprehend the concepts presented in their subject area classes.

Concrete thinkers benefit from exposure to common instructional media such as graphs, pictures, charts, photographs, videotapes, laser videodiscs, slides, television, motion pictures, film loops, filmstrips, artifacts, historical maps, overhead projectors and transparencies, language laboratories, and sound recordings. Some educators believe, however, that to benefit fully, students must be skilled in *visual literacy.*

According to Kerr (1989), teaching students to become visually literate means moving them beyond the mere comprehension of images to focusing their attention "on the intents and attempted manipulations of [media] producers" (p. 206). Teachers themselves must be visually literate if they are to become adept at matching different forms of instructional media with the learning outcomes they have in mind for their students. Media specialists who are involved in cooperative planning with classroom teachers can serve a vital role in developing teachers' visual literacy (Holt & Cashman, 1990).

The following examples of some different media matched to specific learning outcomes will illustrate the point we are making about the need for teachers to be visually literate. Keep in mind that these are only examples; other combinations of media and outcomes also exist.

Pictures, Photographs, and Artifacts

If you want your students to remember the details of a person's life or an event,

> it is important that you present the information within a larger, more meaningful context. . . . For example, rather than merely describing the physical characteristics of Abraham Lincoln to your students, it would be more effective to accompany such a description with pictures of the man. (Dick & Reiser, 1989, p. 90)

Photographs and/or artifacts, such as those housed in museums or traveling exhibits, are especially effective media to use when you want to develop a sense of reality for students.

Slides, Motion Pictures, and Filmstrips

Sometimes you may want students to develop concepts of complex systems, such as the animal kingdom or the plant classification system. Slides, motion pictures, and filmstrips, which can be used to reach this outcome, are effective for the following reasons: (1) slides can be grouped and regrouped at will, thus providing students with opportunities to try different classification schemes; (2) motion pictures bring to life, through sights and sounds, concepts such as the animal kingdom; and (3) filmstrips typically combine the visual image, the printed word (and sometimes even sound), a combination that is particularly helpful to students who are trying to learn complex classification systems.

Charts, Graphs, and Historical Maps

Seeing relationships among various things is a visual literacy skill that is aided by the use of charts, graphs, and historical maps. Charts can be used to present information in a hierarchical format and graphs and historical maps can be used to compare and contrast information.

Overhead Projector and Transparencies

This medium is unique in that "material may be shown graphically in segments and overlays, revealed progressively, annotated with student comments, and/or revised as the lesson progresses" (Kerr, 1990, p. 197). The overhead projector might be the medium of choice if you wanted to model for students how you, yourself, go about revising and editing a rough draft that you have written.

Videotapes, Television, and Sound Recordings

A number of outcomes can be facilitated through the use of videotapes, television, and sound recordings. If you want students to express their feelings about substance abuse, propaganda techniques, war, hunger, poverty, environmental clean-up campaigns, and so on, these three types of media are excellent devices for stimulating discussion. Stop-action and slow-motion capabilities make videotapes and television particularly valuable when teaching concepts such as the circulatory or digestive system, the trajectory of a missile, or the passage of a bill through Congress. Sound recordings are valuable resources when used in language labs or in combination with any of the other instructional media mentioned earlier.

Common instructional media can stimulate young adolescents' motivation to learn.

Laser Videodiscs

Although laser videodiscs might have been included in the discussion on motion pictures and videotapes, we decided to treat it in a class by itself for two reasons. First, advocates of laser videodisc (e.g., Van Horn, 1987) claim that educators have largely ignored this technology. By singling it out, we hope to draw attention to its unique capabilities. Second, a laser videodisc has many special features that distinguish it from other common forms of instructional media.

Laser videodisc technology has been available to the public since 1978. However, despite the fact videodiscs are 10 to 20 times cheaper than film and are practically indestructible, they have generally not found their way into school libraries and classrooms, at least not on any grand scale. With the advent of consistently lower costs of videodisc players and a growing number of titles, the 1990s may see an influx of this technology into the nation's schools. Van Horn (1987), in calling film "an outdated medium" (p. 697), recommended that all film libraries should convert to videodisc libraries:

> Film is an archaic medium with sprocket holes that tear and leaders that break. . . . Projectors often "lose their loop," and the film must be periodically cleaned and lubricated. . . . Videodiscs, on the other hand, never need rewinding or maintenance, and do not wear out. . . . Because videodisc players are not mechanical, they typically operate more than 4,000 hours before they need repair. (p. 697)

Videodiscs contain a wealth of information. For example, there are discs called *video glossaries* that contain collections of still pictures on a variety of topics. Over 54,000 pictures can be stored on one side of a videodisc, and when it is placed on a videodisc player, any one of these 54,000 pictures can be accessed in approximately two seconds. Some samples of video glossaries include: *National Air & Space Museum Archival Discs*, *History Disquiz*, the *Louvre* disc, *Bio-Science* disc, *Space Archive* discs (Van Horn, 1987), and *ABC News Interactive* discs, which "contain hundreds of video segments and thousands of photographs, maps, and graphics of the most significant events of our times" (*The New York Times*, 1990, p. 29).

If one of your goals is to make your subject area come alive for students, and if you want to have images out of the past (sometimes complete with sound) readily available, then the videodisc is one medium that you will want to consider using in your classroom. Learner outcomes that depend on students having access to "concrete" learning materials are well served by laser videodisc technology. Although this medium will never replace a class fieldtrip to the National Air and Space Museum, it can be a suitable substitute.

Multimedia

When a videodisc player is used as a computer peripheral, this new medium is known as *computer-assisted video instruction* (CAVI). CAVI "combines slides, television, and stereo with computer programming" (Van Horn, 1987, p. 698). As such, CAVI is an example of what is known in the world of technology as *multimedia*.

CAVI

How does CAVI work? What does it look like in a real classroom setting? To give you a sense of the types of learner outcomes possible through CAVI, consider the following excerpt from an article on Compton's MultiMedia Encyclopedia (Schwartz, 1990):

> Don't give up hope for educating our kids, America. Carol Sammans says her students are "jazzed." The Chandler, Arizona . . . teacher is gushing about *Compton's Multi-Media Encyclopedia,* a new reference work designed for personal computers. She had assigned her kids to prepare a debate on whether the American Revolution was a "justifiable mutiny" or a "traitorous rebellion." . . . They called up articles, paged through a detailed "timeline" and took notes on the computer as they went along. With the help of their PCs, she said, "they did a really great debate." . . . Thanks to ingenious design, the program is so simple that, literally, a child can use it. Click the mouse at a given point on the world atlas or a timeline and an appropriate article will be summoned; students can even browse through pictures, bringing up stories about each one. The computer will also call up articles suggested by key words such as "American Revolution." Hit a difficult word? A click will bring up the definition—and if your PC has sound capability, the machine will even pronounce it for you. . . . Does computer software this good mean an end to books? Happily no. Sammans says that in the debate project, "I looked around and there were tons of books in my room." Once the computer had whetted their appetites, the students checked books out of the library so they could find out more. Talk about a revolution. (p. 45)

Multimedia Publishing Centers

Most schools have as standard equipment personal computers, tape recorders, videocassette recorders, and television sets. Some may even have camcorders. When you combine all of these, you have what D'Ignazio (1988) calls a *multimedia publishing center*:

> The multimedia centers enable students to create classroom presentations in wholly new ways—video term papers and book reports, radio documentaries in science, electronic slide shows, animations of math word problems, publications, banners, ads, and so on. Students dramatically increase their productivity and get the most out of the equipment they already have. (p. 27)

Student learning outcomes that are fostered by using multimedia publishing centers include cooperative learning, pride of authorship, and self-directed learning. According to D'Ignazio (1988), cooperative learning is the most powerful of the three because of its ability to transform existing social organizational patterns. For example, he noted that "teachers encourage students to collaborate . . . across classrooms, across grades, and across subjects" (p. 27). Pride of authorship comes from being able to communicate in a variety of new ways, with even the most reluctant writer finding something of value to use in the multimedia approach. Self-directed learning results when students see ways to integrate the publishing centers into math, science, social studies, and so on. They become what D'Ignazio calls "producers" of learning, rather than consumers.

Hypermedia

The word *hypermedia* is more easily described than defined. Hypermedia is "a system of audio-visual and textual communication that allows users to interactively navigate through a multimedia information base using their intuition, memory, and interest as a guide" (Paske, 1990, p. 54).

An example might be a student, who having learned the term *relief* in social studies, is confused by the use of the term in art. The student consults a computer terminal to define the word. The dictionary program presents several meanings of the word *relief*. When the student highlights "painting," several examples are displayed of paintings that depict contrast. The student presses another key and listens to a curator demonstrate and explain relief paintings. Before the end of the session, the student reviews the meaning of *relief* in relation to *surface elevations* for social studies and views an on-screen film clip of relief painting.

New alternatives in instructional media, such as hypermedia, can offer advantages over the more common forms of educational technology. With the medium itself as an assessor of students' work, teachers are free to work in more productive ways with students. Hypermedia can also individualize instruction for students. For example, using Apple's Hypercard Program for the Macintosh, students "might 'zoom in' on one section of the material, request a condensed version of another section, look for examples to illustrate the reading, and so on" (Kerr, 1990, p. 209).

More advances involving hypermedia are on the drawing board, including what Perelman (1988) refers to as *brain-enhancement technology,* which is the product of applied research on the brain and cognition. How this technology will work and what it will offer in the way of learner outcomes is an unknown at this time.

Summary

The predicted technology revolution in education may affect middle-grades education in at least one of two ways. It may, as Kerr (1990) suggests, "wash over the schools, leaving little change in educational practice . . . [which] has been the fate of many earlier 'revolutions' in schooling" (p. 217), or it may become what he describes as an evolutionary process.

In the latter case, middle-grades teachers and administrators would work with the changes now in progress to bring them to fruition. At the same time, they would work with designers and developers of instructional media to ensure that new alternatives to the textbook fit the cultural and social organizational patterns of the middle grades.

In this chapter we provided a historical overview of the different ways instructional media have been used in the schools. Although programmed instruction and educational television have not fared well, there is reason to believe that computer-assisted instruction will have a greater impact on how teachers teach and students learn. At the very least, educators have learned that computer-assisted instruction can be effective without necessarily revolutionizing the way teaching and learning occur in the classroom.

REFERENCES

Bruce, B. C. (1986). *Computers and language: A look to the future.* (Technical Report No. 371). Champaign: University of Illinois, Center for the Study of Reading.

Cawelti, G. (1988, November). Middle schools a better match with early adolescent needs, ASCD survey finds. *ASCD Curriculum Update,* pp. 1–12.

Center for Research on Elementary and Middle Schools. (1987, June). Instructional effectiveness of computers remains an open question. *CREMS* (A Special Report) (pp. 17–19). Baltimore, MD: The Johns Hopkins University, Center for Research on Elementary and Middle Schools.

Clark, R. E., & Salomon, G. (1986). Media in teaching. In M. C. Wittrock (Ed.), *Handbook of research on teaching* (3rd ed., pp. 464–478). New York: Macmillan.

Conran, P. C. (1989). Using technology to cope with "all-at-once-ness." *ASCD Update, 31*(8), 2.

Dick, W., & Reiser, R. A. (1989). *Planning effective instruction.* Englewood Cliffs, NJ: Prentice-Hall.

D'Ignazio, F. (1988). Bringing the 1990s to the classroom of today. *Phi Delta Kappan, 70,* 26–27.

Holt, L. C., & Cashman, J. S. (1990). Is the media professional an underused instructional resource? *Middle School Journal, 21*(2), 14–15.

Hunter, B., Dearborn, D., & Snyder, B. (1983). Computer literacy in the K–8 curriculum. *Phi Delta Kappan, 65,* 115–118.

Kerr, S. T. (1989). Pale screens: Teachers and electronic texts. In P. W. Jackson & S. Haroutunian-Gordon (Eds.), *From Socrates to software: The teacher as text and the text as teacher.* (Eighty-eighth yearbook of the National Society for the Study of Education, Part I) (pp. 202–223). Chicago: University of Chicago Press.

Kerr, S. T. (1990). Alternative technologies as textbooks and the social imperatives of educational change. In D. L. Elliott & A. Woodward (Eds.), *Textbooks and schooling in the United States.* (Eighty-ninth yearbook of the National Society for the Study of Education, Part I) (pp. 194–221). Chicago: University of Chicago Press.

Kinzie, M. B., Sullivan, H. J., & Berdel, R. L. (1988). Learner control and achievement in science computer-assisted instruction. *Journal of Educational Psychology, 80,* 299–303.

Levin, H. M., & Meister, G. (1986). Is CAI cost-effective? *Phi Delta Kappan, 67,* 745–749.

Lloyd, L. A. (1984). Computers and science teaching. In D. Holdzkom & P. B. Lutz (Eds.), *Research within reach: Science education* (pp. 109–120). Charleston, WV: Appalachia Educational Laboratory.

Luke, A. (1989) Literacy as curriculum: Historical and sociological perspectives. *Language, Learning and Literacy, 1*(2), 1–16.

Mathison, C., & Lungren, L. (1989). Using computers effectively in content area classes. In D. Lapp, J. Flood, & N. Farnan (Eds.), *Content area reading and learning: Instructional strategies* (pp. 304–318). Englewood Cliffs, NJ: Prentice-Hall.

Mecklenburger, J. A. (1988). What the ostrich sees: Technology and the mission of American education. *Phi Delta Kappan, 70,* 18–19.

Michaels, S., & Bruce, B. (1989). *Classroom contexts and literacy development: How writing systems shape the teaching and learning of composition* (Technical Report No. 476). Champaign: University of Illinois, Center for the Study of Reading.

National Council of Teachers of Mathematics. (1989). *Curriculum and evaluation standards for school mathematics.* Reston, VA: Author.

New York Times. (1990, August 5). ABC News presents an idea that can change the course of history (and reading, writing, science and the arts, too). *The New York Times,* Education Life (Section 4A, p. 29).

Niemiec, R. P., Blackwell, M. C., & Walberg, G. J. (1986). CAI can be doubly effective. *Phi Delta Kappan, 67,* 750–751.

Paske, R. (1990). Hypermedia: A brief history and progress report. *T.H.E. (Technological Horizons in Education), 18*(1), 53–56.

Perelman, L. J. (1988). Restructuring the system is the solution. *Phi Delta Kappan, 70,* 20–24.

Pogrow, S. (1990). A Socratic approach to using computers with at-risk students. *Educational Leadership, 47*(5), 61–66.

Reinking, D. (1988). Computer-mediated text and comprehension differences: The role of reading time, reader preference, and estimation of learning. *Reading Research Quarterly, 23,* 484–498.

Reinking, D., & Schreiner, R. (1985). The effects of computer-mediated text on measures of reading comprehension and reading behav-ior. *Reading Research Quarterly, 20,* 536–552.

Saettler, P. A. (1968). *A history of instructional technology.* New York: McGraw-Hill.

Saracho, O. N. (1982). The effect of a computer-assisted instruction program on basic skills achievement and attitude toward instruction of Spanish speaking migrant children. *American Educational Research Journal, 19,* 201–219.

Schwartz, J. (1990, March 19). A computer encyclopedia. *Newsweek,* p. 45.

Skinner, B. F. (1986). Programmed instruction revisited. *Phi Delta Kappan, 68,* 103–110.

Upchurch, R. L., & Lochhead, J. (1987). Computers and higher-order thinking skills. In V. Richardson-Koehler (Ed.), *Educators' handbook: A research perspective* (pp. 139–164). New York: Longman.

Van Horn, R. (1987). Laser videodiscs in education: Endless possibilities. *Phi Delta Kappan, 68,* 696–700.

Wagschal, P. H. (1984). A last chance for computers in the schools? *Phi Delta Kappan, 66,* 251–254.

11

Teaching Strategies

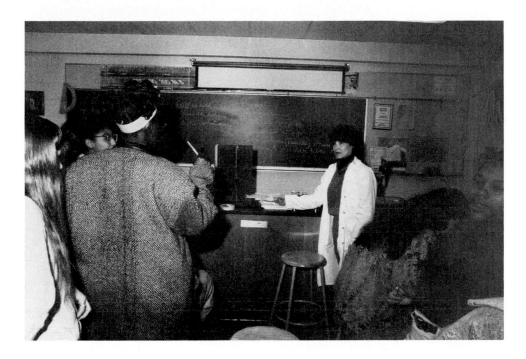

This chapter on teaching strategies and the next chapter on learning strategies are closely related. Simply put, *teaching strategies* are concerned with what teachers do while they teach and *learning strategies* are concerned with what students do while they learn. Teaching strategies and learning strategies are both integral components of the teaching-learning process.

This chapter is divided into three sections. In the first section, we discuss the nature of the teaching-learning process so that you will have an understanding of the roles that teaching and learning strategies play in this process. In the second section, we discuss the nature of the content that you will be teaching. The nature of the content will help you select the most appropriate strategy for teaching that content. Last, we discuss the various teaching strategies that you can use to teach the content.

Nature of the Teaching-Learning Process

Weinstein and Mayer (1986) provide us with an excellent framework for analyzing the teaching-learning process (see Figure 11.1). Weinstein and Mayer define the components of their framework in the following way:

- *Teacher characteristics:* including the teacher's existing knowledge concerning the subject matter and how to teach, that may be required for the teaching strategy selected.
- *Teaching strategies:* including the teacher's performance during teaching such as what is presented, when it is presented, and how it is presented.
- *Learner strategies:* including the learner's existing knowledge concerning facts, procedures, and strategies, that may be required for the learning strategy selected.
- *Learning strategies:* including behaviors that the learner engages in during learning that are intended to influence affective and cognitive processing during encoding.
- *Encoding process:* including internal cognitive processes during learning such as how the learner selects, organizes, and integrates new information.
- *Learning outcome:* including the newly acquired knowledge that depends on both teaching and learning strategies.
- *Performance:* including behavior on tests of retention and transfer. (p. 316)

As you can see in Figure 11.1, teacher characteristics influence the strategy that the teacher selects and the way in which he or she implements that strategy. Learner characteristics influence the learning strategy that the learner selects and the way in which he or she implements that strategy. Both teaching and learning strategies influence the encoding process of the student, which in turn influences what the student learns and how he or she demonstrates that learning.

FIGURE 11.1   Framework for Analyzing the Teaching-Learning Process

Teacher Characteristics	*Learner Characteristics*
What the teacher knows	What the learner knows
Teaching Strategy	*Learning Strategy*
What the teacher does during teaching	What the learner does during learning

Encoding Process
How information is processed

Learning Outcome
What is learned

Performance
How learning is evaluated

Source: From "The Teaching of Learning Strategies" by C. E. Weinstein and R. E. Mayer. Reprinted with permission of Macmillan Publishing Company from *Handbook of Research on Teaching,* Third Edition (pp. 315–327), edited by Merlin C. Wittrock. Copyright © 1986 by the American Educational Research Association.

As mentioned, teacher characteristics influence which particular strategy a teacher selects to teach the subject matter. One important teacher characteristic that has a great influence on the strategy that a teacher selects is the teacher's knowledge of the nature of the content and how to best teach it. In order to prepare you to better select among the various teaching strategies, we now discuss the nature of the content.

Nature of the Content

In general, the content that you teach can be classified as either declarative knowledge or procedural knowledge. *Declarative knowledge* is knowledge about something, whereas *procedural knowledge* is knowledge about how to do something. Declarative knowledge involves knowledge of *facts, concepts,* and *generalizations.*

Knowledge that Harrisburg is the capital of Pennsylvania; that the lower the pH, the higher the acidity; that your brother's name is Jim; and that you don't like brussels sprouts are all examples of declarative knowledge. Procedural knowledge involves the acquisition of *skills.* Knowing how to graph a quadratic equation, how to locate China on a map, how to write a poem in iambic pentameter, and how to measure the mass of an object are all examples of procedural knowledge. When a student becomes proficient at a certain procedure, he or she is said to be skillful at it.

As you may have noticed, in many instances declarative knowledge and procedural knowledge do not occur in isolation of each other. Oftentimes, the two types of knowledge interact. For example, just because you can list the steps involved in changing the oil in your car does not mean that you can actually do it. When you are first learning how to change the oil, you may actually write down the steps (declarative knowledge) and refer to them as you go about changing the oil (procedural knowledge). Students frequently use this procedure when they are learning how to do something new, such as solving a quadratic equation. In order to give you a better sense of the nature of the content that you will be teaching, we now discuss three types of declarative knowledge—facts, concepts, and generalizations—and one type of procedural knowledge—skills.

Facts

Facts are arbitrary associations that usually occur in isolation and have no predictive value. The following statements are examples of facts:

1. George Washington was the first president of the United States.
2. A rectangle has four sides.
3. Cervantes' *Don Quixote* was published in 1605.
4. The symbol for potassium is K.

The teaching of facts is a controversial issue. On the one hand, many educators consider facts to be the foundation for future higher-order learning. Recall from our discussion of Bloom's taxonomy that learning at the higher levels, such as analysis, synthesis, and evaluation, frequently depends on having a firm grasp of the facts. For example, students cannot be expected to evaluate a play or movie without first knowing the criteria on which to base their evaluation. In addition, as we discuss later in this section, knowledge of facts leads to concept learning, which in turn leads to the ability to understand and make generalizations.

On the other hand, in and of themselves, facts are not very useful. This notion is especially important at the middle-grades level, because, contrary to what was previously believed, current research (McCall, 1988) indicates that young adolescents are not at a plateau in mental growth and are quite capable of engaging in higher-order learning and thinking. As the Carnegie Council on Adolescent Development (1989) points out, young adolescents need to be able to "grapple with complexity, think critically, and deal with information as parts of systems rather than as isolated, disconnected facts" (p. 47).

In light of this discussion, our best advice to you is to think carefully about lessons that are little more than the presentation of isolated facts. Facts should be taught in relationship to each other so that students are able to use them to form concepts and make generalizations. In any event, only facts that "will remain important over a long period of time" and that will be "used frequently in everyday living" (Kauchak & Eggen, 1989, p. 237) should be included in the curriculum.

One of the most effective methods of learning facts is through memorization (Kauchak & Eggen, 1989). Students can use drill and practice (which we discuss later in this chapter) to memorize important facts. Keep in mind, however, that memorization need not be a boring or tedious task for students. Games, small-group competitions, and peer tutoring are examples of activities that capitalize on the social nature of young adolescents and that can be used to make drill and practice as well as memorization a more enjoyable task.

Concepts

Concepts are "categories used to group similar events, ideas, objects, or people" (Woolfolk, 1990, p. 264). Love, athlete, independence, circumference, gravity, food, and essay are all examples of concepts. Some concepts are more concrete (e.g., house and dog) than others (e.g., war and integrity). Concepts themselves do not actually exist. They cannot be seen, touched, or heard. Only examples of concepts exist.

There are many strategies that can be used effectively to teach concepts. (We discuss some of these strategies later in this chapter.) However, regardless of the strategy you select, Weil and Joyce (1978) recommend that it includes the following four elements:

1. The name of the concept
2. A definition of the concept
3. Relevant and irrelevant features
4. Examples and nonexamples

In general, lessons in which students are actively involved will be more successful than those in which students are passive recipients of information. Accordingly, notice that we did not say you must supply each of the four preceding elements for your students. Instead, you could use guided discovery to lead your students to a definition. Together, students could brainstorm relevant and nonrelevant features as well as examples and nonexamples.

Effective teaching of concepts is especially important at the middle-grades level because many of the concepts that middle-grades students are expected to learn are abstract. However, as you may recall from our discussion of cognitive development, most young adolescents are still at the concrete operational stage of development. Hence, unless lessons are well planned, a developmental mismatch could occur between what students are expected to learn and what they are capable of learning. By planning lessons that include the four elements, as well as concrete experiences and examples, you can increase the likelihood that your students will better understand abstract concepts.

Generalizations

Generalizations are statements that identify relationships between and among concepts. Rules and principles are two types of generalizations frequently taught at the middle-grades level.

Rules
Rules are methods or directions for carrying out procedures. The following statements are examples of rules:

1. Multiply half of the altitude by the base to calculate the area of a triangle.
2. To change Celsius temperature to Fahrenheit temperature, multiply by 9/5 and then add 32.
3. To calculate the density of an object, divide its mass by its volume.
4. Use commas to separate words, phrases, or clauses in a series.

Each of these rules contains at least two concepts. For example, the first rule contains the concepts multiply, half, altitude, base, area, and triangle. The fourth rule contains the concepts separate, words, phrases, clauses, and series.

Students can often memorize a rule and implement it without having a thorough understanding of what they are doing or why they are doing it. For example, given a triangle with the altitude and base labeled, students who have memorized the rule could probably calculate the area without understanding what they are doing. In order to have a thorough understanding of a rule and be able to implement in appropriate situations, students must first understand each concept in the rule.

Principles
Principles are basic truths, laws, or assumptions. In a sense, especially where natural phenomena or mechanical processes are concerned, principles provide order in the world. The following statements are examples of principles:

1. Matter expands when heated.
2. Factories turn raw materials into manufactured goods.
3. The farther a phrase departs from ordinary usage, the more readily it becomes a cliché.
4. Estimation can be a useful skill when solving word problems.

As was the case with rules, each of these principles is composed of at least two concepts. For example, the first principle contains the concepts matter, expands, and heated. As was also the case with rules, in order to have a true understanding of a principle, students must first understand each concept in the principle.

Skills

Skills have been defined in a number of ways but the definition we feel best conveys the relationship between skills and classroom learning is "the ability to perform a voluntary physical or intellectual action" (Montague, Huntsberger, & Hoffman, 1989, p. 122). Some of the skills taught in middle-grades classrooms are procedural skills, whereas others are thinking skills.

Procedural skills aid in performing physical actions; *thinking skills* aid in performing intellectual actions. In actual classroom practice, students are frequently required to integrate their procedural and thinking skills in order to perform a particular action. For example, when solving arithmetic word problems, students must possess procedural skills in order to carry out the appropriate operations, but they also must possess thinking skills in order to determine which operations to perform and the sequence in which to perform them. We will now discuss basic, complex, and higher-order skills.

Basic Skills

Basic skills are usually single actions, either physical or intellectual, that are necessary for carrying out more complex skills. For example, being able to move your foot is a basic skill that is ultimately necessary for being able to kick a ball. Similarly, counting is a basic skill that is necessary for being able to solve arithmetic word problems.

In general, basic skills are best taught by actively involving students in lessons that stress drill and practice as well as memorization. As Kauchak and Eggen (1989) point out, the most effective basic-skills lessons usually contain the following three components:

1. Opportunities for students to observe someone (e.g., the teacher, another student) performing the skill correctly. Frequently, this component involves teacher modeling.
2. Opportunities for students to practice the skill. In middle-grades classrooms, this component frequently involves small groups or pairs of students practicing together. Allowing students to practice skills together is an excellent mechanism for capitalizing on the social nature of young adolescents.
3. Corrective feedback from someone on whether or not the student is performing the skill correctly.

When teaching basic skills, the ultimate goal of the teacher is to lead students toward independence. Initially, students depend on modeling the teacher in order to perform the skill. However, in order to be able to use the skill in combination with other basic skills, students must be able to perform them automatically on their own. Pearson and Gallagher (1983) refer to this method of instruction as the *gradual release of responsibility model*.

According to the model, the teacher initially has most of the responsibility but, through a gradual release of responsibility on the part of the teacher, students assume more and more responsibility until independence is achieved. Once independence is achieved, students are able to perform the skill on their own. Recall from Chapter 2 our discussion of the zone of proximal development (Vygotsky, 1978). The gradual release of responsibility model moves students from one end of the zone of proximal development to the other.

Complex Skills

Complex skills are skills that combine two or more basic skills. For example, swimming the butterfly stroke can be considered a complex skill because it combines arm strokes and leg strokes with skilled breathing. Similarly, two-digit multiplication can be considered a complex skill because it combines addition and multiplication and, in some cases, carrying.

Before students can be taught complex skills, they must first be proficient at all of the basic skills involved in the complex skill. Using our two-digit multiplication example, students must be skilled at addition and one-digit multiplication before they are taught two-digit multiplication.

Because complex skills can be broken down into their component basic skills, complex skills can be taught in much the same way as basic skills. One of the most effective strategies for teaching complex skills is explicit teaching (Rosenshine, 1986), which we discuss later in this chapter.

Higher-Order Skills

Higher-order skills are the mental operations necessary for engaging in higher-level learning. They are frequently called *thinking skills* or *critical-thinking skills*. The ability to form hypotheses, to make predictions, and to solve problems are examples of higher-order skills that are essential for higher-level learning.

Unfortunately, because higher-order skills are mental operations, they are difficult to observe and evaluate. For example, since we cannot directly observe whether or not students comprehend what they read, we tend to evaluate their comprehension based on what they recall or how they answer certain questions we ask them. Similarly, since we cannot directly observe the processes students use when they solve arithmetic word problems, we tend to evaluate them based on whether or not they get the correct answer.

However, this procedure for evaluating students' higher-order skills does not always accurately reflect their abilities. Consider the think-aloud protocol (Muth, 1988) in Figure 11.2. This actual protocol was collected as Jennifer, an eighth-grade student, solved a word problem containing extraneous information.

FIGURE 11.2 Think-Aloud Protocol of Jennifer Solving a Word Problem

---

Problem: Bill exercises by jogging around a circular building. The building is 75 yards high and has a radius of 50 yards. How far does Bill jog every time he goes around the building?

(Reads problem out loud.)
(Doesn't say anything for about 8 seconds.)

Teacher: What are you thinking right now?
Jennifer: Um, that I multiply, um, the radius, which is, um, and I square, um, 50 so it'd be 50 times itself, and I get 2500 times . . . 75.

(Works for a long time on the multiplication.)

Teacher: So do you have an answer?
Jennifer: Um, . . . 197,500

(Long pause)

Teacher: What are you thinking right now?

(Long pause)

Jennifer: It doesn't really sound right.
Teacher: Why does it not sound right?
Jennifer: Sounds too big. The number's too big.
Teacher: So what are you thinking?

(Long pause)

Teacher: You think that it's not right but you're not sure what to do? Is that what it is?
Jennifer: Yeah.
Teacher: So you want to leave it at that?
Jennifer: Yes m'am, I don't know what it is.
Teacher: Ok.

As indicated in Figure 11.2, Jennifer did not get the problem correct. She did, however, engage in the higher-order skill of monitoring her performance. When Jennifer got her final answer, she considered its size in relation to the other numbers in the problem and remarked, "It's too big. The number's too big." Granted, Jennifer did not know how to proceed to correct her answer, but she did know her answer was incorrect. If we had looked only at Jennifer's final answer, we might have assumed that she was not engaging in any higher-order thinking.

Higher-order skills can be taught either directly or indirectly. When higher-order skills are taught directly, the lesson focuses exclusively on the skill or skills and no subject matter is taught. When higher-order skills are taught indirectly, they are integrated with the particular subject matter being taught. Figure 11.3 (adapted from Kauchak & Eggen, 1989) illustrates the direct teaching of higher-order skills. In this lesson, Mrs. Winkowsky's goal is to teach her students how to classify. Notice that the lesson focuses exclusively on teaching the students how to classify. Mrs. Winkowsky does not teach any science content during the lesson.

In Figure 11.4, Eggen and Kauchak (1988) present an actual lesson in which the

FIGURE 11.3 Direct Teaching of Higher-Order Skills

Mrs. Winkowsky begins by writing the following definition on the board:

Classify—Put things into groups and label the groups

"This is an important skill that we'll be using all year long, not only in science but in other areas as well, so everyone needs to learn it. First I'm going to show you how I classify. Then I'm going to ask one of you to do it in front of the rest of the class. Then, I'm going to ask each of you to do it on your own.

"When we classify, here are the steps to follow." She then wrote the following on the board:

Steps in Classifying

1. Skim over all objects.
2. Choose two that are alike.
3. Label that group.
4. See if any others belong in that group.
5. Find two more that belong together.
6. Label that group.
7. See if any others belong in that group.
8. Do steps 5, 6, 7, until all items are in a group.

"Now, I'm going to show you how to classify using these steps. Listen very carefully because I'm going to ask you to do it next. When we're all done, each of you will be able to classify on your own.

"First, what should we classify? We can classify anything because classification is a skill that works with all kinds of things. Let's see, since it's getting close to lunch, let's classify the things in my lunch bag. Everyone watch while I put these on the table." She then placed the following items on the table for the class to see:

sandwich	apple
fork	milk
salad	straw

"Hmm, now let's go back to the steps that I wrote on the board. First we skim over everything we're going to classify. *Skim* means look. Okay . . . sandwich, fork, salad, apple, milk and straw. Now, step 2. Which two of these go together? Hmm? How about sandwich and salad. They go together because they're things to eat. That's the label for the group. To help us remember that, let's put *Es* in front of them and put 'E—Things to eat' on the board.

"Now we're ready for step 4. Are there any other things that belong in that group? Hmm, things to eat. Fork, no. Apple, yes. So let's put an *E* by it." The lesson continued until all the items were classified. "Now that you've seen me classify, let's see if you can do it now. I'm going to put some things up on the board, and I want each of you to see if you can classify them using the steps on the board. Everyone try to classify these, then I'll call on someone to explain how they did it."

car	boat
plane	jet
bus	

After a short pause, Mrs. Winkowsky continued, "Who would like to come up here and show us how they did it? Jeremy?"

"Well, first I put *car* and *bus* together and put an *L* by them for *land*. Then I put *plane* and *jet* together and put an *A* by them for *air*. Then I didn't know where to put boat so I made a new group called *water*."

"Excellent, Jeremy, you did a fine job of classifying all the items. How many people classifed it like Jeremy? Thirteen, fourteen, fifteen. Good. How about the rest of you? Phil?"

"I put *car, plane, bus* and *jet* together because they all have wheels. Then I put *boat* in its own group like Jeremy and called it *water*."

"Did anyone else do that? Martha, you did. Sam, okay. That's something I forgot to mention before. It's okay to classify things in different ways—just so your system makes sense. Now, let's try another one."

Source: Donald P. Kauchak and Paul D. Eggen, *Learning and Teaching.* Copyright © 1989 by Allyn and Bacon. Reprinted with permission.

FIGURE 11.4 Lesson Integrating Higher-Order Skills with Subject Matter

At the beginning of the lesson, Mrs. Soo displayed a chart that identified the characteristics, food, and habitat of frogs and toads.

After directing the class to study the chart for a moment she began the activity by saying, "Look carefully at the part that tells what toads eat. What do you notice here? Mike?"

"Well, they eat earthworms," Mike responded.

"And what else? Kathy?"

"Spiders," Kathy answered.

"Also grasshoppers," David volunteered.

"Yes, very good, everyone," Mrs. Soo smiled. "Now look at the frogs. What can you tell me about what they eat? Judy?"

"They eat insects," Judy replied.

"Also earthworms," Bill added.

"Now, let's go a bit farther," Mrs. Soo encouraged. "Look at both the frogs and toads. How would you compare what they eat? How is it the same or different?"

"They both eat insects," Tom noticed.

"John?"

"They both eat earthworms too," John offered.

"The food for each seems to be almost the same," Kristy added tentatively.

"Very good, Kristy," Mrs. Soo smiled. "Why do you suppose that the food seems to be the same?"

After some hesitation Brad volunteered, "The frog and toad live in about the same places."

"What tells you that, Brad? Mrs. Soo probed.

". . . It says on the chart that the frog lives on land, in the water and in trees, and it says for the toad that he lives on land and in the water," Brad responded.

"Yes, excellent, Brad," Mrs. Soo praised. "You have supported your conclusion with information that you observed on the chart. Very well done."

"Also, the frog and the toad are very much alike," Sonya offered.

"What do you see that tells you that, Sonya?" Mrs. Soo continued.

"From the pictures we see that they look about the same," Sonya replied.

"Also, they both start from eggs and then become tadpoles." Jim added. "On the chart we see pictures of the eggs and the tadpoles."

"Very good everyone!" Mrs. Soo enthused. "You're all thinking very well. Now here's a tough one. Suppose that frogs and toads were quite different rather than being very similar. What might happen to them then? Donna?"

". . . Maybe the food that they would eat would be different," Donna suggested.

"Can you give me an example of where that would be the case, Donna?" Mrs. Soo queried.

". . . A frog and a mouse are different and they eat different foods," Donna replied.

"Yes, excellent example, Donna," Mrs. Soo smiled. "Anything else, anyone?"

Sue noted, "Perhaps they wouldn't live in the same places. Frogs and mice don't live in quite the same places."

"Yes, good suggestion, Sue," Mrs. Soo commented.

"You've all done very well everyone. Now try and summarize what we've discussed about frogs and toads here and talk about animals in general."

After some prompting Joel said, "Animals that are pretty much the same, such as living in the same place and looking about the same, eat the same food."

"Yes, Joel, that's a good summary. Could we go a bit further?"

Again, with prompting the class finally derived the statement, "Animals with similar characteristics will have similar habits, such as living in the same place and eating similar food."

teacher integrated higher-order skills with the subject matter being taught. In this lesson, Mrs. Soo integrates the higher-order skills of forming hypotheses and drawing conclusions with the content being taught about frogs and toads.

In summary, we need to point out that it is often difficult to classify a particular skill as either basic, complex, or higher order. Quite often, a skill might fall between two of the categories. Think of skill development as occurring on a continuum, with basic skills at one end, complex skills in the middle, and higher-order skills at the other end. Given this continuum, many skills can fall between the ends.

Teaching Strategies

Now that you are familiar with the nature of the content, we will discuss teaching strategies. As we mentioned in the beginning of this chapter, teaching strategies are what the teacher does as he or she teaches. And, as you have just learned, the nature of the content plays a critical role in helping you select the most appropriate strategy to teach that content.

Over the years, teaching strategies have been classified in a variety of ways by a variety of educators. Most likely, you have heard the categories inductive, deductive, expository, didactic, implicit, explicit, direct, indirect, integrative, interactive, teacher centered, learner centered, teacher directed, and learner directed applied to teaching strategies. Many of these categories overlap; in some cases (e.g., explicit and direct), they actually mean the same thing. Accordingly, we will not needlessly confuse you by defining and explaining each of these categories. Instead, we discuss only two categories: teacher directed and learner directed. These two particular categories were chosen because, in the past, we have found that they are the most easily understood and remembered by pre- and in-service teachers.

Teacher-directed strategies are strategies that require the teacher to manage instruction and to make decisions about how to proceed. Such strategies are useful for teaching facts and basic skills. In addition, teacher-directed lessons that are well planned can also help students understand concrete concepts and generalizations. With teacher-directed strategies, the timing and pace of the lesson is controlled by the teacher. On the whole, these strategies allow for very little input from students nor do they provide much opportunity for students to play an active role in their own learning.

Learner-directed strategies are strategies that require the learners to manage their own instruction and to make their own decisions about how to proceed. Such strategies are particularly useful for helping students to understand abstract concepts and generalizations and to develop their complex and higher-order skills. Learner-directed strategies allow students to participate in their own learning by providing them with opportunities to integrate and apply their knowledge. One disadvantage of these strategies is that they generally require more time than teacher-directed strategies. But many educators feel this is time well spent because it leads to greater understanding on the part of the students.

In actual classroom practice, the distinction between teacher-directed strategies and learner-directed strategies is not always clear; many strategies are a combination of the two. For example, during classroom discussions, control of the discussion frequently shifts from the teacher to the students. Oftentimes, a discussion is carried on among the students themselves, with the teacher playing a very small role. In these instances, both the teacher and the students are managing the instruction and making decisions about how to proceed. For the sake of organization, we have labeled such strategies *teacher/learner-directed strategies.* We now discuss a variety of teacher-directed, teacher/learner-directed, and learner-directed strategies that are appropriate for use in middle-grades classrooms.

Teacher-Directed Strategies

In this section, we discuss the teacher-directed strategies of lecture, explicit teaching, demonstration, and recitation.

Lecture

A *lecture* is a teaching strategy "in which the teacher presents information by telling or explaining, and students receive and record it in essentially the same form in which it was presented" (Kauchak & Eggen, 1989, p. 285). Unfortunately, when many of us hear the word *lecture,* we tend to conjure up the worst possible image—the teacher who, in a barely audible voice, rambles on and on in a completely unorganized manner. Fortunately, most lectures do not fit this image. Lectures are very common in most middle-grades classrooms and are quite often interwoven with other teaching strategies such as discussions, recitations, and demonstrations. They are an effective means of presenting a body of facts to students.

Lectures can be formal or informal. During *formal lectures,* students do very little except listen. Except for clarification, the teacher discourages student questions and comments. Formal lectures are used quite often when the audience is large and time is limited. During *informal lectures,* student participation in the form of questions and comments is allowed and oftentimes encouraged. Most lectures in middle-grades classrooms tend to be informal. Short, spontaneous lectures that occur as a result of student confusion or lack of understanding are called *explanations.* Lectures, both formal and informal, and explanations are extremely versatile in that they can be used in virtually any of the content areas.

Advantages.   Lectures that are well organized, well implemented, and up to date can be extremely effective. Such lectures can be advantageous because they allow teachers to:

1. Provide students with large amounts of information that otherwise might take them a great deal of time to locate, read, and organize.
2. Present large amounts of information in a short amount of time.
3. Adapt the material to the particular background, interests, and ability levels of the students.
4. Motivate students and arouse their interest.
5. Tie together related facts and ideas.
6. Control the timing and pace of the presentation.

The use of visual aids during lectures helps young adolescents better understand abstract concepts and ideas.

Disadvantages.   Unfortunately, lectures also have several disadvantages that should be considered by teachers. They:

1. Encourage passive learning on the part of the students.
2. Usually center around facts and are generally not effective for teaching abstract concepts and generalizations or higher-order skills. In general, lectures are not effective for teaching basic or complex skills since lectures do not provide for student practice of the skills.
3. Assume that all students learn at the same rate and need the same information.
4. Are generally not effective with low-ability learners who require more individual attention.
5. Frequently outlast students' attention spans.
6. Are difficult to evaluate since student participation and feedback are low.

Appropriate Uses.   The most appropriate times to use lectures include when:

1. The purpose of the lesson is to disseminate basic information to students.
2. Important information is not easily available to students.
3. Time is limited.
4. Students have encountered conflicting information.
5. A change of pace or variety is needed.
6. An introduction, background information, or directions are needed for an upcoming activity.

Guidelines for Implementation.   Lectures can be an effective means of conveying information to students if the following guidelines are kept in mind:

1. Plan ahead so that the lecture is well organized. The purpose of the lecture should be clear to students. Some teachers provide an outline or write one on the chalkboard.
2. Plan an interesting opening so that student interest and curiosity are quickly captured.
3. Stay on the topic. Interesting facts, stories, and anecdotes can be interspersed throughout the lecture but they should not take precedent over the content. Also, do not permit student questions and comments to allow you to stray off the topic.
4. Use your voice to convey enthusiasm and maintain student interest. Vary the volume, rate, and intonation of your speech. Enunciation should be clear so that students can understand everything you say. Unobtrusively tape record yourself during a lecture and listen to it later. This is usually an eye-opening experience for most teachers. Enthusiasm can also be conveyed through eye contact, facial expressions, and gestures.
5. Do not lecture too long. Lectures should be well timed to coincide with students' attention spans. We recommend lectures between 15 to 20 minutes, as young adolescents have difficulty listening for much longer than that.
6. Intersperse short lectures with other teaching strategies such as discussion, recitation, and demonstration. Use lectures in conjunction with activities such as small-group work, films or videos, and field trips.
7. Throughout the lecture, provide concrete examples whenever possible. Use instructional aids such as charts, models, and outlines to reinforce key ideas. Emphasize major points or potential areas of difficulty.
8. Throughout the lecture, monitor student attention. Young adolescents are particularly adept at appearing very attentive when they have actually tuned you out. (We discuss monitoring student attention in detail in Chapter 15.)
9. Provide students with a summary at the end of your lecture so they are clear about the main points of the lecture.
10. Solicit feedback about the effectiveness of your lectures. Invite team members or other teachers to sit in and evaluate your lectures. Be receptive to their constructive criticism and implement their suggestions.

Explicit Teaching

Explicit teaching is a systematic strategy for teaching mastery of facts as well as basic and complex skills. The term *explicit teaching* was coined by Rosenshine (1986). Explicit teaching has also been called *direct instruction* (Rosenshine, 1979) and *active teaching* (Good, Grouws, & Ebmeier, 1983). Explicit teaching "includes presenting material in small steps, pausing to check for student understanding, and requiring active and successful participation from all students" (Rosenshine, 1987, p. 75). Most of the research conducted on explicit teaching was done in the areas of reading and mathematics but the results can be applied to any area in which mastery of facts, basic skills, or complex skills is desirable.

Advantages.   Explicit teaching has the following advantages:

1. It is effective for teaching related facts as well as basic and complex skills.
2. It can be applied to the learning of rules and procedures as well as to the learning of difficult or confusing material if the material can be broken down into small steps.
3. It is especially useful for teaching low-ability learners or students who need structure and continual guidance and feedback from a teacher. It can also be adapted to teach higher-ability students or older students by reducing the amount of review and practice and increasing the amount of new material presented.
4. It allows the teacher to control the pace and timing of the lesson.

Disadvantages.   Along with its advantages, explicit teaching also has several disadvantages:

1. Explicit teaching is not possible in some areas because the processes necessary have not been identified or cannot be explicitly communicated to students. Doyle (1989) uses the example of riding a bicycle. We know that balance is required "but telling or showing someone how to balance a bicycle is virtually impossible" (p. 293).
2. Although explicit teaching can lead to the successful development of skills, it does not necessarily lead to successful use of those skills at the appropriate time. For example, Ralph may be proficient at addition, subtraction, multiplication, and division, but this does not necessarily mean that he will choose the correct operation(s) to solve an arithmetic word problem.
3. At the present time, explicit teaching has not proved effective for teaching abstract concepts and generalizations or for developing higher-order skills. This is a particularly important disadvantage for teaching middle-grades students. Recall that early adolescence is the time when many students are beginning to move from the concrete operational stage into the formal operational stage. Accordingly, they are becoming much more capable of being challenged to develop their higher-order skills.
4. Research conducted on explicit teaching has only looked at its effectiveness in terms of improving student test scores. Hence, there is currently no evidence as to how explicit teaching affects other variables such as student attitudes, creativity, self-confidence, or social development. This has important implications for the teaching of young adolescents because they are at an age when their social and emotional development are as equally important as their cognitive development.

Appropriate Uses.   Current research indicates that explicit teaching is effective when:

1. The objective of the lesson is to teach a related body of facts or a basic or complex skill.

1. The material being taught is well structured.
2. The material can best be taught in small steps.
3. The students are low-ability learners or novices at the material or skill being taught.

Guidelines for Implementation.   Rosenshine (1987) provides the following guidelines for implementing explicit teaching:

1. Begin a lesson with a short statement of goals.
2. Begin a lesson with a short review of previous, prerequisite learning.
3. Present new material in small steps, with student practice after each step.
4. Give clear and detailed instructions and explanations.
5. Provide a high level of active practice for all students.
6. Ask many questions, check for student understanding, and obtain responses from all students.
7. Guide students during initial practice.
8. Provide systematic feedback and corrections.
9. Provide explicit instruction and practice for seatwork exercises and, when necessary, monitor students during seatwork.
10. Continue practice until students are independent and confident. (p. 79)

Within these guidelines, Rosenshine (1987) identified six teaching functions: review, presentation, guided practice, corrections and feedback, independent practice, and weekly and monthly reviews. Figure 11.5 provides a detailed description of the six teaching functions. Keep in mind, however, that the functions do not have to occur in the order they are listed but rather should occur when necessary for student understanding.

Demonstration

Demonstration is a teaching strategy in which a teacher engages "in a learning task rather than just talking about it" (Lorber & Pierce, 1990, p. 72). When we think of demonstrations, most of us tend to think of science labs or physical education classes. But a demonstration can be an effective teaching strategy in a variety of content areas. For example, a mathematics teacher can demonstrate the process of doing three-digit long division by going through each step for the students. Similarly, a social studies teacher can use a map to demonstrate how to determine the tributaries of a river.

Demonstration is frequently a component of explicit teaching. Notice under the *presentation* function in Figure 11.5 the statement "Model procedures." If you were using explicit teaching, it is at this point that you would use a demonstration. Keep in mind, however, that a demonstration can be used on its own. It does not always have to be used in conjunction with explicit teaching. It is frequently used in middle-grades classrooms in conjunction with other teaching strategies such as lecture or discussion.

FIGURE 11.5   Teaching Functions in Explicit Teaching

1. Review
    - Review homework
    - Review relevant previous learning
    - Review prerequisite skills and knowledge for the lesson
2. Presentation
    - State lesson goals and/or provide outline
    - Teach in small steps
    - Model procedures
    - Provide concrete positive and negative examples
    - Use clear language
    - Check for student understanding
    - Avoid digressions
3. Guided practice
    - More time
    - High frequency of questions or guided practice
    - All students respond and receive feedback
    - High success rate
    - Continue practice until students are fluid
4. Corrections and feedback
    - Give process feedback when answers are correct but hesitant
    - Give sustaining feedback, clues, or reteaching when answers are incorrect
    - Reteach when necessary
5. Independent practice
    - Students receive help during initial steps, or overview
    - Practice continues until students are automatic (where relevant)
    - Teacher provides active supervision (where possible)
    - Routines are used to give help to slower students
6. Weekly and monthly reviews

Source: From "Explicit Teaching" by B. Rosenshine. From *Talks to Teachers,* D. C. Berliner and B. Rosenshine, Eds., Copyright © 1987 by Random House. Reprinted by permission of McGraw-Hill, Inc.

Advantages.   Demonstrations have the following advantages:

1. They are extremely versatile because they can be used in a variety of content areas and in a variety of settings. In addition, they can be used to introduce new material, review previously learned material, or show students how to apply material in new situations.
2. They can be used to teach facts, concepts, and generalizations, as well as basic and complex skills.
3. They are an excellent means of making abstract material more concrete since they have both an auditory and a visual component.
4. If well planned and carried out, demonstrations can increase student motivation and interest.

5. Because only the teacher needs materials, financial costs can be reduced through the use of demonstrations.

Disadvantages.   As you will quickly learn when you use demonstrations, they also have several disadvantages:

1. Demonstrations are time consuming, both in terms of teacher planning as well as use of class time.
2. Demonstrations are not usually effective for the development of higher-order skills.
3. Since all students must be able to see, demonstrations cannot be used for large classes unless some type of overhead video display can be arranged.
4. If students do not understand the demonstration, it can lead to rote memorization and inability to apply what was learned in appropriate situations.
5. There is no evidence that demonstrations help students develop either socially or emotionally.

Appropriate Uses.   A demonstration is an appropriate teaching strategy when:

1. The body of material being taught is easily broken down into steps that can be visually illustrated to students.
2. All students can easily see and hear.
3. Dangerous materials or procedures must be used. In this event, a demonstration will either eliminate students having to work with the materials or procedures themselves, or will show them how to handle the materials or carry out the procedures later themselves.

Guidelines for Implementation.   In order to conduct demonstrations that are well planned and implemented, the following guidelines are suggested:

1. Break down the body of knowledge or skill to be demonstrated into its component parts and decide which parts to include in your demonstration.
2. Plan far enough in advance so that you can collect all necessary materials. Before you begin the demonstration, make sure all materials are available and in working condition.
3. Make sure that students have the background knowledge necessary for understanding the demonstration. For example, before you demonstrate how to determine the pH of a solution, students should know what pH is and why it is important.
4. If the demonstration is particularly difficult or dangerous, or if the time you have for your demonstration is limited, practice the demonstration several times on your own before you conduct it in front of the class.
5. If necessary, rearrange the seating arrangement in your classroom so that all students can see and hear.

6. Throughout the demonstration, solicit student questions and comments so you can involve them and also informally evaluate their understanding of the demonstration.
7. At the end of the demonstration, summarize the key points or review the major steps.

Recitation

Recitation, a form of questioning, is a teacher-directed strategy in which a series of questions posed by the teacher are answered by students interacting only with the teacher, one at a time or sometimes in a chorus. Recitation is used primarily to elicit knowledge of facts from students. We do not discuss recitation in detail here because we do so later in Chapters 13 and 14.

Teacher/Learner-Directed Strategies

In this section, we discuss the teacher/learner-directed strategies of drill and practice, discovery learning, brainstorming, and discussion.

Drill and Practice

Drill and practice is a teaching strategy in which speed and accuracy are developed through repetition. We have classified drill and practice as a teacher/learner-directed strategy because the drill component is typically teacher directed while the practice component has the *potential* for being learner directed. Many teachers tend to think that drill and practice is only for very young children. But there are many instances at the middle-grades level in which drill and practice can be effective. For example, multiplication facts, state capitals, and chemical symbols for the elements of the periodic table can all be learned effectively through drill and practice.

We mentioned that the practice component of drill and practice has the potential for being student directed. Unfortunately, it also has the potential to be teacher directed. When practice is nothing more than busywork that the teacher has assigned, then the students really have no role in their own learning. Hence, practice is not student directed. However, when students plan an active role in practice, as they might with certain computer programs or when working in pairs or groups to design their own method of practice, then practice is more student directed.

Advantages.   Drill and practice has the following advantages:

1. It can be used to develop speed and accuracy in the recall of facts, concepts, and generalizations and in the performance of basic and complex skills.
2. It is especially useful for developing proficiency in psychomotor skills.
3. It aids long-term retention of facts.
4. It can be used to fill in short slots of time.
5. When pair or small-group practice is used, it can help develop social skills.

6. When individual practice is used, it allows students to work at their own pace.
7. When designed appropriately, it can provide the teacher with useful diagnostic information.

Disadvantages.   Drill and practice has the following disadvantages:

1. If the task is too easy or too hard for the students, or if drill and practice is used to the exclusion of other strategies, then it becomes nothing more than busywork.
2. If inappropriately designed or implemented, drill and practice can be boring and tedious for students.
3. If students do not understand what they are being drilled in or what they are practicing, then it can lead to rote memorization and students will be unable to apply what they have learned in appropriate situations.
4. Unless they are used frequently in the context of real situations, information and skills learned through drill and practice will not be remembered for very long.

Appropriate Uses.   Drill and practice is appropriate when:

1. Speed and accuracy are desired in the recall of facts, concepts, or generalizations, or in the performance of basic and complex skills.
2. Low-ability or older students lack basic skills that can be developed through repetition,
3. Computer programs are available to help students practice.

Guidelines for Implementation.   When using drill and practice with middle-grades students, keep the following guidelines in mind:

1. Keep the length of drill and practice short and the pace brisk. Young adolescents tend to become bored quickly from repetition and, as Lorber and Pierce (1990) point out, "Students gain most from the use of drill and practice programs during the first 15 minutes of use" (p. 106).
2. Vary the nature of drill and practice by having students work as a whole class, in small groups, in pairs, and individually when appropriate. Use games or contests.
3. Remember that drill and practice does not typically lead to higher-order thinking, so its use should be minimal.
4. Make sure students understand what they are being drilled in or what they are practicing.
5. Monitor students constantly during practice to ensure that they are recalling the information or implementing the skill correctly. Provide them with feedback about their progress.

Discovery Learning

Henson (1988) provides an excellent summary of discovery learning and much of the information in our discussion of it here draws from his summary. Discovery learning means different things to different people. The definition we feel succinctly captures the essence of *discovery learning* is "intentional learning through problem solving under the supervision of a teacher" (Henson, p. 102). Thus, *intentional* and *supervision* are two essential criteria for discovery learning to take place. Both the teacher and the students play an active role in discovery learning. Depending on how active a role the teacher plays in supervising and guiding students, discovery learning can range anywhere on a continuum from strict supervision (guided discovery or inquiry) to very little supervision (free or pure discovery).

In using discovery learning, the teacher designs a scenario that forces the students to answer a question or solve a problem. As mentioned, teacher supervision and guidance can range from great to almost none. However, even if very little supervision or guidance occurs, the teacher still plays an active role in discovery learning because it is he or she who designs the scenario.

The ultimate goal of discovery learning is that students learn *how* to learn rather than *what* to learn. Accordingly, discovery learning is an effective strategy for helping students understand concepts and generalizations and for developing their higher-order skills. Figure 11.6 illustrates a lesson in which discovery learning was used to "lead" eighth-grade students to a definition of *poetry*. This lesson was designed and taught by Dierdra Jackson, a University of Georgia student teacher. This lesson was the first in a 10-day unit on poetry.

Advantages.   Discovery learning has the following advantages:

1. Understanding and retention of information and skills is usually greater than with many other strategies because students play an active role in discovering their new knowledge.
2. Intrinsic motivation is frequently enhanced since students are involved in the discovery.
3. By participating in discovery learning, students learn valuable higher-order skills such as forming and testing hypotheses, making predictions, and drawing conclusions.
4. If carefully planned, discovery learning helps students make connections between school and the real world.
5. Discovery learning provides students with opportunities to work together to solve common problems. It also allows students to see that sometimes there are various solutions to a problem and that their peers do not always have the same ideas they do. This is a big advantage for young adolescents, many of whom are still egocentric and are just beginning to accept the fact that multiple opinions and viewpoints exist.
6. Discovery learning frequently leads to incidental or unplanned learning on the part of the students.

FIGURE 11.6 Dierdra Jackson's Lesson Plan

NAME _Dierdra Jackson_   "Exploring Poetry"   DATE _10·31_

Day 1

OBJECTIVES	ACTIVITIES	MATERIALS	EVALUATION
1. Students will define the term poetry.	Students will be introduced to poetry by the teacher. The teacher will give students a ditto with a number of poems on it. Students will then be placed in 4 groups. Each group will choose a poem off of the ditto sheet to present to the class. Students will be allowed to "rap" with the poem to show rhyme, beat, and sound effects. Others will do choral reading with their poems, etc. The teacher will read other poems written by kids who are 12, 13, 14 years of age to the students, and will try to get students to give a definition of poetry. The teacher will lead students in the direction that she is looking for. By using this definition, students will determine why poems are forms of poetry. Homework: Students will be required to bring in one poem each for class on Day 2.	chalk chalkboard pencil/pen paper text	1. End of Unit Assessment *6 Teacher observation of response. Teacher will look for the following points in definitions: – concentrates on language – transmits poet's feeling or thoughts – builds on observation of definition image – contains musical quality

Source: Used with permission of Dierdra Jackson.

7. Discovery learning focuses on cooperative learning rather than competitive learning.

Disadvantages. The following disadvantages are associated with discovery learning:

1. Lessons involving discovery learning tend to be more time consuming than most other lessons. Especially when lessons include very little supervision from the teacher, the timing and pace of the lesson is controlled by the students.
2. Teachers who have little knowledge of their students' capabilities or do not provide the appropriate amount of supervision and guidance during discovery learning run the risk of frustrating their students instead of helping them.
3. Discovery learning places enormous demands on teachers. In order to use discovery learning effectively, teachers must have a thorough knowledge and understanding of the content, they must be aware of each student's strengths and weaknesses, and they must be extremely capable of making interactive decisions.
4. Discovery learning is not an effective strategy for covering large amounts of material.

Appropriate uses. Discovery learning is best used when:

1. The teacher is familiar with the students and the content to be taught.
2. Instructional goals focus on teaching students how to learn.
3. Higher-order skills are being developed.
4. Time is not a critical factor.

Guidelines for Implementation. The following guidelines are offered for implementing discovery learning:

1. Plan ahead and in sufficient enough detail so the problem, your role, and the role of the students are clear before you begin.
2. At the end of the lesson, take time to review the process of discovery with the students. Discovery learning loses much of its value when students do not understand what they are doing and why they are doing it.
3. Allow time at the end of the lesson for individual students or groups of students to share their discoveries, products, or answers with other students. Young adolescents need to have their accomplishments recognized by their peers.
4. When appropriate, use discovery learning in conjunction with other teaching strategies such as demonstrations and discussions.
5. When using discovery learning with students for the first time, plan a short, simple problem or scenario to increase the chance of student success. Some students who are not successful initially might get discouraged and be unwilling to try this approach again. Be supportive, encouraging, and helpful when students encounter difficulty.

Brainstorming

Brainstorming is a teaching strategy in which the teacher elicits from the students as many ideas as possible but refrains from evaluating them until all possible ideas have been generated. Both the teacher and the students play an active role in brainstorming. Though there are many variations, brainstorming usually occurs in four phases: (1) problem identification, (2) idea generation, (3) idea evaluation, and (4) solution implementation and evaluation. We discuss how to implement these phases later in this section.

Because all possible ideas are accepted, brainstorming is an excellent strategy for stimulating creativity in students. In addition, since brainstorming is used in all walks of life, ranging from business and industry to law and athletics, it is important to expose students to it in the classroom so they are better prepared to use it in real life.

Advantages.   Brainstorming has the following advantages:

1. It is an extremely versatile strategy in that it can be used in any content area and with any size group.
2. It is cost effective because, in most instances, it can be implemented without any materials or equipment.
3. It is effective for encouraging creativity and for developing higher-order skills such as generating hypotheses, considering alternatives, and synthesizing information.
4. It is especially helpful for developing social skills in young adolescents. Through brainstorming, students learn to take turns, consider the ideas and viewpoints of their peers, and work with their peers towards a common goal.
5. It can help develop many areas of the affective domain such as self-confidence and self-esteem. All too frequently, young adolescents who feel their thoughts

The teacher and students play an active role in brainstorming.

and ideas are strange or not as good as those of their peers refrain from speaking up or sharing their ideas with others. Through brainstorming, young adolescents are provided with a vehicle for having their thoughts and ideas accepted by their peers and also having their ideas contribute to the solution of a problem.

6. It can be used during advisor/advisee time to generate ideas and solutions to actual social, emotional, or moral problems that students may be experiencing.

Disadvantages.   The following disadvantages are associated with brainstorming:

1. It can take longer than some other strategies because timing and pace are frequently controlled by the number of ideas students generate.
2. If students do not follow the rules and procedures, some students may be hurt if their ideas are criticized or laughed at by their peers.
3. It is not an effective strategy for teaching facts or basic skills.

Appropriate Uses.   Brainstorming is most appropriate when:

1. The goal of the lesson is to encourage creativity and/or develop higher-order skills.
2. A realistic problem or scenario is identified or is serendipitously generated by the students.
3. Multiple perspectives or ideas can lead to better solutions to the problem or the scenario.

Guidelines for Implementation.   Following these guidelines will increase the effectiveness of brainstorming:

1. Students should be made aware of the goal of brainstorming and should also know that the more ideas generated, the better their solution will probably be.
2. The teacher should identify the problem and make sure that students know exactly what it is. Problems come from a variety of sources. For example, some problems might be related to the content (e.g., "What can we do if we have 12 people and our pizza is cut into 5 pieces?"); others might be related to managing the classroom (e.g., "As you know, we are having such a problem with too many people talking at once during discussions that it has gotten to the point where it is almost impossible to hear what anyone is saying. What shall we do?"); and still others might be related to extracurricular activities of the students (e.g., "At the dance last night, seven students were caught with alcohol. How do you think we could avoid this in the future?").
3. The teacher should act as a facilitator of the idea-generation stage and should record *all* responses. The teacher should encourage everyone to participate and should accept all suggestions regardless of how silly or strange they seem.
4. During the idea-generation stage, no criticism or evaluation of the students' ideas is permitted.

5. When the idea-generation stage is over, the teacher facilitates the evaluation of the ideas that the students generated. Criteria for evaluating the ideas are solicited from the students (e.g., Which ideas can be easily and quickly implemented and are cost effective?). Students weigh each idea against the established criteria. They then pick the best ideas, combine ideas, and come up with the best possible solution to the problem.

6. The teacher and/or the students then try out or implement the solution to determine its effectiveness. In some cases, implementation and evaluation of the solution can be done immediately; in other cases, this process may take a long time (as in the preceding alcohol at the dance example).

7. If the class size is large, students can work in small groups to generate group ideas. Each group can then present its ideas to the whole class.

Discussion

Discussion, as used in most middle-grades classrooms, is a teacher/learner-directed strategy in which students are free to address their peers and to ask their own questions of each other and of the teacher. (In instances when the teacher plays no role in a discussion, then it would be a student-directed strategy. In most middle grades classrooms, however, the teacher does play a role, so we have chosen to include discussion here rather than in the next section on student-directed strategies.)

During discussions, teachers have neither the right nor the responsibility to direct the flow of the questioning. Discussions are ideal for teaching facts, concepts, and generalizations as well as basic, complex, and higher-order skills. Discussions can be organized in a variety of formats such as whole-class discussions, small-group discussions, panel discussions, debates, and forums. The role of the teacher varies in each of these formats. In general, the teacher plays a larger role in whole-class discussions than in some of the other formats such as panel discussions and debates. We do not discuss discussions in detail here because we do so in Chapters 13 and 14.

Learner-Directed Strategies

In this section, we discuss the learner-directed strategies of roleplaying and problem solving. As mentioned earlier, learner-directed strategies are strategies that require the learners to manage their own instruction and to make their own decisions about how to proceed. In actual classroom practice, however, there are very few instances of *pure* learner-directed strategies because it is rare that students are completely in charge of managing and making decisions about their own instruction.

So-called pure learner-directed strategies place enormous responsibility on students, and many young adolescents are not prepared to be completely responsible for their own learning. Hence, as you will probably notice, the teacher does play a role in the strategies we discuss in this section, but it is a much smaller role than he or she plays in the strategies we discussed in the two previous sections.

Roleplaying

Roleplaying is a student-directed strategy in which students act out a particular idea, circumstance, or situation. True roleplaying is spontaneous; that is, students do not write or practice their dialogue ahead of time. In classroom use, however, roleplaying does not have to be completely spontaneous.   *get into the role!*

In order for roleplaying to be effective, students must express themselves in a manner consistent with the characters they are playing. For example, if Patrick is playing a father looking at his son's poor report card, Patrick must react as a father would react, not as he himself would react. As you can see, roleplaying requires students to assume the feelings and ideas of the characters they are playing. It is this aspect of roleplaying that helps young adolescents recognize and understand other people's points of view.

Unfortunately, many middle-grades teachers fail to use roleplaying because they feel it is appropriate for elementary school students but not for middle-grades students. This is not the case, and there is even evidence that roleplaying can help alleviate depression in young adolescents (Butler, Miezitis, Friedman, & Cole, 1980). In addition, roleplaying is becoming more widely used outside of the classroom in areas such as business, law, counseling, and labor relations.

What type of learning typically takes place in roleplaying? As Torrance (1970) points out, that depends on the roles that the students select. For example:

> If occupational roles are chosen, the content involves concepts and experiences in the occupational world. If family roles are chosen, the content becomes family relationships and problem solving. If fantasy roles are chosen, the subject matter becomes the literature from which these roles come. Almost always, there is practice in human relationships, psychomotor skills, and social skills. (p. 5)

Advantages.   Given the number and the nature of the advantages of roleplaying, it is unfortunate that it is not used more often in middle grades.

1. Roleplaying helps students better express their feelings.
2. It can help students develop a better understanding of other people's feelings and problems, particularly people from different cultures and ethnic groups.
3. Cognitive, affective, and psychomotor skills can be practiced and enhanced through the use of roleplaying.
4. Roleplaying can encourage creativity and imagination. Oftentimes, quiet or withdrawn students respond to roleplaying. Also, students who create management problems (e.g., the class clown) frequently are very effective roleplayers because they are able to channel their energies into creative activities.
5. Roleplaying provides students with an opportunity to practice interpersonal and social skills in a safe environment. For example, young adolescents can practice a particularly stressful or embarrassing conversation they anticipate having with a peer or a parent. Advisor/advisee sessions can be used for roleplaying to develop these skills.

Disadvantages.   Despite its many advantages, roleplaying also has several disadvantages:

1. Lessons involving roleplaying can be time consuming. Students generally control the timing and pace of such lessons. The length of the lesson varies according to the nature of the situation and the numbers of roles.
2. Some students (particularly young adolescents who want to impress their peers) may tend to act silly or disruptive.
3. Roleplaying can be boring for those students who are only watching and not actually involved in the acting.
4. Some students may get so involved with their acting or the acting of their peers that they miss the point of the lesson. Roleplaying is not the same as acting in a play.

Appropriate Uses.   Roleplaying is best when:

1. The goal of the lesson is to develop interpersonal skills.
2. Students express concern, embarrassment, or apprehension about an upcoming situation.
3. The content being taught can be best understood by students if they portray the various characters involved. For example, Dennis Rowley, a middle-grades student teacher at the University of Georgia, used roleplaying in a lesson on conservation. As part of the lesson, Dennis had students roleplay a local developer who wanted to clear trees to build homes and an environmentalist who wanted to save the trees.

Guidelines for Implementation.   The following guidelines should help you implement roleplaying into your classroom:

1. Begin slowly and provide students with help and support. Young adolescents who are trying roleplaying for the first time may be embarrassed or nervous in front of their peers.
2. When using roleplaying for the first time, the teacher should plan the situation and the roles. Roles should be assigned to capable students and they should be allowed a brief amount of time to plan and rehearse their lines. After students are familiar with how roleplaying is carried out, future roleplaying situations should be generated by the students.
3. Do not force any student to take on a role. Initially, some students may be apprehensive about roleplaying, but we have found that as they watch their peers several times, most young adolescents eventually want to participate.
4. Actively involve the students who are in the audience in some aspect of the roleplaying. For example, audience members could take notes on key points made, logical arguments generated, and misconceptions of the various roleplayers.

5. At the end of roleplaying, provide time for students to summarize what they learned, express their feelings, and/or evaluate the credibility of the various roleplayers.
6. Some situations can be roleplayed several times with different students playing the various roles. This reenactment frequently results in new ideas and alternatives.
7. When appropriate, certain roleplaying situations can be tape recorded or videotaped so students have an opportunity to watch and evaluate their own performances.
8. The teacher's role in roleplaying should be kept at an absolute minimum.

Problem Solving

Problem solving can best be defined as a learner-directed strategy in which students "think patiently and analytically about complex situations in order to find answers to questions" (Montague, Huntsberger, & Hoffman, 1989, p. 136). A *problem* is defined as "a situation in which you are trying to reach some goal, and must find a means for getting there" (Chi & Glaser, 1985).

As these two definitions illustrate, students are responsible for their own learning during problem solving. It is the students who must think about the situation and must find their own means for reaching their goal. Thus, *problem solving* is not synonymous with *discovery learning*. In discovery learning, the teacher leads the students toward the answer or the solution. In a sense, during discovery learning, students are actually "discovering" what the teacher already knows. This is not always the case in problem solving because part of the students' responsibility is to identify the problem.

One type of problem solving that is particularly popular with young adolescents is future problem solving in which students brainstorm and evaluate possible solutions to future problems. During future problem solving, students typically work on teams of four or five. The steps in problem solving are:

1. Brainstorm possible problems.
2. Identify the main problem.
3. Brainstorm possible solutions to the main problem.
4. Establish criteria for evaluating solutions.
5. Evaluate solutions.
6. Describe the best solution.

As you can see, brainstorming is a critical component of problem solving. Figure 11.7 illustrates a future problem that middle-grades students could use for problem solving. When students engage in problem solving of this type, they are obviously not expected to come up with a solution in one class period. They might be allowed a month or several weeks to work on their problem.

Students are often provided with a reference list on their topic. Figure 11.8 illustrates a reference list on shrinking tropical forests, the topic of the problem illustrated in Figure 11.7.

FIGURE 11.7   Future Problem for Middle-Grades Students

Shrinking Tropical Forests

The year is 1999. The world is facing a crisis. About 18 million acres of tropical rain forests are being destroyed each year. Many of the animals that had lived in the forests are also dying, because their homes are being destroyed. Thousands of types of plants and animals are becoming extinct each year, which means they will never exist again anywhere on earth.

Scientists are very concerned about this loss of plant and animal life. Many of the important medicines to cure diseases come from plants in the tropical forests. Scientists know that many tropical forest plants that can cure serious diseases have yet to be discovered. They also know that the destruction of the forests means that many of these plants will become extinct before they can ever be discovered.

There are many nations that have tropical rain forests. They are located in a band around the earth, close to the equator. They all are very hot and have heavy rainfalls almost every day. Brazil is one of the largest of these countries.

Brazil has millions of very poor people. Until the 1970s most of these people lived in the big cities in slums. In the 1970s Brazil's leaders wanted to help the poor people. They also wanted to try to rebuild the economy of the nation. So they offered free land in the rain forest to people who would settle there, clear the land, and farm it. Ranchers were encouraged to clear the rain forest to create ranches. People of the mining and timber industries were urged to use the resources found in the rain forest.

Unfortunately, the leaders of Brazil did not realize the terrible effects that clearing the rain forest would have on Brazil, and on the entire world. Something must be done to halt this terrible destruction.

Use the information you have gathered about tropical rain forests and your problem solving skills to examine the situation and develop a set of solutions.

Source: From Anne B. Crabbe, *1989–91 FPS Practice Problems*. Laurinburg, NC: Future Problem Solving Program, 1989. Reprinted by permission.

Keep in mind that all problems need not be this elaborate or detailed. Students can work on quite simple problems that their teachers may actually design themselves. Many textbooks provide sample problems that can be used for problem solving. Also, school district curriculum centers or local college or university libraries usually have books containing problems.

Advantages.   Problem solving has the following advantages:

1. Because students are actively involved in their own learning, understanding and retention of material is usually longer than with many other strategies. For example, students who work on the shrinking tropical forests problem will most likely remember what they learn longer than if they had been presented with this information during a lecture.
2. Student interest and motivation are usually increased through the use of problem solving.

FIGURE 11.8   Reference List for Shrinking Tropical Forests

Begley, Sharon, "The World's Largest Lab," *Newsweek*. February 20, 1989, pp. 46–47.

Borrell, John, "Trouble Ahead for the Canal?" *Time*. March 2, 1987, p. 63.

Breck, Henry R., "Rain Forests for Rent?" *Newsweek*. December 5, 1988, p. 12.

Brower, Kenneth, "Out on a Limb," *Omni*. April 1987, pp. 56–64, 119–124.

Conniff, Richard, "Inventorying Life in a 'Biotic Frontier' Before It Disappears," *Smithsonian*. September 1986, pp. 80–84•.

Copeland, Jeff B. and others, "Buying Debt, Saving Nature," *Newsweek*. August 31, 1987, p. 46.

Curtis, S., "Rain Forests Lost," *Boy's Life*. November 1987, p. 5.

Dwyer, Victor, "Cheap Conservation at $25 an Acre," *Macleans*. April 4, 1988, p. 52.

Ellis, William T., "Rondonia: Brazil's Imperiled Rain Forest," *National Geographic*. December 1988, pp. 772–779.

"Into the Rain Forest!" *Junior Scholastic*. December 16, 1988, p. 16.

Kurlansky, Mark J., "Woman in Love with a Jungle," *International Wildlife*. September/October 1985, pp. 34–39.

Levin, Bob, "The Last Frontier," *Macleans*. January 19, 1987, p. 28.

Linden, Eugene, "The Death of Birth," *Time*. January 2, 1989, pp. 32–35.

McIntyre, Loren, "Last Days of Eden," *National Geographic*. December 1988, pp. 800–817.

Murphy, Jamie, "The Quiet Apocalypse," *Time*. October 13, 1986, p. 80.

Nalley, Richard, "Is It Too Late for the Rain Forests?" *Science Digest*. April 1986, pp. 56–61•.

Nations, James D. and Komer, Daniel I., "Chewing Up the Jungle," *International Wildlife*. September/October 1984, pp. 14–16.

Page, Jake, "Clear-cutting the Tropical Rain Forest in a Bold Attempt to Salvage It," *Smithsonian*. April 1988, pp. 106–12•.

Quammen, David, "Brazil's Jungle Blackboard," *Harper's*. March 1988, pp. 65–70.

"Shrinking Tropical Forests," *Futurist*. August 1984, p. 40.

Steinhart, Peter, "Trouble in the Tropics," *National Wildlife*. December 1983/January 1984, pp. 16–20.

Tangley, Laura, "Studying (and Saving) the Tropics," *BioScience*. June 1988, pp. 375–385.

White, Peter, "Nature's Dwindling Treasures," *National Geographic*. January 1983, pp. 2–47.

Source: From Anne B. Crabbe, *1989–91 FPS Practice Problems*. Laurinberg, NC: Future Problem Solving Program, 1989. Reprinted by permission.

3. Problem solving is an effective method of developing higher-order skills such as distinguishing relevant from irrelevant information, forming and testing hypotheses, evaluating ideas, and drawing conclusions.

4. Through problem solving, students can think about and work on problems that they may actually confront in their future.

5. In problem solving, the responsibility for learning is placed on the students. This is especially important for young adolescents who are at an age where they are beginning to accept more and more responsibility for themselves.

6. When students work on problems in teams, they are provided with an opportunity to develop interpersonal and social skills. Young adolescents have a need to belong to a group and to be needed by others. Team problem solving provides outlets for both of these needs.

Disadvantages.   Problem solving does have several disadvantages that should be kept in mind:

1. Problem solving, especially the type of problem solving we described here, is difficult for many students. Having students work on teams helps but does not always eliminate this problem.
2. If the necessary resources are not available, problem solving cannot be effective. For example, if students could not locate any of the suggested sources of information on shrinking tropical forests, then that particular situation would not be a good one to have students work on.
3. Problem solving is a very time-consuming strategy for the students. In addition to using class time, students frequently must work on the problem together after school or at night.
4. Teachers must spend a great deal of time either preparing a problem or selecting an appropriate one for their students. Thus, teachers should know their students' capabilities and interests well before engaging in problem solving.

Appropriate Uses.   Problem solving is an appropriate strategy to use when:

1. The goal of the lesson is to increase students' understanding of concepts and generalizations and/or to develop their higher-order skills.
2. An appropriate problem is available or the teacher can design one. Students must be interested in the problem and should view it as important.
3. Students are capable of working together on a project.

Guidelines for Implementation.   The following guidelines are suggested for successful use of problem solving with middle-grades students:

1. When using problem solving for the first time, select a simple problem that can be completed in a short amount of time. Guide the students through each step and make sure they understand what they are doing and why they are doing it. The purpose of this first session is to familiarize students with the process of problem solving.
2. Plan student teams carefully and thoughtfully. Team members should be able to work together without significant conflict. Each team should have at least one student whom you see as a leader. (You do not have to identify the leader to the other students; just make sure each team has one.) Teams should be well balanced in terms of high- and low-ability students.

3. Take student interest, ability level, and maturation level into account when selecting or designing problems. Make sure resources are available for the problems you select or design.
4. Make sure that students are familiar with brainstorming before you implement problem solving.
5. Allow each team of students to share their solution with the whole class. If possible, display each team's solution somewhere in the classroom such as on a bulletin board or in a class book.

Summary

In the first part of this chapter, we discussed the nature of the content you will be teaching and presented information about declarative and procedural knowledge. Three types of declarative knowledge were discussed: facts, concepts, and generalizations. We also presented one type of procedural knowledge—skills. In particular, we talked about basic, complex, and higher-order skills.

A variety of teacher-directed, teacher/learner-directed, and learner-directed strategies were discussed next. For each strategy, we familiarized you with its advantages and disadvantages, and suggested when it can be used most effectively and how to implement it.

It is our hope that as you begin to plan lessons for young adolescents, you will integrate what you learned about the nature of the content with what you learned about the various teaching strategies. In short, we hope that you will consider the nature of the content when selecting among the various teaching strategies.

REFERENCES

Butler, L., Miezitis, S., Friedman, R., & Cole, E. (1980). The effect of two school-based intervention programs on depressive symptoms in preadolescents. *American Educational Research Journal, 17,* 111–119.

Carnegie Council on Adolescent Development. (1989). *Turning points: Preparing American youth for the 20th century.* Washington, DC: Carnegie Council of New York.

Chi, M. T. H., & Glaser, R. (1985). Problem-solving ability. In R. J. Sternberg (Ed.), *Human abilities* (pp. 227–250). New York: W. H. Freeman.

Doyle, W. A. (1989). Academic work. In L. W. Anderson (Ed.), *The effective teacher* (pp. 291–300). New York: Random House.

Eggen, P. D., & Kauchak, D. P. (1988). *Strategies for teachers* (2nd ed.). Englewood Cliffs, NJ: Prentice Hall.

Good, T. L., Grouws, D., & Ebmeier, H. (1983). *Active mathematics teaching.* New York: Longman.

Henson, K. T. (1988). *Methods and strategies for teaching in secondary and middle schools.* New York: Longman.

Kauchak, D. P., & Eggen, P. D. (1989). *Learning and teaching.* Boston: Allyn and Bacon.

Lorber, M. A., & Pierce, W. D. (1990). *Objectives, methods, and evaluation for secondary teaching* (3rd ed.). Englewood Cliffs, NJ: Prentice Hall.

McCall, R. B. (1988). Growth periodization in mental test performance. *Journal of Educational Psychology, 80,* 217–233.

Montague, E. J., Huntsberger, J. P., & Hoffman, J. V. (1989). *Fundamentals of elementary and middle school classroom instruction.* Columbus, OH: Merrill.

Muth, K. D. (1988, November). *Effects of extraneous information and multiple steps on the problem-solving performance of middle school students*. Paper presented at the meeting of the North American Chapter of the International Group for the Psychology of Mathematics Education, DeKalb, IL.

Pearson, P. D., & Gallagher, M. C. (1983). The instruction of reading comprehension. *Contemporary Educational Psychology, 8*, 317–344.

Rosenshine, B. (1979). Content, time, and direct instruction. In P. Peterson, & H. Walberg (Eds.), *Research on teaching: Concepts, findings, and implications*. Berkeley, CA: McCutchan.

Rosenshine, B. (1986). Synthesis of research on explicit teaching. *Educational Leadership, 43*(7), 60–69.

Rosenshine, B. (1987). Explicit teaching. In D. C. Berliner & B. Rosenshine (Eds.), *Talks to teachers* (pp. 79–92). New York: Random House.

Torrance, E. P. (1970). *Encouraging creativity in the classroom*. Dubuque, IA: Wm. C. Brown.

Vygotsky, L. S. (1978). *Mind in society: The development of higher mental processes*. Cambridge, MA: Harvard University Press.

Weil, M., & Joyce, B. (1978). *Information processing models of teaching*. Englewood Cliffs, NJ: Prentice Hall.

Weinstein, C. E., & Mayer, R. E. (1986). The teaching of learning strategies. In M. C. Wittrock (Ed.), *Handbook of research on teaching* (3rd ed., pp. 315–327). New York: Macmillan.

Woolfolk, A. E. (1990). *Educational Psychology* (4th ed.). Englewood Cliffs, NJ: Prentice Hall.

_12_

Learning Strategies

Learning is a collaborative effort between what the teacher does during teaching (teaching strategies) and what the learner does during learning (learning strategies). In other words, learning is not totally dependent on how the teacher presents the information. Students can, and should, play an active role in their own learning. In the last chapter, we focused on teaching strategies. In this chapter, we focus on learning strategies.

As you are probably aware, some students learn faster than others, some students learn more than others, and some students remember what they learn longer than others. At one time, educators believed there was not much they could do about these differences among students. However, as Gagné (1985) points out, we now have a much better understanding of how students learn and of the processes that account for some of these differences among students. As a result, we are now aware of strategies that students can use to enhance their own learning. These strategies are aptly named learning strategies.

Weinstein and Mayer (1986) define *learning strategies* as "behaviors that the learner engages in during learning that are intended to influence affective and cognitive processes during encoding" (p. 316). The ultimate goal of teaching learning strategies to students is to make them self-directed, autonomous learners. Because young adolescents are at an age when they are beginning to assume more responsibility for their own lives, this is an excellent age to introduce them to the idea of becoming more responsible for their own learning.

As you will discover in this chapter, there is a variety of learning strategies that middle-grades students can be taught to use to enhance their learning. In the first part of this chapter, we describe and give examples of these learning strategies. We then provide suggestions and guidelines for teaching these strategies to young adolescents so that they can begin to use them on their own.

Learning Strategies

Before beginning our discussion of learning strategies, the following is a description of students who are good strategy users:

> Good strategy users know many strategies and much information about when and where to use them. They are reflective and have low anxiety. They possess beliefs about themselves and performance that are compatible with good strategy use (e.g., that they can do well by using the right approaches). These beliefs motivate use of strategies. Good strategy users can combine strategies proficiently and often execute strategic sequences automatically. (Pressley, Goodchild, Fleet, Zajchowski, & Evans, 1989, p. 301)

Just what are these strategies that good strategy users use so effectively and efficiently? In their summary of the research on learning strategies, Weinstein and Mayer (1986) identify eight major categories of learning strategies:

1. Basic rehearsal strategies
2. Complex rehearsal strategies
3. Basic elaboration strategies
4. Complex elaboration strategies
5. Basic organizational strategies
6. Complex organizational strategies
7. Comprehension monitoring strategies
8. Affective and motivational strategies

Notice that categories 1, 3, and 5 refer to strategies that can be used for basic learning tasks, whereas categories 2, 4, and 6 refer to strategies that can be used for complex learning tasks. *Basic learning* typically includes the learning of new words or items on a list such as the names of the letters of the alphabet, new spelling words, the multiplication tables, and the chemical symbols for the elements in the periodic table. *Complex learning*, on the other hand, generally involves learning from prose, either oral prose such as what students hear in lectures, or written prose such as what students read in textbooks or what they write themselves. We now discuss each of Weinstein and Mayer's (1986) eight categories of learning strategies.

Basic Rehearsal Strategies

When students are engaged in basic learning tasks, such as learning the chemical symbols for the elements in the periodic table, one of the most effective strategies they can use to learn the new information is rehearsal. Weinstein and Mayer (1986) define *rehearsal* as "actively reciting or naming the presented information during learning" (p. 317). Rehearsal is usually used when verbatim recall of information is desired. It is an effective strategy for recalling (or not forgetting) new information because, through rehearsal, new information can stay in short-term memory for an indefinite period of time.

You have probably had the experience of looking up a phone number and closing the telephone book only to find that you forgot the number as soon as you began to dial the phone. Most people use the rehearsal strategy of reciting the number over and over again until they dial and they no longer need to remember the number. Rehearsal is an effective strategy for helping students remember information that they have already learned. Rehearsal can be used with the whole class or with small groups or pairs of students. Students can also use rehearsal alone, such as when they are studying for a test.

Recall from Chapter 11 that drill and practice is a teaching strategy in which rehearsal is typically used. For example, as the teacher goes up and down the rows, calling on students to identify the capitals of the 50 states, Miguel might reply "The capital of Georgia is Atlanta" and Melissa might reply, "The capital of Oregon is Salem." In this example, Miguel and Melissa are engaging in rehearsal.

When using rehearsal to help students with basic learning tasks, keep the following guidelines in mind:

1. Make sure students rehearse all of the information, not just the "answer." In the preceding example, notice that Miguel and Melissa both rehearsed the entire statement, including the word *capital* along with the state and its capital. They did not just answer "Atlanta" or "Salem."
2. Whenever possible, use visual aids, such as flashcards, when students are engaged in rehearsal. Visual aids add a visual modality to the auditory modality of repeating the information. When visual aids are used, make sure students still rehearse all information and not just the answer. For example, in response to a flashcard that shows $12 \times 12 = $ ___ , students would say, "$12 \times 12 = 144$," and not just "144."
3. Allow students to use rehearsal in small groups or pairs. Allowing students to work together is an excellent strategy for capitalizing on the social nature of young adolescents.

Complex Rehearsal Strategies

In both of the examples used (i.e., state capitals and multiplication tables), rehearsal was used to help students learn lists of facts. Quite often, though, students may need to recall larger chunks of information, such as short passages from their textbooks. For example, for a class play, speech, or performance, students might be required to memorize Robert Frost's "The Road Not Taken" or the Preamble to the

Constitution. When verbatim recall of information of this type is required, students can use the complex rehearsal strategy of repeated reading.

Dowhower (1989) defines *repeated reading* as "multiple reading of connected text" (p. 502). Research (e.g., Barnett & Seefeldt, 1987; Howe & Singer, 1975; Bromage & Mayer, 1986) has shown that repeated reading is an effective study strategy for students of all ages and abilities when recall of short passages is desired.

Dowhower (1989) suggests the following guidelines when using repeated reading of passages with students:

1. A passage selected for repeated reading should be relatively short (i.e., 50 to 300 words).
2. Students should be able to read the passage with about 85 percent accuracy. If the passage is too difficult for students to read, retention may be hindered.
3. Students should be able to read the passage at a minimum rate of about 60 words per minute (wpm). If their reading rate is slower than 60 wpm, the teacher can read along with the students.
4. The passage should be read a minimum of three to five times. The more often the passage is read, the greater the recall.
5. Students should be encouraged to read for meaning rather than speed. Reading for meaning increases recall of the passage.
6. Students can use repeated reading in pairs. Each student in the pair should read the passage a minimum of three to five times while the other student follows along. Using pairs of students is an especially appropriate strategy for use with young adolescents who enjoy working with each other.

When students are engaged in complex learning tasks, such as verbatim recall of *important* information from a lecture or a textbook, rehearsal strategies become a bit more elaborate. Students sometimes still actively recite the new information, but they are selective about what they recite. That is, they do not recite everything they read or hear; they recite only the important pieces of information that they want to remember.

Rehearsal strategies for complex learning tasks can also include several types of rehearsal that are different from the verbal rehearsal just described. For example, students can use strategies such as **copying**, selective **notetaking**, or **underlining** (Weinstein & Mayer, 1986) to help commit important information to memory. In a sense, these strategies are almost a form of psychomotor rehearsal because students are using their psychomotor skills to help them learn and remember the new information. Using psychomotor rehearsal in conjunction with verbal rehearsal (e.g., reciting the words to yourself as you copy them) typically results in increased learning.

Using Complex Rehearsal Strategies
with the Help of the Teacher

Unfortunately, effective use of many of these rehearsal strategies for complex learning tasks depends on first being able to identify the important information to be rehearsed. For instance, in order to take notes selectively during a lecture, students must be able to determine which information is important so they can write it down. Similarly, in order to use underlining effectively as they read a textbook, students must be able to determine which information is important so they can underline it.

Being able to determine important information is a difficult task for many middle-grades students. Fortunately, there are a number of things teachers can do so their students can still use these complex rehearsal strategies even if they have difficulty identifying important information. To help students identify important information from your lectures, try to implement as many of the following suggestions as possible:

1. Point out important or key information to students. Make sure they know why it is important. Some teachers even tell students when they should write information in their notebooks.
2. Provide students with an outline or a guide that identifies the important information from your lecture or discussion. The outline or guide can be given to students ahead of time so they can follow along or it can be put on the chalkboard so students can copy it. Remember that the act of copying the information adds an additional modality to the rehearsal process. If copying is to be used as a rehearsal strategy, make sure that it is not just used as busywork to fill time. Students should copy information only if it is important and you want them to commit it to memory.
3. At the end of lectures and discussions, summarize key points or important facts so that students know exactly what the important information is so they can rehearse it.

To help students identify important information when they read their textbooks, try to implement the following suggestions:

1. During the first few days of school, spend time demonstrating and explaining the key features of the textbook to the students. Most textbooks for middle-grades students contain most, if not all, of the following features: objectives, headings, chapter outlines, chapter summaries, bold print, underlining, and review questions. All of these features are intended to help students identify important information as they read. Unfortunately, many middle-grades students are not aware of these features and their purpose. If teachers take time to explain these features to their students, then students will be more able to take advantage of them.

2. The teacher's edition of most textbooks usually contains a list of a description of the unique features of the book. By reading and planning ahead, before the first day of school, you can prepare short lessons to introduce these features to your students during the first few days of school. Figure 12.1 illustrates the key features of the Prentice Hall General Science textbook *A Voyage of Exploration* (1989) as described in the teacher's edition of the textbook.

Figures 12.2 and 12.3 illustrate some of these key features as they appear in the student edition of the textbook. In particular, Figure 12.2 shows chapter sections and objectives, and Figure 12.3 shows a chapter summary that highlights the important information in the chapter.

FIGURE 12.1   Key Features of a Middle-School Science Textbook

Prentice Hall General Science has been set up to provide a flexible and varied approach to teaching science. The text is divided into six units, sufficiently self-contained to be taught separately and in any order. Since science cannot be compartmentalized into discrete packets of information, there are areas in which topics in one unit overlap with topics in other units. However, in order to retain the flexibility of the program and allow the teacher to begin with any unit he or she desires, any concept or definition introduced for the first time in any unit is considered unfamiliar and taught as if the topic is a new one.

One exception to this flexibility is Chapter 1. This chapter introduces students to the scientific method, the various branches of science, the metric system, the tools of measurement, and the need for safety in the laboratory. It is recommended that all students complete Chapter 1 first. At that point, the teacher may jump to the unit in the text that best fits his or her curriculum needs.

UNIT OPENERS

Each unit begins with a two-page spread that includes a large dramatic photograph or illustration. Accompanying the visual is a short overview that both introduces the topics to be discussed in the unit and provides motivational text to capture student interest. A listing of the chapters in the unit is also included in the unit-opening spread.

CHAPTER OPENERS

Each chapter begins with a two-page spread. Like the unit openers, large photographs and illustrations are employed to grab student attention immediately. A short, concise caption informs the reader as to the nature of the visual. The visual can also be readily identified through the chapter-opening text. This text, often written in an anecdotal style, serves to entice the student to read further. Intriguing questions and unusual data are employed to hold the student's attention and to motivate the student to find out more about the topic.

Also included in the chapter-opening spread is a list of the main sections in each chapter. This listing serves as an instructional outline for both student and teacher. Moreover, chapter objectives are in the chapter-opening spread. Thus, the chapter opener serves the dual purpose of initiating the student's desire to learn more about the material and of alerting the student to the specific objectives, or goals that he or she is expected to grasp when the chapter is completed.

CHAPTER SECTIONS

As noted, each main chapter section is listed in the chapter opening. These sections are numbered consecutively on both the chapter-opening page and in the text itself. Numbering the main sections helps distinguish the main topics in the chapter from the subtopics. Subtopics in each main section are set apart and boldfaced.

In most sections, the students will find in-text questions based on the material just presented. Some in-text questions require simple factual recall. Other in-text questions employ more advanced-critical thinking skills such as predicting and relating.

With each main section are numerous photographs and illustrations that help teach and reinforce the topic found in the section. Most visuals are large and in color, to further hold student interest. Data charts and graphs are interspersed in the text as well, to provide further information. Each numbered section also contains one sentence that is set apart in boldfaced type. This sentence alerts the student to the key idea of that section.

SECTION REVIEWS

At the end of every numbered section is a Section Review. These review questions, usually short-answer questions, allow the teacher to quickly verify whether the important topics in that section have been grasped by the student. In general, at least one review question relates back to the Section Objective listed at the beginning of the chapter.

CHAPTER REVIEWS

Chapter Summaries and Vocabularies

At the end of every chapter is a chapter summary section. The summary is divided into groupings based on the main numbered sections in the chapter. Under each grouping is a list of key sentences that describe the most important concepts presented in the chapter. The chapter summary might be considered a detailed outline of the chapter content.

Following the summary is a listing of the vocabulary words included in the chapter. The vocabulary words include all the boldfaced terms from the chapter.

Source: From D. Hurd et al., *Prentice Hall General Science: A Voyage of Exploration,* © 1989. Reprinted by permission of Prentice Hall, Inc., Englewood Cliffs, New Jersey.

FIGURE 12.2 Chapter Sections and Objectives in a Students' Science Textbook

CHAPTER SECTIONS
7-1 Fuels and Their Use
7-2 Solar Energy
7-3 Wind and Water
7-4 Nuclear Power
7-5 Energy: Today and Tomorrow

CHAPTER OBJECTIVES
After completing this chapter, you will be able to:

7-1 Define combustion.
7-1 Describe the types of fossil fuels and their various uses.
7-2 Compare direct and indirect uses of solar energy.
7-2 Describe a typical solar heating system.
7-3 Discuss the types of locations in which wind generators can be used.
7-3 Relate hydroelectric power to the movement of water.
7-4 Compare nuclear fission and nuclear fusion.
7-5 Describe geothermal energy and its uses.
7-5 Discuss the need for all people to conserve energy and to use nonpolluting energy resources.

Source: From D. Hurd et al., *Prentice Hall General Science: A Voyage of Discovery,* © 1989. Reprinted by permission of Prentice Hall, Inc., Englewood Cliffs, New Jersey.

Using Complex Rehearsal Strategies Independently
When the preceding guidelines are followed, students are actually told, by either the teacher or the authors of the textbook, what the important information is so they can rehearse it. However, in real life, students are not always going to have teachers or textbook authors around to tell them what is important and what is not important. Middle-grades students are at an age when they should be beginning to develop this skill so they can use it independently.

Middle-grades students can be taught simple underlining and notetaking strategies that they can use when they read and study on their own to increase the likelihood that when they use rehearsal, they actually rehearse the most important information. Figure 12.4 provides guidelines for teaching students **selective underlining**, a complex rehearsal strategy that is appropriate for novice underliners.

Figure 12.5 illustrates how to teach **two-column notes**, another complex rehearsal strategy, to students. Two-column notes is best used after students are familiar with and proficient at selective underlining. Santa, Havens, and Harrison (1989) recommend introducing "two-column notes with material that students have already underlined" (p. 145). In a sense, two-column notes actually takes students beyond mere recall because it also helps them organize information.

Basic Elaboration Strategies

As mentioned in the last section, rehearsal strategies are used primarily when verbatim recall is the desired outcome. Keep in mind, however, that verbatim recall is achieved primarily through rote memorization. In many cases, however, rote

FIGURE 12.3 Chapter Summary in a Students' Science Textbook

CHAPTER REVIEW

Summary

2-1 Molecules and Motion

- Heat is a form of energy related to the motion of molecules.
- Conduction is the transfer of heat by the direct contact of one molecule with another.
- Convection is the transfer of heat by molecules of liquids and gases moving in currents.
- Radiation is the transfer of heat through space in the form of infrared light.

2-2 Temperature and Heat

- Work is defined as a force acting on an object and causing it to move.
- Kinetic energy is energy of motion.
- Temperature is a measure of the average kinetic energy of molecules.
- A thermometer is the instrument used to measure temperature.
- The metric scales of temperature are the Celsius and Kelvin scales.
- Absolute zero is the lowest possible temperature.
- Most objects expand when heated.

- Water expands as it is cooled from 4° C to 0° C.
- A calorie, the unit used to measure heat, is the amount of heat needed to raise the temperature of one gram of liquid water one degree Celsius.
- Potential energy is stored energy.
- The specific heat of a substance is the number of calories needed to raise the temperature of one gram of that substance one degree Celsius.
- The law of conservation of energy states that energy can be neither created nor destroyed but can only be changed from one form to another.

2-3 Heating and Refrigeration Methods

- Common heating systems include steam heat, hot water, forced air, and electric heat.
- Insulation reduces heat transfer that occurs by conduction.
- Refrigerators and air conditioners contain liquid coolants that absorb heat from an area as they change from liquids to gases.

Source: From D. Hurd et al., *Prentice Hall General Science: A Voyage of Discovery,* © 1989. Reprinted by permission of Prentice Hall, Inc., Englewood Cliffs, New Jersey.

FIGURE 12.4 Selective Underlining

Selective Underlining

Underlining is a powerful tool for processing main ideas if students know how to underline. Novice underliners typically take their magic marker and hemorrhage across the page, underlining practically everything. Underlining has to be taught. Because students cannot write in their text, use consumable materials such as magazine articles, laboratory manuals, and photocopies of reading assignments.

Begin with a demonstration. Photocopy the selection for the students and make a transparency of the assignment. Demonstrate how to underline the material selectively by highlighting key ideas, capturing the essence of the material. Talk aloud, explaining your underlines. Students underline their photocopy as you demonstrate. As you underline, develop guidelines with the class for students to use when underlining an assignment on their own. Sample guidelines might include (1) underline key ideas, (2) do not underline whole sentence, (3) put an * by underlined main points, and (4) make up study questions over main points. Students will need several demonstrations before they can succeed independently.

An intermediary step is to divide students into groups of two or three. Give each group a transparency containing a selection from their reading assignment. Each group selectively underlines the material on the transparency and then presents their underlines on the overhead for class discussion. Once students have success underlining key points and details in their reading, you can begin assigning students to underline assignments on their own.

Source: From Diane Lapp, James Flood, and Nancy Farnan, *Content Area Reading and Learning: Instructional Strategies.* Copyright © 1989 by Allyn and Bacon. Reprinted with permission.

FIGURE 12.5   Two-Column Notes

Two Column Notes

Two-column notes should be a part of every science curriculum. This form of note taking provides a simple system for organizing information and encourages self-testing. Students learn two-column note taking more easily if they have had some direct instruction in noting main ideas and details through selective underlining. In fact, it is often a good idea to introduce two-column notes with material that students have already underlined.

Make a transparency of a selection. Talk aloud while you demonstrate. Have students divide their paper lengthwise into two columns. As noted in the following example, the left column contains key words naming an essential concept or main idea, and the right portion elaborates on main points. Then, covering the information on the right, students can test themselves using the key words on the left.

Sample Two-Column Notes

1. Variations among flowers   Size, shape and color
2. Parts of flower
   receptable   Modified stem
   sepals   Leaflike petals at base of flower
   calyx   Made from petals to form protective coating for
                                       outer flower
   petals   Brightly colored structures protecting reproductive
                                       structures
   corolla   All petals together
3. Male parts of the flower
   stamens   Slender, knoblike ends
   anthers   Knoblike ends of stamens
   filament   Thin stalk that supports anther
   pollen grains   Male gametophytes
4. Female parts of flower
   carpels   Reproductive organ
   ovary   Thickened base of carpel
   ovule   Female gametophyte
   style   Narrow stalk on top of ovary
   stigma   Traps pollen

Source: From Diane Lapp, James Flood, and Nancy Farnan, *Content Area Reading and Learning: Instructional Strategies.* Copyright © 1989 by Allyn and Bacon. Reprinted with permission.

memorization is difficult for students because the information to be learned is not in a form that is meaningful to them. Through the use of elaboration strategies, students can make learning more meaningful. You elaborate automatically everyday when you say, "Oh, that reminds me of . . ." or when you put something in your own words. **Elaboration strategies** involve "adding some sort of symbolic construction to what the student is trying to learn in an attempt to make it more meaningful" (Weinstein, 1987, p. 590). Elaboration is an effective learning strategy because it helps students build connections between the items being learned.

One elaboration strategy that middle-grades students can use for basic learning tasks (e.g., learning the capitals of the 50 states) is mental imagery. This strategy can help students form associations between the new words or facts being learned, in this case the state and its capital. For example, to help them remember that Olympia is the capital of Washington, students might form a mental image of George *Washington* pole vaulting at the *Olympics*. Obviously, it is easier to create images for some states and their capitals than it is for others. Thus, this strategy is effective only when a meaningful image can be created.

Middle-grades students are capable of creating their own images in many situations. In fact, it appears that students in the sixth grade and beyond may even be distracted by images that their teachers may provide for them (Reese, 1977). Creating mental images is a strategy that can also be extended to more complex learning tasks, as we discuss in the next section.

Complex Elaboration Strategies

Middle-grades students can also use elaboration when they are engaged in more complex learning tasks such as listening to a lecture or reading a textbook. As we just mentioned, mental imagery can be used but students can also use a variety of other elaboration strategies such as "paraphrasing, summarizing, creating analogies, generative notetaking, and question answering" (Weinstein & Mayer, 1986, pp. 319–320). In order to demonstrate how these elaboration strategies can be used with middle-grades students, we provide specific examples of three of these strategies: guided imagery, summarizing, and creating analogies. (In Chapter 13, we describe another elaboration strategy in detail, Raphael and Pearson's [1982] question answering strategy, QAR.)

Guided Imagery

If you have spent any time in middle-grades classrooms lately, you have probably noticed that young adolescents tend to daydream frequently. Unfortunately, when they daydream, young adolescents are not always thinking about their schoolwork or reflecting on what they are reading or what the teacher is saying. But middle-grades teachers can capitalize on early adolescents' ability to daydream by guiding them to turn their daydreams into mental images about what they read in their textbooks and hear during lectures and discussions.

Imagery allows students to make associations or connections between the new facts or words being learned. When imagery is used in complex learning tasks, it also prompts students to make connections between the new information being learned and what they already know. Encouraging middle-grades students to form images before and while they read increases their learning and recall (Gambrell & Bales, 1986; Gambrell & Koskinen, 1982). Creating mental images during reading is particularly helpful for below-average students.

Unfortunately, despite its effectiveness in all content areas, most middle-grades students fail to use imagery spontaneously unless they are taught to do so. Wood (1989) developed a strategy in which the teacher guides middle-grades students in the use of imagery during reading. The steps of this guided imagery strategy are detailed in Figure 12.6.

Summarizing

Without being aware of it, middle-grades students engage in summarization everyday. For example, when Ralph gets home, he tells his parents what he did in school that day; on Monday, Jacinta tells Becky about the movie she saw Saturday night; after talking on the phone with Charlie, Carmen calls Anita and retells the

---

FIGURE 12.6   Guided Imagery

FIRST   Help the students develop their visualization skills by having them create visual images of familiar objects. Simple concrete objects such as a rose, a pier or a frog may be most beneficial for this early modeling phase. Tell the students to close their eyes and form a picture from these words by trying to sense how the object looks, sounds, feels and smells. Discuss more of the varied images with the class, being certain to reinforce the individualization of their responses.

SECOND   Proceed from individual key words to complete sentences by following the same procedures. For example, have students develop images for sentences such as: "A grandmother is cooking a turkey in the kitchen." Before eliciting their responses, have students underline the words in the sentence which were needed to help them form a mental picture. (The likely choices in this sentence are grandmother, turkey and kitchen.) Students can be asked to describe their own or a relative's kitchen and elaborate on what else and why she may be preparing this meal.

From these personally relevant examples, the teacher can move to sentences which are more content specific. These sentences can be drawn from material to be read in class.

"An amoeba will move slowly across a slide." (Science)

"Custer told his men to stop on the hill before they reached the campsite." (History)

Again, have the students underline or at least select the words with the most "picture potency" and then close their eyes to form their images.

Probing questions can be asked such as, "What do you see in your mind?" "Are there any prevalent smells?" "What do you feel—emotionally or tactily?"

THIRD   *Before Reading:* Have students turn to a short selection or excerpt in their textbook or other classroom reading material. Tell them they are going to make "pictures" or a "movie" as they read through the passage. Instruct the class to select the key words in the title and try to describe everything that comes to their minds. Discuss the contributions made by the class.

FOURTH   *During Reading:* Assign the students to pairs and tell them to underline lightly in pencil or put a check over the key words in the first topically relevant section, often signalled by subheadings. After each dyad has discussed their images with their partners, elicit some responses from the class. The teacher should proceed in this manner for a few more sections until the class seems to have a comfortable grasp on the concept of applying this process to longer discourse. They can continue working in pairs, discussing their images, using probing questions, and even making graphic representations of the information if necessary.

FIFTH   *After Reading:* Follow up with a classwide discussion of the content, asking for elaborations and inferred details whenever appropriate. Another option to further extend the lesson is to engage the students in a writing activity or to give them an objective or subjective test.

Source: From K. D. Wood, 1989, "Using Guided Imagery to Enhance Learning." *Middle School Journal,* *21*(2), 26–28. Reprinted with permission of the National Middle School Association.

conversation to her. In all of these examples, the students are summarizing because they are organizing "material by indicating the superordinate-subordinate relationships in a set of information" (Gagné, 1985, p. 338). In other words, they are not telling everything; they are telling the most important information and skipping the fine details. Summarization is an effective strategy for complex learning tasks because it helps students reorganize information into a format that is meaningful for them, thus making it easier to remember.

Some middle-grades students are able to summarize quite well, whereas others ramble on and on. But middle-grades students can be taught to be better at it when they read by using a hierarchical summarizing strategy developed by Taylor (1982). When they use this strategy, students create a summary by using the headings in their textbook. As was the case with the imagery strategy described previously, teachers introduce students to this summarizing strategy by initially guiding them in its use. The teacher's goal, however, is to teach students how to develop their own summaries when they read and study text independently. Muth (1987a) summarized the steps of this strategy as follows:

> First, students generate a "skeleton" outline consisting of a main idea statement (formed from the title of the text) and a list of numbers (one for every subheading in the text) down a sheet of paper. Next, students read each subsection of the text and write a main idea for each one next to the appropriate number on their paper. Then, students list a few important details under each main idea. Finally, students show relationships among main ideas by listing key ideas which connect related main ideas. (pp. 67–68)

Figure 12.7 illustrates a hierarchical summary generated from a social studies text.

Creating Analogies

Another type of elaboration strategy that middle-grades students can use is analogy. Through the use of analogies, students are able to put new ideas and concepts into familiar terms. Teachers can introduce students to analogies by using them when they lecture or explain new concepts to students or by pointing them out when they are used in textbooks. As the following examples illustrate, analogies are powerful learning strategies because they can be used and applied in all content areas:

- A mathematics teacher explaining the concept of an equation by drawing an analogy to the balance used in science lab.
- A geography teacher explaining the concept of a glacier by drawing an analogy to a river of ice.
- A music teacher explaining the concept of harmony (i.e., musical background) by drawing an analogy to the concept of perspective in painting.
- An English teacher explaining the concept of a hierarchical outline by drawing an analogy to a tree and its branches. (Glynn, 1989, pp. 190–191)

By using analogies when they teach and by pointing out and explaining textbook analogies to their students, teachers are taking the first step toward

FIGURE 12.7 Hierarchical Summary

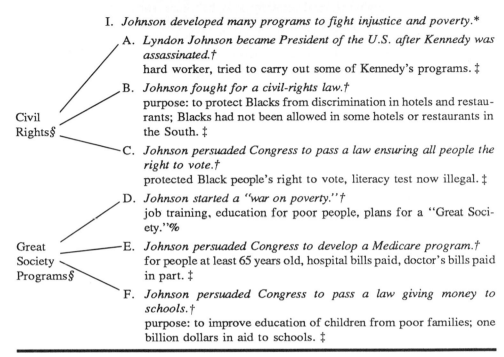

**Hierarchical Summary for Social Studies Text Selection
Containing One Heading and Six Subheadings**

I. *Johnson developed many programs to fight injustice and poverty.**

  A. *Lyndon Johnson became President of the U.S. after Kennedy was assassinated.†*
  hard worker, tried to carry out some of Kennedy's programs. ‡

Civil Rights§

  B. *Johnson fought for a civil-rights law.†*
  purpose: to protect Blacks from discrimination in hotels and restaurants; Blacks had not been allowed in some hotels or restaurants in the South. ‡

  C. *Johnson persuaded Congress to pass a law ensuring all people the right to vote.†*
  protected Black people's right to vote, literacy test now illegal. ‡

  D. *Johnson started a "war on poverty."†*
  job training, education for poor people, plans for a "Great Society."%

Great Society Programs§

  E. *Johnson persuaded Congress to develop a Medicare program.†*
  for people at least 65 years old, hospital bills paid, doctor's bills paid in part. ‡

  F. *Johnson persuaded Congress to pass a law giving money to schools.†*
  purpose: to improve education of children from poor families; one billion dollars in aid to schools. ‡

Source: From B. M. Taylor, 1982, "A Summarizing Strategy to Improve Middle School Students' Reading and Writing Skills," *The Reading Teacher, 36,* 202–205. Reprinted with permission of Barbara M. Taylor and the International Reading Association.

* Topic sentence for entire selection as designated by a heading

† Main ideas for subsections as designated by subheadings

‡ Supporting details for main ideas

§ Key phrases connecting subsections

encouraging students to use analogies on their own. Students who are knowledgeable about the usefulness of analogies are more likely to use them as a learning strategy when they encounter them in their textbooks. In the long run, these students will also be more likely to generate their own analogies.

Basic Organizational Strategies

Organizational strategies are strategies that convert new information into a meaningful arrangement that is easier for students to understand and remember. Organizational strategies are effective for at least two reasons (Weinstein, 1987). First, when students use organizational strategies, they are actively involved in the process of converting the information into the new arrangement. Being actively involved in learning tends to increase learning. Second, the new arrangement that results from using organizational strategies makes information easier to remember.

One organizational strategy that has been shown to be effective for basic learning tasks is **clustering**. When students use clustering, they arrange the information to be learned into meaningful groups or categories. Clustering can be used in all content areas and research (e.g., Moely, Olson, Hawles, & Flavell, 1969) has shown that at about age 10, students begin to use clustering spontaneously.

An example of clustering that teachers use in mathematics is the multiplication tables. Students could be taught their multiplication tables randomly. But since information is better remembered when it is organized in a meaningful manner, students learn their multiplication tables in clusters. That is, in the words of the students, they learn their "two times tables, three times tables, four times tables," and so on.

Students can use clustering for a variety of basic learning tasks. For example, suppose students were required to memorize the names of the 50 states. Students could put the states into alphabetic clusters and then learn the states in each cluster. Thus, students could remember three *A* states (Alabama, Alaska, and Arkansas), three *C* states (California, Colorado, and Connecticut), and so on. Similarly, students could cluster the states geographically and then memorize the New England states, the Mid-Atlantic states, the Southern states, and so on. In both examples, the names of the 50 states will be easier for the students to remember because they are organized in a meaningful arrangement.

Complex Organizational Strategies

Perhaps two of the most difficult academic tasks middle-grades students face are reading and understanding their textbooks and identifying the main ideas and important details. Science, social science, and mathematics textbooks are particularly challenging for middle-grades students because they are generally written in an expository fashion rather than a narrative or story format with which students are more familiar.

One factor that appears to be important in the comprehension of expository text is the student's ability to detect the organizational pattern or structure of the text (Meyer, Brandt, & Bluth, 1980; Taylor, 1980). Authors of expository texts arrange their ideas by means of structures. An author chooses a particular structure or combination of structures because it is the one that is best suited to frame the ideas he or she wants to present.

Some of the structures that are used most frequently in content area textbooks include analysis, cause/effect, chronology or time order, compare/contrast, definition/example, description, enumeration, illustration, and problem/solution. Two types of organizational strategies that are particularly effective for helping students use the organizational pattern or structure of a text to identify main ideas and details are outlines and graphic organizers.

Graphic Organizers

Graphic organizers are schematic diagrams that use the vocabulary words in the text to help students identify key concepts and the relationships among those concepts. Graphic organizers are helpful because they visually convey the structure of a text. Figure 12.8 illustrates a simple graphic organizer used for a science text about the various types of volcanoes.

There are many uses for graphic organizers. They can be used at the beginning of a lesson as part of the introduction, during the lesson to guide students as they read, and at the end of the lesson to help students summarize what they read. They can also be used as a study aid to help students review and prepare for tests. In addition, graphic organizers can show relationships among ideas in a single paragraph, a page, a chapter, or even several chapters on related topics.

Constructing graphic organizers can be a difficult task for many middle-grades students. Therefore, we recommend a technique developed by Smith and Tompkins (1988) that slowly introduces students to the idea of text structure and how it can help them better understand what they read. Figure 12.9 illustrates graphic organizers developed by Smith and Tompkins for text structures that are commonly found in content area textbooks.

Smith and Tompkins recommend explicit teaching of the various text structures, one at a time, by the teacher. Through guided practice and the use of the graphic organizers illustrated in Figure 12.9, students eventually achieve independence from the teacher and are able to generate their own graphic organizers as they read and study their textbooks.

Once students are proficient at using the graphic organizers supplied by Smith and Tompkins, they are generally able to construct their own, more informal graphic organizers. Many content area textbooks for middle-grades students contain graphic organizers that teachers can use to help students organize information. Figure 12.10 illustrates a graphic organizer included in a sixth-grade social studies textbook.

The chart in Figure 12.10 helps students compare and contrast information

FIGURE 12.8   Graphic Organizer of a Science Text about Volcanoes

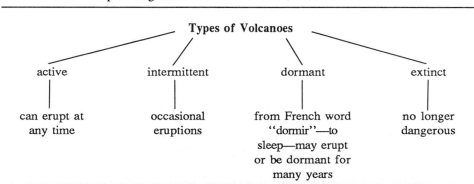

Source: From K. D. Wood, 1987, "Teaching Vocabulary in the Subject Areas." *Middle School Journal, 19,* 11–13. Reprinted with permission of the National Middle School Association.

FIGURE 12.9   Graphic Organizers for Common Text Structures

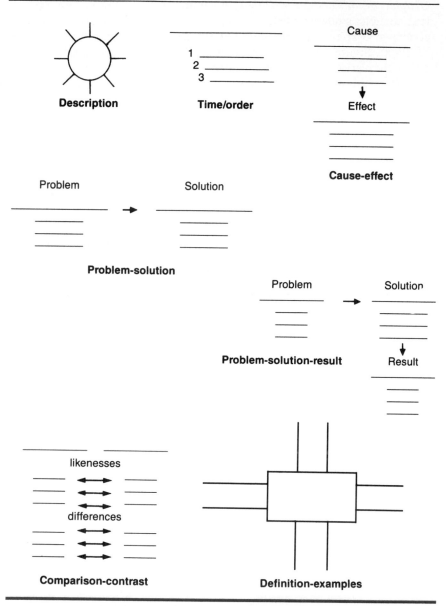

Source: From P. L. Smith and G. E. Tompkins, 1988, "Structured Notetaking: A New Strategy for Content Area Readers." *Journal of Reading, 32,* 46–53. Reprinted with permission of Patricia L. Smith and the International Reading Association.

about the first four river valley civilizations. As you can see, to help students get started, the chart is partially completed. When students become skilled at filling in charts such as this one, they can begin to fill in charts in which no information has been supplied for them.

FIGURE 12.10 Partially Completed Compare/Contrast Graphic Organizer

	LOCATION	GOVERNMENT	RELIGION	WRITING
Mesopotamia				Cuneiform on clay tablets
Egypt		Ruled by a powerful pharaoh		
India	Indus River valley			
China	Huang He River valley			

Source: From *Exploring Our World, Past and Present,* by C. L. Ver Steeg et al. Copyright © 1991 by D. C. Heath and Company. Reprinted by permission.

Figure 12.11 shows a blank chart that asks students to compare and contrast the two colonies of Jamestown and Plymouth. Eventually, students become less and less dependent on the visual aid portion of the graphic organizer—such as the charts illustrated in Figures 12.10 and 12.11—and are able to move into more formal outlining.

Outlining

Outlining is an organizational strategy in which "major concepts and pertinent details are hierarchically organized" (Moore, Readence, & Rickelman, 1982, p. 50). In formal outlining, Roman numerals, upper-case letters, Arabic numbers, and lower-case letters are used to identify the relationships among the concepts and ideas in the text.

Constructing formal outlines is extremely difficult for many middle-grades students, so we recommend introducing them to it gradually and beginning with short, well-organized texts. Initially, middle-grades students should be provided with a framework in which the teacher has already filled in many of the major concepts. Figure 12.12 illustrates such a framework for a science chapter on sound waves.

After students have become proficient at filling in frameworks such as the one illustrated in Figure 12.12, they should be provided with frameworks in which less and less information has been filled in. Eventually students can complete blank

FIGURE 12.11 "Blank" Compare/Contrast Graphic Organizer

	JAMESTOWN	PLYMOUTH
Reason for starting colony		
Group who started colony		
Date colony began		
Location		
Problems faced by settlers		
Leader of colony		
Chief crops grown		

Source: From *Exploring America's Heritage,* by C. L. Ver Steeg et al. Copyright © 1991 by D. C. Heath and Company. Reprinted by permission.

FIGURE 12.12 Framework for an Outline on Sound Waves

Sound Waves

I. Characteristics

    A. _____

    B. _____

    C. _____

    D. _____

II. Interaxtions

    A. _____

    B. _____

        1. _____

        2. _____

    C. _____

        1. _____

        2. _____

frameworks and then begin to generate their own outlines. When students first begin to generate their own outlines, they should use short, well-organized texts so they can be successful. Later, they can move to more difficult and less well-structured texts.

Comprehension Monitoring Strategies

Comprehension monitoring strategies help students meet their goals "effectively and efficiently" (Gagné, 1985, p. 173). These strategies are not only useful when students are reading their textbooks but whenever they are engaged in any activity in which comprehension is necessary. For example, middle-grades students could use comprehension monitoring strategies as they try to follow directions for completing a science experiment, as they listen to a lecture on the Renaissance, as they watch a stage production of *Our Town*, and as they solve mathematics word problems.

According to Weinstein and Mayer (1986) comprehension monitoring has three components: "to establish learning goals for an instructional unit or activity, to assess the degree to which these goals are being met, and, if necessary, to modify the strategies being used to meet the goals" (p. 323). Recall from Chapter 11 the thinking-out-lout protocol of Jennifer trying to solve the word problem about the circumference of a circle. Jennifer was clearly able to establish a learning goal (i.e., to solve the problem). She was also able to assess whether or not she was meeting that goal (i.e., she knew she did not get the correct answer because "the number was too big"). But, in this situation, Jennifer was not able to implement the third component of comprehension monitoring. That is, she was not able to modify her strategy so she could reach her goal. Although Jennifer knew her answer was not correct, she did not know what to do to get the correct answer.

Jennifer's inability to remedy the situation is not surprising in light of research findings that suggest "it is not until mid to late adolescence that children exhibit spontaneously the kinds of self-monitoring and self-management behaviors that are central to productive, self-directed learning" (Thomas, Strage, & Curley, 1988, p. 314). Even when they reach late adolescence, many students do not spontaneously begin to monitor their own comprehension processes. Given this fact, many educators are recommending that comprehension monitoring be taught to students throughout their elementary and middle-grades years. Recall our discussion of the *gradual release of responsibility* model of instruction in Chapter 11. By teaching students to monitor their own comprehension, teachers are gradually shifting the responsibility of learning from themselves to their students.

Weinstein and Mayer (1986) point that there are a variety of techniques that have been used to teach students how to monitor their own comprehension. These techniques range from having students create questions before they read to having them covertly question themselves about what they are doing and why they are doing it. We now describe two techniques that have been shown to be effective for teaching comprehension monitoring to middle-grades students: reciprocal teaching and K-W-L.

Reciprocal teaching helps students learn how to collaborate and to respect each other's ideas and opinions.

Reciprocal Teaching

Reciprocal teaching (Palincsar & Brown, 1984) is a technique for teaching comprehension strategies to students. In particular, reciprocal teaching teaches students the four skills of forming questions, summarizing, making predictions, and anticipating and clarifying problems as they read. Reciprocal teaching has been shown to be particularly effective with small groups of low-achieving, middle-grades students (Palincsar, 1987). When students use reciprocal teaching in small groups or pairs, in addition to cognitive benefits, they also gain many social and affective benefits as a result of interacting with their peers. For example, students learn to respect each other's ideas and opinions and how to collaborate their efforts toward a common goal.

When reciprocal teaching is first introduced, students are taught the four skills just mentioned. Initially, students model the teacher but responsibility gradually shifts to the students, who act as the teacher during much of the lesson. Figure 12.13 provides an example of a reciprocal teaching lesson.

K-W-L

K-W-L (Ogle, 1986, 1989), a technique for teaching comprehension strategies to students, is particularly applicable to expository text. K-W-L involves three steps: "assessing what I Know, determining what I Want to learn, and recalling what I did Learn as a result of reading" (Ogle, 1986).

The first step of K-W-L begins by having students brainstorm what they already know about the topic or key concept about which they are reading. The teacher writes down all student responses on the chalkboard or an overhead projector. Then students record what they think they know on their own individual strategy sheets. Next, students are asked to categorize the information they have brainstormed. For example, if students were reading an article about dolphins, and three comments were made about how they looked, then students might generate the category *appearance*. At this time, students can also suggest other categories of information that they think might be in the article.

During the second step of K-W-L, students generate questions that they want answered as they read. Then students write their own personal questions on their

FIGURE 12.13 Example of a Reciprocal Teaching Lesson

TEACHER: The title of this story is "Genius with Feathers." Let's have some predictions. I will begin by guessing that this story will be about birds that are very smart. Why do I say that?

FIRST STUDENT: Because a genius is someone very smart.

SECOND STUDENT: Because they have feathers.

TEACHER: That's right. Birds are the only animals that have feathers. Let's predict now the kind of information you might read about very smart birds.

THIRD STUDENT: Parrots or blue jays.

FIRST STUDENT: A cockatoo like the bird on *Baretta*.

TEACHER: What other information would you want to know? *(No response from students.)*

TEACHER: I would like to know what these birds do that is so smart. Any ideas?

SECOND STUDENT: Some birds talk.

FOURTH STUDENT: They can fly.

TEACHER: That's an interesting one. As smart as people are, they can't fly. Well, let's read this first section now and see how many of our predictions were right. I will be the teacher for this section. *(All read the section silently.)*

TEACHER: Who is the genius with feathers?

FIRST STUDENT: Crows.

TEACHER: That's right. We were correct in our prediction that this story would be about birds, but we didn't correctly guess which kind of bird, did we? My summary of the first section would be that it describes the clever things that crows do, which make them seem quite intelligent. Is there anything else I should add to my summary?

FIRST STUDENT: How they steal corn?

TEACHER: That's a detail that described one of the ways in which they are clever. For our summary we will not include details. I think I found a word that needs clarification. What does "resourceful" mean?

ALL STUDENTS: *(No response.)*

TEACHER: If I say that you are a resourceful person, I mean that you are able to deal with problems and difficulties easily. Being resourceful is another way in which crows are intelligent. I would like to make a prediction now. The section's last sentence says, "One major reason they have mastered survival against heavy odds is their amazing communication system." My prediction is that the next section will describe this communication system. How do you think crows communicate with one another?

ALL STUDENTS: Caw-Caw.

FIRST STUDENT: With a special song.

TEACHER: Let's read on. Who will be the teacher for this section? *(Dialogue follows in which the student Jim is chosen to lead the discussion, with the teacher providing corrective feedback.)*

JIM: How do crows communicate with one another?

TEACHER: Good question! You picked right up on our prediction that this is about the way crows communicate. Whom do you choose to answer your question?

JIM: Barbara.

BARBARA: Crows have built-in radar and a relay system.

JIM: That's a good part of it. The answer I wanted was how they relay the messages from one crow to the other crow.

TEACHER: Summarize now.

JIM: This is about how crows have developed a system of communication.

TEACHER: That's right. The paragraph goes on to give examples of how they use pitch and changes in interval, but these are supporting details. The main idea is that crows communicate through a relay system. Jim?

JIM: It says in this section that crows can use their communication system to play tricks, so I predict the next section will say something about the tricks crows play. I would like Sue to be the next teacher.

TEACHER: Excellent prediction. The last sentence of a paragraph often suggests what the next paragraph will be about. Good, Jim.

Source: From Anne Marie S. Palincsar, "Reciprocal Teaching: Working within the Zone of Proximal Development." Paper presented at the annual convention of the American Educational Research Association, New Orleans, April 1984. Reprinted by permission of the author.

strategy sheet. These questions are important because they give students a purpose for reading. Students then read on their own. If the material or article being read is relatively short, students can read it all at once. However, if it is long, the teacher may want to break it into several smaller sections.

During the third step, after the students have finished reading, they record what they learned on their strategy sheets. Students should check the questions they wrote down before reading and see if they were answered. If some questions were not answered, students should have an opportunity to raise their unanswered questions for class discussion. The teacher may also want to suggest additional readings so unanswered questions can be researched further. Figure 12.14 illustrates what a fourth-grade student's strategy sheet looked like after the class used K-W-L while reading an article on wolves.

Affective and Motivational Strategies

Affective and motivational strategies help students "in creating, monitoring, and controlling a suitable learning environment" (Weinstein & Mayer, 1986, p. 324). As shown in Figure 12.15, Thomas, Strage, and Curley (1988) have identified and categorized a number of these affective and motivational strategies.

As you can see in Figure 12.15, many of these strategies relate to being well organized and being able to manage time effectively. These are difficult tasks for many middle-grades students. Recall from Chapter 2 our discussion of young adolescents' perspective on time. At this age, many students deal primarily with the present and are unconcerned with future events. They have difficulty planning ahead and often are unaware of how their present performance can affect their future.

In order to help their students develop these skills, middle-grades teachers must be organized themselves. They should have clear goals and these goals should be communicated to the students. Long-range assignments should be broken into smaller tasks, each with their own due date. Techniques should be developed for helping students keep track of their own progress. These and other techniques for helping students develop effective self-management strategies are discussed in detail in Chapter 15.

Teaching Learning Strategies

As we have mentioned throughout this chapter, it is possible and desirable to teach effective learning strategies to middle-grades students. Throughout this chapter we have also discussed various ways that teachers can integrate the teaching of learning strategies into their instructional routines. Unfortunately, however, as Derry (1990) points out, many "students who can correctly execute learning strategies when instructed to do so will fail to use them spontaneously when appropriate situations arise outside of class" (p. 371).

In this section, we discuss guidelines for maintaining a classroom environment that encourages middle-grades students to become more responsible for their own learning and leads them toward autonomy in learning situations outside of the

FIGURE 12.14   K-W-L Strategy Sheet

Terry

What we know	What we want to find out	What we learned/ still need to learn
Wolves live in Canada they like the woods They are dangerous & wild, gray & howl fangs & long ears eat meat-carnivorous dangerous to people	Do they attack people? Where do they live? Are they endangered? How do they care for their babies?	Wolves are endangered, People killed them because they eat sheep & horses. They don't attack humans They live mostly in Canada in the mountains They are intelligent. wolf families live together and help each other.

Categories of information we expect to use
A. Habitat
B. Appearance
C. Characteristics
D. Endangered
E. Homes
F. self-defense
G. Family life

Source: From D. M. Ogle, 1989, "The Know, Want to Know, Learn Strategy." In
K. D. Muth, Ed., *Children's Comprehension of Text.* Reprinted with permission of
the International Reading Association.

classroom. The following guidelines are drawn from the research of Thomas,
Strage, and Curley (1988) and Pressley and colleagues (1989):

1. *Maintain appropriate academic demands.*   Academic demands should be appropriate for the students' developmental needs (i.e., they should be compatible with the students' age and ability). Middle-grades students need to be challenged but not to the point of frustration. Learning strategies should be introduced

FIGURE 12.15 Affective and Motivational Learning Strategies

Time management (activities that provide the opportunity to learn) →	Establishing sufficient time to complete activities Keeping track of time Scheduling time Meeting time commitments Distributing time over tasks
Effort management (activities that serve to promote and maintain the disposition to learn) →	Establishing a productive study environment Setting learning and achievement goals Initiating effort Securing the necessary materials Maintaining attention and avoiding distractions Providing incentives to learn
Volitional monitoring (activities that serve to monitor and evaluate the productivity of one's study habits →	Keeping track of the adequacy of time and effort management activities Monitoring attention Assessing strengths and weaknesses in study habits

Source: From J. W. Thomas, A. Strage, and R. Curley, 1988, "Improving Students' Self-Directed Learning: Issues and Guidelines." *The Elementary School Journal, 88,* 313–326. Copyright © 1988 by the University of Chicago. Reprinted by permission of the University of Chicago Press.

gradually and in such a way as to build on each other. Meaningful and useful strategies should be taught so that students can see their effectiveness almost immediately.

2. *Give adequate instructional support.* Thomas, Strage, and Curley (1988) distinguish between *support* and *compensation.* Instructional supports help students develop effective learning strategies and encourage them to use these strategies on their own. If used appropriately, the aids we discussed in this chapter, such as graphic organizers, diagrams, and outlines, should support students in their efforts toward being self-directed.

However, all too often teachers used aids to compensate for students' problems. For example, some teachers try to circumvent students' inability to read their content area textbooks by "avoiding the textbook and substituting lectures, films, tapes, and games. As as result, some middle grades students get little instruction in how to read their textbooks" (Muth, 1987b, p. 6). The aids we discussed in this chapter should be used in conjunction with strategy instruction and not as substitutes for it.

3. *Provide frequent opportunities for learning and practicing new strategies.* In order to enhance students' abilities to eventually use a variety of learning strategies on their own, they must be provided with frequent opportunities to learn and practice these strategies in a risk-free environment with constant feedback about their progress. By using the *gradual release of responsibility* model of instruction, teachers can create such a risk-free environment. By incorporating the use of learning strategies into classroom and homework activities, teachers can provide students with frequent and appropriate opportunities to practice what they have learned.

4. *Design appropriate classroom goals.*   As you probably recall from our discussion in Chapter 3, appropriate goals for young adolescents are those that encourage learning rather than performance. As mechanisms for designing appropriate goals, Thomas, Strage, and Curley (1988) suggest a variety of strategies such as

> grading students on the basis of improvement . . . rather than on a norm-referenced basis, providing special instructions to students in order to encourage them to attribute success and failure to effort rather than ability, and developing procedures whereby students can take responsibility for scheduling their own work and dispensing their own rewards. (p. 323).

5. *Teach a few learning strategies well.*   Rather than trying to teach a great many strategies to students, who may or may not remember how or when to use all of them, teachers are encouraged to select a few strategies and teach them well. When selecting among the various strategies, teachers should give highest priority to those that can be used in a variety of content areas (Pressley et al., 1989). Emphasis should also be placed on those strategies that students can use immediately. For example, students should not be taught how to outline unless they will be involved in activities in which they will be expected to be able to outline. In short, teaching learning strategies is not an end in itself.

6. *Find out more about learning strategies.*   In this chapter we have described only a few of the many learning strategies that can be taught to middle-grades students. Teachers are encouraged to continue to learn as much as possible about the many learning strategies available. This can be done by taking additional courses and reading professional journals and books. Teachers who are familiar with a variety of learning strategies are more able to select those that are most appropriate for their students. Pressley and colleagues (1989) also suggest that teachers observe the strategies that their more capable students use; such strategies may be worth teaching to all students.

7. *Encourage other teachers to learn about and teach learning strategies.* Teachers who have been successful at teaching learning strategies to their students should encourage other teachers to do the same. The team organization of many middle-grades schools is an excellent mechanism for encouraging all teachers to learn about and teach learning strategies. For example, during team planning, teachers can discuss a variety of strategies and decide which ones are most appropriate and most timely for teaching to middle-grades students. Then, all teachers on the team could teach and provide opportunities for their students to practice the strategies. As a result, students would get constant practice and reinforcement in using the strategies. They would also become more aware of how the learning strategies can be used in all of the content areas.

Summary

This chapter has explained the role that learning strategies play in the teaching-learning process. A variety of learning strategies can and should be taught to middle-grades students. In particular, these students can be taught to use rehearsal, elaboration, organization, comprehension monitoring, and affective and motivational strategies to enhance their own learning. We have provided several specific examples of each of these categories of learning strategies but there are many more that teachers can learn about and teach to their students.

Some students use a variety of learning strategies spontaneously, but many students are unaware of the numerous strategies available to them. By following the guidelines provided throughout the chapter, middle-grades teachers can teach many of these strategies to their students. By doing so, teachers are helping their students toward becoming more autonomous, self-directed learners.

REFERENCES

Barnett, J. E., & Seefeldt, R. W. (1987, April). *Read something once, why read it again?* Paper presented at the meeting of the American Educational Research Association, Washington, DC.

Bromage, B. K., & Mayer, R. E. (1986). Quantitative and qualitative effects of repetition on learning from technical text. *Journal of Educational Psychology, 78,* 271–278.

Derry, S. J. (1990). Learning strategies for acquiring useful knowledge. In B. F. Jones & L. Idol (Eds.), *Dimensions of thinking and cognitive instruction* (pp. 347–379). Hillsdale, NJ: Erlbaum.

Dowhower, S. L. (1989). Repeated reading: Research into practice. *The Reading Teacher, 42,* 502–507.

Gagné, E. D. (1985). *The cognitive psychology of school learning.* Boston: Little, Brown.

Gambrell, L. B., & Bales, R. J. (1986). Mental imagery and the comprehension-monitoring performance of fourth and fifth grade poor readers. *Reading Research Quarterly, 21,* 454–464.

Gambrell, L. B., & Koskinen, P. S. (1982, March). *Mental imagery and the reading comprehension of below average readers: Situational variables and sex differences.* Paper presented at the meeting of the American Educational Research Association, New York.

Glynn, S. M. (1989). The teaching with analogies model. In K. D. Muth (Ed.), *Children's comprehension of text* (pp. 185–204). Newark, DE: International Reading Association.

Howe, M. J. A., & Singer, L. (1975). Presentation variables and students' activities in meaningful learning. *British Journal of Educational Psychology, 45,* 52–61.

Meyer, B. J. F., Brandt, D. M., & Bluth, G. J. (1980). Use of top-level structure in text: Key for reading comprehension of ninth grade students. *Reading Research Quarterly, 16,* 72–103.

Moely, B., Olson, F., Hawles, T., & Flavell, J. H. (1969). Production deficiency in young children's clustered recall. *Developmental Psychology, 1,* 26–34.

Moore, D. W., Readence, J. E., & Rickelman, R. J. (1982). *Prereading activities for content area reading and learning.* Newark, DE: International Reading Association.

Muth, K. D. (1987a). Structure strategies for comprehending expository text. *Reading Research and Instruction, 27,* 66–72.

Muth, K. D. (1987b). What every middle school teacher should know about the reading process. *Middle School Journal, 19*(1), 6–7.

Ogle, D. M. (1986). K-W-L: A teaching model that develops active reading of expository text. *The Reading Teacher, 39,* 564–570.

Ogle, D. M. (1989). The know, want to learn, learn strategy. In K. D. Muth (Ed.), *Chil-*

dren's comprehension of text (pp. 205–223). Newark, DE: International Reading Association.

Palincsar, A. S. (1987, April). *Reciprocal teaching: Field evaluations in remedial and content-area reading.* Paper presented at the meeting of the American Educational Research Association, Washington, DC.

Palincsar, A. S., & Brown, A. L. (1984). Reciprocal teaching of comprehension-fostering and monitoring activities. *Cognition and Instruction, 1,* 117–175.

Pressley, M., Goodchild, F., Fleet, J., Zajchowski, R., & Evans, E. D. (1989). The challenges of classroom strategy instruction. *The Elementary School Journal, 89,* 301–342.

Raphael, T. E., & Pearson, P. D. (1982). *The effects of metacognitive awareness training on children's question answering behavior.* Technical Report #238. Urbana, IL: Center for the Study of Reading, University of Illinois.

Reese, H. W. (1977). Imagery and associative memory. In R. V. Kail & J. W. Hagen (Eds.), *Perspectives on the development of memory and cognition.* Hillsdale, NJ: Erlbaum.

Santa, C., Havens, L., & Harrison, S. (1989). Teaching secondary science through reading, writing, studying, and problem solving. In D. Lapp, J. Flood, & N. Farnan (Eds.), *Content area reading and learning.* Englewood Cliffs, NJ: Prentice Hall.

Smith, P. L., & Tompkins, G. E. (1988). Structured notetaking: A new strategy for content area teachers. *Journal of Reading, 32,* 46–52.

Taylor, B. M. (1980). Children's memory for expository text after reading. *Reading Research Quarterly, 15,* 399–411.

Taylor, B. M. (1982). A summarizing strategy to improve middle school students' reading and writing skills. *The Reading Teacher, 36,* 202–205.

Thomas, J. W., Strage, A., & Curley, R. (1988). Improving students' self-directed learning: Issues and guidelines. *The Elementary School Journal, 88,* 313–326.

Weinstein, C. E. (1987). Fostering learning autonomy through the use of learning strategies. *Journal of Reading, 30,* 590–595.

Weinstein, C. E., & Mayer, R. E. (1986). The teaching of learning strategies. In M. C. Wittrock (Ed.), *Handbook of research on teaching* (3rd ed., pp. 315–327). New York: Macmillan.

Wood, K. D. (1989). Using guided imagery to enhance learning. *Middle School Journal, 21*(2), 26–28.

13

Classroom Questions

"Do you think he was just talking about *one* year passing?" the teacher went on.

"Or do you think, Lennie, that the poet was seeing his whole life as a year, that he was seeing his whole life slipping past?"

"I'm not sure." Lennie's hand was still on his chin as if ready to stroke a long gray beard.

"Class?"

"His whole life slipping past," the class chorused together. They had had this teacher so long that they could tell, just from the way she asked a question, what they were supposed to answer.

In this excerpt from Betsy Byars's *The TV Kid* (1976, p.70), the teacher's question elicited a *performance* rather than any real thinking or learning on the students' part. Like the students in this fictionalized class, the young adolescents whom we have taught and observed rarely respond in thoughtful ways when pseudoquestions, or questions for which the answer is already known, are asked. Why would anyone ask such questions in the first place? According to Paul (1984), "Teachers have learned to insinuate, often quite unwittingly, their own favored answers in so many ways that children are typically discouraged from suggesting or considering their own" (p. 63).

Research, which spans nearly three decades and includes Durkin's (1978–79) and Guszak's (1967) well-known studies on the types of questions teachers ask, suggests that teachers ask students questions to assess or evaluate their understanding of course content. Far too many of these questions test students' memory or recall of details; far too few challenge them to think.

Questions that stimulate students' thinking are difficult to form. Such questions require much knowledge about the students and the content. However, effort spent in learning to ask questions that tap a variety of comprehension levels is effort well spent. Teachers who have at their disposal a repertoire of questioning strategies are likely to ask questions that go beyond merely assessing or evaluating their students' responses. They are likely to move students to higher levels of thinking.

In this chapter, we subscribe to Vaughan and Estes' (1986) notion about the purpose and role of classroom questions; namely that "questions should . . . stimulate rather than evaluate" (p. 181). In keeping with this view of classroom questioning, we emphasize the value of questions in promoting the growth of young adolescents' cognitive, affective, and expressive abilities.

We begin the chapter with a brief overview of different question types. Next, we look at the various functions questions serve and how these functions are mediated by young adolescents' developmental needs. We then explore ways of knowing when it is appropriate and inappropriate to question, as well as some alternatives to questioning. In the final section, we present several questioning strategies that are known to be effective with young adolescents.

Types of Questions

Questions can be classified by a variety of dimensions. These multidimensional classification schemes are useful in distinguishing between the nature of questions asked in recitations and those asked in discussions; in framing questions that can be used to stimulate different levels of thinking; and in planning lessons that incorporate questioning strategies before, during, and after reading.

Questions in Recitations and Discussions

According to Dillon (1983, 1984), recitations are characterized as teacher-student verbal exchanges in which a series of questions posed by the teacher are answered by students interacting only with the teacher, one at a time or sometimes in a chorus. Typically, these exchanges are short, fast paced, and aimed at eliciting the mere recall of facts. It is said that in recitations, "the teacher speaks in questions and the students in answers" (Dillon, 1983, p. 12).

Recitationlike questioning of young adolescents can produce some rather serious consequences. For example, young adolescents may perceive their contributions so insignificant and so undervalued that they simply resort to saying nothing, to becoming passive rather than active learners. Or they may find their freedom of expression and curiosity for learning so sharply curtailed, even stifled in some instances, that they elect to drop out of school at the earliest opportunity.

On the other hand, the type of questioning that goes on in discussions may have just the opposite effect. In discussions, teachers and students are engaged in a different form of questioning. Rather than addressing only the teacher and the teacher's questions, students are free to address their peers and to ask their own questions of each other and of the teacher. Teachers do not assume that they have the right or the responsibility to direct the flow of all classroom talk. Instead, they are free to defer to students' lines of thinking and reacting, breaking in only with an occasional question or statement designed to refocus or clarify the topic under discussion. (See Chapter 14 for examples of a recitation and a discussion taken from actual middle-grades classrooms.)

Questions and Levels of Thinking

Taxonomies such as the *Taxonomy of Educational Objectives: Cognitive Domain* (Bloom, Englehart, Furst, Hill, & Krathwohl, 1956) have provided teachers and researchers with a convenient means for examining the role of questions in stimulating different levels of thinking. Bloom identified six levels of cognitive functioning, which Vacca and Vacca (1986, pp. 148–149) have equated with six types of student behaviors (see Table 13.1).

Using these six cognitive processes as the basis for their own classification of question types, Pearson and Johnson (1978) developed a taxonomy that enables teachers and students to identify sources of information needed to answer different types of questions. The Pearson and Johnson taxonomy differs from other types of classification schemes in that it focuses attention on the *information* students will need to *answer* the questions rather than on the *types of questions* per se.

For example, answers to textually explicit questions, or questions that tap information from the knowledge level of Bloom's taxonomy, can be found right in the text, either in paraphrase or verbatim form. Raphael and Pearson (1982) have labeled this type of question/answer relationship (QAR) "Right There." That is, the words used to phrase a knowledge-level question and the words used to answer it are stated explicitly in the text, typically in the same sentence of the text.

In a similar manner, the answers to textually implicit questions, or questions that tap information from the comprehension level of Bloom's taxonomy, can be found in what Raphael and Pearson have labeled the "Think and Search" QAR. Textually implicit questions will also have their answers stated in the text, but the words used in the question and those needed to answer the question will typically not be in the same sentence. Instead, the reader will have to integrate ideas across sentences, paragraphs, and perhaps even pages; hence, the label "Think and Search."

TABLE 13.1   Bloom's Levels of Cognitive Functioning

COGNITIVE PROCESSES	STUDENT BEHAVIORS	SAMPLE QUESTIONS
1. Knowledge	The student recalls or recognizes information.	1. Who was Harriet Beecher Stowe?
2. Comprehension	The student changes information into a different symbolic form of language, and discovers relationships among facts, generalizations, definitions, values, and skills	2. What was the relationship of Ms. Stowe's book (*Uncle Tom's Cabin*) to the Civil War?
3. Application	The student solves a lifelike problem that requires the identification of the issue and the selection and use of appropriate generalizations and skills.	3. How is Lois Lenski's *Strawberry Girl* similar to *Uncle Tom's Cabin*?
4. Analysis	The student solves a problem through conscious knowledge of the parts and forms of thinking.	4. Why was slavery an issue in the westward expansion of the U.S.?
5. Synthesis	The student solves a problem that requires original, creative thinking.	5. Why would freed slaves choose to remain in the South?
6. Evaluation	The student makes a judgment of good or bad, or right and wrong, according to designated standards.	6. Did the South have the right to threaten secession?

Source: From *Content Area Reading* (2nd ed.), by R. T. Vacca and J. L. Vacca, Boston: Little, Brown, 1986. Copyright © 1986 by Little, Brown. Reprinted by permission of HarperCollins, Publishers.

Finally, the answers to questions that tap information from the application, analysis, synthesis, and evaluation levels of Bloom's taxonomy can be found in what Raphael and Pearson have called the "On Your Own" QAR. That is, the information needed to answer these questions is not in the text; rather the reader will have to provide the answers from his or her own background of experiences or prior knowledge.

To give you a feel for what we mean by "Right There," "Think and Search," and "On Your Own" question/answer relationships, we have developed a set of questions based on an excerpt from a social studies text, *America Past and Present* (Schreiber, Stepien, Patrick, Remy, Gay, & Hoffman, 1986). First, read the brief excerpt and the questions that follow it. Then identify the source of information that you will need to answer each of these questions. For example, is the information that you need stated explicitly in the text ("Right There" QAR), is it stated implicitly in the text ("Think and Search" QAR), or is it information that must come from your own background of experiences ("On Your Own" QAR)? Answers to these questions can be found at the end of this chapter.

The Antislavery Movement

From the 1820s to the 1860s, many blacks and whites worked together. They spoke, wrote, and acted against slavery. They wanted the United States government to abolish slavery. These people were called abolitionists. By 1985, the movement had about 200,000 members. The abolitionists were led by a number of people. Some, such as David Walker, William Lloyd Garrison, and Frederick Douglass wanted immediate change. They wanted slavery ended at once.

Walker, a black abolitionist, told slaves to strike violently if they were not freed. Garrison printed a newspaper called the *Liberator*. In it, he spoke out against northerners who did not try to help free the slaves. Douglass, an ex-slave, told crowds what it was like to be freed from slavery.

A number of women were leaders of the abolitionist movement. Angelina and Sarah Grimke were daughters of a southern slaveholder. They left their home in South Carolina to speak out against slavery. Harriet Tubman, a runaway slave, helped over three hundred slaves escape. She was a "conductor" on the "underground railroad." This really wasn't a railroad. And it wasn't underground. It was abolitionists who secretly hid runaways in their "stations," their homes and barns. Harriet Beecher Stowe, writer, also worked to abolish slavery. She wrote a book called *Uncle Tom's Cabin*. Her characters made the horrors of slavery come alive for many people who had never seen it. (Schreiber et al., 1986, pp. 241–242)

1. What was the name of the newspaper Garrison printed?
2. How widespread were the activities of the abolitionists?
3. Why do you think the abolitionists included both blacks and whites?

Distinctions also are drawn between question types on the basis of their being *closed* or *open* (Swift, Gooding, & Swift, 1988). Closed questions typically have only one correct answer, which may or may not be at the factual or knowledge level of Bloom's taxonomy. A closed question, for example, could be at the synthesis level and still have only one right answer, as in: How did the abolitionists work together to abolish slavery? Open questions, which may have several equally valid answers, usually involve reasoning and judgment (Hargreaves, 1984), as in: Why do you think the abolitionists included both blacks and whites?

Questions Before, During, and After Reading

Most instruction can be broken down into three phases: that which prepares students for learning, that which guides the learning, and that which follows up in some way on what is learned. This is true of instruction in the social studies, language arts, sciences, mathematics, and other subject areas, especially when that instruction includes reading from assigned texts. Questions that prepare students for reading typically are of the type that help them access or activate knowledge related to the topic to be learned. Sometimes before-reading questions alert students to elements in their background knowledge that are inaccurate or that will be incompatible with the information presented in the text. When this is the case, it is important that these questions be thoroughly explored prior to reading the text so that accurate background knowledge is built.

Questions asked during reading are frequently of the self-monitoring type. That is, they serve to alert students to comprehension failures. Self-monitoring questions can be generated by either students or teachers. Typically, they are used for the following reasons: to check for understanding or breakdowns in understanding; to test the accuracy or inaccuracy of predictions; to compare what is known with the unknown; and to determine if the relationships drawn among ideas presented in the text are reasonable ones. The following is an example of a self-monitoring question that a student might generate while reading the preceding passage, "The Antislavery Movement":

> Do the examples of people working together to abolish slavery in the 1800s remind me of anything I know that is happening today?

After-reading questions make up the most common type of questioning. These questions should be used to do more than provide a check on comprehension, however. When used properly, they should serve to focus students' attention on the need to summarize answers to questions that they have generated for themselves. Reading to answer self-generated questions is one of the highest forms of independent learning.

After-reading questions should also be used to encourage students to elaborate on what they have learned and to apply this new learning to their own lives. In this way, the information gained is made meaningful and stands a chance of being transferred to new or similar situations. For example, an after-reading question that might be used with "The Antislavery Movement" passage is:

> How were the attempts to abolish slavery in the United States in the 1800s similar to those used by the people of Eastern Europe to gain their freedom from the Soviet Union in 1990?

A recent review of the research (Andre, 1987) on the effects of pre- and postquestioning suggests the following findings:

1. Strong support is found in [the] literature for the direct effect of before and after adjunct questions . . . Although this effect can be interpreted as a simple practice effect, it has instructional utility and should be considered in the design of instructional materials.
2. The recent studies add confirmation to the hypothesis that low level before adjunct questions reduce the learning of unrelated information, and they have demonstrated that this effect occurs in typical classroom settings. (p. 81)

Functions of Questions

In this section of the chapter, we concentrate on a variety of functions that questions are assumed to serve. Certainly one of the most commonly held assumptions is that teachers' questions have an impact on what students learn. A second and less explored assumption is that questions serve affective functions. A third assumption, which has been challenged recently, is that people ask questions to obtain information.

Effect of Teacher Questioning on Student Learning

The research literature linking teachers' use of higher cognitive-level questions to student learning is limited in at least two major ways. One problem has been the failure to use standardized definitions in determining what separates higher-level questions from their lower-level counterparts. Another problem is that relatively few experimental or quasi-experimental studies have been conducted on the effectiveness of higher- versus lower-level questions on student learning.

Despite these limitations, efforts have been made over the past three decades to synthesize the available evidence. For example, Winne (1979) concluded from his synthesis of the literature that "whether teachers use predominantly higher cognitive questions or predominantly fact questions makes little difference in student achievement" (p. 43).

Other researchers (Andre, 1987; Andre, Mueller, Womack, Smid, & Tuttle, 1980; Hamaker, 1986) have also studied the effect of application- versus factual-level questions on student learning. Although the results of these studies should be interpreted with caution, generally they suggest that merely asking a higher-level question will not guarantee that students will use higher-order thinking to answer that question. For example, a higher-level question based on "The Antislavery Movement" passage might be the following:

> *Why did the abolitionists speak, write, and act out against slavery in other ways?*

At first glance, this question might appear to tap higher-order thinking, but a close perusal of the first paragraph of the passage will show that the answer to this question is stated explicitly in the third sentence (*"They wanted the United States government to abolish slavery"*). At most, this is an inference.

The point being made is that the source of the information needed to answer a particular question will determine whether or not the question is tapping higher-order thinking. Information stated explicitly in the text is not generating higher-order thinking. Consequently, if you want to ask questions of young adolescents that will engage them in thinking beyond the factual levels, you should consider carefully the source of information they will need to answer your questions. Becoming familiar with and using Raphael and Pearson's (1982) question/answer relationships discussed earlier in this chapter will provide you with an effective approach to asking higher-level questions.

Affective Functions of Questions

Up to this point, we have dealt primarily with the cognitive functions of questions. We have suggested that by engaging students in different levels of questioning, students are being helped to comprehend and remember what they have learned.

However, as Sigel and Kelley (1988) maintain, questions can have an affective function as well; that is, questions can arouse personal feelings that range from the mild to the intense. According to Sigel and Kelley, questions may be perceived as "hostile, disparaging, seductive or warm, friendly, supportive" (p. 113).

Although the affective impact questions may have on young adolescents is difficult to determine, it behooves middle-grades teachers to be aware of the potential for such impact. For example, Sigel and Kelley (1988) point out that probing questions can generate tension as a function of who asks them and under what conditions they are asked. If a teacher asks a question that is intended to clarify a student's thinking, the affective impact that question will have is determined by the relationship established between the teacher and student, by the teacher's tone in asking the question, and by the student's sense of security in attempting to answer it.

Typically, teacher-student exchanges are affectively benign. However, if students feel threatened by the teacher, or if the teacher's intent is to interrogate the student and the student is rarely successful in responding, the affective impact that is generated may be destructive.

Interestingly, research on the impact of questions on students' learning reveals that follow-up questions produce a greater psychological effect than do initial questions (Rosner, 1978). In fact, Sigel and Kelly (1988) argue that the impact of follow-up questions can produce a sense of tension among students:

> When a question is answered and followed by another question, it might suggest to the student that the initial response was unsatisfactory and therefore the need to provide a more satisfactory answer is required. If the inquiry goes on, then the student may get increasingly dissatisfied and frustrated, feeling he/she is always on the spot. Questions may inhibit learning rather than facilitate it because the intent of the inquirer is perceived as critical and non-accepting of the respondent's response. If the teacher answers a question with a question, the student wonders, "What did I say wrong?" (p. 114)

Questions That Function as Requests for Answers

The assumption that people ask questions to get information, which will allow them to achieve some goal requiring that information, is being challenged by a number of researchers (Dillon, 1982b; Riesbeck, 1988; Smith, Tykodi, & Mynatt (1988). Riesbeck, for instance, has produced a list of questions that functions as requests for answers, which he claims is not equivalent to functioning as requests for information. Consider the following examples that Riesbeck gives:

- *Leading questions*, e.g., "Are you sure that's the right answer?";
- *Argumentative questions*, e.g., "Isn't that the point I was trying to make?";
- *Test questions, where the asker knows the answers*, e.g., "What are three causes of civilization?";
- *Rhetorical questions*, e.g., "But if a question is not just a request for information, what is it?";

Young adolescents' self-concepts are influenced by their interactions with teachers and peers.

- *Wondering out loud questions*, e.g. "Now why didn't I think of that?";
- *Riddles*, e.g., "Why is a raven like a writing desk?" (p. 18)

In all but one of these examples (*wondering out loud questions* being the exception), questions appear to function as prompts to get the hearer to agree with the inquirer or to test the hearer's ability to respond. In short, they are questions in search of answers rather than information.

A problem in using these kinds of questions with young adolescents is that they pose a threat to developing positive self-concepts among students. As we noted in Chapter 2, young adolescents' self-concepts are greatly influenced by their experiences in interacting with teachers and peers. When teachers ask too many socially normative questions, such as the ones just listed, young adolescents may feel that their opinions are undervalued and inappropriate. From there, it is only a step to becoming passive rather than active learners.

To Question or Not to Question

When is it appropriate to question? This is more than a rhetorical question, for the importance of finding an answer to it can be inferred from the attention paid to questioning in the teaching education literature. As early as 1847, Page stated that questions "wake up [the] mind" (cited in Dillon, 1982a, p. 128). "To know how to question is to know how to teach" was a popular adage in the methods textbooks of 1910 (Betts, cited in Dillon, 1982b, p. 152). The tendency to equate the ability to question with the ability to teach is still with us today, according to Hyman (1979). Furthermore, according to Johnston and Markle (1986), ''The questions teachers ask in class are the best clues students have to determine what they should be learning'' (p.89). Clearly, then, middle-grades teachers must be knowledgeable in the art of questioning.

According to Krieger (1990), who writes a newspaper column for middle-grades teachers,

> during the middle school years, students should be developing the ability both to recognize how an author structures a text and to read aesthetically. In other words, they should be learning to read with a sense of writer . . . Through the use of effective questioning, teachers can help their students to develop author awareness and critical reading ability. (p. 22)

From the perspective of some experts on classroom questioning practices, and most notably Dillon (1981a), there is only one reason for asking questions: *to acquire information in situations where we are personally and truly perplexed.* Dillon goes on to note that this reason, when turned into a recommendation, ''may be especially difficult for a teacher to do, in that a 'perplexity' question exposes ignorance, confusion and need, ordinarily not the action of an authoritative, self-sufficient, knowledgeable personage'' (p. 54). Asking questions that one does not know the answers to is viewed as equally risky business among young adolescents. Thus, fearful of asking questions that will mark them as confused or ignorant in the eyes of their peers, young adolescents frequently prefer to engage in passive rather than active learning strategies.

Although Dillon (1981a) is adamant in his recommendation that it is appropriate to ask questions only when we are in genuine need of information, he does acknowledge that questions can be used by teachers as mechanical, or procedural, devices in the following three situations:

1. Questions may be put *to define the issue*, as in posing the question for discussion . . . No one takes these utterances as anything but foci for topical comments.
2. Like any other participant, the teacher may use questions *to ensure hearing rightly.* ''I'm sorry, what did you say?'' ''Who was it that mentioned *X* a moment ago?''
3. Finally, the teacher may revert to questioning in order *to regain control of the class* . . . The suggestion relates to the teacher's grip on the class and it reveals the effectiveness of questioning as means of social and verbal control. (p. 55)

A fuller description of teachers' use of questions in actual classroom discussions will follow in Chapter 14. For the present, however, it is important that we focus our attention on the appropriate and inappropriate times to ask questions outside of discussions.

According to some researchers (e.g., Miyake & Norman, 1979), ''To ask a question, one must know enough to know what is not known'' (p. 357). Although this statement seemed a bit convoluted when we first encountered it and tried to make sense of its message, we include it here because we believe that an important lesson can be learned from it. The most interesting finding to emerge from Miyake and Norman's investigation of the questions asked by novice and advanced learners was that there is a definite relationship between the knowledge level of the learners and the difficulty level of the material to be learned.

Novice learners ask more questions on easier material than do advanced learners; conversely, advanced learners ask more questions on harder material than do novice learners. Stated in another way, "People do not appear to be able to cope with material too far beyond their present knowledge" (Miyake & Norman, 1979, p. 362). Thus, it is probably unwise to assume that middle-grades students will ask questions when there is an inappropriate match between their ability level and the difficulty level of the material being presented.

Miyake and Norman (1979) concluded from their study, "The results also show that any theory of question asking in learning cannot simply use the gaps in a person's knowledge as the source of questions. To ask a question, knowing too little is just as disadvantageous as knowing too much" (p. 364).

Frequently, we are struck by the number of instances in which students in our own preservice teacher-education classes fail to ask the inquiring types of questions that we would like them to generate. Some days, when there is a virtual lack of any type of questioning on the part of students in our preservice classes, it is particularly discouraging. However, if one is to believe the research on norms against student questioning, there may be good reasons for preservice teachers' reluctance to ask questions.

In a study reported by Dillon (1981b), a questionnaire was distributed to 166 student teachers. The respondents were asked to explain why students ask so few questions in their college education classes. The 100 preservice teachers in the study who responded to the questionnaire cited the following reasons:

1. First, the question may not be clear or pressing enough to ask (10% of responses).
2. Second, the situation or the teacher may prevent the question from being asked (18%).
3. Third, the student may be afraid to ask the question (72%). (p. 136)

In an elaboration of these reasons, Dillon noted that students who fell into the first category felt unsure of what they wanted to ask, they were insecure about how to phrase their questions, or they deemed their questions too trivial to pursue. Students in the second category explained that class size, the availability of time, and the type of activity could be deterrents to asking questions in class. Some students indicated that when teachers used the phrase, "Ask me after class," they were less likely to pose questions of their own. By far, however, the largest number of responders fell into the third category. Generally, preservice teachers in this category stated that they were afraid to ask questions because they feared a negative reaction from their teachers and/or peers. "As one respondent put it: 'They think that everyone else knows it [the answer to their question] so they will keep quiet and not look the fool' " (p. 137).

Several points can be learned from this study of preservice teachers. First, teachers should presume that students have questions, though indeed they may not be asking them in class. Next, teachers should make sure that the first students to ask questions in class are rewarded and encouraged for their willingness to share their thinking. Doing this will make it more likely that others will follow suit. Third, teachers have to establish a nonthreatening environment so students will feel free to ask questions. Students need to be reminded that the only dumb question is the one they don't ask. Fourth, teachers must make sure that students have adequate time to phrase their responses (this topic is dealt with more fully later in this chapter). Finally, as Dillon (1981) recommends, it may be worthwhile to tape record a few class sessions to get some idea of how frequently or infrequently students are asking questions in class.

Teachers in the middle grades who are faced with the decision of whether to question a student who is not participating may take their cues from what Maier (cited in Dillon, 1983) calls the five reasons for not asking questions of an individual who is not participating:

1. The question may threaten the individual.
2. The individual may have nothing worthwhile to contribute at the moment.
3. Others will wonder why this individual was picked out for special treatment.
4. The questioner's behavior suggests that spontaneous contributions are not in order.
5. The technique causes participants to be ready with a response in case called upon, rather than to think about the problem under discussion. (p. 34)

Alternatives to Questioning

One of the simplest things teachers can do to limit the amount of teacher talk and increase the amount of student talk is to stop asking questions. Following are seven alternatives to questioning.

1. Make a *declarative statement*. According to Dillon (1983), "Contrary to what some people think, declarative statements do evoke responses. Moreover, the responses may be both longer and more complex than responses to questions" (p. 30). Young adolescents typically find declarative statements easier to respond to because the person making the declarative statement comes to the point directly, rather than hinting at it through a question. This circumvents tension-producing situations in which young adolescents are likely to feel ill at ease.

2. Make a *reflective statement*. To do this, simply restate what you understood a student to say. In essence, you are merely saying that you were attentive to what a student was trying to say and that you don't intend to evaluate immediately the correctness or incorrectness of that student's contribution. According to Dillon (1983), "The reflective statement encourages students to say more with, perhaps, more substance" (p. 32). Consequently, by encouraging your students to say more, you may be helping them to elaborate upon and improve their initial responses.

3. Express your *state of mind*. This alternative works well when you are truly confused about what a student has said but you don't want to ask a question and put the student on the defensive. It also works well when you want to ponder

something that was said, perhaps for the purpose of encouraging the student to elaborate on an earlier response.

4. Make an *invitation to elaborate* (Dillon, 1983). Using this technique, you might say, "I would be interested in hearing more about what you think on this topic," Or you might phrase the invitation to elaborate in such a way that it extends a mixed declarative-interrogative message, such as, "Perhaps you could improve our understanding by giving an example." However, a note of caution is needed when using this alternative to questioning. If students perceive that you are merely attempting to trick them into participating, they may withdraw even further.

5. Request that a student formulate what Dillon (1983) calls the *speaker's question*. This technique is particularly valuable when a student has difficulty getting a point across. Rather than asking a series of questions yourself, all aimed at helping the student clarify his or her thinking, you might step back and give the student a chance to self-question. Quite often when the pressure is off to answer a series of teacher questions, students will be able to clarify their own thought processes through self-questioning.

6. Encourage your students to use *class questions*. That is, provide opportunities for students to ask questions of each other.

7. Maintain *deliberate silence*. Putting this alternative into practice will require plenty of patience, both on your students' part as well as your own. According to Dillon, who recommends that teachers maintain a deliberate silence for 3 to 5 seconds after a student pauses or has finished speaking, this technique encourages "not only more talk but also more complex thought" (p. 39).

The following is a portion of a transcript in which a middle-grades teacher practices the seven alternatives to questioning. The setting for this transcript was a seventh-grade social studies class. The topic of study was the Great Compromise.

TEACHER: Think a minute. It wouldn't be practical, it wouldn't even be possible, for 12 states—and eventually 13 of them—to get everything they wanted. (This is a *declarative statement.)*

LEIGH: 'Cause some states might want something, um, that would make the other states real mad and they wouldn't . . . (pause of over 5 seconds)

TEACHER: (maintains *deliberate silence*) You might try to think of an example of where some states might want something that would harm other states. (This is an *invitation to elaborate.)*

LEIGH: Oh, uh, whoever lived in the larger states would get more representatives and the smaller states wouldn't like being outvoted.

TEACHER: All right. They had to compromise. They had to do some giving and taking. There is a name for the plan. (This is a *declarative statement.)*

JIMMY: Democracy.

TEACHER: Well, democracy was certainly at the heart of the plan. (This is a *reflective statement.)*

JIMMY: The Great Compromise, that's it. The delegates had to give and take. They decided that each state would get two senators, but the bigger states could get more representatives.

TEACHER: But I am confused because you say the larger states still get more representatives than the smaller states. (This is a *state of mind* statement.)

JIMMY: Yes, but the little states don't mind because they have equal votes in the Senate, and if the big states don't like that, they have to like the idea of having more votes in the House of Representatives.

TEACHER: Thank you. I see what you mean now.

ROBIN: So we have 10 representatives from Georgia and 2 senators. Isn't that right?

EDWIN: How do you get that? We have 10 congressional districts, that's what my dad says. That's not the same thing as 10 representatives.

LANELLE: But if the population changes, like Mrs. Garner (the teacher) says, then how do you know it's 10 representatives?

(These *class questions* posed by students occurred because the teacher stopped asking questions herself. Note, however, how the teacher helps Robin clarify her thinking in the next exchange.)

TEACHER: Robin, think about the 10 representatives and the 10 congressional districts. Take some time and ask yourself what that would mean—in terms of the total number of representatives from each congressional district. (The teacher encourages Robin to formulate a *speaker's question.*)

Effective Questioning Strategies

Numerous questioning strategies exist in the research literature. In making decisions about which to include in this chapter, we were guided by four lines of thinking: (1) We wanted to address the importance of asking questions that follow the storyline and structure of texts. (2) We wanted to include a question-probing strategy that essentially "slices" complex text into manageable units. (3) We were interested in providing guidelines for asking questions, such as knowing when to follow up on a question and where to place questions. (4) Because research tells us that self-questioning is one of the most effective means of improving young adolescents' learning (Wong, 1985), we wanted to include a self-questioning strategy that involves teachers and students in modeling problem-solving behaviors.

Asking Storyline and Text-Structure Questions

When teachers focus attention on central story content, sometimes called the *storyline*, they help students improve their ability to remember and answer questions about a selection. Research (e.g., Beck, Omanson, & McKeown, 1982; Winograd, 1984) has shown that when students' attention is focused on important, rather than unimportant, information in a selection, they are able to comprehend the selection better. In some selections the theme is developed through a problem/solution storyline. For example, one of the characters may have a problem and several attempts may be made to solve that problem before the final solution is reached. Asking questions that focus students' attention on the various attempts to solve the problem is an effective way of developing comprehension.

Likewise, asking questions that reflect the text structure of an expository piece of writing can also enhance students' understanding (Armbruster, Anderson, & Ostertag, 1987; Berkowitz, 1986). Selections that have a comparison/contrast structure lend themselves to questions that reflect that structure. The same is true for selections in which an author has decided to use a cause/effect structure or a time/order sequence. In each case, potential comprehension problems are alleviated when questions reflect the text structure.

Slicing Questions

When students are unable to respond to a certain question, it often helps to ''slice'' the question by using a probed questioning approach. Often this involves breaking down the initial question into a series of questions that cue readers about the relationships among ideas. There are two ways to slice a question. The more common way is to recast the question, asking for a smaller part of the original question.

In the example that follows, an inferential question is sliced into two literal probe questions. If students had difficulty answering the original question, the two literal questions would serve to probe, or cue, their responses.

Original question:	How did Sequoya show he was determined to write his syllabary?
Probe question:	What happened when Sequoya's wife became angry and burned the bark picture-words?
Probe question:	How did Sequoya react when other Indians burned the cabin in which he was developing his syllabary, thus destroying all he had accomplished?

Another way to slice the original question is to change the task by having students *recognize*, rather than *recall*, the information requested. For example:

Probe question:	Which of these events reinforced Sequoya's determination to complete his syllabary?

He started over again after his wife burned the bark picture-words.

He received many honors for creating the syllabary.

He overcame the disappointment of losing his syllabary in the cabin fire.

Guidelines for Asking Questions

Knowing when to follow up on a previously asked question is governed in part by where students are in the process of responding to the question. Research (Rowe, 1974) has shown that pauses between teachers' and students' utterances, referred to as *wait time*, can influence higher cognitive learning. Typically, the average teacher's wait time is 1 second or less. For example, in a study of middle-grades science teachers, Tobin (1980) observed a wait time of only 0.5 seconds.

A recent review of the research on wait time (Tobin, 1987) has demonstrated the importance of allowing adequate time between teachers' and students' utterances. When the average wait time has been 3 seconds or longer, higher cognitive-level achievement has been observed both in middle-grades science and middle-grades mathematics. According to Tobin (1987), "Wait time appears to facilitate higher cognitive level learning by providing teachers and students with additional time to think" (p. 69).

Like wait time, placement of questions is another powerful factor in determining what is learned. In general, prequestions tend to improve students' learning of targeted information. To illustrate, a selection might describe the disasters that slowed Sequoya's completion of the Cherokee syllabary. By asking the question, What disasters delayed Sequoya in completing his work on the syllabary? *before* reading, we could expect students to remember the several disasters but at the expense of other incidental information. If the goal is to help students gain an overall or general understanding of a selection, postquestions would be preferable to prequestions.

Another example of how the placement of questions affects young adolescents' learning can be found in Wood's (1986) research on interspersed questions. In her study involving over 100 seventh-grade students, Wood found that interspersing questions in science, social studies, and basal reading texts reduced the amount of print students had to deal with at any one time. This "slicing of the task" (as Wood termed it) resulted in improved learning not unlike that observed when teachers slice questions.

A Self-Questioning Strategy for Solving Problems

If young adolescents are taught how to question themselves as they engage in problem-solving activities, they have learned one of the most valuable independent learning tools around. In a review of the research on self-questioning among young adolescent learners, Alvermann and Moore (1991) concluded:

Knowing when to follow up on a previously asked question is part of a teacher's knowledge of "wait time."

Generally, instruction in self-questioning improves students' processing of text. However, those with low verbal ability and/or poor reading skills tend to profit more from this instruction than do those with high verbal ability and/or better reading skills. Although MacDonald's (1986) work provides additional evidence that improving below-average and average readers' self-questioning ability leads to improved recall, it appears to do so only for readers who possess certain prerequisite abilities, such as the ability to perform well on free-recall measures. MacDonald noted some instances in which self-questioning instruction actually depressed below-average students' performance. Regardless of students' ability level, successful self-questioning instruction typically involves either direct instruction in the strategy or explicitly written instruction with examples of good questions. (pp. 961–962)

In creating the following self-questioning starters, we borrowed heavily from an idea that we saw in a book titled *How to Evaluate Progress in Problem Solving* (Charles, Lester, & O'Daffer, 1987). Instead of using the italicized stems as elements of teacher-directed questions, which the authors of that book had done, we turned the stems into self-questioning probes that young adolescents can use on their own in a variety of content area classes.

1. *How did I know* which information was necessary for solving the problem?
2. *What did I do first* when I tried to solve the problem?
3. *Have I used* what I know about other problems to solve this one?
4. *How did I decide* whether to multiply or divide to find the answer?
5. *Am I sure* that I have answered the question in the problem?
6. *Can I describe* what I did to someone else?
7. *What do I think* is the most important thing I have learned from solving the problem?
8. *How do I feel* about the effort I put into solving the problem?

Although these questions are intended for students to use on their own, middle-grades teachers should not expect them to do so initially. We suggest that teachers use the stems to model their own problem-solving approach. If the modeling is done by thinking aloud, students will be provided with a form of scaffolded learning in which the teacher serves as a model of effective self-questioning before turning over this responsibility to students.

Summary

If we have been successful in communicating our views on the purpose and role of questions in classroom learning, you have no doubt come away from this chapter with the idea that questions should be used to stimulate young adolescents' thinking, not merely to evaluate it. Classifying questions by types is useful when you need to distinguish recitations from discussions, when you want to stimulate different levels of thinking, and when you plan lessons to incorporate before-, during-, and after-reading strategies. Teacher questioning can have an impact on student learning, questions can serve affective as well as cognitive functions, and teachers can ask questions for reasons that extend beyond merely testing students' ability to respond.

Our views on questioning take into account when it is appropriate and inappropriate to question young adolescents. We subscribe to the notion that alternatives to questioning may provide a welcome relief in many middle-grades classrooms. These alternatives can foster greater student participation and even increase the substantive nature of students' responses. Young adolescents who possess a repertoire of effective questioning strategies are better equipped to deal with their textbook assignments and a variety of problem-solving activities.

Answers to QARS

The answer to the first "Right There" QAR is: Garrison printed the *Liberator*.

The answer to the second "Think and Search" QAR is: The abolitionists spoke and wrote publicly about the evils of slavery, and they even hid runaway slaves in their own homes.

One answer to the third "On Your Own" QAR is: Denying people their freedom is an issue that people of all races have fought down through the ages, and the struggle continues even today.

REFERENCES

Alvermann, D. E., & Moore, D. W. (1991). Secondary school reading. In R. Barr, M. Kamil, P. Mosenthal, & P. D. Pearson (Eds.), *Handbook of reading research Volume II* (pp. 951–983). New York: Longman.

Andre, T. (1987). Questions and learning from reading. *Questioning Exchange: A Multidisciplinary Review, 1*, 47–86.

Andre, T., Mueller, C., Womack, S., Smid, K., & Tuttle, M. (1980). Adjunct application questions facilitate later application, or do they? *Journal of Educational Psychology, 72*, 533–543.

Armbruster, B. B., Anderson, T. H., & Ostertag, J. (1987). Does text structure/summarization instruction facilitate learning from expository text? *Reading Research Quarterly, 22*, 331–346.

Beck, I. L., Omanson, R. C., & McKeown, M. G. (1982). An instructional redesign of reading lessons. *Reading Research Quarterly, 17*, 462–481.

Berkowitz, S. J. (1986). Effects of instruction in text organization on sixth-grade students' memory for expository reading. *Reading Research Quarterly, 21*, 161–178.

Bloom, B. S., Englehart, M. B., Furst, E. J., Hill, W. H., & Krathwohl, D. R. (1956). *Taxonomy of educational objectives: The classification of educational goals. Handbook I: Cognitive domain.* New York: Longman, Green.

Byars, B. (1976). *The TV kid.* New York: Viking Press.

Charles R., Lester, F., & O'Daffer, P. (1987). *How to evaluate progress in problem solving.* Reston, VA: National Council of Teachers of Mathematics.

Dillon, J. T. (1981a). To question and not to question during discussion: Questioning and discussion. *Journal of Teacher Education, 32*(5), 51–55.

Dillon, J. T. (1981b). A norm against student questions. *The Clearing House, 55*, 136–139.

Dillon, J. T. (1982a). The effect of questions in education and other enterprises. *Journal of Curriculum Studies, 14*, 127–152.

Dillon, J. T. (1982b). The multidisciplinary study of questioning. *Journal of Educational Psychology, 74,* 147–165.

Dillon, J. T. (1983). *Teaching and the art of questioning.* Bloomington, IN: Phi Delta Kappa Educational Foundation.

Dillon, J. T. (1984). Research on questioning and discussion. *Educational Leadership, 42*(3), 50–56.

Durkin, D. (1978–79). What classroom observations reveal about reading comprehension instruction. *Reading Research Quarterly, 14,* 481–533.

Guszak, F. (1967). Teacher questioning and reading. *The Reading Teacher, 21,* 227–234.

Hamaker, C. (1986). The effects of adjunct questions on prose learning. *Review of Educational Research, 56,* 212–242.

Hargreaves, D. H. (1984). Teachers' questions: Open, closed and half-open. *Educational Research, 26*(1), 46–50.

Hyman, R. T. (1979). *Strategic questioning.* Englewood Cliffs, NJ: Prentice-Hall.

Johnston, J. H., & Markle, G. C. (1986). *What research says to the middle level practitioner.* Columbus, OH: National Middle School Association.

Krieger, E. (1990). Effective questioning for critical reading. *Reading Today* (Oct./Nov.), p. 22

MacDonald, J. D. (1986). Self-generated questions and reading recall: Does training help? *Contemporary Educational Psychology, 11,* 290–304.

Miyake, N., & Norman, D. A. (1979). To ask a question, one must know enough to know what is not known. *Journal of Verbal Learning and Verbal Behavior, 18,* 357–364.

Paul, R. W. (1984). The Socratic spirit: An answer to Louis Goldman. *Educational Leadership, 42*(1), 63–64.

Pearson, P. D., & Johnson, D. (1978). *Teaching reading comprehension.* New York: Holt, Rinehart & Winston.

Raphael, T. E., & McKinney, J. (1983). An examination of fifth- and eighth-grade children's question-answering behavior: An instructional study in metacognition. *Journal of Reading Behavior, 15*(3), 67–86.

Raphael, T. E. & Pearson, P. D. (1982). *The effect of metacognitive awareness training on children's question-answering behavior.* (Tech. Rep. No. 238). Urbana, IL: Center for the Study of Reading, University of Illinois.

Riesbeck, C. K. (1988). Are questions just function calls? *Questioning Exchange: A Multidisciplinary Review, 2,* 17–24.

Rosner, F. C. (1978). An ecological study of teacher distancing behaviors as a function of program, context, and time. *Dissertation Abstracts International, 39,* 760A (University Microfilms, No. 7812235).

Rowe, M. B. (1974). Wait-time and rewards as instructional variables, their influence on language, logic, and fate control. Part I. Wait-time. *Journal of Research in Science Teaching, 11,* 81–94.

Schreiber, J., Stepien, W., Patrick, J., Remy, R., Gay, G., & Hoffman, A. (1986). *America past and present.* Glenview, IL: Scott, Foresman.

Sigel, I. E., & Kelley, D. D. (1988). A cognitive developmental approach to questioning. In J. T. Dillon (Ed.), *Questioning and discussion: A multidisciplinary study* (pp. 105–134). Norwood, NJ: Ablex.

Smith, K. H., Tykodi, T. A., & Mynatt, B. T. (1988). Can we predict the form and content of spontaneous questions? *Questioning Exchange: A Multidisciplinary Review, 2,* 53–60.

Swift, J. N., & Gooding, C. T. (1983). Interaction of wait time feedback and questioning instruction on middle school science teaching. *Journal of Research in Science Teaching, 20,* 721–730.

Swift, J. N., Gooding, C. T., & Swift, P. R. (1988). Questions and wait time. In J. T. Dillon (Ed.), *Questioning and discussion: A multidisciplinary study* (pp. 192–211). Norwood, NJ: Ablex.

Tobin, K. (1980). The effect of an extended wait time on science achievement. *Journal of Research in Science Teaching, 17,* 469–475.

Tobin, K. (1987). The role of wait time in higher cognitive level learning. *Review of Educational Research, 57,* 69–95.

Vacca, R. T., & Vacca, J. L. (1986). *Content area reading* (2nd ed.). Boston: Little, Brown.

Vaughan, J. L., & Estes, T. H. (1986). *Reading and reasoning beyond the primary grades.* Boston: Allyn and Bacon.

Winne, P. H. (1979). Experiments relating teachers' use of higher cognitive questions to student achievement. *Review of Educational Research, 49*, 13–50.

Winograd, P. N. (1984). Strategic difficulties in summarizing texts. *Reading Research Quarterly, 19*, 404–425.

Wong, B. Y. L. (1985). Self-questioning instructional research: A review. *Review of Educational Research, 55*, 227–268.

Wood, K. D. (1986). The effect of interspersing questions in text: Evidence for "slicing the task." *Reading Research and Instruction, 25*, 295–307.

_14

Classroom Interaction

Young adolescents enjoy opportunities to interact with their peers. Many times these opportunities present themselves in informal settings, such as before and after school, during advisory group meetings, and in extracurricular activities. Opportunities also arise in more formal settings, within the context of a lesson or in an interdisciplinary team project.

Regardless of the setting, young adolescents are particularly conscious of the need to fit in with other students in their age group. In their attempts to conform to peer norms, young adolescents do not value being seen as different or siding with the teacher and other authority figures. Consequently, it is essential that middle-grades teachers acknowledge these needs and plan instruction that fosters the interpersonal and cognitive growth of their students.

This chapter begins with an overview of the characteristics of talk that make up a majority of classroom interactions in the middle grades. Included are the roles and responsibilities of teachers and students in these interactions. From there we move to a more focused look at recitations and discussions, two of the more common forms of classroom interaction in the middle grades. The criteria for well-developed discussion are laid out and clarified. Next, we describe the interpersonal needs and cognitive growth of young adolescents that are served by the give-and-take nature of well-developed discussions. The chapter concludes with an example of a discussion strategy that is theoretically grounded and wholly suited to developing interpersonal and cognitive growth in young adolescents.

Overview of Classroom Interaction

Teachers play significant roles in classroom interaction. They are the directors, facilitators, and evaluators of all that transpires among themselves and students and frequently among students and students. This topic has been the subject of several books. For example, Jackson (1968) describes teachers as being alone and in control of many aspects of students' lives, including their speech. Along with this sense of autonomy, and coupled with the need to react immediately to large numbers of students, teachers take for granted their role as arbiters of classroom talk (Delamont, 1983).

Stubbs (1983) also acknowledges the central role teachers play in what he calls "chalk-and-talk" lessons. He stated, "One thing which characterizes much classroom talk is the extent to which the teacher has *conversational control* over the topic, over the relevance or correctness of what pupils say, and over when and how much pupils may speak" (p. 105).

Holt (1986) asked:

> Do teachers talk too much? I'm afraid we do. Much too much. From the time we enter the school in the morning till we leave it at night, we hardly stop talking. We only realize how much we talk when we come to school with a sore throat.
>
> What do we talk about? Some of the time we hand out information. Perhaps we read something from a text. Or we tell students something we think they ought to know—certain rules of grammar, facts about a place or event, what a poem means, why this book is important, and so on. We like handing out information. It's our pleasure as well as our business. (pp. 47–48)

Although written more than two decades ago, Holt's observation that classroom talk is teacher dominated is still true today. Moreover, teacher talk varies little in the form it takes. Goodlad (1984), for instance, found in his large-scale study that less than 1 percent of all teacher talk deals with information above the literal level. Alvermann, O'Brien, and Dillon (1990) found that the majority of the 24 middle-grades teachers whom they observed reported that it was difficult, and in many instances impossible, to relinquish control of classroom talk, even when their goal was to involve students more actively in a variety of classroom interactions.

The following section provides a detailed look at two common forms of classroom interaction: recitations and discussions. In recitations, teacher-dominated talk is the norm, but in discussions, it is less so, especially in small-group discussions.

Common Forms of Classroom Interaction

Although talk among teachers and students during lessons can take a variety of forms, recitation and discussion are two of the most commonly observed forms. The roles and responsibilities assumed by teachers and students in each of these forms of classroom talk are governed by what Erickson and Shultz (1981) describe as social participation structures.

The social participation structure for a recitation is one in which students are expected to answer a series of rapid-fire questions posed by the teacher for the purpose of reviewing, drilling, and quizzing literal-level information. The student's responsibility is to listen passively until called on to speak by the teacher. In essence, the teacher is the sole gatekeeper, regulating who will talk, when, and on what topic. Despite the criticism that has been leveled against this form of classroom interaction, it has shown no sign of abating over the past 60 or so years (Stodolsky, Ferguson, & Wimpelberg, 1981).

Although we favor discussions over recitations, there are times when recitations are useful. For example, in their review of the research on recitation, Corno and Snow (1986) pointed out that in presenting lessons, the same instructional objectives and materials can be used for all students. In soliciting student response, teachers need to attend to only one student at a time. In providing feedback to one student, essentially the entire class benefits, thus saving time and energy for all concerned. When recitations are conducted in conjunction with other forms of interaction and for a relatively short period of time, they are pedagogically sound (Stodolsky, Ferguson, & Wimpelberg, 1981). Recitations also help teachers maintain a learning environment in which everyone is expected to be on task and attentive (Doyle, 1986). Guidelines for effective recitations appear in Figure 14.1

FIGURE 14.1   Guidelines for Effective Recitations

1. Presenting Lesson Information
   - Typically, choose to use recitation with large-group instruction.
   - Enhance your instruction by using a variety of media and other materials.
   - Plan to deliver information sequentially.
2. Soliciting Student Response
   - Vary calling on students by stating their name first followed by the question and vice versa.
   - Provide at least 3 to 5 seconds for a student to respond.
3. Providing Feedback to Student Responses
   - Give feedback as to the accuracy and/or explicitness of the response.
   - Monitor the progress of the students who initially shy away from participating in the recitation.
   - Encourage students to remain on task and attentive even if they have had a turn recently.

Source: From L. Corno and R. E. Snow, "Adapting Teaching to Individual Differences among Learners" (pp. 605–629). Adapted with permission of Macmillan Publishing Company, a Division of Macmillan, Inc., from *Handbook of Research on Teaching,* Third Edition, edited by Merlin C. Wittrock. Copyright © 1986 by the American Educational Research Association.

The social participation structure for a discussion is one in which students ask questions of each other and of their teacher. In well-developed discussions, students are actively involved in refining and enriching their own understandings by observing how their ideas are interpreted by others. Although the social participation structure for a discussion entails some degree of gatekeeping to allow listeners and speakers their turns at talking, the allocation of turns is distributed more representatively between students and teachers in a discussion than in a recitation. The type of information shared also differs. Unlike a recitation, a discussion is more apt to evoke higher-level thinking, such as that involved in solving problems or debating issues.

According to Bridges' (1979) definition of a discussion, it is distinguishable from a recitation in three important ways: (1) in a discussion, participants put forth multiple points of view; (2) they are willing to change their minds if presented with convincing evidence; and (3) they have the intention of developing an in-depth understanding of the topic under discussion. In line with Bridges' thinking, we view a well-developed classroom discussion as being a give-and-take dialogue that encourages sustained talk about a concept for the purpose of exploring its different aspects. This view of discussion implies that communicating with others (social interaction) plays an important role in the way knowledge is acquired and organized.

Classroom Interaction Exercise

Following are several excerpts from actual classroom interactions involving two groups of seventh-grade students and their respective social studies teachers, Ms. Morton and Ms. Gannett. Each of the excerpts is preceded by a short description of the setting in which the interaction occurred. Using the descriptions provided, the classroom talk contained within the excerpts, and your understanding of what constitutes the participation structures of recitations and discussions, decide which excerpt has more recitationlike qualities and which one has more discussionlike qualities. Write your answers on a separate sheet of paper, making sure that you give reasons for your choices.

Description of the setting: *Ms. Morton is seated in front of the class, which consists of 24 average-ability, seventh-grade students. In her hand is a worksheet that contains questions about the men who met in Philadelphia to frame the Constitution of the United States. As the students rummage through their book bags for their assignment (the answers to the worksheet), Ms. Morton reminds them that they should keep their books open to the pages where they found their answers.*

MS. MORTON: Okay, the first question says, "What were two reasons some people were against the Constitution?" Robert? List two reasons.
ROBERT: Well, they said . . . they thought they were missing something important and it was the Bill of Rights and such a bill would protect citizens from their government by guaranteeing their rights.
MS. MORTON: Okay, very good. Right there in the first section of the book. They had just come out of a situation where England had had a ruler, a

strong ruler, a lot of power, and they didn't want to give the, uh, government strong power again. And, they felt that a very important part of human rights was the Bill of Rights. Okay, number 2, um, Kelly? Why were some people in *favor* of the Constitution?

KELLY: They realized that if the United States was to grow and prosper as a united country . . .

MS. MORTON: (interrupting) All right, but if it wants to grow and prosper, what?

KELLY: A strong government was needed.

MS. MORTON: A strong government was needed. Good, that was the important thing. They needed to have a strong government. All right, number 3. You had to define *ratified.* Celeste?

CELESTE: To approve.

MS. MORTON: To approve. Now, what did they ratify, or what did they approve?

CELESTE: The Bill of Rights.

MS. MORTON: The Bill of Rights. And all of those Bill of Rights separately, uh, were what? What were each of those little things called?

SONNY: The Ten Commandments?

MS. MORTON: (laughing) No, not commandments, not ten commandments, but . . .

KEITH: (interrupting) Amendments.

MS. MORTON: Amendments. That's right, you got it, but it ends the same. The number's the same. That's right, that's okay. Uh, number 4, define *Bill of Rights.* James?

JAMES: The bill that will protect the citizens from government, and freedom to . . . freedom such as to speak and stand trial in court.

MS. MORTON: All right, we said it was human rights. Some of those things were the right to free speech, the right for what?

JAMES: Fair trial.

MS. MORTON: Keith?

KEITH: Free, uh (looking down at his worksheet), free religion.

MS. MORTON: Right. Freedom to worship as you want to. What else? What were some of the others? What?

TED: (barely audible) Tax goods.

MS. MORTON: No, not in the Bill of Rights.

DIANE: Freedom to vote.

MS. MORTON: All right, voting. What was another important thing that goes back . . .

KEITH: (interrupting) Wasn't there one about slavery?

MS. MORTON: No, not in the Bill of Rights, I don't think.

MARY ANN: Freedom of the press?

MS. MORTON: All right, press, Right.

(*Note: The teacher continued to question the students over the remaining items on their worksheets. Near the end of the class period, the students took a short, closed-book quiz on the information on their worksheets.*)

In the next set of excerpts, a different group of average-ability, seventh-grade students and their teacher, Ms. Gannett, are talking about the Constitution and its guarantee of freedom of religion. The students had read about the separation of church and state, particularly as it applied to a legal battle over the right of an individual to set up a nativity scene on public property.

Description of the setting: *Ms. Gannett is leaning against the corner of her desk in front of the classroom. Her 23 students are seated in rows facing the front. They have on their desks a worksheet on a case that came before the Supreme Court involving a group of people in Pawtucket, Rhode Island, who wanted to put a nativity scene on public property.*

MS. GANNETT: Okay, now here we go. What do you think about this? Do you think the people in Pawtucket have the right to say, "We believe in God— we're Christians—and we want to put up a nativity scene. It doesn't hurt anybody, and we've been doing it for 40 years." And the other group says, "No, no, this is public property, and the Constitution says you can't establish a state religion. We pay taxes, and we don't want a nativity scene on public property." What do you think about that?

PAUL: If it's the law, they shouldn't do it.

STEVE: If they want to put it up, they oughta find someone who will let them put it up in town, or somebody like that.

MS. GANNETT: All right, so take it and put it on private property. You think that's the solution?

JEFFREY: People who want to put it up *also* pay taxes, and if there are more of them, I think they should just put it there.

MS. GANNETT: Are you saying that the majority rules if there are more people that want it?

JEFFREY: Yeah, if more people want it, then they should be able to put it there.

MS. GANNETT: Okay, but what does the Constitution say?

JEFFREY: They're not trying to *establish* a religion. They're just *showing* it— same way that Buddhists can go out and burn statues down in front of their homes.

STEVE: What if someone, uh, built, uh, a nice tall Buddha and put it in front of the court house? How would you feel about it?

(Several students begin to talk at once among themselves.)

JEFFREY: It wouldn't bother me.

KATHERINE: I think they could ask somebody if they could put it *close* to the state court house—like the bank. So it would be close.

MS. GANNETT: So, move it *off* public property to business property or private property? Well, that's a solution, but these people do not want to do that. They say, "We've been doing this for 40 years, and most of us like it." Just like Jeffrey said, the majority probably wants it, and it's the minority who doesn't.

(*Note: The talk took a detour at this point when someone asked whether school prayer is in violation of the separation of church and state. Kayleen offered information about a boy who had been denied his Eagle Scout badge because he was an atheist. Then Skip commented that when he went to public school in Florida, "We used to say the flag every morning.")*

MS. GANNETT: (in an attempt to refocus the talk) The pledge of allegiance, right? But, does it have anything to do with religion?

(*Note: The students ignored the teacher's attempt to focus on the Pawtucket case. Instead, they brought up the possibility that people might define religion differently. For example, Jeffrey asked, "Aren't atheists practicing a form of religion when they say they want no god?")*

MS. GANNETT: Well, I don't know. Maybe we—you—should say it's a lack of religion. It is a *belief*. I see what your point is, Jeffrey. Your point is that these people (people in Pawtucket who oppose erecting the nativity scene on public property) are imposing their beliefs on the rest of us. Is that what you're saying?

JEFFREY: Same thing.

BRIDGETT: An atheist is doing nothing wrong as far as the Constitution is concerned—only upholding it, and that's what they (people in Pawtucket opposing the nativity scene) say they're doing!

JEFFREY: But I still don't see any difference between our pressing our religion on them and them pressing their beliefs on us.

LINDA JO: Well, you see, they say you can practice any religion you want, but do it in your church, not on public property.

JOHN: They (the atheists) do it on public property . . . going to the Supreme Court and all. Wouldn't that cost more tax dollars than putting up a simple nativity scene?

(*Note: The students continued to explore the two sides of the Pawtucket case. At one point, the talk digressed to devil worship, but the teacher brought them back to the topic by asking Richard to read a section of the worksheet on spending public money for religious purposes. By the end of the class period, most of the students (Jeffrey being one exception) agreed that the idea of majority rule does not hold if what the majority wants is against the Constitution.)*

Reflection on the Exercise

At the start of this exercise, we asked you to read the excerpts from Ms. Morton's and Ms. Gannett's classroom interactions and to decide which teacher interacted with her students in a way that resembled a recitation more than a discussion, and conversely, a discussion more than a recitation. We also asked you to write your answers on a separate sheet of paper and to give your reasons for your choices. You may want to refer to your paper in preparation for reflecting on the exercise.

First, we think you will agree that if the two teachers' excerpts were placed on a continuum whose two end points were *recitation* and *discussion*, Ms. Morton's classroom interactions would resemble a recitation more than a discussion. By way of contrast, Ms. Gannett's classroom interactions probably reminded you of a discussion more than a recitation. Why? And what are your reasons for believing as you do?

Several characteristics stand out as indicators of why we believe Ms. Morton's class was involved in a recitation and Ms. Gannett's in a discussion. These include, but are not limited to, the following:

1. Although Ms. Morton appeared to have established a positive social climate in her classroom, a large subset of her students remained passive during the question-and-answer session. Even those students who did participate tended to answer in short two- and three-word phrases, or they attempted to paraphrase longer answers from their texts and study sheets.

Students in Ms. Gannett's class, on the other hand, were generally more involved in the talk and the topic. It is true, however, that relatively few students participated in Ms. Gannett's room. In fact, Jeffrey appears to have dominated the discussion, although we did not find this to be the case when we examined other excerpts from the same class discussion. Certainly neither teacher appeared to curtail extended student talk in order to elicit a response from every individual in the class.

2. The purpose of Ms. Morton's interactions with her students appeared to differ from Ms. Gannett's. In Ms. Morton's class, students were engaged in a subject-mastery recitation in preparation for a quiz that followed at the end of the period. In contrast, students in Ms. Gannett's room were engaged in an issue-oriented discussion. Her purpose was to inform students of the diverse nature of people's responses to the separation of church and state, and, at the same time, to elicit from students their own feelings and beliefs about the issue.

3. The amount and type of teacher talk also led us to characterize Ms. Morton's interactions as being recitationlike. She directed the turntaking throughout the entire lesson. At no point in the lesson, not even at the end, did she emphasize key concepts or encourage students to share their insights in the framing of the Constitution.

Because responsibility for much of the talk rested with the students in Ms. Gannett's room, she frequently exercised the right to step in and refocus what she considered was a straying discussion. At times, however, students' interests were so strong that they took the discussion along the path they wanted it to go. When this happened, Ms. Gannett did not immediately try to wrest control of the talk from the students. However, as facilitator of the discussion, she did intervene whenever there was danger of it breaking down due to misunderstanding or confusion.

How generalizable these observations are to the larger universe of middle-grades classrooms is difficult to measure. We do know, however, from a study involving 24 middle-grades classroom teachers and their students, that because of perceived pressures from outside forces, most teachers believed in covering content, or the facts, as opposed to encouraging students to question the reasons behind the facts (Alvermann, O'Brien, & Dillon, 1990).

Although there are appropriate uses for recitations in middle-grades classrooms, as noted earlier, the remainder of the chapter focuses on discussions.

Research suggests that recitations are easier to conduct than discussions. Teachers tell us the same thing (Alvermann, O'Brien, & Dillon, 1990). We also know from an analysis of teaching methods texts that guidelines for conducting classroom discussions are rarely provided (Moore, Alvermann, & O'Keefe, 1990). Hence, our emphasis on discussion in this chapter seems well founded.

Interpersonal Needs and Cognitive Growth

Well-developed discussions can facilitate young adolescents' interpersonal needs and cognitive growth in the following five ways:

1. Discussions can serve as sounding boards for young adolescents' beliefs and value systems.
2. By participating in discussions, young adolescents can gain experience in learning how to overcome their egocentric views.
3. Discussions that involve constructive controversy can facilitate young adolescents' growth in learning, problem solving, and decision making.
4. Discussions can provide opportunities for young adolescents to expand and refine their oral language skills.
5. Because well-developed discussions tend to focus on higher-order thinking rather than on rote learning, young adolescents can gain invaluable practice in adjusting to the increased cognitive demands of the middle grades.

Using Discussion as a Sounding Board

Young adolescents benefit from classroom discussions that enable them to test out their beliefs and values against those of significant others—their peers and their teachers. If discussions are to serve as sounding boards for students' beliefs and value systems, they must be structured in ways that help students develop a tolerance for points of view that may differ from their own. They also must be structured in ways that promote sensitivity to other people's views, interests, and needs.

Structuring of this type is a tall order for any instructional approach, but particularly discussion, given that young adolescents need to be accepted by their peers and at the same time be recognized as individuals with unique qualities and abilities. As you will recall from earlier sections, acceptance by one's peers is of paramount concern among young adolescents (George & Lawrence, 1982; Ingersoll, 1989). It is easy to see, therefore, how failing to consider the importance of structuring discussions—so that they foster young adolescents' tolerance and sensitivity toward others—could cause emotional and even physical harm.

The middle grades provide an interesting context in which to study the effects of discussions as sounding boards for students' beliefs and values that lead to new learning because of the complex mix of communicative demands placed on students and teachers at this level. For example, students who have been accustomed to listening to their teachers talk throughout most of their school years find it difficult to assume responsibility for generating task-related talk when they are in small-group discussions.

Teachers, on the other hand, who have long been accustomed to doing the talking, find it difficult to relinquish control of classroom interactions. They may fear that in giving up the floor to student talk, valuable time will be lost and content coverage will be slowed. In short, learning will be hindered. Yet, according to a comprehensive report of the Task Force on the Education of Young Adolescents, "Learning often takes place best when students have opportunities to discuss, analyze, express opinions, and receive feedback from peers" (Carnegie Council on Adolescent Development, 1989, p. 43).

Classroom discussions that serve as safe sounding boards for young adolescents' beliefs and values can be positive forces in shaping their motivation and enthusiasm for learning. Good, Reys, Grouws, and Mulryan (1990) found in their study, for instance, that using work groups in mathematics instruction led to increased opportunities for peer interaction. They reported that "students were developing the ability to work with others and use strengths that others bring to a task—as well as becoming more sensitive to others' needs and interests" (p. 58). Opportunities for higher-level mathematical thinking and skill development were also enhanced by the discussions that took place in the work groups, although, as Good and colleagues (1990) noted, "The extent to which students began to develop these skills and sensitivities varied considerably from classroom to classroom" (p. 58).

In sum, although it is possible to structure discussions so that they serve as sounding boards for students' beliefs and value systems, the task is not a simple one. Consideration must be given to the nature of young adolescent development and to the complex mix of communicative demands placed on students and teachers who are unaccustomed to classroom discussion as an instructional approach.

Interpersonal understanding is a building block for discussions that include different points of view.

Overcoming Egocentric Views

At the same time that a majority of young adolescents are responding largely in a concrete operational fashion, they are also growing into a period of interpersonal understanding that includes valuing a friend for what he or she can offer beyond satisfying their immediate needs (Selman, 1980). In this period of their interpersonal growth, young adolescents are also able to take on and appreciate another's point of view; they are no longer confined to believing that because they see the world in a certain way, everybody else does as well.

Even as egocentrism begins to give way to a more mature outlook on interpersonal understanding in the middle-grades years, young adolescents' concerns that everyone is watching and evaluating them become more intense. These concerns, which have been described as being more symptomatic of limited interpersonal skills than limited thinking ability, can be addressed through well-structured discussions in which students learn how to cooperate and collaborate with their peers (Lapsley, Milstead, Quintanta, Flannery, & Buss, 1986). Through cooperation and collaboration, young adolescents gain experience in overcoming their egocentric views in three important ways.

First, discussions that are designed to encourage cooperation and collaboration support the student who is fearful of failure. The results of a study involving a questionnaire administered to 1,168 middle-grades students in four states (Arth, 1990) showed that of seven major concerns identified by these students, fear of failure was the greatest. Over 41 percent of their responses were focused on this concern, although it could not be determined if they feared failure due to personal, social, intellectual (or a combination of all three) factors. Discussions that are designed to teach students how to cooperate and collaborate lessen the possibility that failure will result from a general lack of knowledge, assuming of course that there is any truth to the old adage that two heads are better than one.

Second, discussions involving cooperative and collaborative learning can help young adolescents overcome their egocentric concern that everyone is watching and evaluating them. Giving a presentation in front of classmates was the third most rated concern among young adolescents in Arth's (1990) study. This concern can be alleviated somewhat by discussions that are structured so that students pair and share first in groups of two and then in groups of four before an individual is required to speak before the whole class.

Third, participation in well-structured discussions can assist young adolescents in overcoming their egocentric views that because they think in a certain way, everybody else must think the same way (Elkind, 1967; Irvin, 1989). In discussions where students pair and share, there is ample opportunity for them to hear divergent points of view. How accepting they are of each other's views will depend to a great extent on the teacher's expertise in grouping students and pacing the lesson.

Initially, at least, the teacher might want to avoid pairing students who are apt to become behavioral problems if placed within the same group. Likewise, to avoid problems associated with stray talk, the teacher might want to set a time limit on discussion activities. A rule of thumb that works for some teachers is to plan discussions that last no longer (in minutes) than the average of their students' chronological ages, plus one. For example, if the average age of an eighth-grade class is 13, then discussions should go no longer than 14 minutes. Although this rule of thumb has no empirical backing (of which we are aware) we offer it here as a reminder that discussions are most focused and successful when they are paced appropriately.

To summarize, by participating in discussions, young adolescents can be helped to overcome their egocentric views. Discussions that encourage cooperation and collaboration tend to alleviate students' fear of failure, their perception that everyone thinks like they do, and their concern that everyone is watching and evaluating them.

Engaging in Constructive Controversy

In the past, research has shown that teachers generally suppress situations that might lead to verbal conflict in classrooms. Perhaps this is largely due to teachers' lack of understanding of the benefits that such conflict can produce and because their students lack the experience and skills to deal with controversy (DeCecco & Richards, 1974; Johnson, 1970). More recently, however, evidence has begun to mount suggesting that constructive controversy has the potential to spark students' transition to higher levels of cognitive and moral reasoning (Johnson & Johnson, 1979) and to enable students to generalize what they have learned in one situation to new situations (Alvermann & Hynd, 1989).

Controversy, as defined by Johnson and Johnson (1979), "exists when one person's ideas, information, conclusions, theories, or opinions are incompatible with those of another person, and the two seek to reach an agreement" (p. 53). According to their description of the process by which controversy improves learning, problem-solving, and decision-making abilities, it is necessary for a student first to recognize that his or her views are not shared by others—a condition that produces conceptual conflict or uncertainty. This uncertainty, in turn, is hypothesized to motivate the student's search for a more accurate understanding of what the opposing views are. In this search for greater understanding, the student's own cognitive perspective and reasoning processes are changed as he or she engages in debate or argument with peers and teachers alike.

Discussions lend themselves nicely to the learning process if teachers structure them in ways that enable middle-grades students to save face and avoid destructive controversy. One way to promote face-saving and constructive controversies is to structure discussions so that they are cooperative, rather than competitive, in nature. For example, students should be encouraged to work together to solve a problem or reach a conclusion rather than be pushed to engage in individualized win-lose tactics that are divisive in nature.

Another way to promote constructive controversies is to make certain that students deal with their feelings as well as the content or ideas that tend to focus their discussions. This is especially true of discussions that have problem solving as their goal. "In successful problem solving," Johnson and Johnson (1975) note, "feelings, intuition, and hunches play an important part" (p. 17).

Finally, teachers need to create contexts for constructive controversies. Discussions that provide supportive climates in which students and teachers feel free to challenge each other's ideas are excellent contexts for learning, problem solving, and decision making. At the same time, teachers need to teach young adolescents how to recognize similarities as well as differences among their views and the views of others (Dole & Smith, 1989; Johnson & Johnson, 1979).

There is considerable evidence that supports the use of constructive controversy to foster young adolescents' transition to higher levels of cognitive and moral reasoning. Moreover, discussions appear to be excellent vehicles for exploring differences of opinion and arriving at shared understandings when certain guidelines are followed.

Expanding and Refining Oral Language Skills

When students enter the middle grades, their competence in oral language development may lag significantly behind their intellectual and social growth (Elkind, 1967; Johnson & Johnson, 1979). When this is the case, they may appear inarticulate and incompetent because they cannot express in a meaningful way what it is that they know.

Although small-group discussions are thought to provide relatively safe settings for students to expand and refine their verbal repertoires (Taylor, 1989), groupings of this sort may result in practices that decrease, rather than increase, learning through discussion. For example, teachers who assign students to small work groups for mathematics instruction may find that they are giving students work of a drill-and-practice nature to keep from being interrupted as they work with various groups (Good et al., 1990). Thus, rather than providing opportunities for students to expand and refine their oral language skills, small work groups may actually curtail the quality and quantity of student talk.

Small-group discussions followed by whole-class debriefings, where a spokesperson from each small group reports back to the class, are effective means for helping students expand and refine their oral language skills. The effectiveness of combining small- and large-group discussions is further enhanced if the following three guidelines are considered.

1. Insist that students express themselves clearly and completely. Deemphasize the importance of remembering technical vocabulary, at least initially; it is preferable that students demonstrate an understanding of the concepts they are discussing.
2. Stress the need for collecting evidence outside the textbook or primary information source used in presenting a concept. The task of stimulating students to put forth multiple points of view is made easier when they are provided with multiple information sources.
3. Emphasize important linkages among the discipline areas. By concentrating on ways to strengthen interdisciplinary links, there is less opportunity for students to infer that what is discussed in one content area has little or no connection with what is discussed in another area. For example, as aptly pointed out by

the Carnegie Council on Adolescent Development (1989), "The concept of evolution is demonstrable in stars, organisms, and societies" (p. 44).

In review, it is important to bear in mind that young adolescents' oral language development may belie their levels of intellectual and social maturity. To assist students in elevating their language skills so they are on a par with their other abilities, teachers may resort to a combination of small- and large-group discussions. These discussions will be effective in expanding and refining students' oral language only to the point that they adhere to certain principles having to do with clarity of expression, multiple information sources, and interdisciplinary linkages.

Adjusting to Increased Cognitive Demands

One of the strongest endorsements for using discussion to help students adjust to the increased cognitive demands of the middle grades came from a report of the National Assessment of Educational Progress (NAEP, 1981). The major conclusion drawn by the individuals responsible for summarizing the massive amounts of data collected on U.S. 9-, 13-, and 17-year-olds was that we have failed to teach more than 5 to 10% of the student population in the United States to use higher-order thinking skills. One of several recommendations for addressing this deficiency, which has continued to plague us throughout subsequent administrations of the NAEP, is to provide students with opportunities for discussion.

Because a discussion is assumed to be technically simple to orchestrate, it has received little attention in methods textbooks. Consequently, it is not surprising to find that many of the discussions we have observed in the middle grades are ineffective. Typically, the problem is one of expecting students to discuss at a level of abstractness that they simply are not prepared to do (Alvermann, O'Brien, & Dillon, 1990).

According to cognitive developmental theory, young adolescence is a period in which individuals are just beginning to make the transition from thinking in terms of concrete reality to thinking in terms of abstract reality and abstract possibility (Ingersoll, 1989). As we pointed out in Chapter 2, cognitive developmental theory predicts that not all individuals will reach the same level of functioning at the same time. Thus, the need to provide for individual differences within discussion activities is of paramount concern to middle-grades educators.

One way to individualize discussions so that students at all developmental levels gain practice in adjusting to the increased cognitive demands of middle-grades curricula is to choose activities that allow for multiple levels of responding. For example, in the Discussion Web that follows in the next section of this chapter, questions representing different levels of concreteness and abstractness can be inserted in the Web's center box. Even better, students can be encouraged to provide their own questions for use in the box. Webs can be exchanged among friends and completed first as individual homework and then elaborated upon in small-group discussions the next day.

In sum, young adolescents generally are in the process of making the transition from concrete to more abstract levels of reasoning. Discussions are viewed as valuable in helping students complete the process, though it is understood that individual differences within the young adolescent period make it necessary to adjust discussion activities so that they match students' ability levels as closely as possible.

The Discussion Web

The idea for developing the Discussion Web stemmed from an article written by a social studies teacher named James Duthie (1986). In the article, Duthie described a strategy for teaching students how to avoid what he called the ''narrative trap'' (p. 232); that is, how to avoid describing *what* happened, and instead, analyzing *why* it happened. To counteract his students' tendencies to write in the narrative form when he had assigned them the task of writing an analytical essay, Duthie developed the Web Outline. In its present form, the Discussion Web is an adaptation of the Web Outline. It differs from Duthie's original web in that all four of the language arts (reading, writing, speaking, and listening) are incorporated into the strategy, and the focus is on higher-order reasoning skills rather than on essay writing alone.

The Discussion Web (see Figure 14.2) consists of a *yes* and a *no* strand to encourage students to think about both sides of an issue before drawing a conclusion in response to the question in the center box. A box containing the word *Reasons* is a reminder that all conclusions must be backed by evidence either gathered from the text, another information source, or one's own background knowledge. The Discussion Web is a simple strategy to learn. After a few short exposures to the process, middle-grades students can independently create their own.

In addition to providing structure for a discussion, the Discussion Web can be used to highlight an imbalance in one's argument (e.g., the evidence in the *yes* and *no* strands is unevenly developed), to point out places where an argument is unsupported in the text, or to provide a visual reminder of the focus of the discussion.

As a follow-up to a discussion, the Web can serve as a guide for writing about why some event occurred. For example, reasons can be turned into topic sentences or main ideas. Evidence in the form of brief notes or key words in the *yes* and *no* strands can be turned into supporting details, and the conclusion can become the summary statement.

Discussion Web Exercise

We have created a Discussion Web for you to use with John Reynolds Gardiner's well-known story, *Stone Fox* (see the Appendix at the end of this chapter). Participating in this exercise will enable you to get both a sense of the strategy and a feeling for how easy it is to use and adapt. First, read the chapter titled ''The Race'' adapted from Gardiner's book to determine who won—Little Willy or Stone Fox. The introduction at the start of the chapter will provide you with a bit of background on the story up to this point. Then follow the directions given at the bottom of Figure 14.2 when you have finished reading.

FIGURE 14.2   A Discussion Web

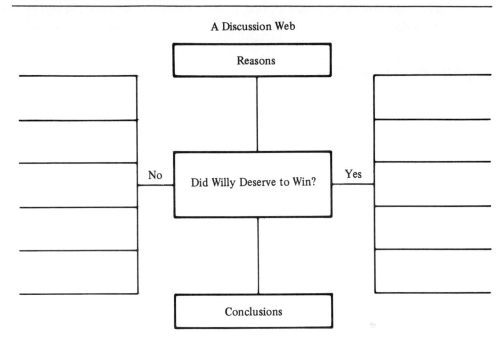

A Discussion Web

1. After reading a selection (silently or orally to a partner), form groups of two students each.
2. Together with your partner, discuss the question in terms of the evidence that can be found to support the yes/no columns. Remember to jot down only key words or phrases in the yes/no boxes. You do *not* have to fill all boxes.
3. After time is called, join another group of two students. In your new group of four, try to come to consensus by stating your conclusion and reason(s) for your conclusion. It is perfectly acceptable to have a dissenting view, but the discussion process will be more effective if you try to reach consensus.
4. Finally, after time is called again, appoint a person from your group to present your group's conclusion and reason(s) for that conclusion. Be sure to include the minority viewpoint if consensus was not reached.
5. As a follow-up activity to the discussion, write your own answer to the question. You may include your group's ideas as well as the ideas expressed by other groups.

Source: Adapted with permission from J. Duthie, 1986, "The Web: A Powerful Tool for the Teaching and Evaluation of the Expository Essay." *The History and Social Science Teacher, 21,* 232–236.

Follow-Up Activity

As you moved through the various steps of the Discussion Web, you may have been aware of how your own understanding of the story was refined and enriched through the ideas expressed by other members of your group. You also may have wondered how this activity would work in a classroom filled with young adolescents. Feedback from teachers who have tried the Discussion Web with young adolescents is generally positive. When difficulties arise, they are mostly attributed to students' inexperience in working independently in small groups or to teachers' forgetting to limit the discussion time.

Following is a checklist for your use. Think back to your participation in the discussion that followed the reading of *Stone Fox*. How many of these descriptors applied? Place a check mark beside each one that applied to you or someone in your group. If some descriptors did not apply, but you wish they had, place an asterisk beside them.

_____ relevant to topic or theme

_____ active involvement of everyone

_____ time to review and restate

_____ patience in listening

_____ accepting and open

_____ turntaking acknowledged

_____ controversy encouraged

_____ comfortable environment

_____ positive and constructive

_____ time for wrap-up

If you have a checkmark in front of each of these descriptors, chances are that members of your group were involved in a first-rate discussion. On the other hand, if you have several blanks and/or asterisks, it is likely that the discussion group did not function as it should. Giving some attention to those areas that need improvement may pay off the next time you are involved in a discussion.

Summary

Traditionally, it has been teacher talk, not student talk that has played a significant role in classroom interaction. The situation might best be described as one in which the rich get richer while the poor get poorer, to paraphrase an old saying. That is, the teachers learn the material better each time they are actively involved in presenting it, whereas the students become more and more complacent about their own involvement with school learning. Although there are some signs that the recitation approach to classroom instruction is waning, by and large it is still the most prevalent form of classroom interaction among young adolescents and their teachers.

Why this is so is difficult to determine. The literature on young adolescent development leads us to conclude that well-developed discussions can facilitate young adolescents' interpersonal needs and cognitive growth. Indeed, a recent report from the Carnegie Council on Adolescent Development specifically mentions discussion as a means by which students can learn to analyze information, express themselves, and receive feedback on their input.

Discussions have also been linked to helping students overcome their egocentric views, engage in constructive controversy, expand and refine their oral language skills, and adjust to the increased cognitive demands of the middle grades. Perhaps one reason discussions are conducted less frequently than recitations in middle-grades classrooms is that young adolescents are accustomed to taking a relatively passive role in classroom interaction, that is, they are content to let their teachers do most of the talking.

The Discussion Web was introduced as a strategy for structuring classroom interactions so that they become contexts in which students learn to value the importance of taking an active role in their own schooling. Working first is twos and then in fours, students have the opportunity to enrich and refine their own understandings before they are asked to reach consensus and report that consensus (plus any dissenting views) to the whole class. From this experience, they gain a sense of peer support and, at the same time, a feel for what it means to participate actively in classroom interactions.

REFERENCES

Alvermann, D. E., & Hynd, C. R. (1989, December). *The influence of discussion and text on the learning of counterintuitive science concepts.* Paper presented at the annual meeting of the National Reading Conference, Austin, TX.

Alvermann, D. E., O'Brien, D. G., & Dillon, D. R. (1990). What teachers do when they say they're having discussions following content reading assignments: A qualitative analysis. *Reading Research Quarterly, 25,* 296–322.

Arth, A. A. (1990). Moving into middle school: Concerns of transescent students. *Educational Horizons, 68,* 105–106.

Bridges, D. (1979). *Education, democracy, and discussion.* Windsor, England: NFER Publishing.

Carnegie Council on Adolescent Development. (1989). *Turning points: Preparing American youth for the 21st century.* New York: Carnegie Corporation.

Corno, L., & Snow, R. E. (1986). Adapted teaching to individual differences among learners. In M. C. Wittrock (Ed.), *Handbook of research on teaching* (3rd ed., pp. 605–629). New York: Macmillan.

DeCecco, J., & Richards, A. (1974). *Growing pains: Uses of school conflict.* New York: Aberdeen Press.

Delamont, S. (1983). *Interaction in the classroom* (2nd ed.). London: Methuen.

Dewey, J. (1959). The school and society: The school and life of the child. In M. S. Dworkin (Ed.), *Dewey on education* (pp. 50–70). New York: Teachers College, Columbia University.

Dillon, J. T. (1984). Research on questioning and discussion. *Educational Leadership, 42,* 50–56.

Dolan, T., & Dolan, E. (1979). Improving reading through group discussion activities. In E. Lunzer & K. Gardner (Eds.), *The effective use of reading.* London: Heinemann Educational Books.

Dole, J., & Smith, E. L. (1989). Prior knowledge and learning from science text: An instructional study. In S. McCormick & J. Zutell (Eds.), *Cognitive and social perspectives for literacy research and instruction* (38th Yearbook of the National Reading Conference) (pp. 345–352). Chicago: National Reading Conference.

Doyle, W. (1986). Classroom organization and management. In M. C. Wittrock (Ed.), *Handbook of research on teaching* (3rd ed., pp. 392–431). New York: Macmillan.

Duthie, J. (1986). The web: A powerful tool for the teaching and evaluation of the expository essay. *The History and Social Science Teacher, 21,* 232–236.

Elkind, D. (1967). Egocentrism in adolescence. *Child Development, 38* 1025–1034.

Erickson, F., & Shultz, J. (1981). When is a

context? Some issues and methods in the analysis of social competence. In J. Green & C. Wallat (Eds.), *Ethnography and language in educational settings.* Norwood, NJ: Ablex.

George, P., & Lawrence, G. (1982). *Handbook for middle school teaching.* Glenview, IL: Scott, Foresman.

Good, T. L., Reys, B. J., Grouws, D. A., & Mulryan, C. M. (1990). Using work-groups in mathematics instruction. *Educational Leadership, 47*(4), 56–62.

Goodlad, J. I. (1984). *A place called school.* New York: McGraw-Hill.

Holt, J. (1969). *The underachieving school.* New York: Dell.

Ingersoll, G. M. (1989). *Adolescents* (2nd ed.). Englewood Cliffs, NJ: Prentice-Hall.

Irvin, J. L. (1989). *Reading and the middle school student: Strategies to enhance literacy.* Boston: Allyn and Bacon.

Jackson, P. W. (1968). *Life in classrooms.* New York: Holt, Rinehart & Winston.

Johnson, D. W. (1970). *The social psychology of education.* New York: Holt, Rinehart & Winston.

Johnson, D. W., & Johnson, R. T. (1975). *Learning together and alone.* Englewood Cliffs, NJ: Prentice-Hall.

Johnson, D. W., & Johnson, R. T. (1979). Conflict in the classroom: Controversy and learning. *Review of Educational Research, 49,* 51–70.

Lapsley, D. K., Milstead, M., Quintana, S. N., Flannery, D., & Buss, R. R. (1986). Adolescent egocentrism and formal operations: Tests of a theoretical assumption. *Developmental Psychology, 22,* 800–807.

McTighe, J., & Lyman, F. T., Jr. (1988). Cueing thinkers in the classroom: The promise of theory-embedded tools. *Educational Leadership, 45,* 18–24.

Moore, D. W., Alvermann, D. E., & O'Keefe, K. (1990). Discussion practices: An historical overview. *Reading Psychology, 11*(2), 115–130.

National Assessment of Educational Progress. (1981). *Reading, thinking and writing.* (Report No. 11-L-01). Denver: National Assessment of Educational Progress.

Selman, R. L. (1980). *The growth of interpersonal understanding: Developmental and clinical analyses.* New York: Academic Press.

Sternberg, R. J. (1987). Most vocabulary is learned from context. In M. G. McKeown & M. E. Curtis (Eds.), *The nature of vocabulary acquisition.* Hillsdale, NJ: Erlbaum.

Stodolsky, S. S., Ferguson, T. L., & Wimpelberg, K. (1981). The recitation persists, but what does it look like? *Journal of Curriculum Studies, 13,* 121–130.

Stubbs, M. (1983). *Language, schools and classrooms* (2nd ed.). London: Methuen.

Taylor, R. (1989). The potential of small-group mathematics instruction in grades 4 through 6. *Elementary School Journal, 89,* 633–642.

APPENDIX: THE RACE

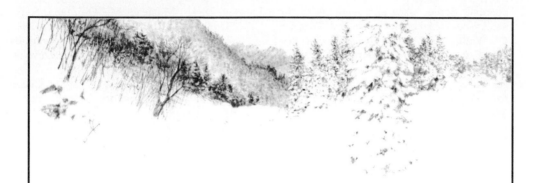

*Unless he can come up with five hundred
dollars for the bank, little Willy's grandfather
is going to lose his farm. Little Willy thinks
he has a way to get the money, but it is
a race against all odds.*

THE RACE

from STONE FOX
by John Reynolds Gardiner

Little Willy went to see Mayor Smiley at the city
hall building in town to sign up for the dogsled race.

The mayor's office was large and smelled like hair
tonic. The mayor sat in a bright red chair with his
feet on his desk. There was nothing on the desk
except the mayor's feet.

18

"We have a race for you youngsters one hour before," Mayor Smiley said.

"I wanna enter the *real* race, Mr. Mayor."

"You must be funning, boy." The mayor laughed. "Anyway, there's an entrance fee."

"How much?"

"Fifty dollars."

Little Willy was stunned. That was a lot of money just to enter a race. But he was determined. He ran across the street to the bank.

"Don't be stupid," Mr. Foster told little Willy. "This is not a race for amateurs. Some of the best dog teams in the Northwest will be entering."

"I have Searchlight! We go as fast as lightning. Really, Mr. Foster, we do!"

"Willy . . . the money in your savings account is for your college education. You know I can't give it to you."

"You have to."

"I do?"

"It's *my* money!"

Little Willy left the bank with a stack of ten-dollar gold pieces—five of them, to be exact.

He walked into the mayor's office and plopped the coins down on the mayor's desk. "Searchlight and I are gonna win that five hundred dollars, Mr. Mayor. You'll see. Everybody'll see."

Mayor Smiley entered Willy in the race.

When little Willy stepped out of the city hall building, he felt ten feet tall. He looked up and down the snow-covered street. He was grinning from ear to ear. Searchlight walked over and stood in front of the sled, waiting to be hitched up. But little Willy wasn't ready to go yet. He put his thumbs in his belt loops and let the sun warm his face.

He felt great. In his pocket was a map Mayor Smiley had given him showing the ten miles the race covered. Down Main Street, right on North Road—little Willy could hardly hold back his excitement.

Five miles of the race he traveled every day and knew with his eyes closed. The last five miles back into town were mostly straight and flat. It's speed that would count here, and with the lead he knew he could get in the first five miles, little Willy was sure he could win.

As little Willy hitched Searchlight to the sled, something down at the end of the street—some moving objects—caught his eye. They were difficult to see because they were all white. There were five of them. And they were beautiful. In fact, they were the most beautiful Samoyeds little Willy had ever seen.

The dogs held their heads up proudly. They pulled a large but lightly constructed sled. They also pulled a large—but by no means lightly constructed—man. Way down at the end of the street the man looked normal, but as the sled got closer, the man got bigger and bigger.

The man was an American Indian—dressed in furs and leather, with moccasins that came all the way up to his knees. His skin was dark, his hair was dark, and he wore a dark-colored headband. His eyes sparkled in the sunlight, but the rest of his face was as hard as stone.

The sled came to a stop right next to little Willy.
The boy's mouth hung open as he tilted his head
way back to look up at the man. Little Willy had
never seen a giant before.

"Gosh," little Willy gasped.

The Indian looked at little Willy. His face was
solid granite, but his eyes were alive.

"Howdy," little Willy blurted out, and he gave a nervous smile.

But the Indian said nothing. His eyes shifted to Searchlight, who let out a soft moan but did not bark.

The giant walked into the city hall building.

Word that Stone Fox had entered the race spread throughout the town of Jackson within the hour, and throughout the state of Wyoming within the day.

Stories and legends about the awesome mountain man followed shortly. Little Willy heard many of them at Lester's General Store.

Little Willy learned that no white man had ever heard Stone Fox talk. Stone Fox refused to speak with the white man because of the treatment his people had received. His tribe, the Shoshone, who were peaceful seed gatherers, had been forced to leave Utah and settle on a reservation in Wyoming with another tribe called the Arapaho.

Stone Fox's dream was for his people to return to their homeland. Stone Fox was using the money he won from racing to simply buy the land back. He had already purchased four farms and over two hundred acres.

That Stone Fox was smart, all right.

In the next week little Willy and Searchlight went over the ten-mile track every day, until they knew every inch of it by heart.

Stone Fox hardly practiced at all. In fact, little Willy only saw Stone Fox do the course once, and then he was sure he wasn't going very fast.

The race was scheduled for Saturday morning at ten o'clock. Only nine sleds were entered. Mayor

Smiley had hoped for more contestants, but after Stone Fox had entered, well . . . you couldn't blame people for wanting to save their money.

It was true Stone Fox had never lost a race. But little Willy wasn't worried. He had made up his mind to win. And nothing was going to stop him. Not even Stone Fox.

Grandfather was out of medicine. Little Willy went to see Doc Smith.

"Here." Doc Smith handed little Willy a piece of paper with some scribbling on it. "Take this to Lester right away."

"But it's nighttime. The store's closed."

"Just knock on the back door. He'll hear you."

"But . . . are you sure it's all right?"

"Yes. Lester knows I may have to call on him any time—day or night. People don't always get sick just during working hours, now, do they?"

"No, I guess they don't." Little Willy headed for the door. He sure wished he could stay and have some of that cinnamon cake Doc Smith was baking in the oven. It smelled mighty good. But Grandfather needed his medicine. And, anyway, he wouldn't think of staying without being asked.

"One other thing, Willy," Doc Smith said.

"Yes, ma'am?"

"First, I want you to know that I think you're a darn fool for using your college money to enter that race."

Little Willy's eyes looked to the floor. "Yes, ma'am."

"But, since it's already been done, I also want you to know that I'll be rooting for you."

Little Willy looked up. "You will?"

"Win, Willy. Win that race tomorrow."

Little Willy beamed. He tried to speak, but couldn't find the words. Embarrassed, he backed over to the door, gave a little wave, then turned quickly to leave.

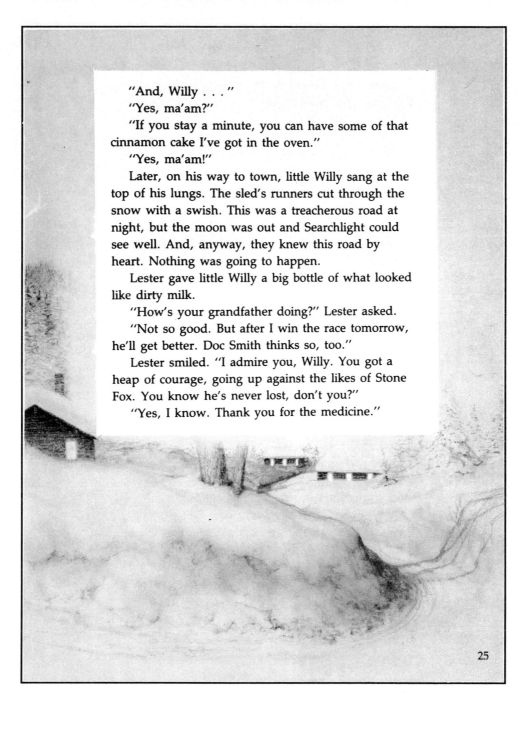

"And, Willy . . ."

"Yes, ma'am?"

"If you stay a minute, you can have some of that cinnamon cake I've got in the oven."

"Yes, ma'am!"

Later, on his way to town, little Willy sang at the top of his lungs. The sled's runners cut through the snow with a swish. This was a treacherous road at night, but the moon was out and Searchlight could see well. And, anyway, they knew this road by heart. Nothing was going to happen.

Lester gave little Willy a big bottle of what looked like dirty milk.

"How's your grandfather doing?" Lester asked.

"Not so good. But after I win the race tomorrow, he'll get better. Doc Smith thinks so, too."

Lester smiled. "I admire you, Willy. You got a heap of courage, going up against the likes of Stone Fox. You know he's never lost, don't you?"

"Yes, I know. Thank you for the medicine."

25

Little Willy waved good-bye as Searchlight started off down Main Street.

Lester watched the departing sled for a long time before he yelled, "Good luck, son!"

On his way out of town, along North Road, little Willy heard dogs barking. The sounds came from the old deserted barn near the schoolhouse.

Little Willy decided to investigate.

He squeaked open the barn door and peeked in. It was dark inside and he couldn't see anything. He couldn't hear anything either. The dogs had stopped barking.

He went inside the barn.

Little Willy's eyes took a while to get used to the dark, and then he saw them. The five Samoyeds. They were in the corner of the barn on a bed of straw. They were looking at him. They were so beautiful that little Willy couldn't keep from smiling.

Little Willy loved dogs. He had to see the Samoyeds up close. They showed no alarm as he approached, or as he held out his hand to pet them.

And then it happened.

There was a movement through the darkness to little Willy's right. A sweeping motion, fast at first; then it appeared to slow and stop. But it didn't stop. A hand hit little Willy, sending him over backwards.

"I didn't mean any harm, Mr. Stone Fox," little Willy said as he picked himself up off the ground.

Stone Fox stood tall in the darkness and said nothing. Searchlight barked outside. The Samoyeds barked in return.

27

Little Willy continued, "I'm going to race against you tomorrow. I know how you wanna win, but . . . I wanna win too. I gotta win. If I don't, they're gonna take away our farm. They have the right. Grandfather says that those that want to bad enough, will. So I will. I'll win. I'm gonna beat you."

Stone Fox remained motionless. And silent.

Little Willy backed over to the barn door. "I'm sorry we both can't win," he said. Then he pushed open the barn door and left, closing the door behind him.

In the barn, Stone Fox stood unmoving for another moment; then he reached out with one massive hand and gently petted one of the Samoyeds.

That night little Willy couldn't sleep. And when little Willy couldn't sleep, Searchlight couldn't sleep. Both tossed and turned for hours, and whenever little Willy looked over to see if Searchlight was asleep, she'd just be lying there with her eyes wide open, staring back at him.

Little Willy needed his rest. So did Searchlight. Tomorrow was going to be a big day. The biggest day of their lives.

The day of the race arrived. Little Willy got up early and fed Grandfather his oatmeal. After adding more wood to the fire, little Willy kissed Grandfather, hitched up Searchlight, and started off for town.

At the edge of their property he stopped the sled for a moment and looked back at the farmhouse. The roof was covered with freshly fallen snow. A trail of smoke escaped from the stone chimney. The jagged peaks of the Teton Mountains shot up in the background toward the clear blue sky overhead. "Yes, sir," he remembered Grandfather saying. "There are some things in this world worth dying for."

Lost in his thoughts, little Willy got to town before he knew it. As he turned onto Main Street, he brought the sled to an abrupt halt.

He couldn't believe what he saw.

Main Street was jammed with people, lined up on both sides of the street. They must have all come to see Stone Fox.

Searchlight pulled the sled down Main Street past the crowd. Little Willy saw Miss Williams, his teacher,

and Mr. Foster from the bank, and Hank from the post office. And there were Doc Smith and Mayor Smiley. The city slickers were there. And even Clifford Snyder, the tax man, was there. Everybody.

Lester came out of the crowd and walked alongside little Willy for a while. It was one of the few times little Willy had ever seen Lester without his white apron.

"You can do it, Willy. You can beat him," Lester kept saying over and over again.

They had a race for the youngsters first, and the crowd cheered and rooted for their favorites. It was a short race. Just down to the end of Main Street and back. Little Willy didn't see who won. It didn't matter.

And then it was time.

The old church clock showed a few minutes before ten as the contestants positioned themselves directly beneath the long banner that stretched across the street. They stood nine abreast. Stone Fox in the middle. Little Willy right next to him.

Little Willy had read all about the other contestants in the newspaper. They were all well-known mountain men with good racing records and excellent dog teams. But, even so, all bets were on Stone Fox. The odds were as high as a hundred to one that he'd win.

Not one cent had been bet on little Willy and Searchlight.

But little Willy was smiling. He still felt like a winner. Searchlight knew the route as well as he did. They were going to win today, and that was final. Both of them knew it.

Stone Fox looked bigger than ever standing next
to little Willy. In fact, the top of little Willy's head
was dead even with Stone Fox's waist.

"Morning, Mr. Stone Fox," little Willy said, looking practically straight up. "Sure's a nice day for a
race."

Stone Fox must have heard little Willy, but he did
not look at him. His face was frozen like ice and his
eyes seemed to lack that sparkle little Willy remembered seeing before.

The crowd became silent as Mayor Smiley stepped out into the street.

Miss Williams clenched her hands together until her knuckles turned white. Lester's mouth hung open, his lips wet. Mr. Foster began chewing his cigar. Hank stared without blinking. Doc Smith held her head up proudly. Clifford Snyder removed a gold watch from his vest pocket and checked the time.

Tension filled the air.

Little Willy's throat became dry. His hands started to sweat. He could feel his heart thumping.

Mayor Smiley raised a pistol to the sky and fired.

The race had begun!

Searchlight sprang forward with such force that little Willy couldn't hang on. If it weren't for a lucky grab, he would have fallen off the sled for sure.

In what seemed only seconds, little Willy and Searchlight had traveled down Main Street, turned onto North Road, and were gone. Far, far ahead of the others. They were winning. At least for the moment.

Stone Fox started off dead last. He went so slowly down Main Street that everyone was sure something must be wrong.

Swish! Little Willy's sled flew by the schoolhouse on the outskirts of town, and then by the old deserted barn.

Swish! Swish! Swish! Other racers followed in hot pursuit.

"Go, Searchlight! Go!" little Willy sang out. The cold wind pressed against his face. The snow was

33

well packed. It was going to be a fast race today. The fastest they had ever run.

The road was full of dangerous twists and turns, but little Willy did not have to slow down as the other racers did. With only one dog and a small sled, he was able to take the sharp turns at full speed without risk of sliding off the road or losing control.

Therefore, with each turn, little Willy pulled farther and farther ahead.

Swish! The sled rounded a corner, sending snow flying. Little Willy was smiling. This was fun!

About three miles out of town the road made a half circle around a frozen lake. Instead of following the turn, little Willy took a shortcut right across the lake. This was tricky going, but Searchlight had done it many times before.

Little Willy had asked Mayor Smiley if he was permitted to go across the lake, not wanting to be disqualified. "As long as you leave town heading north and come back on South Road," the mayor had said, "anything goes!"

None of the other racers attempted to cross the lake. Not even Stone Fox. The risk of falling through the ice was just too great.

Little Willy's lead increased.

Stone Fox was still running in last place. But he was picking up speed.

At the end of five miles, little Willy was so far out in front that he couldn't see anybody behind him when he looked back.

He knew, however, that the return five miles, going back into town, would not be this easy. The trail along South Road was practically straight and very smooth, and Stone Fox was sure to close the gap. But by how much? Little Willy didn't know.

Doc Smith's house flew by on the right. The tall trees surrounding her cabin seemed like one solid wall.

Grandfather's farm was coming up next.

When Searchlight saw the farmhouse, she started to pick up speed. "No, girl," little Willy yelled. "Not yet."

As they approached the farmhouse, little Willy thought he saw someone in Grandfather's bedroom window. The someone was a man. With a full beard.

It couldn't be. But it was! It was Grandfather! Grandfather was sitting up in bed. He was looking out the window.

Little Willy was so excited he couldn't think straight. He started to stop the sled, but Grandfather indicated no, waving him on. "Of course," little Willy said to himself. "I must finish the race. I haven't won yet."

"Go, Searchlight!" little Willy shrieked. "Go, girl!"

Grandfather was better. Tears of joy rolled down little Willy's smiling face. Everything was going to be all right.

And then Stone Fox made his move.

One by one he began to pass the other racers. He went from last place to eighth. Then from eighth place to seventh. Then from seventh to sixth. Sixth to fifth. He passed the others as if they were standing still.

He went from fifth place to fourth. Then to third. Then to second.

Until only little Willy remained.

But little Willy still had a good lead. In fact, it was not until the last two miles of the race that Stone Fox got his first glimpse of little Willy since the race had begun.

The five Samoyeds looked magnificent as they moved effortlessly across the snow. Stone Fox was gaining, and he was gaining fast. And little Willy wasn't aware of it.

Look back, little Willy! Look back!

But little Willy didn't look back. He was busy thinking about Grandfather. He could hear him laughing . . . and playing his harmonica . . .

Finally little Willy glanced back over his shoulder. He couldn't believe what he saw! Stone Fox was nearly on top of him!

This made little Willy mad. Mad at himself. Why hadn't he looked back more often? What was he doing? He hadn't won yet. Well, no time to think of that now. He had a race to win.

"Go, Searchlight! Go, girl!"

But Stone Fox kept gaining. Silently. Steadily.

"Go, Searchlight! Go!"

The lead Samoyed passed little Willy and pulled up even with Searchlight. Then it was a nose ahead. But that was all. Searchlight moved forward, inching *her* nose ahead. Then the Samoyed regained the lead. Then Searchlight . . .

When you enter the town of Jackson on South Road, the first buildings come into view about a half a mile away. Whether Searchlight took those buildings to be Grandfather's farmhouse again, no one can be sure, but it was at this time that she poured on the steam.

Little Willy's sled seemed to lift up off the ground and fly. Stone Fox was left behind.

But not that far behind.

The crowd cheered madly when they saw little Willy come into view at the far end of Main Street, and even more madly when they saw that Stone Fox was right on his tail.

"Go, Searchlight! Go!"

Searchlight forged ahead. But Stone Fox was gaining!

"Go, Searchlight! Go!" little Willy cried out.

Searchlight gave it everything she had.

She was a hundred feet from the finish line when her heart burst. She died instantly. There was no suffering.

The sled and little Willy tumbled over her, slid along the snow for a while, then came to a stop about ten feet from the finish line. It had started to snow—white snowflakes landed on Searchlight's dark fur as she lay motionless on the ground.

The crowd became deathly silent.

Lester's eyes looked to the ground. Miss Williams had her hands over her mouth. Mr. Foster's cigar lay on the snow. Doc Smith started to run out to little Willy, but stopped. Mayor Smiley looked shocked and helpless. And so did Hank, and so did the city slickers, and so did Clifford Snyder, the tax man.

Stone Fox brought his sled to a stop alongside little Willy. He stood tall in the icy wind and looked down at the young challenger, and at the dog that lay limp in his arms.

"Is she dead, Mr. Stone Fox? Is she dead?" little Willy asked, looking up at Stone Fox.

Stone Fox knelt down and put one massive hand on Searchlight's chest. He felt no heartbeat. He looked at little Willy, and the boy understood.

Little Willy squeezed Searchlight with all his might. "You did real good, girl. Real good. I'm real proud of you. You rest now. Just rest." Little Willy began to brush the snow off Searchlight's back.

Stone Fox stood up slowly.

No one spoke. No one moved. All eyes were on the Indian, the one called Stone Fox, the one who

41

had never lost a race, and who now had another vic-
tory within his grasp.

But Stone Fox did nothing. He just stood there,
like a mountain.

His eyes shifted to his own dogs, then to the finish line, then back to little Willy, holding Searchlight.

With the heel of his moccasin Stone Fox drew a
long line in the snow. Then he walked back over to
his sled and pulled out his rifle.

Down at the end of Main Street, the other racers
began to appear. As they approached, Stone Fox fired
his rifle into the air. They came to a stop.

Stone Fox spoke.

"Anyone crosses this line—I shoot."

And there wasn't anybody who didn't believe him.

Stone Fox nodded to the boy.

The town looked on in silence as little Willy, carrying Searchlight, walked the last ten feet and across
the finish line.

_15

Classroom Management

According to a recent Gallup Poll (Elam, 1989), teachers cite discipline as one of the major problems that public school teachers face today. Specifically, among elementary school (grades K–8) teachers, lack of discipline ranked second (after drug use) out of a list of 25 problems. In addition, discipline problems ranked third (after low salary and low status of the profession) among reasons why teachers leave the profession. Examples of discipline problems cited by teachers include schoolwork and homework not completed, behavior that disrupts class, talking back to and disobeying teachers, inappropriate dress, and cheating on tests. In a similar Gallup Poll (Elam, Rose, & Gallup, 1991), the general public also ranked lack of discipline second (after drug use) out of 25 problems facing public schools.

The results of these and similar polls are particularly distressing for middle-grades teachers because young adolescents are frequently identified as being harder to manage than students at other levels (Kauchak & Eggen, 1989). Middle-grades students are particularly hard to manage because they are at an age when they are seeking peer approval and are beginning to challenge authority and test their assertiveness in the classroom. Unfortunately, many prospective middle-grades teachers are unprepared to manage their classrooms effectively. In fact, many potentially good teachers are lost their first year of teaching because they are not prepared to implement the basic principles of effective classroom management. In particular, many teachers are not able to answer students' questions about classroom rules, procedures for completing assignments, and expectations concerning appropriate behavior and good work.

Our goal in this chapter is to familiarize you with the basic principles of classroom management so that you are better prepared to manage an effective middle-grades classroom and to deal with any discipline problems that may arise. First, we will provide you with some important definitions and discuss some general characteristics of effective classroom managers.

Definitions

In the beginning of this chapter, we used two terms related to effective classrooms: *management* and *discipline*. However, these two terms were not used interchangeably. How are management and discipline related? According to Emmer (1987), *management* "is a set of teacher behaviors and activities directed at engaging students in appropriate behavior and minimizing disruptions" (p. 233). *Discipline*, on the other hand, is "the degree to which students behave appropriately, are involved in activities, are task-oriented, and do not cause disruptions" (Emmer, p. 233). Thus, the goal of effective management is good discipline.

Management involves teacher behaviors, whereas discipline involves student behaviors. How are these two terms related to instruction? As we have mentioned previously in other chapters, effective instruction has many components, including plans, strategies, assessment, questions, management, and discipline. Thus, management and discipline are two necessary (but not sufficient!) components of effective instruction. In actuality, however, in well-managed classrooms, management and instruction take place simultaneously. "As students and teacher work together to construct lessons and to reach instructional goals, management and instructional processes are co-occurring" (Weade & Evertson, 1988, p. 189).

Effective Middle-Grades Classroom Managers

In general, effective classroom managers are well organized, have high expectations for their students, and maintain a positive learning atmosphere in their classrooms (Kauchak & Eggen, 1989). Among middle-grades teachers, Moskowitz and Hayman (1976) found that effective managers use the first few days of school to convey their rules and expectations to their students. Along similar lines, Emmer and Evertson (1980) found that effective middle-grades managers are capable of monitoring their students' behavior, maintaining appropriate behavior, and dealing with inappropriate behavior quickly and effectively.

As you can see, well-run classrooms don't just happen. They are the result of careful planning, implementing, and monitoring of rules, procedures, and expectations. Thus, effective middle-grades management takes place in three stages: planning before school starts, implementing during the first few days of school, and maintaining during the school year. The remainder of this chapter will provide you with important information about strategies that effective middle-grades managers use during each of these three stages.

Before School Starts

The first day of school is not the time to be thinking about how to run your classroom. Important decisions must be made well in advance of opening day. Three important criteria for a well-run classroom that should be planned before school starts include: (1) the physical setting of your classroom, (2) the expectations for appropriate behavior in your classroom, and (3) the expectations for routines in your classroom.

Physical Setting

Arrange the classroom thoughtfully!

Seating arrangements, material storage, and placement of the teacher's desk are important aspects of the physical setting of your classroom that can affect your classroom management. However, before presenting specific guidelines on each of these aspects, we will discuss several important characteristics of young adolescent development that you should consider when planning the physical setting of your classroom.

Young Adolescent Development

First, as you may recall from Chapter 2, young adolescents are at various stages of physical development. Therefore, you will need desks, tables, and chairs of various sizes in your classroom. Accomplishing this may take a bit of ingenuity on your part. Middle-grades teachers frequently resort to scavenging storerooms and arranging trades with other teachers. But, in most cases, middle-grades principals and administrators are well aware of early adolescent physical development, and reasonable requests are usually acted upon when funding is available.

Second, as George and Lawrence (1982) point out, physical growth in young adolescents "occurs at a different tempo for various body parts" (p. 28). Disproportionate growth can result in clumsiness and awkwardness in some students. Keeping this in mind, you should design traffic patterns that allow students to move about easily without tripping over and walking into furniture and materials. You can also help your students by arranging the furniture in your classroom in such a way that provides a variety of comfortable places in which they may work.

Third, young adolescents are at a stage where they are beginning to seek recognition among their peers. You can help them gain this recognition in a positive way by providing space around your classroom to display their work and allowing them time to walk around and view each other's work. You can also provide students with opportunities to design their own displays such as bulletin boards and learning centers.

An important part of the physical setting of a classroom involves instructional bulletin boards.

Finally, social interaction among peers is always on the minds of young adolescents. Thus, you may want to consider arranging the furniture in your classroom in a way that allows for some interaction among students at appropriate times.

Seating Arrangements

The one aspect of the physical setting of classrooms that comes to most teachers' minds is the seating arrangement. As you probably know from your own school experiences, there are a variety of ways to arrange desks in classrooms, and some arrangements are better than others. Probably the best recommendation we can make to you about your seating arrangement is to ensure that it is conducive to the types of activities you do in your classroom. For example, if students work primarily in groups in your classroom, then the seats should be arranged in small clusters. On the other hand, if you lecture to the whole class most of the time, then rows are probably more appropriate. If you conduct your class lessons primarily through whole-class discussion, then a large circle is the most effective arrangement for keeping middle-grades students on task and involved in the discussion (Rosenfield, Lambert, & Black, 1985).

The majority of middle-grades teachers engage their students in a variety of activities that can be carried out individually, in pairs, in small groups, or as a whole class. Using a variety of activities and grouping procedures is one of the best ways to operate a middle-grades classroom but it does lead to some problems with the seating arrangement. Probably the most effective way to arrange furniture in this case is to have a variety of seating arrangements in the classroom. For example, have several small groups of desks in one part of the room and individual desks scattered throughout the room.

The obvious limitation of this type of seating arrangement is that you need a large classroom and a large number of desks or tables. If you do not have the luxury of a large classroom and many desks, then you will probably want to arrange your desks or tables to suit the activity you do most frequently. Students will then have to move their desks when you switch from one activity to another. On one of the first few days of school, students can be taught how to move their desks, chairs, or tables quietly and efficiently.

Regardless of how you arrange the desks in your classroom, keep in mind that students should always be able to see you when you teach and they should also be able to see any instructional aids or materials such as the blackboard, the overhead projector, charts, and films when they are in use. Similarly, you should be able to see all students at all times. Figure 15.1 illustrates a classroom seating arrangement. Can you identify the advantages and disadvantages associated with this type of seating arrangement?

Another important aspect of the seating arrangement is who decides where the students sit. One question that middle-grades students routinely ask on the first day of school is: Can we sit anywhere we want? Hopefully, you will have planned for this question before school started and will be ready either with a yes or a seating chart. For the first few weeks of school (or longer if you anticipate problems), it is a good idea to assign students to seats. Later, if no major discipline problems arise, Kauchak and Eggen (1989) recommend allowing students to sit where they want as a privilege, which can be withdrawn if they misbehave.

Material Storage

Part of running an effective classroom involves using closets, bookcases, cabinets, and other storage spaces appropriately so that materials and supplies are ready and handy when you need them. Middle-grades students who are forced to sit and wait several minutes while you hunt in a closet for books tend to become bored and misbehave. Figure 15.2 provides suggestions for storing materials and supplies in your classroom. Many of these suggestions come from the research of Emmer, Evertson, Sanford, Clements, and Worsham (1989).

Placement of the Teacher's Desk

Traditionally, teachers have placed their desks at the front of the classroom, based on the assumption that they could best monitor their students from that location. But with more and more teachers arranging student desks in groups and circles, the optimal place for the teacher's desk is not always the front of the classroom. The most important thing for you to consider when deciding where to place your desk is how you will use it. Many teachers never sit at their desks except after school when their students are gone. Some teachers only use their desks for conferences with students. Others sit at their desks to work while students are taking tests. And, unfortunately, some teachers sit at their desks all the time. Decide what your desk will be used for and place it accordingly. In fact, it is a good idea to have two desks

FIGURE 15.1   Sample Classroom Arrangement

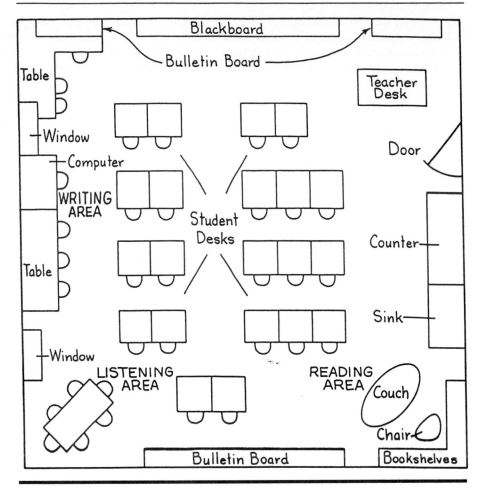

Source: From Karen D'Angelo Bromley, *Language Arts: Exploring Connections,* Second Edition. Copyright © 1992 by Allyn and Bacon. Reprinted with permission.

(or a desk and a table) so you can place them in different locations for different purposes.

In summary, keep in mind that the way you initially arrange your classroom does not have to be permanent. If seating arrangements and assignments do not work out as planned, change them. If your materials and supplies turn out to be stored ineffectively, rearrange them. If you do not like the placement of your desk, move it. Most teachers change the physical arrangement of their classrooms several times during the school year. Teachers as well as middle-grades students enjoy a change of scenery every once in awhile.

FIGURE 15.2   Suggestions for Classroom Storage

1. Keep frequently used materials and supplies near your desk where you have easy and quick access to them.
2. Store all media equipment, such as overhead projectors, tape players, and filmstrip projectors, together in one place (e.g., a locked cabinet).
3. Place reference materials, such as dictionaries and encyclopedias, together on one or two shelves of a bookcase.
4. Put your own personal materials, such as gradebook, pens, pencils, and a planbook, in your desk drawers.
5. Store all student work and confidential information in a filing cabinet that can be locked if necessary.
6. Reserve one shelf of a bookcase or the top of a file cabinet near your desk for the plans and materials you will need each day. At the end of each day, you can return these things to their regular place and replace them with plans and materials for the next day.
7. Decide which cabinets, closets, bookcases, and desk drawers students are allowed to access. For example, if you absolutely do not want students to have access to your desk drawers, they should be aware of this rule.

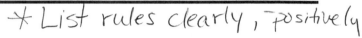

✱ List rules clearly, positively

Expectations for Behavior

Before students enter your classroom on the first day of school, you should know exactly how you expect them to behave. On the whole, young adolescents will do what is expected of them but they must know what those expectations are. The most effective classroom managers are very clear about how they expect their students to behave (Brophy, 1983). This means that you will have to think about and plan your expectations before school starts. These expectations are usually written in the form of classroom rules and penalties. Before discussing rules and penalties, we will review several characteristics of young adolescent development that you may want to keep in mind when you plan your rules and penalties.

Young Adolescent Development

First, young adolescents are beginning to question and challenge authority. Be prepared to explain the rationale behind each of your rules, as some students will automatically question them and challenge you to explain them. For example, if one of your rules is "Only one person talks at a time," you can explain that each of them has something important and worthwhile to say. Therefore, when one of them is talking, everyone else (including yourself) should be listening.

As we mentioned before, most students will follow rules if they see a logical reason for the rules. Similarly, students should know exactly why they are being corrected. Correcting students randomly and inconsistently only antagonizes them and does little to enhance your authority in the classroom. Research shows that middle-grades students expect their teachers to be consistent in enforcing rules, and they do not want their teachers to ignore misbehavior (Lovegrove, Lewis, Fall, & Lovegrove, 1985).

Second, young adolescents are extremely conscious of their status among their peers. Whenever possible, correct or reprimand students in private. If a student misbehaves during a class, try eye contact, moving close to the student, or whispering to the student first before correcting or reprimanding him or her in front of peers.

Third, young adolescents are at a stage where they should be assuming responsibility for their actions. They must know that they are responsible for adhering to class rules. They also must be made aware of the relationship between privileges and responsibilities. With each privilege comes a responsibility, and privileges can be withdrawn if students do not live up to their responsibilities.

Classroom Rules

Leinhardt, Weidman, and Hammond (1989) define rules as "statements of what is not permitted" (p. 185). Even though this definition is worded in negative terms, it should be noted that the rules themselves can (and should) be worded in positive terms (e.g., "We respect the property of others"). Despite the fact that no teacher can effectively manage a classroom without rules, we are constantly amazed when we visit schools and find middle-grades classrooms without rules. The research on classroom rules (e.g., Sanford & Evertson, 1981) is quite explicit: Rules that are clear and consistently enforced are usually effective. Based primarily on the research of Emmer and Evertson (Emmer et al., 1989; Evertson, Emmer, Clements, Sanford, & Worsham, 1989), we have several suggestions on how to design rules for your classroom. These suggestions are summarized in Figure 15.3.

Penalties

Students should know what the penalties are for breaking rules. It is extremely difficult to enforce a rule when you have not thought about a penalty. Merely saying "You broke the rule" will not deter most students from breaking it again. Thus, you will need to think about and plan penalties before school starts. Figure 15.4 provides guidelines for you to keep in mind about penalties.

In summary, have a few, short, simple rules. Make sure that students know the rationale for the rules as well as the penalty for violating the rules. And, most important, enforce rules consistently.

Expectations for Routines

Routines, as defined by Leinhardt, Weidman, and Hammond (1989) are "fluid, paired, scripted segments of behavior that help movement toward a *shared goal*" (p. 184). In a sense, routines are procedures that have become automatic. As the definition indicates, routines are helpful to both the teacher and the students. According to these researchers, routines can be categorized as either management, support, or exchange. Before discussing each of these three types of routines, we will review several characteristics of young adolescent development that you should bear in mind when you plan your classroom routines.

Young Adolescent Development

The majority of middle-grades students are not yet capable of establishing long-term goals or of doing much long-range planning. Therefore, your routines for classroom procedures and especially for planning and completing assignments

FIGURE 15.3   Suggestions for Classroom Rules

1. Find out what the school rules are. Many classroom behaviors may already be covered by school rules. For example, your school may have a rule forbidding gum chewing. If so, then you will not have to make a class rule about gum. Many middle-school teachers establish the first classroom rule as "Obey all school rules."
2. If you work on a team, it is a good idea to have team rules that are enforced by all teachers on the team. Team rules are especially appropriate in the middle grades where students may first experience changing classrooms and dealing with several teachers. Team rules let students know that they are expected to behave regardless of whose classroom they are in. Team rules also help avoid situations where students are allowed to do something in one room but not in another. No teacher enjoys constantly hearing "But Mrs. Billips lets us do it, why won't you?"
3. Have a few short, general rules instead of a long list of complicated rules. As Kauchak and Eggen (1989) point out, students frequently break rules because they forget them. A short, simple rule such as "Only one person talks at a time" covers a multitude of behaviors.
4. Whenever possible, rules should be stated positively instead of negatively. For example, it is more effective to say "Only one person talks at a time" than to say "Do not talk when someone is talking."
5. Rules should be written down and posted in the classroom. Merely telling students the rules is not as effective as also posting them in the room and referring to them whenever necessary. For example, if several students are talking at once, you should be able to point to the classroom rules and say, "What is our rule about talking in the classroom?"
6. Make sure *you* obey all rules. Young adolescents need good role models. It is difficult to expect them to obey rules if you do not obey them. For example, if food or drinks are not allowed in the classroom, then you should not have a cup of coffee or a soda at your desk.
7. You may want to have your students add one or two rules of their own to the rules you have already identified. This method of involving students in the decision-making process may lead to increased responsibility on the part of the students. However, keep in mind that this method has several limitations. First, as Evertson and colleagues (1989) point out, there is a limit in the amount of student participation allowed in most schools. Second, many school and classroom rules can not be changed or left up to the discretion of the students. Third, if you have several different classes throughout the day, posting different rules for different classes becomes a problem.

---

should be geared toward helping students develop these skills. For example, your routine for completing a quarter-long project should help students break the assignment into small pieces, each with its own due date. A routine such as this will help students with long-range planning as well as with time management.

Also, as mentioned earlier, young adolescents are beginning to assume more responsibility for their own behavior as well as their own work. Established classroom routines should aid students in becoming more responsible and should lead to eventual independence. If each student has a job (e.g., watering the plants, erasing the board, collecting books) at the end of the day, students may need to be reminded of their jobs for the first week or two of school. But, after a reasonable amount of time, students should be responsible for their jobs without any reminder

FIGURE 15.4 Suggestions for Classroom Penalties

1. Find out about school and team penalties. Your school or team may already have a penalty for breaking certain rules and you should administer these penalties when appropriate.
2. The penalty should fit the rule. Penalties that are too harsh or too lenient will not help you gain the respect of your students. For example, assigning a student to a month of detention for talking in class is too harsh a punishment in most cases. On the other hand, having a student stay after school for an hour for punching a student at recess is too lenient a punishment.
3. One of the most effective penalties if students abuse a privilege is to withdraw the privilege. For example, if students are allowed to sit near their friends in your class but you find some of them tend to talk too much, make them sit in assigned seats. In general, if students know that a privilege can be easily withdrawn, they tend not to abuse it.
4. Avoid using grades or extra academic work as penalties for misbehavior. As we mentioned in Chapter 9, when extraneous variables such as behavior affect students' grades, the grades no longer are a reflection of achievement. If necessary, grades can be given specifically for behavior. Along similar lines, a student who misbehaves during mathematics class should not be required to solve 20 extra word problems as a punishment. This practice only serves to negate the students' interest in the subject area involved.
5. Avoid group penalties. Some teachers penalize the whole class when they cannot identify the culprit. Other teachers ask the class to identify the culprit. Given the importance of peer acceptance among young adolescents, neither of these is a good practice. Both practices increase the likelihood that the students will turn against the teacher as well as each other.

Have a management routine !

from you. The same logic applies to other routines such as completing homework and doing seatwork.

Management Routines

Management routines are "housekeeping, discipline, maintenance, and people-moving tasks" (Leinhardt, Weidman, & Hammond, 1989, p. 189). As such, this type of routine helps you manage your classroom and leads to better discipline among your students. In general, management routines are nonacademic. Typically, middle-grades teachers spend a great deal of time in the beginning of the year explaining and providing opportunities for their students to practice management routines, such as jobs in the classroom, entering and leaving the classroom, and storing personal materials (books, lunches, umbrellas, etc.).

When establishing management routines, keep in mind that the routines should be simple enough for students to understand and remember. Long, complex routines that do not make sense to your students are not very likely to be carried out. Management routines should also be efficient in terms of time. A routine that requires you to get a key and unlock a closet every time a student needs a piece of paper does not save anyone time. Finally, as much as possible, management routines should be delegated to the students. This practice will save you time and will also help students develop a sense of responsibility and independence.

Support Routines

Support routines are "behaviors and actions necessary for a learning-teaching exchange to take place" (Leinhardt, Weidman, & Hammond, 1989, p. 189). In short, support routines enhance the teaching-learning process in the classroom. Examples of support routines include routines for distributing and collecting materials, completing and correcting homework, and knowing what to do when seatwork is completed.

Usually, support routines will vary from classroom to classroom because teachers have their own personal preferences about how they want things done. As a result, most middle-grades teachers spend a great deal of time in the beginning of the school year explaining and providing practice in support routines. The guidelines for designing support routines are similar to the guidelines for designing management routines: They should be simple and logical enough for students to follow and remember, they should be time efficient, and they should be delegated to the students as much as possible.

Exchange Routines

Exchange routines "specify the interactive behaviors that permit the teaching-learning exchange to take place" (Leinhardt, Weidman, & Hammond, 1989, p. 189). These routines pertain to the language contacts and interactions that occur between the teacher and the students and among the students themselves. Exchange routines facilitate communication in the classroom by ensuring that both the teacher and the students are listening to whomever is talking. Examples of exchange routines include routines for asking and answering questions, interacting in small groups, and participating in class discussions.

The previous chapters on classroom questions and classroom interactions provided many suggestions for establishing exchange routines. In general, exchange routines should be specific enough to maintain orderly classroom communication but not so rigid as to stifle spontaneity and inhibit a student's desire to speak up and participate in oral exchanges.

In summary, classroom routines are an important component of a well-managed classroom. Simple, logical routines can enhance management, provide support, and encourage exchanges in the classroom. Most routines must be taught to students and should eventually lead to increased responsibility and independence among students. Despite the importance of establishing routines, they should not become so important that they become the primary focus in the classroom. Classroom routines are a means to an end, not an end in themselves.

Beginning of School

Now that you have spent time arranging your classroom and planning your rules, penalties, and routines, you are ready to begin the school year. As you begin the first day of school, keep in mind that many of your students will be nervous and apprehensive because they do not know what is expected of them. It is your job to put them at ease by conveying your expectations to them.

Group work should begin with one small group of students while the rest of the students in the class work individually.

Effective middle-grades managers usually spend a significant amount of time during the first few days of school familiarizing their students with the classroom rules, penalties, and routines. This is time well spent because it usually results in a well-managed classroom throughout the rest of the year. So, do not expect to jump too deeply into the content right away. There will be plenty of time for that later. It is also a good idea to conduct your lessons and activities with the whole class for the first week or two. Begin group work only when you are able to manage the whole class.

Since you probably will not be spending a great deal of time on the content during the first few days of school, what should you do? Evertson and colleagues (1989) provide some excellent suggestions: introductions; room descriptions; get-acquainted activities; administrative activities such as distributing books; time fillers such as games, puzzles, and songs; brief, easy, content activities or seatwork; and implementation of rules and routines.

How do you go about implementing your rules and routines? A great deal of research (e.g., Anderson, Evertson, & Emmer, 1980; Emmer, Sanford, Clements, & Martin, 1982; Evertson, Emmer, Sanford, & Clements, 1983) has been conducted on this topic. The results of this research suggest implementation should involve three stages: communicating your expectations to the students, providing practice, and providing feedback.

Communicating Your Expectations to Students

Communicating your expectations to students involves more than just telling them what you expect. You must *describe* and *demonstrate* your expectations. For example, if students are allowed to whisper only when they are doing seatwork, describe exactly what you mean by seatwork. Provide them with examples of when they may and may not whisper. Provide a rationale for why they can only whisper during seatwork. Them demonstrate exactly what you mean (and do not mean!) by whispering. If there is a penalty associated with breaking the rule or not carrying out the routine correctly, let them know exactly what the penalty is. For example, if students talk too loudly, seatwork will be done in silence.

Providing Practice

After you have communicated you expectations to your students, provide immediate opportunities for them to practice. Using our whispering example again, you could ask students to whisper several times so that you are sure they know what you mean by whispering. If you are teaching students how to enter and leave the classroom properly, you could have them get up and practice it several times.

Providing Feedback

When students practice a rule or a routine, provide them with immediate and specific feedback. In our whispering example, you might say, "No, that's a little too loud. Try it again a bit lower." "Good! That's just right. Do it one more time." It is also important to praise them when they do it correctly. For example, "Excellent! That was just perfect. Remember, that's exactly how you should whisper when doing your seatwork." It is a good idea to provide them with some short seatwork activity later in the day so you can determine if they can whisper correctly. Remember to give them specific feedback and praise when appropriate.

During the Year

Assuming that the first week of school has gone as planned, management now becomes a matter of maintaining good discipline throughout the rest of the year. Emmer and Evertson (1980) found that incidences of misbehavior in middle-grades classrooms are generally low during the first week of school. Then, during the next few weeks, misbehavior increases in the classrooms of ineffective managers but not in the classrooms of effective managers. Clearly, these few weeks are critical in terms of maintaining the good discipline that you established during the first week of school.

We will now discuss six strategies that you can use to maintain good discipline in your classroom: (1) monitoring student behavior, (2) beginning group work appropriately, (3) timing your lessons appropriately, (4) encouraging appropriate behavior, (5) dealing with inappropriate behavior, and (6) evaluating your management system.

Monitoring Student Behavior

Kounin (1970) has conducted much of the research on monitoring student behavior. One of his most important findings was that effective managers "project an image of being in charge in the classroom" (Charles, 1983, p. 51). How do effective managers project such an image? Kounin identified three components of effective monitoring: "withitness," overlapping, and desist strategies.

"Withitness"

"Withitness" is defined as "the ability to know what is going on in all parts of the room at all times" (Moore, 1989, p. 206). This task is not as simple as it sounds. It is quite easy to lose track of what is going on in the back of the room when you are in the front. It is also quite easy to lose track of what the rest of the class is up to when you are working with a small group of students. Middle-grades students are extremely adept at determining whether or not their teachers are "withit."

In order to demonstrate withitness, Kounin (1970) provides several recommendations. First, stop misbehavior as soon as it happens rather than wait until it spreads. It is easier to deal with one student than with four or five. Second, make sure you identify the right student for correction. Nothing upsets middle-grades students more than getting corrected for something they did not do. Third, when two or three misbehaviors are occurring simultaneously, attend to the most serious first. For example, if Susie is talking to Elliott while Joe is punching Melvin, attend to Joe first.

Overlapping

Overlapping is defined as "the ability to attend to two issues at the same time" (Charles, 1985, p. 22). For example, teachers frequently have to work with a small group of students while ensuring that the rest of the class stays on task. Effective classroom monitors are able to scan the classroom, correct students when appropriate, answer questions when necessary, and still conduct the lesson with the small group.

Desist Strategies

Desist strategies are defined as "means of systematically communicating the teacher's desire to stop or alter the behavior of a student" (Orlich, Harder, Callahan, Kravas, Kauchak, Pendergrass, & Keogh, 1985, p. 342). Desist strategies can be low (e.g., eye constant), average (whisper or conversational tone) or high (e.g., screaming) in force. Desist strategies can also be private (e.g., after class) or public (e.g., in front of the class). In most situations, teachers should start with a "low-private" form of communication and proceed from there for more serious instances of misbehavior. Effective classroom monitors are able to assess a situation in order to know how and when to communicate their wishes to the students.

In addition to identifying components of effective monitoring, Kounin (1970) identified four critical errors that ineffective monitors tend to make: (1) thrusts, (2) dangles, (3) flip-flops, and (4) fragmentations.

Thrusts

Thrusts can occur when a teacher stops or interrupts a lesson with little or no warning. For example, your students are working in small groups on word problems and you suddenly say, "Okay, what's the answer to the first one?" Students should know how long they have to complete an activity and should be given a warning several minutes before their time is up (e.g., "You have three minutes left so try to finish up"). Similarly, you should monitor your students as they work so that you are aware if they finish before the end of their allotted time. When this happens, make sure you do not let students sit there with nothing to do.

Dangles

Dangles are made when a teacher stops in the middle of a lesson to attend to something else. Dangles can occur at any time throughout a lesson, such as when you do not have materials handy, when you get involved with individual students in the middle of whole-class instruction, or when you spend too much time talking to another teacher in your doorway. Inevitably, students get bored and misbehave. You can avoid dangles by being prepared with lessons and materials and by having a routine for students to follow when there are interruptions.

Flip-Flops

Flip-flops happen when a teacher returns to a previous activity in the middle of a new activity. For example, you would be guilty of flip-flopping if you stopped in the middle of a reading lesson to remind students to bring in their parental approval slips for tomorrow's field trip. You can avoid flip-flops by writing yourself short notes when you think of something out of context. Then, at the end of the lesson, you can tell the students.

Fragmentations

Fragmentations occur when you begin a lesson or activity without all the students being ready. For example, a fragmentation would happen if you start your social studies lesson while six students are still hanging up their coats or while half of the students are still looking for their books. Granted, you cannot wait forever for every student to be ready, but within reason, you should gain the attention of all students when you start a lesson or activity.

Beginning Group Work Appropriately

In light of the social needs of young adolescents, grouping students together in middle-grades classrooms has several advantages. First, it increases the interaction and communication among students. Second, it helps students develop important social skills such as cooperation, responsibility, and decision making. Third, it provides you with the opportunity to work with small numbers of students who have a particular strength, weakness, or interest.

Group work can be conducted in a variety of ways. For example, students can work in small groups while you circulate throughout the room helping, answering questions, and providing feedback and encouragement. Students can also work in small groups while you work with one small group. Or students can work individually while you work with one small group. Regardless of how you group students, we have several suggestions for beginning group work after the first few weeks of school. These recommendations were adapted from those designed by Joyce Johnston, a teacher in Clarke County, Georgia. Keep in mind our recommendation in the previous section to hold off on group work until you feel you can effectively manage the whole class. When you are ready to begin group work, keep in mind the suggestions in Figure 15.5

Before you initiate any group work in your classroom, make sure all students know exactly how they are expected to behave. You may even want to have two or three special rules for working in groups. For example, you will need to decide what students should do if they need your help while you are working with a small group. Should they interrupt you, ask another student, or go on to something else until you can help them? You will also need to decide if students who are working individually can talk while you are working with a small group.

Timing Lessons Appropriately

Timing your lessons appropriately is critical for maintaining good discipline. Appropriate timing involves knowing when to begin a lesson, how to make a transition from one activity to another within a lesson or from one lesson to another, how fast or slow to pace a lesson, and when to end a lesson. Again, much of the research on timing lessons was conducted by Kounin (1970).

Beginning a Lesson

If teachers do not have their students' attention when they start a lesson, the odds of getting it during the lesson are pretty slim. Unfortunately, many teachers fail to get the attention of all students before starting lessons. Good and Brophy (1984) recommend having a signal that you always use to start lessons. Examples of signals include "Okay, we're ready to begin" and "All right, everything out of your hands, everyone still, and all eyes up here." Regardless of what you say, your students

---

FIGURE 15.5   Suggestions for Beginning Group Work in the Classroom

---

1. Begin slowly. Start with a small group of students you know are well behaved. They should work together (or you can work with them) on an activity that can be completed in a few days.
2. Let the other students work at their seats individually, rather than in groups. These students should work on a simple activity that they can complete successfully without help from you.
3. Even if you are not working with the students in the small group, meet with them for a few minutes every day to ensure they get off to a good start.
4. After a few days, when this first small group finishes its activity or lesson, the students in it should go back to doing their work individually so you can work with another small group.
5. Select another small group of students and repeat steps 1 through 4.
6. When all students have had a chance to work in a small group, you can have two small groups work at the same time. After several weeks, all students can be working in small groups at the same time.

A good classroom manager makes smooth transitions from one activity to the next.

should get the idea that you are ready to begin. Effective managers then wait several seconds to ensure that they have the attention of all students. If one or two students are not paying attention, make eye contact with them, gesture, or call their names. Then begin the lesson.

Making Transitions

Transitions are defined as "the times when students are finishing one activity and preparing for actually starting another activity" (Grossman, 1990, p. 48). Ordinarily, students are not working during transitions but they are engaged in getting books, collecting papers, and other similar activities. Effective classroom managers have smooth transitions, meaning that students know exactly what to do and they do it quickly. Ineffective classroom managers have rough transitions, meaning that one activity tends to blend in with the next activity.

Sanford and Evertson (1983) found that as the amount of time taken for transitions increases in junior high school classes, so do the number of disruptions and the amount of off-task behavior. Accordingly, transitions should be as short as possible and should clearly indicate that one activity has ended and another has begun. This is especially important in low-ability classes, as research (Evertson 1982) suggests that the ability level of the students in the class plays a role in transition time, with low-ability students taking more time for transitions than high-ability students. Suggestions for smooth transitions include having supplies and materials handy, having an established routine for transitions, and letting students know at the beginning of the day if there are any changes in the schedule.

Pacing a Lesson

Determining how fast or slow to move through a lesson can be difficult until you get to know your students. In fact, we find that appropriate pacing is one aspect of teaching with which our student teachers tend to have the most difficulty. Effective managers have a knack for reading the faces and body language of their students to determine if they are pacing their lesson appropriately. Puzzled, frowning faces may indicate confusion and a need to slow down or rephrase what you have just said. You can confirm this by asking strategic questions at appropriate times. Bored, yawning faces, slouching bodies, and general restless among students may indicate that you are going too slowly or spending too much time on things students already know.

Effective managers are capable of immediately changing pace when the need is indicated. In order to pace your lessons effectively, Kounin (1970) recommends that you avoid *overdwelling*. This occurs when you spend too much time giving directions, attending to materials, correcting students, overteaching the content, and focusing on small details rather than main ideas. All of these examples of overdwelling lead to loss of interest among the students and eventual misbehavior.

Ending a Lesson

Deciding when to end a lesson is an important aspect of maintaining good discipline. Ideally, we all like to hold our students' interest throughout the entire lesson and end the lesson at the exact minute planned. Unfortunately, this does not always happen. There are at least two instances of times when you will have to decide when to end a lesson.

In one instance, you run out of time before you finish the lesson. We have all been in classrooms when the bell rings, the students get up and begin to leave, and the teacher shouts to deaf ears, "Your homework is. . . ." Effective classroom managers watch their time and are aware of when they are running out of time. Then they have to decide whether or not to (1) rush the rest of the lesson so they fit it in before time runs out, or (2) stop, summarize, tell the students that they'll pick up at this place tomorrow, and get the students ready to move on to the next subject or class. Nine times out of ten, choice 2 is the better choice.

In another instance, you are only halfway through the lesson but you can sense that your students have absorbed all they are going to. For a variety of reasons, they may be inattentive and bored. Because you are probably going to have to spend a great deal of time maintaining student interest rather than teaching the lesson, Good and Brophy (1984) recommend that you terminate such lessons or move on to the next part of the lesson. For example, suppose you are having all of the students in your writing class read their essays aloud. You sense that after about six or seven essays have been read, students are getting restless and inattentive. It is time to move on the next part of the lesson.

Encouraging Appropriate Behavior

One of the most effective ways to decrease the likelihood of misbehavior is to encourage appropriate behavior. Unfortunately, many ineffective classroom managers do not consciously encourage appropriate behavior. Instead, they wait for misbehavior to occur and then try to deal with it. Effective classroom managers, on the other hand, do not take good behavior for granted. They do everything they can to ensure that their students' good behavior continues. Two techniques that you can use to encourage appropriate behavior among your students are to stress appropriate behavior and to reinforce appropriate behavior.

Stressing Appropriate Behavior

There are several ways that you can stress appropriate behavior in your classroom. First, when communicating your expectations about classroom behavior to your students, be certain that you are very specific about what you want. Students should know exactly what you expect of them and they should not learn it after the fact. Second, state your expectations in positive rather than negative terms. Most students would rather hear what they should do than what they should not do. For example, if Billy is running down the hallway, it would be more effective to say "Walk in the hallway" instead of "Do not run in the hallway."

Reinforcing Appropriate Behavior

In Chapter 2, we explained that behavior that is reinforced is likely to continue and behavior that is not reinforced is likely to stop. Although this principle appears to apply to appropriate behavior in the classroom, the issue of reinforcement in the classroom is a controversial one among educators. Some educators feel students should not be reinforced because reinforcement will decrease their intrinsic motivation to behave appropriately. Other educators feel that students should be reinforced when they behave appropriately because it increases their self-concept and further motivates them to behave appropriately.

Despite the controversy, the majority of educators believe that appropriate use of reinforcement can be effective. Good and Brophy (1984) offer several guidelines for using reinforcement in the classroom. First, keep in mind that your students are already reinforced in a variety of ways (e.g., grades) and by a variety of people (e.g, peers, parents). Thus, quantity in not as important as quality. Too much reinforcement can be counterproductive.

Second, for some young adolescents, reinforcement from you may not be as important as reinforcement from others, such as their peers. If fact, some young adolescents may view reinforcement from you in a negative way. Thus, try to become aware of how each of your students reacts to your reinforcement.

Third, be careful that students do not become dependent on your reinforcement to the extent that "their behavior is controlled externally" (Good & Brophy, 1984, p. 192). Eventually, students should behave because it is the acceptable thing to do, not because they need reinforcement from you.

We would like to add an additional guideline: Be careful not to reinforce inappropriate behavior. Strange as it sounds, some teachers do this unconsciously. For example, you probably all remember the teacher who said "All right, we'll just sit here until you're all quiet." Then, you all sat for a long time. In effect, for some students, that teacher was reinforcing inappropriate behavior because these students really did not care if the lesson went on or not. In fact, for some students, it may have been more fun and less hassle just to sit there.

Two specific types of reinforcement that teachers use in their classrooms are praise and rewards. Nafpaktitis, Mayer, and Butterworth (1985) report that the use of approval, such as praise and rewards, by middle-grades teachers "has been found to maintain or increase various pupil behaviors" (p. 365).

Teacher praise has a different effect on each student. Some students respond positively to praise and others respond negatively. Some young adolescents like being praised in front of their peers; others are embarrassed by it. Praise also has differential effects on those students who observe one of their peers being praised. Some observers become jealous, others become more competitive, and others feel pride for their peers. Knowing exactly how your praise will affect each student in your classroom is a difficult job, even for most experienced teachers. Woolfolk (1990) provides several excellent guidelines for using praise appropriately in the classroom. These suggestions are summarized in Figure 15.6.

Rewards are also used by many teachers to reinforce appropriate behavior. This practice has several advantages. Research indicates that rewards, if used appropriately, can enhance classroom behavior. Rewards can also enhance student interest in routine or tedious activities. For example, Lepper (1983) found that student motivation can be increased by rewards that are dependent on performance rather than on participation. Social rewards have been found to be more effective than material rewards (Deci, 1975). Accordingly, young adolescents might be more motivated by 5 minutes of free time at the end of a class period than by candy bars or stars on their papers.

There are also several disadvantages of rewards. Rewards can decrease students' intrinsic motivations to behave appropriately or engage in a certain activity (Lepper, Greene, & Nisbett, 1973). When this happens, appropriate behavior or performance may disappear after students have been rewarded. For example, if Daryl already enjoys writing poems in language arts class, he may lose interest in this activity if he is rewarded for it. Also, in some cases, the effects of rewards are only temporary. Even if the reward continues, some students may lose interest in it and revert back to their old behavior. In addition, rewards can be costly in terms of time and money.

Rewards, then, should be tailored to the individual student. Students who are already being rewarded in some way (e.g., good grades, peer recognition, interest in the activity) should not receive additional social or material rewards. However, students who have no interest in an activity may benefit from rewards.

Emmer (1987) categorizes rewards as social, activity, or tangible. Examples of *social rewards* include "good behavior" honor role, certificates, written comments, and verbal approval. *Activity rewards* can include games, extra recess, and field trips. Activity rewards are especially effective for encouraging appropriate behavior from the whole class. *Tangible rewards* include food, prizes, money, and other material things that are not necessarily associated with school.

Grossman (1990), Good and Brophy (1984), and Evertson and colleagues (1989) offer several excellent guidelines for using rewards to reinforce or encourage appropriate behavior. First, most rewards, especially tangible rewards, should be used on a temporary basis. Young adolescents are at the stage where they should be assuming responsibility for their own behavior and should not be encouraged to

FIGURE 15.6   Guidelines for Using Praise Appropriately

Be clear and systematic in giving praise.

Examples
1. Make sure praise is tied directly to appropriate behavior and doesn't happen randomly.
2. Make sure the student understands the specific action or accomplishment that is being praised. You could say, "You brought the materials I lent you back on time and in excellent condition. Well done!" instead of saying, "You were very responsible."

Recognize genuine accomplishments.

Examples
1. Reward the attainment of specified goals, not just participation, unless participation is the major goal of the activity.
2. Be especially careful not to reward uninvolved students just for being quiet and not disrupting class.
3. Tie praise to students' improving competence or to the value of their accomplishment. You might say, "You are working more carefully now. I noticed that you double-checked all your problems. That is a very important habit to develop. Your score reflects your careful work," instead of simply, "Good for you. You have the top grade in your group."

Set standards for praise based on the individual abilities and limitations of the student involved.

Examples
1. Praise progress or accomplishment in relation to the individual student's past efforts.
2. Focus the student's attention on his or her own progress, not on comparisons with others.

Attribute the student's success to effort and ability, so the student will gain confidence that success is possible again.

Examples
1. Avoid implying that the success may be based on luck, extra help, or easy material.
2. Ask students to describe the problems they encountered and how they solved them.

Make praise really reinforcing.

Examples
1. Avoid singling out students for praise in an obvious attempt to influence the rest of the class. This tactic often backfires, since students know what's really going on. In addition, if you say, "I like the way Ken is . . ." too many times, Ken will be embarrassed and may be seen as the teacher's pet.
2. Don't give undeserved praise to students simply to balance failures. (Brophy calls this "praise as a consolation prize.") It is seldom consoling and calls attention to the student's inability to earn genuine recognition.

Source: Anita E. Woolfolk, *Educational Psychology*, Fourth Edition. Copyright © 1990 by Allyn and Bacon. Reprinted with permission.

depend on rewards. Second, your students should know the exact behavior you are rewarding. Third, no reward should be too easy or too difficult to gain.

Next, make sure that the reward is really a reward. Some young adolescents may be thrilled to receive a smiley face at the end of the week, whereas others might think it is silly or babyish. And last, rewards should be distributed in a timely manner. Rewarding students either too frequently or too infrequently will not encourage good behavior. For example, promising middle-grades students a popcorn party at the end of three months of good behavior will not motivate very many of them.

Dealing with Inappropriate Behavior

We would like to be able to tell you that if you follow all the guidelines we have presented so far in this chapter, students will always behave appropriately in your classroom. Unfortunately, that is not the case. Despite your best intentions, some young adolescents will still misbehave for a variety of reasons, many of which are beyond your control.

Some young adolescents will misbehave just for the sake of misbehaving. As Callahan and Clark (1988) point out, many "classroom situations are somewhat unnatural, restrictive situations, so pupils like to relieve the tension" (p. 160). Some students will misbehave by showing off in an attempt to gain peer approval. Recognition among peers and peer approval are extremely important to young adolescents and some of them will use misbehavior as a means to gain that recognition and acceptance. Also, because young adolescents are at a stage when they are beginning to question any authority figure, some of them will deliberately break classroom rules in an attempt to challenge you and find out just how far they can push you.

Early intervention can prevent more serious classroom managment problems.

Because of the unique interaction between young adolescents' physical development and social/emotional development, some students will use aggression as a means of getting what they want in the classroom. Also, despite all your good planning and organization, some students will just not be interested in some of your lessons. Frequently, these students become bored and misbehave. Last, due to background or homelife situations that you might be unaware of, some students will misbehave in your classroom.

How do you deal with students who act inappropriately in your classroom? Good classroom managers are skilled in a variety of techniques that are effective for dealing with students who misbehave. They are also aware of and try to avoid using certain techniques that are ineffective for dealing with students who misbehave.

Effective Techniques

Researchers such as Evertson and colleagues (1989), Good and Brophy (1984) and Emmer (1987) offer several suggestions for dealing with inappropriate behavior effectively. These suggestions are summarized in Figure 15.7.

Ineffective Techniques

There are several techniques to avoid when dealing with inappropriate classroom behavior. These techniques are summarized in Figure 15.8.

Evaluating Your Management System

Research conducted by Evertson and colleagues (1989) indicates that frequent evaluation of your management system is an essential component of maintaining appropriate classroom behavior. When things are not going as planned, effective managers find out why and make changes. These researchers identified several components of the evaluation process: (1) deciding if changes are needed, (2) identifying the cause of the problem, and (3) implementing changes.

Are Changes Needed?

There are several factors that will help you determine if changes are needed. First, are your students on task? Do they listen to you and to each other during lectures and discussions? Do they participate in activities? Off-task students are not necessarily misbehaving; they are just not on task. Evertson and colleagues (1989) note that, in well-managed classrooms, approximately 90 percent of the students are on task.

Second, is disruptive behavior happening in your classroom? Are there students who are behaving in a way that hinders the learning of others? In effectively run classrooms, few instances of disruptive behavior happen, but when they do occur, teachers handle them very quickly and efficiently.

Third, do you have the cooperation of your students? Are your students generally happy with the way things operate in your classroom? Do they follow the rules and procedures you set up? In well-managed classrooms, students generally cooperate and follow rules and procedures without constant reminders.

FIGURE 15.7 Effective Techniques for Dealing with Inappropriate Behavior

1. Before deciding what to do if a student (or the class) misbehaves, first decide if anything needs to be done. Effective managers do not correct every instance of misbehavior. In fact, teachers who constantly correct students are not necessarily the best managers. How do you decide when to act and when not to act? In general, behavior that is potentially harmful to you or other students, behavior that hinders learning, behavior that is likely to spread, and behavior that blatantly violates classroom rules should be stopped immediately. On the other hand, Grossman (1990) recommends that behavior involving minor infractions, unintentional misbehavior, and misbehavior caused by out of the ordinary circumstances may not require intervention by you.

2. For minor misbehavior, use the least amount of intervention possible. For example, physical proximity, eye contact, whispers, and gestures are extremely effective in the right situation.

3. For misbehavior that you decide needs immediate intervention, act quickly. This will let students know you are aware of what is going on. In a brief and direct manner, demand appropriate behavior. Stress the appropriate behavior rather than the inappropriate behavior. For example, if Shanna is talking to her neighbor in a situation where students are supposed to be working quietly on their own, it is more effective to say "Do your own work, Shanna" instead of "Don't talk, Shanna." You should raise your voice only in situations where it is absolutely necessary (e.g., the entire class is yelling and screaming).

4. Always be consistent and fair when intervening, correcting, or punishing students. Respect students and their rights and avoid playing favorites. Young adolescents can quickly get the feeling that the teacher is always picking on them.

5. Correct the problem, not the student. For example, if Larry has yelled out loud in class several times, avoid saying "Larry, there you go again. Why can't you do what you're supposed to? How many times do I have to tell you?" Notice that in this example, you only corrected Larry and really did not do or say anything about his yelling out loud.

6. If a student consistently exhibits the same type of misbehavior, try to find out if there is a reason for it and correct it if you can. For example, Amanda may not be turning in her homework because she has to babysit her two younger brothers until her mother gets home from work. By the time her mother gets home, Amanda may be too tired to do homework.

7. As much as possible, be responsible for your own classroom management. Constantly sending students to the principal does little to enhance your authority with students (or you reputation with the principal).

8. Refer serious misbehavior or infractions of classroom or school rules (e.g., bringing drugs or weapons to school) to the principal immediately. You are not in a position of authority to deal with these types of problems.

9. Whenever you are confronted with misbehavior, either minor or major, remain calm and professional. Avoid giving students the impression that you do not know what to do or that you are threatened by or afraid of them. You may have one or two students who, if they sense inexperience or fear, will continue to agitate you.

Fourth, do your students complete their assignments? Do they follow your procedures for completing assignments correctly and on time? Or do they frequently fail to turn in assignments or turn them in late or poorly done? In the classrooms of effective managers, most students follow the procedures for completing assignments without being constantly reminded.

FIGURE 15.8   Ineffective Techniques for Dealing with Behavior Problems

1. Avoid reinforcing inappropriate behavior. For example, in an attempt to get Frank to stop talking and get back to his work, it is quite tempting to say "Frank, will you take this book to Mrs. Miller's room, please." Now Frank is getting rewarded for talking by being able to get out work and wander around the hallways. Such practices send the wrong messages to students.

2. Avoid tolerating inappropriate behavior. Young adolescents quickly learn whether you will enforce your rules or give in to inappropriate behavior. For example, in a study conducted by Mergendoller and Packer (1985), one seventh-grade student described a teacher in the following way: "She warns you a lot. And she says, 'This is my final warning.' About 15 minutes later she says the same thing" (p. 588).

3. Avoid confronting a student or giving him or her an ultimatum in front of the rest of the class. This practice only puts you and the student on the spot. Young adolescents do not like to lose face in front of their peers and some will not back down to you. On the other hand, you cannot afford to lose face in front of your students by giving in to the culprit. Situations like this are best handled by saying "Alice, please see me after class." This will provide both you and Alice with time to cool down and possibly negotiate a compromise without an audience.

4. Avoid making threats that you cannot enforce. Young adolescents are quick to spot idle threats. Such threats will not correct misbehavior and may only serve to provoke some students to misbehave more.

5. When misbehavior occurs, do not waste time asking questions with obvious answers. For example, if Mike is clearly pulling Deborah's hair, avoid asking "What are you doing, Mike?" Questions such as these only provide an opportunity for students to lie. In this example, it would be more effective to say "Mike, keep your hands to yourself."

6. Avoid overdwelling on misbehavior and constantly nagging students about their behavior. Also avoid getting into arguments with students about what they may or may not have done. Correct the misbehavior quickly and get on with the lesson or class.

7. Avoid displays of authority when students misbehave. Remind them of the rules and get back to the task at hand. Constantly reminding students "I'm in charge here and you'll do as I say in the classroom" may only provoke some young adolescents to challenge your authority.

If you notice problems in any of the four factors we just discussed, you will probably need to start thinking about making some changes in your management system. Your first job is to identify the exact nature of the problem.

What Is Causing the Problem?

One of the most effective ways to identify your problem is to conduct a detailed review of the various components of your management system. Evertson and colleagues (1989) suggest carrying out the following review:

1. Examine the physical setting of your classroom. Is the seating arrangement or the placement of your desk causing or contributing to the problem? Are materials stored in places where both you and your students have access to them? Have you taken the needs of young adolescents into account when you designed the physical setting of your classroom?

2. Examine your rules and routines for behavior and assignments. Are you consistently enforcing them? Do the students really understand them? Are your rules, procedures, and penalties appropriate for young adolescents?
3. When misbehavior does occur, are you reacting to it quickly and effectively? Or are you waiting until it involves several students or develops into something more serious? When misbehavior happens, do you find out why? Are you consistently monitoring your students' behavior? Are you timing your lessons appropriately? Are you encouraging appropriate behavior?

Assuming that you have now identified the specific problem, you should start to make changes that will help eliminate it. Evertson and colleagues (1989) identified some simple changes and some more complex changes that you may want to make in your classroom management system.

What Changes Should Be Made?

The simplest changes to make are those that involve only you. For example, maybe you need to be more consistent in enforcing your classroom rules. This is not something that you need to discuss with your students. You just need to do it. Research suggests that you should carefully plan ways to make the change. This may involve written notes or reminders to yourself of the exact changes you plan to make. Some simple changes do involve your students, such as the schedule and the physical setting of your classroom.

Some changes, however, are more complex. In most complex changes, students must make significant and frequent modifications in their behavior. These changes generally take more time than the simple changes just described. In order to make complex changes effectively, you should discuss the change and its rationale with your students. You may also want to design new forms of reinforcement or penalties to accompany the change. After implementing the change, you should be consistent in monitoring, encouraging, and enforcing it.

Summary

Hopefully, we have achieved our goal of familiarizing you with the basic principles of classroom management so that you are better prepared to run an effective middle-grades classroom and deal with any discipline problems that may arise. Effective classroom management does not just happen. It is the result of careful planning, implementation, and maintenance. The physical, intellectual, social, and emotional development of young adolescents should be carefully considered as you plan, implement, and maintain your classroom management system.

REFERENCES

Anderson, L., Evertson, C., & Emmer, E. (1980). Dimensions in classroom management derived from recent research. *Journal of Curriculum Studies, 12,* 343–356.

Brophy, J. E. (1983). Classroom organization and management. *The Elementary School Journal, 83,* 265–285.

Callahan, J. F., & Clark, L. H. (1988). *Teaching*

in the middle and secondary schools (3rd ed.). New York: Macmillan.

Charles, C. M. (1983). *Elementary classroom management.* New York: Longman.

Charles, C. M. (1985). *Building classroom discipline.* (2nd ed.). New York: Longman.

Deci, E. L. (1975). *Intrinsic motivation.* New York: Plenum.

Elam, S. M. (1989). The second Gallup/Phi Delta Kappan poll of teachers' attitudes toward the public schools. *Phi Delta Kappan, 70,* 785–798.

Elam, S. M., Rose, L. C., & Gallup, A. M. (1991). The 23rd annual Gallup poll on the public's attitudes toward the public schools. *Phi Delta Kappan, 73,* 41–56.

Emmer, E. T. (1987). Classroom management and discipline. In V. Richardson-Koehler (Ed.). *Educators' handbook: A research perspective* (pp. 233–258). New York: Longman.

Emmer, E., & Evertson, C. (1980). *Effective classroom management at the beginning of the year in junior high school classrooms* (Report No. 6107). Austin: University of Texas, Research and Development Center for Teacher Education.

Emmer, E. T., Evertson, C. M., Sanford, J. P., Clements, B. S., & Worsham, M. E. (1989). *Classroom management for secondary teachers* (2nd ed.). Englewood Cliffs, NJ: Prentice Hall.

Emmer, E. T., Sanford, J. P., Clements, B. S., & Martin, J., (1982). *Improving classroom management and organization in junior high schools: An experimental investigation* (Report No. 6153). Austin: University of Texas, Research and Development Center for Teacher Education.

Evertson, C. M. (1982). Differences in instructional activities in higher- and lower-achieving junior high English and math classes. *Elementary School Journal, 82,* 329–350.

Evertson, C. M., Emmer, E. T., Clements, B. S., Sanford, J. P., & Worsham, M. E. (1989). *Classroom management for elementary teachers* (2nd ed.). Englewood Cliffs, NJ: Prentice Hall.

Evertson, C. M., Emmer, E. T., Sanford, J. P., & Clements, B. S. (1983). Improving classroom management: An experiment in elementary classrooms. *The Elementary School Journal, 84,* 173–188.

George, P., & Lawrence, G. (1982). *Handbook for middle school teaching.* Glenview, IL: Scott, Foresman.

Good, T. L., & Brophy, J. E. (1984). *Looking in classrooms* (3rd ed.). New York: Harper & Row.

Grossman, H. (1990). *Trouble-free teaching.* Mountain View, CA: Mayfield.

Kauchak, D. P., & Eggen, P. D. (1989). *Learning and teaching.* Boston: Allyn and Bacon.

Kounin, J. (1970). *Discipline and group management in classrooms.* New York: Holt, Rinehart and Winston.

Leinhardt, G., Weidman, C., & Hammond, K. M. (1989). Introduction and integration of classroom routines by expert teachers. In L. W. Anderson (Ed.), *The effective teacher* (pp. 185–194). New York: Random House.

Lepper, M. R. (1983). Extrinsic reward and intrinsic motivation: Implications for the classroom. In J. M. Levine & M. C. Wang (Eds.), *Teacher and student perceptions: Implications for learning* (pp. 281–317). Hillsdale, NJ: Erlbaum.

Lepper, M. R., Greene, D., & Nisbett, R. E. (1973). Undermining children's intrinsic interest with extrinsic rewards: A test of the overjustification hypothesis. *Journal of Personality and Social Psychology, 28,* 129–137.

Lovegrove, M. N., Lewis, R., Fall, C., & Lovegrove, H. (1985). Students' preferences for discipline practices in schools. *Teaching and Teacher Education, 1,* 325–333.

Mergendoller, J. R., & Packer, M. J. (1985). Seventh graders' conceptions of teachers: An interpretive analysis. *The Elementary School Journal, 85,* 581–594.

Moore, K. M. (1989). *Classroom teaching skills: A primer.* New York: Random House.

Moskowitz, G., & Hayman, M. L. (1976). Success strategies of inner-city teachers: A yearlong study. *Journal of Educational Research, 69,* 283–289.

Nafpaktitis, M., Mayer, G. R., & Butterworth, T. (1985). Natural rates of teacher approval and disapproval and their relation to student behavior in intermediate school. *Journal of Educational Psychology, 77,* 362–367.

Orlich, D. C., Harder, R. J., Callahan, R. C., Kravas, C. H., Kauchak, D. P., Pendergrass, R. A., & Keogh, A. J. (1985). *Teaching strategies.* Lexington, MA: D. C. Heath.

Rosenfield, P., Lambert, N., & Black, A. (1985). Desk arrangement effects on pupil classroom behavior. *Journal of Educational Psychology, 77,* 101–108.

Sanford, J. P., & Evertson, C. M. (1981). Classroom management in a low SES junior high: Three case studies. *Journal of Teacher Education, 32,* 34–38.

Sanford, J. P., & Evertson, C. M. (1983). Time use and activities in junior high classes. *Journal of Educational Research, 76,* 140–147.

Weade, R., & Evertson, C. M. (1988). The construction of lessons in effective and less effective classrooms. *Teaching and Teacher Education, 4,* 189–213.

Woolfolk, A. E. (1990). *Educational psychology* (4th ed.). Englewood Cliffs, NJ: Prentice Hall.

AFTERWORD

As teachers, curriculum specialists, supervisors, and administrators, we are continually making decisions that influence teaching and learning in the middle grades. Fortunately, we have at our disposal a variety of information sources that we can call upon in making those decisions. Research reports presented at professional meetings, methods texts, professional advice columns in newsletters and journals, and current reform movements are but a few of the available sources.

In writing this book, we have selected what we believe is some of the best thinking available on effective teaching and learning in the middle grades. Our primary goal in using research to ground the information presented in the book was twofold: (1) we wanted to provide you with the most reliable and valid information that is currently available, and (2) we wanted to point out areas that are in need of further research. To the extent that we have succeeded in reaching our goal, you should be relatively well informed about the knowledge base for effective teaching and learning in the middle grades.

For example, you have a sense of how middle-grades schools began, their present stage of development, and where they need to go in the future if they are to meet the needs of young adolescents. You also have knowledge of the various stages of physical, cognitive, social, personality, and moral development that young adolescents experience, though not necessarily in lock-step order. The instructional implications of this knowledge are many, but perhaps none is more important than the knowledge that guides you in treating all students as individuals who need opportunities to experience developmentally appropriate tasks.

Planning is a critical component of effective classroom instruction. Although experienced and novice teachers plan in different ways, most teachers engage in yearly, unit, weekly, and daily planning. Throughout the book, we have made a conscious effort to develop an awareness of the need for educators in the middle grades to plan with a variety of individual differences in mind. Young adolescence marks a period of growth in which differences in ability, cultural background, and motivation play a large role in students' success or lack of success in school.

The call has gone out for a radically different middle-grades curriculum—one that would derive its content from the themes that emerge from the overlap in young adolescents' personal and social concerns. Whether this alternative curriculum, or the more traditional curriculum, prevails is largely dependent on the decisions made by educators like yourselves. Whatever the outcome in curricular matters, rest assured that, as educators, you will face the onerous but necessary task of assessing teaching and learning. In writing this book, we have attempted to make your task of assessing the teaching and learning strategies that are the core of your instructional repertoire a more manageable one.

Finally, as a result of reading this book and participating in its suggested activities, we trust that you have formed some fairly positive notions about the excitement and challenges associated with middle-grades teaching and learning. We share your sense of excitement and wish you the best in meeting the challenges.

AUTHOR INDEX

SUBJECT INDEX